Acknowledgements

This book is dedicated to Ann, without whose assistance the text and illustrations could not have been accomplished, and to Ilene, without whose encouragement it would never have been completed.

The author wishes to express gratitude to the many persons who provided technical assistance, written material, art, advice and support for this book. In particular, thank you to Roy Pritts for criticizing in detail an early draft; to Paul Fidlin and Ray Kirchhoefer of Electro-Voice, for criticizing several important chapters; to John Eargle of JBL and JME Consulting, for some valuable helpful hints; to Cliff Hendrickson of U.S. Sound, for a key encouragement at an important juncture of this project (Dr. Fado DeConsolo? Way to go); and to the following manufacturer's representatives for providing very liberal data and pictorial opportunities: Rita Veix of JBL Professional, Davida Rochman and Tim Vear (nice book) of Shure Bros., Grace Paoli and John Wiggins of Community, Dave Talbot of AKG Acoustics, Bob Lowig of Beyerdynamic, Al Zang of Sennheiser, Bob French of Ashly, Al Lucas of Roland and Paul Hugo of Cetec-Gauss.

Special credit is due to JBL Professional, Electro-Voice Inc. and Yamaha Corporation for helping to lead the way among manufacturers in publishing highly useful information in the field.

English units of measurement are primarily used in this book, though Standard International (metric) equivalents have also been given in most instances. The final chapter of this book uses the term "engineer" in the broadest casual sense to include sound system operators, without intent to diminish the titles of those who have mastered the art and science of sound system design calculations and implementation, or who have earned the title of Engineer in appropriate academic programs.

Table of Contents

PART THREE
Systems: Design and Use

Foreword

In live performance the formula for a truly great show lies in a combination of many elements: discipline, freedom, inspiration, preparation, science and magic. The exact amounts of each may be different in any given production, but they are all necessary for the successful performance and must be taken into account by all participants—no matter what part of the show they are contributing to. When things work, there is a clarity and strength to every gesture. When the situation is fighting against you, it is a struggle to hear yourself let alone other members of the performance—which is frustrating for the musicians or other performers, technicians and the audience. The science of sound reinforcement is one of the most essential elements of this magical combination. It is the medium that performers use to relate their ideas to the audience. Without it, they are relegated to the proverbial tree that falls in the woods: if there is no one there to hear it, does it make a sound?

I have spent most of my musical career on the performance end of the sound reinforcement "stick," battling issues between monitors and the house and trying to make a musician feel intimate with his own sounds and the sounds of his bandmates while he is standing next to a stack of speakers delivering rock and roll to a crowd of sixty thousand. However, it has been my good fortune that, during my tenure in the music business, I have had an opportunity to work with masters. Each one has shown me that taking all elements of the performance seriously is the only way to prepare a situation for the magic to happen. A performer who knows what technology is appropriate for his or her sound is always steps ahead of the one who knows only his or her material and doesn't have a clue as to the best way to get it out to the crowd. Similarly, the sound reinforcement expert who does not understand the nature of the event he or she is reinforcing will often be working out an academic exercise lacking inspiration and artistry. That is not to say that an academic understanding is not essential. If I felt that way, I would not be writing a foreword to this book.

The materials presented here give you a knowledge and understanding of the science of sound reinforcement and a command of the parts of the sound engineer's tools. Knowing what you are talking about always makes it easier to communicate. It is the combination of this science with the art of listening and sensitivity to sound which makes for a great engineer—whether in live situations or in the studio. The sound is not delivered to the audience without being crafted, interrupted, or sculpted by the engineer. Anyone can make a mix, but not just anyone can make a good mix. Learn the science and ideas and keep listening and experimenting. Talk to performers and speakers and find out what they like in their monitors. When you get something they love, don't just look at the knobs—go over and take a listen. Remember that knowledge is just the beginning. ***—Bob Bralove***

General Introduction

In recent years, advancements in studio recording techniques, impressive improvements in home playback systems and the resulting refinements in the listening expectations of popular audiences have created demands in the field of sound reinforcement that could hardly have been imagined only a couple of decades ago. The demands which today's system must meet apply not only to its available loudness level, but also to its compactness and efficiency and, perhaps most importantly, to the clarity, richness and fullness of the output sound.

Expectations for improved sound quality can be seen in P.A. systems ranging from those used for small churches, banquets and other gatherings to the complex installations required in many large transportation centers, sports arenas and other public forums; and in music amplification systems ranging from suitcase systems for weekend bands, to the heavy-duty "portable" systems used by touring rock acts. In short, we have come to want better sound.

Largely in response to these kinds of demands, the modern sound system has evolved into an extremely versatile tool. For all the versatility of the available technology, though, the advances in the audio industry have come so quickly that general knowledge among purchasers and users of the equipment has tended to fall far short of their needs. A lack of thorough and understandable information can sometimes leave system buyers and users at a disadvantage—not only in dealing with the equipment itself, but also in understanding such effects as the acoustic environment and the human factor, and in implementing workable solutions to the problems they present.

Often at stake are the reputations and livelihoods of those who need to use sound reinforcement systems. A poorly designed or improperly operated system can make a talented musical act seem inferior, or cause a public speaker's voice to be lost in a muddle of incoherent sounds. A well-designed and effectively used system, on the other hand, can pleasantly accent a performance or allow a public speaker's message and true ability to come across. Simply put, the sound system can be the critical difference between failure and success.

This book has been written to help close the information gap. It is designed to allow a fairly comprehensive study for those who wish to pursue a relatively detailed understanding of sound reinforcement; both serious students and professionals should find many insights to be useful. It is also meant to be understandable to those who need only the basic facts about how systems work and how they can be used in real-life situations. Liberal explanations accompany the illustrations to assist readers who wish to focus on specifics within this broad subject.

Care has been taken to use the minimum amount of specific mathematics necessary to have a practical and worthwhile working knowledge of sound reinforcement. Much attention has also been given to providing the reader with a foundation that will apply even as the state of the art continues to change in the years ahead.

Part One

BASIC PRINCIPLES

CHAPTER 1

SOUND REINFORCEMENT SYSTEM BASICS

Amplifying sound and delivering it pleasantly and effectively to the ears of an audience—this simple objective known as sound reinforcement is in some ways the most basic task in all of the various audio fields, yet in other respects can be among the most difficult to accomplish in actual practice.

a) Fundamental System Concept.

First, a few of the very basics for the previously unfamiliar reader. Fig. 1.1 shows a diagram of the most basic sound reinforcement system possible, consisting simply of two transducers and an amplifier. The term *transducer* refers to any device which changes one kind of energy to another. A microphone will change sound waves (acoustical energy) into an equivalent audio signal (electrical energy); a speaker of-course changes an audio signal into sound waves. The playback head of a tape recorder or sensor of a CD player, among other devices, also fall into the category of transducers, providing an electrical audio signal which can be fairly easily adapted to an input of any sound reinforcement system.

An *amplifier* makes an electrical copy of an electrical signal (technically it need not be a stronger copy to be termed an amplifier). Certainly a much stronger signal is ultimately required to drive the speaker. This is accomplished in multiple stages, each of which involves one or more amplifiers at each component stage (in simple systems these may be integrated into one chassis). The combined increase in signal strength, known as *gain*, can amount to as much as 1,000,000,000-or-more times the strength of the input signal.

In a sense, each component in a basic system can be thought of as making identical or approximate copies of the signals it receives. Transducers accomplish this through their particular method of transfer from one type of energy to another (such as from acoustical to electrical or vice-versa). Amplifiers produce their output signal with energy supplied by a separate power source, such as is drawn from a standard electrical outlet. The input signal is used only as a guide in producing the correct output signal.

Depending on the need, sound reinforcement systems are normally designed to deal with audio signals in a number of other ways beyond the level controls ("volume/gain/fader"). Once a sound is converted into an equivalent electrical signal, there are numerous possible ways in which it can be mixed, reshaped, split apart and otherwise manipulated. The various additional functions generally are known as *signal processing*.

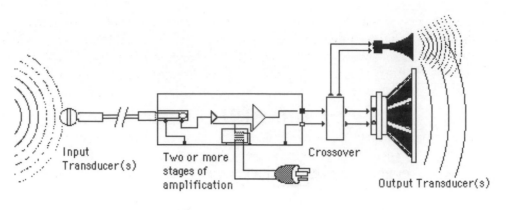

Figure 1.1

When more than one microphone and/or other type of audio source is in use, an audio mixer—as might be expected—serves to allow an input channel for each, and to effectively combine their signals into one or more combined output signals. A mixer normally will also allow for a number of other opportunities to process and reroute the signals it handles. *Equalizers* might consist simply of a couple of tone controls, or may be more finely divided to allow control over a number of narrower frequency ranges, from the deepest bass to the highest treble. A typical system will likely involve additional equalization through one or more separate (outboard) units, the use of effects devices to enhance the sound, and/or the creation of extra signal copies to be sent to additional speakers aimed to allow talkers or performers to monitor themselves—literally called *monitors*.

Commonly more than one—and sometimes all—of the necessary stages of amplification, signal processing, and mixing functions are combined within one chassis; this type of unit is normally intended for relatively basic applications. Beyond this type of basic application, modern systems generally are made up of a series of interacting components which, within certain limits, can be interconnected on an as-needed basis.

b) Microphones and Other Input Transducers.

Microphones, in providing entry for a sound into the electrical realm of the sound system, play a very strategic role in determining the quality of the sound that will finally be delivered by the speakers. Effective use of microphones is considered by many audio engineers to be the single most important step in providing high quality sound reinforcement, with good reason.

Microphones are the first essential step in shaping the tonal quality of sounds as they enter the system. Use of microphones with appropriate tonal-quality-related (frequency response) characteristics can greatly simplify the equalizing and mixing process, particularly with a music performance system. ("Frequency response" is defined in Chapter 4(a). The term "frequency", along with other basic audio terms, is thoroughly explained in Chapter 2. Altering frequency response is, for example, what a simple tone control or equalizer accomplishes.)

A microphone's directional pickup pattern can, when intelligently used, help to provide the best possible pickup of intended sound sources (Fig. 1.3). By the same token, it can also aid in minimizing the pickup of unwanted sounds, including the output sound of the system itself (an excess of which is responsible for what is popularly known as "feedback").

Contact pickups , used mainly for hollow-bodied acoustic instruments, are another commonly used type of input transducer. Signals from *magnetic pickups* (as built into electric bass guitars), and signals from electronic sources such as modern keyboard instruments and guitar processors, ordinarily would enter a sound reinforcement system via *direct input,* also known as *direct injection*. This procedure is further described in Chapters 13 and 16. Instruments such as electric guitars might be either miked or sent direct, depending on whether or not the guitar amp itself plays an important role in the desired sound quality.

Other audio sources might of-course include playback systems for recorded media, such as tape decks, CD players, or in special applications perhaps the audio signal from a videotape or film sound track. Normally such sources can be adapted to the input of any reinforcement system with the use of simple adaptors as described in Chapter 16.

c) Mixers and Related Accessory Units.

Beyond their basic function of mixing different input-signals to form combined output signals, most audio mixers are designed to perform a number of other signal processing functions.

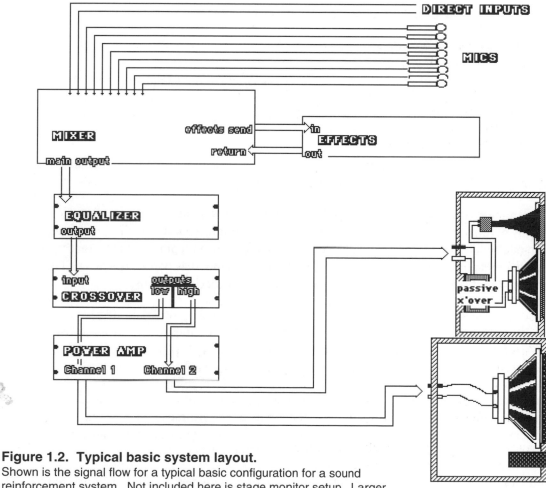

Figure 1.2. Typical basic system layout.
Shown is the signal flow for a typical basic configuration for a sound reinforcement system. Not included here is stage monitor setup. Larger systems essentially tend to be expanded versions of this basic type of layout. A larger system would be likely to include limiters and perhaps other signal processing devices as introduced in Chapter 8.

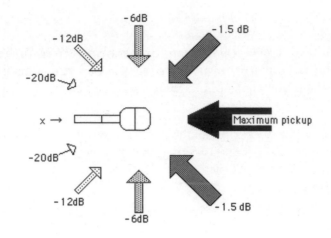

Figure 1.3. Representation of a basic microphone directional pattern as the mic "hears" it. Here, larger thicker arrows represent stronger pickup of sound coming from those directions. The pattern shown is known as a "cardi-oid" pattern, named after the heartlike shape of the pattern on the graphs shown in Chapter 5. A pattern of this type, also known as a "unidirectional" pattern, is useful in reducing pickup of unwanted sounds when properly used. (This pattern is of course three-dimensional, so rotating such a mic without changing its front-to-back orientation would not change this basic scheme. Incidentally, the abbreviation "mic" is used throughout this book—spell it "mike" if you prefer.)

Mixers, for all but the most basic applications, normally allow the signal strength to be adjusted at several stages, to make optimum use of the system's circuitry. Additional outboard devices can also be added to automatically regulate the desired maximum and/or minimum signal levels, called *compressors*, *limiters*, and *gates* (these are described in Chapter 8).

In addition to providing some kind of tone control (EQ) on each individual input channel (see Fig. 1.4), many mixer designs also provide on-board equalizers for the mixed output signals as well.

The vast majority of mixers allow signals to be split into separate electronic paths to allow the addition of any number of effects designed to enhance or modify the sound as well. Current technology has made an overwhelming selection of such devices available for both practical and creative use. The modified signal is then returned to an additional input to be included as part of the mix. (This type of supplementary signal route is usually called an *effects loop* or *auxiliary loop*).

Separately adjustable signal copies may be sent to additional power amplifiers and in-turn to monitor speakers (traditionally called *foldback,* but today usually referred to simply as "stage monitoring". This is a function which all but the most basic mixers ordinarily provide. In high-level systems, separate mixers are often used strictly for the purpose of mixing the monitor sound.

Among other basic features, a mixer may be designed to have multiple outputs to allow signals to be readily sent to different destinations such as to the inputs of a multitrack tape recorder. *Submasters*, if included, can allow the operator to divide input signals into categories at-will and control them in groups (these and other mixer functions are described in Chapter 7).

As indicated before, additional functions are commonly included within the same chassis. The extreme case of this is a mixer with graphic EQ and speaker-level outputs (such a unit is usually called a *mixer/amplifier* or *powered mixer*). A number of currently manufactured units also include features such as built-in digital reverb.

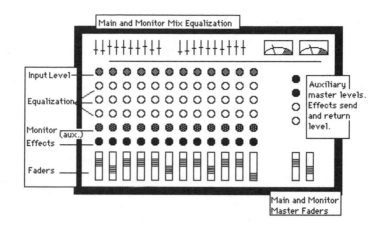

Fig. 1.4. Typical basic mixer layout. Mixers of this size (12 channels and under) and basic design (with graphic EQ) are marketed both with and without internal power amplifiers (speaker level outputs). An all-inclusive design of this kind can of course be quite handy for simple applications, particularly portable ones. Comparatively inexpensive and easy to operate, the compromise is a reduction in flexibility which would be afforded by using separate components for EQ, power amplification, crossover, limiting, etc.

(A mixer with this basic layout commonly uses both output faders and graphic EQ's for left and right in a "stereo" format, somewhat different than shown here. Essential concerns regarding these and larger mixers, as below, are described in Chapter 7 and throughout Part III.)

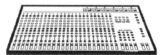

d) Equalizers.

The term *equalization* was originally applied to the process of electronically compensating for deficiencies in the ability of a component or system to accurately reproduce sounds or audio signals. Generally, the term (*EQ* for short) is now applied to any intentional alteration of frequency response—including tone control—whether for practical or creative reasons.

As mentioned, a mixer normally provides the capability to equalize individual channels (this is called "on-board" EQ). An on-board EQ usually allows for control of from 2 to 4 tonal ranges within the entire hearing range. A three-band EQ, for example, would allow emphasis or de-emphasis of bass, midrange and treble frequencies. Commonly, mixers provide *switchable* EQ, which allow the operator to choose between two or more preset frequency ranges for a given knob, or *sweepable* to allow the operator to choose the affected frequency range on a much more gradual basis. The most versatile mixers may include fully *parametric* EQ, which allow control of the three important parameters (aspects) affecting this process. (These basic forms of EQ design are described in Chapter 6.)

A high-power or high-quality system for a large audience or other critical application normally needs to allow fairly precise control over many finely divided tonal ranges (bands). The most common format for outboard EQs is the ubiquitous *graphic* EQ, though other configurations are used as well. Currently manufactured equalizers can provide separate control over as many as 45 separate slices of the human hearing range (in the case of several obscure models many more such slices are provided).

Others allow the operator to "zero in" on the relatively precise audio frequencies necessary for a particular application. The practical applications of this type of finely divided EQ might be to compensate for irregularities in microphones, loudspeakers and room acoustics, to creatively alter a vocal or instrumental sound, or to help eliminate the obnoxious feedback squeals well known to every performer and public speaker.

e) Amplifiers.

An amplifier's basic function, as explained, is to produce a signal copy. Unlike microphones (in which different frequency response curves often are a clearcut advantage) and equalizers (which allow intentional changes of frequency response) the amplifier's task is to make an *accurate* signal copy—one with the least possible alteration of the form of the input signal. The signal's strength may increase, but ideally the essential form (it's "sound") should not.

Amplifiers are normally used in the design of systems and components at every important junction in their often myriad circuitry. Within components such as mixers and other signal processing units, low-level amplifiers serve to isolate circuits from one another, thereby allowing individual circuits to fulfill the various internal signal-processing functions. Amplifiers also serve to compensate for losses of signal strength within the circuitry. These are usually called *line amplifiers* or *line drivers*. Each signal processing component has a line amplifier connected to the ouput jack(s), which generates the output signal that feeds the next component's input via the cable connecting the two. Among other types of low-level amplifiers also utilized are *combining amplifiers*, which perform the actual mixing function within a mixer (see Fig. 1.5). An audio signal being generated into a component's input might, depending on the component's design, be processed through a *differential amplifier*. Generally we need not be concerned with these, except to be aware that they exist, that they should be capable of producing a reasonably accurate signal of adequate strength, and that the inputs and outputs should be electronically compatible with other components in a given system. (The electronic compatibility is fairly easily managed in most cases, while the "adequate strength" occasionally will fall short, particularly with low-budget components.)

Preamplifiers ("pre-amps", for short), serve to boost a signal level prior to power amplification. Preamplifiers serve to produce a signal of sufficient strength to accomodate the input requirements of power amplifiers—that is, to "drive" them to the output level of which they are capable. Ordinarily, separate preamplifier components are used only for certain home-stereo applications. Normally, well-designed sound reinforcement components have line-level outputs sufficiently strong to eliminate the need for additional preamplification. We may, though, encounter the term on the access jacks of musical instrument amplifiers, in which case we can assume it refers to a line level. As well, the term can describe a unit designed to boost a very low-level mic output to a higher mic level or to a line level.

Power amplifiers serve to provide an output signal strong enough to drive the speakers. As mentioned before, several or all of the amplification tasks described in this section can be carried out within one chassis. The extreme case is a mixer with graphic equalization and speaker-level outputs, in which all of the basic electronic processes are accomplished by a single unit. In custom designed systems, the normal procedure is to use standard rack-mountable power amplifiers designed to accomplish only this final stage of amplification. (See also Chapter 4, section "o".)

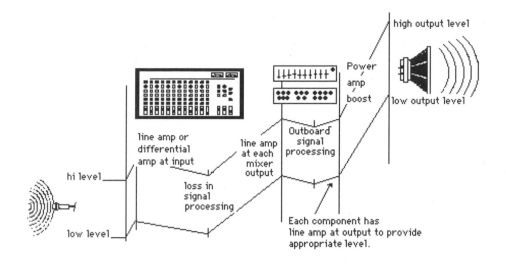

Fig. 1.5. Basic amplification stages in a sound reinforcement system.
Energy loss is involved in both input and output transducers, as well as in each of the signal processing stages, which is compensated for by amplifiers—in addition to the expected increase in sound level provided at the speaker output stage.

Amplifiers also serve in other ways in the internal electronics of components. Below left: A combining amplifier provides an effective summing of individual signals. Below right: A differential amplifier is used at the input stage of many component designs. (Other designs use small input transformers followed by a line amp.) *Note: slight liberty has been used in schematic representations.*

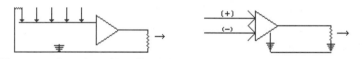

Line amps, also referred to as line drivers, are used within electronic components as well (below).

f) Speakers.

Speaker components, in implementing the final step from the electrical realm back into the acoustical realm, are responsible not only for creating sound waves out of electrical signals, but also for directing the sound in a consistent manner that is appropriate to the application. Over the years, this has represented an immense challenge to the designers of loudspeakers.

At the most basic level, one full-range transducer may be capable of reproducing more or less the whole human hearing range (as in headphone speakers or many inexpensive home stereo speakers). But the behavior of sound does not allow one speaker-element to control the directional pattern in a consistent enough way to be effective for most sound reinforcement applications. (This type of limitation can be experienced with any low-budget home-stereo speaker simply by moving gradually from one side to the other and noting the changes in tonal quality as you move. Directly in front of such a speaker, the very highest treble is readily heard, while off to the side the lower tonal ranges tend to be much more predominant by comparison.) Also, and at least as importantly, at high sound levels it becomes physically impossible for one speaker element to effectively handle such a wide frequency range, from the very low bass to the very high treble.

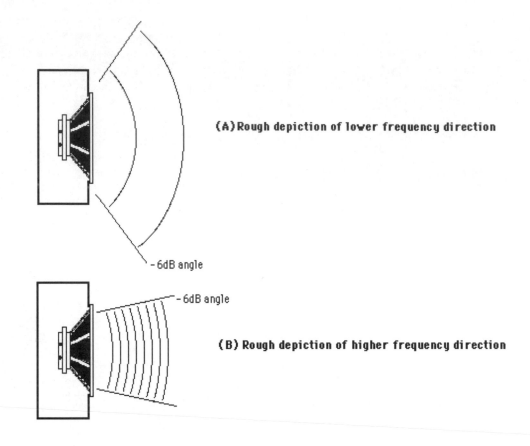

(A) Rough depiction of lower frequency direction

- 6dB angle

- 6dB angle

(B) Rough depiction of higher frequency direction

Fig. 1.6. A single speaker component of this type has massive variations of directivity, and is also unable to effectively reproduce wide tonal ranges at high levels without substantial distortion. These are why multiple components are used in modern sound reinforcment systems. The basic concerns involved in the use of multiple components are discussed in Chapter 9, and throughout Part III.

For all but the most basic applications, the loudspeaker's task is divided among two or more components, each of which is (ideally, at least) best suited for reproducing the frequencies in its intended range. Typical systems involve two, three or four—sometimes as many as five—frequency ranges, each handled by a different type of component. (More is possible but not at all necessary. Commonly, as in most home-stereo units, a multiple system is integrated into one cabinet, though for sound reinforcement applications the design of components often differs greatly from those in typical home-stereo-type applications.) Each basic design approach tends to have its own advantages and drawbacks, outlined in Chapter 9.

When two or more components are used in this way, the signal that powers each component needs to be confined to the band of frequencies for which that component is responsible. This is accomplished by a *frequency dividing network*, commonly referred to as a *crossover*.

g) Crossovers.

The task of the crossover is to divide its output into separate circuits, each covering a fairly specific *band*, or frequency range. This allows each speaker-component to reproduce only the frequency range within which it operates best. As well, the crossover serves to help protect speaker elements from being damaged by operating outside the limits of their designated frequency range.

In systems designed for low-to-moderate-level use, crossovers can easily be installed after the power amplifier stage. When higher sound levels or finer operational control are required, a very significant increase in system efficiency can be achieved by dividing the audio spectrum before the

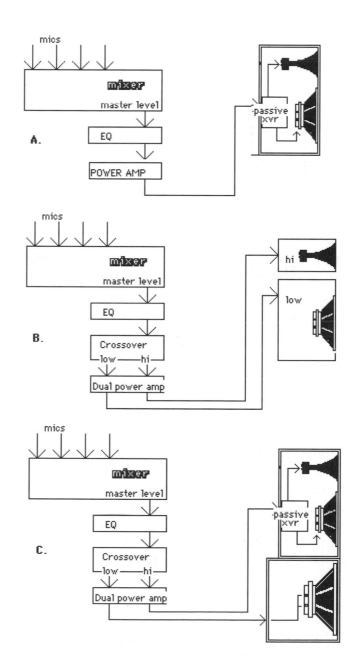

Figure 1.7
Typical crossover
applications in a
simple system.

(A) internal passive crossover, most often built into a standard multiple-component enclosure;

(B) simple "bi-amped" 2-way system with an active cross-over;

(C) standard two-way enclosure, with "sub-woofer".

The factors involved in this aspect of system use and design are discussed in Chapters 9, 10, 11, 13, and 14.

power-amplifier stage. This type of unit is referred to as an *active crossover*, or *electronic crossover*; the former is called a *passive crossover*.

Each has its advantages. Passive crossovers require a smaller number of power amplifiers, less wiring between components, and are generally more convenient for the user. Active crossovers, on the other hand, make more efficient use of total power amplifier output and more readily allow for accurate fine tuning of crossover points, and also can allow control of several other factors involved in dividing frequency ranges. Often, both are used very effectively in the same system, as illustrated in Fig. 1.7.

i) Practical System Concerns.

The overall effectiveness of a system certainly is no better than its weakest link. Beyond the quality of the components themselves, the quality of cables and methods of wiring play fundamental roles in a system's effectiveness. The manner in which the flow of audio signals passes from one stage to another within the system (and/or within a component) also plays a role both in audio quality and in practical aspects of operation. Chapters 5 through 10 overview sound reinforcement components. Chapters 11 through 16 overview system-related aspects of sound reinforcement.

j) The Acoustic Environment.

The acoustical realm is the first and last link in the chain from the sound source(s) to the listeners' ears. While this basic fact is obvious to most, the characteristics of the acoustic environment are often overlooked or misunderstood by many operators and inexperienced designers of sound systems.

Chapter 2 will attempt to introduce an initial perspective on sound in general. Later chapters will attempt to broaden this perspective.

k) Human Factors.

Sound reinforcement systems are oftentimes thought of simply as electronic (or electroacoustic) systems. But there is an often neglected human element involved at both ends of any such system. It is this human element—performers, public speakers and an audience of individuals—for which the system exists, and to which the system is ultimately accountable.

Among other things which are of important concern, the human ear itself behaves very differently than might be expected from looking at electronic measurements and meters. The perception of sound often varies significantly from one individual to another, changes according to the intensity of the sound, and also can change from moment-to-moment and place-to-place in a given arena in some interesting and sometimes almost bizarre ways. Certainly the potential for long term or permanent hearing loss is also of major concern with high-level systems. (Chapter 3 introduces the basics of human hearing and some of the ways it typically affects the process of sound reinforcement.)

In addition, practical considerations involving the various needs of performers and talkers come almost constantly into play. We will attempt to bring these concerns into perspective in later chapters.

CHAPTER 2

THE NATURE OF SOUND

This chapter and the next contain basic information on sound itself, some of which is subject to widespread misconception among more inexperienced trained students of sound reinforcement—indeed, among students of sound in general. The reader is encouraged to double-check this entire chapter thoroughly to ensure that its content is understood.

a) Sound Waves.

Figures 2.1 and 2.2 show the motion of a speaker reproducing a sound of the most basic kind, such as that of a tuning fork or one note in the simplest possible setting of an electronic organ or synthesizer.

When the cone moves outward (Fig. 2.1-B) the air immediately in front is compressed beyond its normal air pressure. The compressed air particles then move outward and exert added pressure on the air particles in front of them, which in turn move outward and compress against the following particles, and so on. In this manner a *wave of compression* is created in which pressure is rapidly passed from one set of air particles to the next as the wave travels outward.

When the cone moves inward (Fig. 2.1-D) it creates a partial vacuum, or expansion (also called "rarefaction"). As the air particles in front of the cone rush back to fill up the expansion, the next particles begin to move back as well, then the following particles, and so on outward. In this way a *wave of expansion* is also passed from one set of particles to the next as it follows behind the compression at the same speed. Each time the cone creates a compression and an expansion (of this most basic type) and then returns to its starting point, it is said to have completed one *cycle*.

As the cone continues to move in the same manner (Fig. 2.2) it creates a series of alternating compressions and expansions that are quickly passed outward in a "ripple effect." Rapid, ripple-like variations of air pressure such as these are what our hearing process detects and a quick instant later interprets to be a particular type of sound. Although the waves travel outward from their source, the air particles themselves do not move any farther out than is necessary to pass a compression onward; instead they are then sucked back by the next outgoing expansion—repeating the process for the duration of the sound.

In an open area, sound waves travel away from their source in a manner which can be roughly likened to the surface waves created in a pond when a pebble is thrown into it. As the waves move outward, they spread their energy over a larger and larger area, diminishing in height until at some distance from

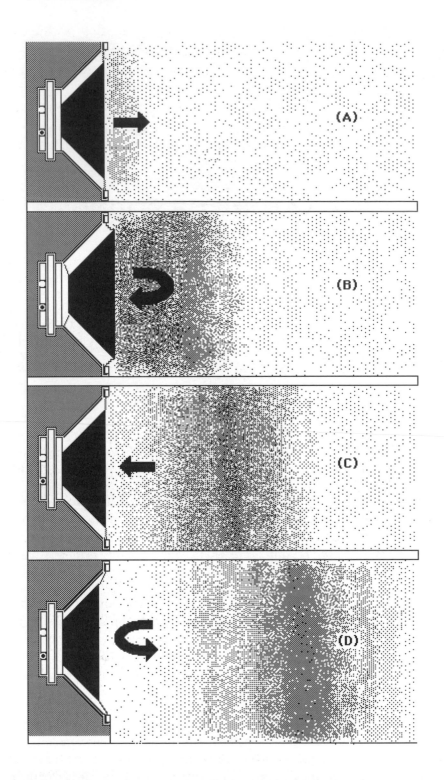

Figure 2.1. One cycle of a speaker cone's movement. (E, cone returns to A) What is illustrated here are not ripples, but compressions and expansions of air, which are sent outward. Shown here is a narrow slice of the outward progress of a wave of one frequency. The actual extent of the "sideways" spread would of-course be three-dimensional (i.e., left, right, upwards and downwards from the direction in which the speaker cone points), and the degree of spread (its dispersion) would normally vary according to the wave's frequency.

the source they can no longer be detected. Sound waves, though, spread out in any of a variety of three-dimensional patterns, rather than on a plane such as the water's surface.

In an enclosed area such as a room or auditorium, sound tends to behave somewhat like the waves created by a pebble dropped into a fishtank (Fig. 2.3). If the walls, floor and ceiling are bare, the sound undergoes numerous reflections before it dies out. (In a highly reflective room, this can be similar to the way light behaves in a room lined with mirrors, except that with light it occurs much more quickly.) The result—called *reverberation*—is a series of echoes so closely spaced they cannot be distinguished apart, sounding instead like a continuous decay following the initial sound.

With each reflection, a certain amount of the energy in the waves is lost to the reflecting surface, until finally it is completely absorbed. A listener in the room hears first the sound directly from the source, then the reflected sound from the surfaces in the room. The manner in which this occurs is in-large-part responsible for what is commonly known as a room's "acoustics."

When furniture, draperies, carpet, etc. are added to the room, the effect becomes more like that which occurs in the fishtank when plants and other porous or irregular objects are allowed to protrude through the surface of the water (Fig. 2.3-B). In such a room, the waves are further diffused and absorbed by the additional objects and porous surfaces, causing the sound to decay more quickly. The degree and type of reverberation in a given room is of great importance to sound reinforcement. Depending on the situation, it is capable of being both a blessing and a curse. An adequate amount of reverberation can add to the pleasantness of a performance. An excessive amount can be a nightmare for both performers and audience alike. The optimum amount of reverberation in any given environment can vary according to whether we are amplifying speech or music, and also according to the type of music involved.

Figure 2.2. This is an actual time-exposure of a slice of sound waves being emitted by a loud-speaker. It was accomplished by an innovative method of sweeping a small microphone—attatched to a tiny neon bulb synchronized to light up instantaneously during the compression phase of each passing wave—gradually swept through the field of the camera. Assuming a 15" speaker, the continuously emitted frequency here would be quite high—on the order of 5000 Hz. Note the extremely narrow pattern of the loudest portion of the waves (the traces on the upper and lower outskirts are many dB lower in intensity, and would be barely audible). This "beaming" characteristic is a primary reason why high frequency horns are used in sound reinforcement, in order to appropriately disperse the high frequencies more evenly throughout an audience. Still, not every system accomplishes this with the same degree of effectiveness, a topic discussed in Chapter 9. Photo reprinted from Seeing Sound, Winston E. Kock. Permission is gratefully acknowledged.

Fig. 2.3
Waves in a fishtank can be used to roughly represent the behavior of sound in a room with reflective walls. In addition to reflections of this type, resonances also occur in a typical room. These can significantly alter the character of sound in a given room.

(B) Porous or irregular objects serve to further reduce reflections. The "shadows" here would vary by frequency—the high frequencies would be more likely to be blocked by such obstructions than would the lows (see also section "e" of this chapter).

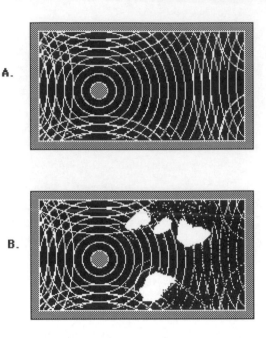

b) The Speed of Sound.

In any given substance, sound travels away from its source at a constant speed. Just how fast this speed is depends upon the substance. In water, for example, sound travels more than four times as quickly as it does in air. In steel or iron, the speed of sound is almost fifteen times as fast as in air. This difference can be fairly easily demonstrated by two people, say fifty meters or so apart, along an iron railing or railroad track. If one person raps on the rail with a hammer, the second person will hear the sound twice—once as the vibrations pass through the railing and again a split second later as they pass at a lower speed through the air. Sound also travels at different speeds through different types of gas. The high-pitched, munchkin-like voice of a person who has just inhaled helium from a balloon is actually a result of the higher velocity of sound waves in helium as it passes through the voicebox and mouth.

In air, the substance we're most concerned with, the speed of sound is about **344 meters per second (1130 feet per second)**. Sound waves travel through air at this speed whether they are soft or loud, low-pitched or high-pitched, of a simple or a complex nature—because this is the normal speed at which air responds to changes in pressure.

The speed of sound does vary very slightly according to temperature, humidity and atmospheric pressure, since these factors affect the physical properties (elasticity and density) of the air somewhat. This can occasionally present problems to musicians playing instruments whose pitch is altered by these changes (primarily wind instruments). For the majority of practical calculations concerning sound reinforcement, though, all sound waves can be assumed to travel at the above mentioned speed.

c) Amplitude.

The strength, or intensity, of a wave at a given instant in time is called its *amplitude*. In Fig. 2.4, amplitude is shown as the vertical distance (height and depth) of the waves above and below the center line. This represents the amount of pressure change (compression (above the center line) and expansion (below center line)) caused in the air by sound waves, and also can represent the electrical signal within the internal circuitry of a sound system. The term "amplitude" has a meaning similar to that of "*volume*," "*loudness*," and "*sound pressure level*," among others. There are subtle-but-important differences between them, though, which will be discussed in Chapters 3 and 4.

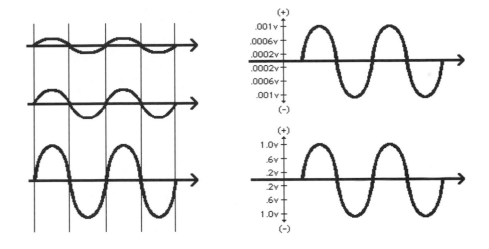

Fig. 2.4 Equivalent waves of different amplitude as shown on a time line or an oscilloscope screen.
Note (on left) that only the height differs, not the length. This would also roughly represent how an amplifier increases the strength of a signal without changing its frequency or essential waveform. This type of amplitude change could also be represented by showing it on an altered vertical scale, such as shown at right. The visual graphs of these same sets of waves could be stretched out or collapsed either vertically or horizontally, depending on the time and amplitude scales used.

d) Frequency.

The rate at which any kind of motion repeats itself is referred to as its *frequency*. For audio waves, frequency is measured in cycles per second, or *hertz*. For example, if a speaker cone were to take one full second to complete the motion described in Fig. 2.1, its frequency would be one cycle per second, or one hertz (*Hz*). If this motion occurred one hundred times per second, its frequency (and that of the resulting sound waves) would be 100 Hz. If the motion occurred one thousand times per second, its frequency would then be 1000 Hz or one *kilo*-hertz (1 *kHz*). When the motion does not last for a full second, "frequency" refers to the number of cycles that would occur if it were to continue for one second at the same rate.

The human ear is capable of hearing throughout a frequency range known as the *audio spectrum*, or simply, the *audio frequency range.* Generally, this range is considered to be from 20 Hz upwards to 20,000 Hz (20 kHz). Within these approximate limits, "frequency" corresponds closely to the sensation of *pitch* created in the ear (the higher the frequency, the higher the musical pitch that is heard).

The audio spectrum is a range which spans roughly ten *octaves*, or doublings of frequency. The concept of an octave is basic in the study of music, but is useful and important in the study of sound in-general as well. The octave represents a proportion (the ratio 2:1), and it is proportions between different frequencies that the hearing process recognizes, rather than the actual number-values between frequencies. As an example, the middle of the audio spectrum is not numerically half-way between 20 and 20,000 (which would be 10,010). Rather, it is half the number of octaves from 20 to 20,000 Hz—which is approximately 640 Hz (see Fig. 2.5).

The ten octaves of the audio spectrum can be thought of as the keyboard upon which all of the sounds heard by human ears are played. *Each sound is given its own character mainly by (1) the frequencies that are involved, (2) their relative intensities, and (3) the manner in which the frequencies and/or intensities vary with time.*

The audio spectrum can also be evenly divided into **decades**, which in audio language refer to a range of frequencies falling within a ratio of ten-to-one. (This is also called an "order-of-magnitude", the span of which can be shown by the addition of a zero to the end of any whole number.) The audio frequency range has a span of three decades: from 20 Hz to 200 Hz, from 200 Hz to 2000 Hz, and from 2000 Hz to 20,000 Hz. This can be a useful way of dividing the audio spectrum, because individual speaker components in many sound reinforcement applications are inherently limited to about one decade of effective frequency range (this is explained in Chapter 9).

It should be noted that the ear's sensitivity to different frequencies varies throughout the spectrum. Some frequency ranges are more readily heard than others, and the upper and lower limits are not by any means hard-and-fast dividing lines. Instead the ability-to-hear gradually lessens towards the extremes (and can also differ widely among individuals). It will be explained in Chapter 3 why this and other special characteristics of the human hearing process have important implications in the use of sound reinforcement systems.

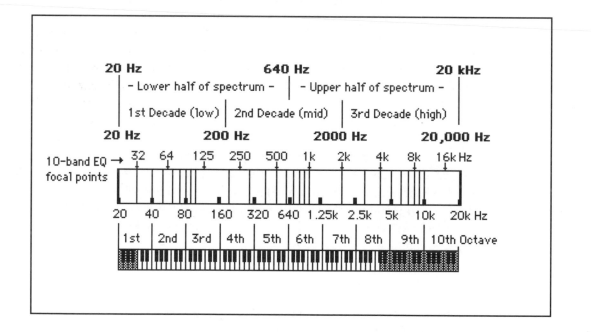

Figure 2.5
The dividing lines of the audio spectrum are actually somewhat arbitrary. Ordinarily, the middle of the spectrum is, for engineering purposes, regarded to be about 1 kHz. A typical very-wide-range sound reinforcement system normally needs to reproduce only from about 40 Hz to 14 kHz. In fact, even these (believe it or not) are very extreme low and high frequencies for most musical applications. However, a specification beyond the needed range can sometimes be an indicator that a component is able to reach the needed frequencies with reasonable effectiveness.

e) Wavelength.

Closely related to the frequency of a sound wave is its *wavelength*. This term describes the distance a wave of given frequency would travel in open air in the time it takes to complete one cycle. It is also the distance between the same point in two consecutive cycles as they travel away from their source. As all sounds travel though air at the same speed, *wavelength varies by inverse proportion to frequency (the higher the frequency, the shorter the wavelength).*

The following analogy may be helpful. Imagine observing a row of people marching out of a doorway, all at the same speed. If these people came out of the doorway at a regular interval (frequency), they would all be spaced the same distance apart (wavelength). If they kept the same speed but doubled the rate at which they came through the doorway (twice the frequency), they would then be spaced only half-the-distance apart (half the wavelength). Considered the other way around, the people in the row with the shorter distance between them could be said to pass an observer with greater frequency than they did when spaced farther apart. This relationship is shown by the formula:

$$\text{Wavelength } (\lambda) = \frac{\text{Speed of sound } (\sim 1130'/\text{second})}{\text{Frequency } (Hz)}$$

A 20 Hz sound wave is about 17 meters (~56 feet) in length, while a 20 kHz wave is only about 17 millimeters (~two-thirds of an inch) long. Wavelengths between the two extremes vary according to the above formula (inversely proportional to frequency). (For easy reference, Chapter 9 includes a chart of approximate wavelengths throughout the spectrum.)

The concept of wavelength is of particular importance in the proper design of speakers, horns and enclosures, as well as in understanding the way sound waves behave in various physical environments. Sound sources which are very small or slender in comparison to the wavelengths they produce do not radiate sound well. This is the primary reason why low-frequency speaker components are so much larger than their high-frequency counterparts. In fact, the ideal low-frequency component would be far too large to be of practical use, so every commonly used type of low-frequency horn or speaker enclosure involves a substantial compromise in size and design.

The length of a sound wave also affects its ability to pass around the various obstacles in its path, such as abutments, pillars and the human body and head. Short wavelengths (high frequencies) tend to be reflected or absorbed by such obstacles, while the longest wavelengths of the spectrum (low frequencies) tend to travel around or through just about everything in their paths.

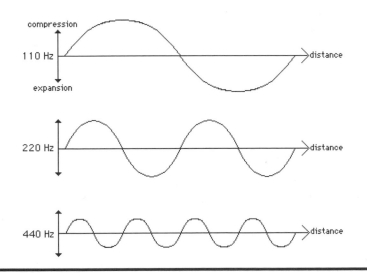

Figure 2.6
Wavelength varies In inverse proportion to frequency. (Twice the frequency=half the wavelength).

Longer wavelengths, among other things, more readily bend around the structure of their source as well as around obstacles in their path.

f) The Sine Wave.

The particular form of the pressure waves that make up a sound, it should be obvious, is determined by the type of vibration which creates them. For the most basic possible physical example, the sound of a tuning fork, used for centuries in tuning musical instruments to their proper pitch, is produced by the most basic type of vibration, known as *simple harmonic motion.*

A pendulum swinging back-and-forth and a weight bobbing up-and-down on the end of a spring are slower, more readily observed examples of this type of motion. Remember that the pendulum was used in clocks of an earlier day because each stroke takes the same amount of time no matter how far out it swings. (In other words, it maintains its characteristic frequency regardless of its amplitude.) The tuning fork, of course, moves back and forth quickly enough to create audible sound waves, but it is very much the same type of movement. When it is struck, the prongs respond by springing back and forth in simple harmonic motion, setting the surrounding air into simple harmonic motion at the same rate. (Concert "A", 440 Hz is the most commonly used frequency, although they are still manufactured for a number of different frequencies corresponding to accepted musical notes—not everyone has switched to electronic tuners.)

Fig. 2.7. Sine-wave motion.

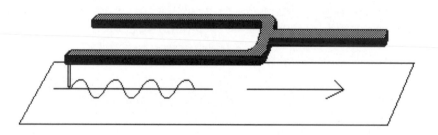

(A) The tuning fork produces the basic waveform called the sine wave, of which all sound waves, without exception, are composed. (The scale of this figure is exaggerated for purpose of illustration.) When the terms "frequency" and "wavelength" are used, they refer to sine waves of which a sound is composed.

(B) Vibration modes of a simple string. Many musicians and soundpersons who are not highly technically oriented have difficulty at-first grasping that these happen simultaneously, each vibration taking the form of sine-wave motion at its particular frequency. (The term "harmonic", by definition, means that its frequency is a whole-number multiple of the fundamental frequency.)

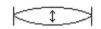 1) Fundamental frequency (f) depends on tension and other physical characteristics.

(Additional harmonics' relative strength depend on how and where string is picked, and on factors such as the thickness of string, type of winding, etc.)

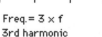

Freq.= 2 x f	Freq.= 3 x f	Freq.= 4 x f	Freq.= 5 x f
2nd harmonic	3rd harmonic	4th harmonic	5th harmonic, etc.
(1st overtone)	(2nd overtone)	(3rd overtone)	(4th overtone, etc.)

A way of graphing this type of motion directly from the vibrations of a tuning fork can be imagined by visualizing an extremely fine-tipped pen attached to one of the prongs as illustrated in Fig. 2.7. If a strip of paper were moved at a regular speed with the pen lightly touching the paper, the back-and-forth motions would be traced.

The resulting waveform, showing simple harmonic motion along a timeline, would be that of a *sine wave. This type of wave is the most elementary "building block" of which all sound waves, **without exception**, are composed.* In fact, due to basic laws of physical and molecular motion, every type of waveform can be mathematically, acoustically and electronically broken down into its sine wave components. **When the terms "frequency" and "wavelength" are used, they are normally assumed to refer to a given sine-wave component in a sound.** As will be seen, the ability to extract the sine-wave components involved in a sound is also of fundamental importance to the human hearing process itself. Before getting into complex waveforms, though, it seems appropriate to first introduce several additional basic concepts.

g) Resonance.

The sound produced by a tuning fork itself is barely audible—capable of being heard only when held very close to someone's ear. In order to be more readily heard, it must be coupled to something more efficient at radiating its particular frequency.

The tines of a tuning fork have an extremely slim surface in comparison to the wavelength they produce. A 440 Hz sound wave, for example, has a wavelength of about 0.75 meters (two-and-a-half-feet), which is overwhelming compared to the thickness of the tines. Consequently, air slips around the sides of the vibrating tines with ease, and very little of the mechanical energy involved in the fork's motion is given to the air in the form of acoustical energy (sound waves).

When the stem of a vibrating tuning fork is placed against an object with a larger surface capable of vibrating at the same frequency, more air is set into motion, resulting in a louder sound. Some of the energy imparted to the fork in striking it is thus used to power a more efficient sound-source. This is an example of *resonance*.

A panel as shown in Fig. 2.8 has certain resonant frequencies at which it will ring when it is struck. These are a result of the panel's *preferred modes of vibration*. In each instance different modes can be emphasized according to where and how it is struck. If one of these frequencies is the same as that of a particular tuning fork, such a panel can serve as a fairly efficient resonator for it. With a properly located contact point, the panel can turn energy from the fork into a relatively large amount of acoustical energy. Often, placing a tuning fork against an object such as a wall panel or table top will have this effect. An object like the sounding board of a piano, which is designed to respond to the frequencies involved in all the notes on the keyboard, will tend to resonate well with a tuning fork of any frequency.

Resonance can also be accomplished through the use of a tube or cavity. The air in a tube or cavity of given internal dimensions and mouth size has its own preferred mode(s) of vibration which, for example, are directly responsible for the note heard when blowing across the mouth of a bottle or test tube. When a tuning fork is placed on its intended resonator box—the cavity of which is designed to respond to its particular frequency—the resulting increase in volume can be surprising. Energy is drawn from the fork through the surface on which it is placed, then radiated efficiently by the cavity. The same effect can be achieved simply by placing the vibrating tines in close proximity to the mouth of the cavity. If a resonator box designed for a tuning fork of a different frequency is used, the effect is usually minimal.

The principle of resonance continually comes into play in sound reinforcement and in the behavior of sound in general, occurring in rooms, speakers and speaker enclosures, acoustic horns, musical instruments and even electrical circuits. In fact, everything in the entire universe has one or more resonant frequencies, though not necessarily within the audio spectrum.

Resonances such as those which are a natural result of the dimensions of a particular room can present an obstacle to the effectiveness of even the highest quality sound reinforcement systems. Such resonances, when present to an extreme, disproportionately accentuate the frequencies that correspond to them, sometimes resulting in a severely altered version of the system's actual output sound. Similar occurences can also be caused by poorly designed horns, speaker enclosures and electronic components, mismatched speaker/enclosure combinations, or by other factors within the system itself. Though disproportionate resonances can sometimes be a source of trouble, the principle of resonance in general is an important and normally desirable influence in the creation of musical and vocal sounds (and as will be explained in Chapter 9, in certain speaker designs as well).

h) Sound Spectra.

While sine waves are the basic building blocks of sound, they are rarely created in pure form by any physical source other than the already mentioned tuning fork. The brief tone heard on many telephone recording machines, the continuous test tone used by off-the-air TV stations, and some of the sounds made by computer-operated game machines are other examples of this type of sound—though these are generated electronically. Because of their status as "building blocks," sine waves are useful for a wide variety of testing purposes (they are used for most hearing tests, as well as in testing audio equipment in general). Pure sine waves of constant frequency and amplitude are commonly perceived as being "lifeless", "monotonous" (they in fact literally **are** monotones), "dull", or simply, "pure". In this sense, hearing a sine wave of constant frequency and amplitude is somewhat like looking at a building block that is not part of a building.

The sounds we hear are normally made up of a mixture of sine-wave components which together can be referred to as the *spectrum* **or** *energy distribution* **of any given sound.** [*] In the case of musical sounds, the frequencies fit together in a way that is orderly enough to have a special pleasing quality when arranged in musical passages. (Sounds that are more noiselike do not have the orderliness we consider musical, instead consisting of more random mixtures of frequencies.) The string, probably the most commonly used type of vibrating element used worldwide, serves as a good illustration of how a musical sound is created.

Consider first the string itself, simply stretched between two solid supports. When it is picked, it of-course springs quickly back and forth, each successive motion becoming slightly smaller than the previous one until it finally comes to rest. *A string that has been set in motion in this way actually vibrates simultaneously in a number of different modes, each of which takes on the form of sine-wave motion at a particular frequency* (see Fig. 2..7-B).

The mode of vibration spanning the entire length of the string, with maximum movement in the center, is the *first harmonic,* usually referred to as the *fundamental*. The fundamental mode produces the primary pitch heard as the musical note of the string.

---

[*] The fact that each sound has its own spectrum of frequencies should not be confused with the idea of the audio spectrum, which refers to all frequencies capable of being heard by human ears. "Spectra" is the plural form of "spectrum."

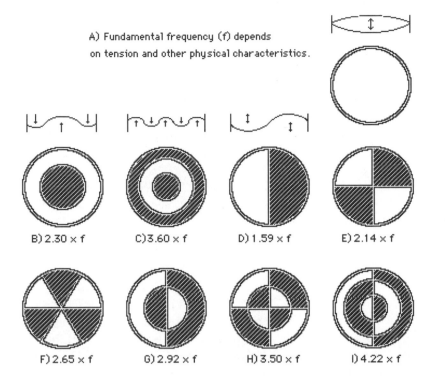

A) Fundamental frequency (f) depends on tension and other physical characteristics.

B) 2.30 × f   C) 3.60 × f   D) 1.59 × f   E) 2.14 × f

F) 2.65 × f   G) 2.92 × f   H) 3.50 × f   I) 4.22 × f

Fig. 2.8 Examples of other types of vibration modes.

Above: Basic vibration modes of a drumhead. Note that these do not bear a harmonic relationship to the fundamental. These particular inharmonic overtones combine to produce the characteristic sound we recognize as that of an undamped (unmuted) drum. Many of the involved frequencies may be enhanced to varying degrees by the resonant characteristics of the drum itself. Of some importance to the discussion in Chapter 17 is the fact that the drum overtones are spaced more closely (in frequency) than harmonics. (illustration derived from Acoustical Engineering, Harry F. Olsen, 1967)

Below: A suspended panel and an enclosed air mass are two examples of fairly efficient resonators. A room is also a kind of enclosed air mass, which has its own resonant frequencies, depending on its shape, size and construction.

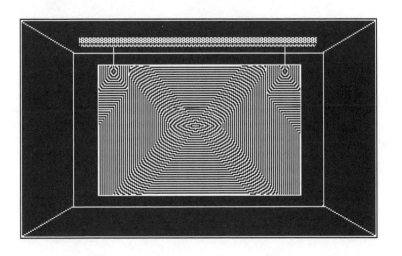

The additional harmonics (2nd, 3rd, 4th, 5th, etc.—also called the string's *overtones*) are the result of vibration modes that involve equal subdivisions of the string's full length. Harmonics, by definition, are frequencies which are integer-multiples (that is, multiplied by a whole number: 1,2,3,4,5, etc.) of the fundamental.

Like the tines of a tuning fork, the string itself slices through the air without giving up much of its energy to the air. If the string is attatched to an acoustic guitar (or other hollow-bodied instrument), the body resonates in response to the string's vibrations. Unlike the resonator box of a tuning fork—which need respond to only one frequency—the body of a guitar must resonate at a large number of frequencies. Its specially curved shape serves to acomplish this.

The guitar body nevertheless responds somewhat more readily to some frequencies than it does to others. The combination of resonances involving all possible vibration modes of the body's wooden plates and the cavity inside can be plotted in the form of a "frequency response curve," or *resonance curve*. This type of graph (Fig. 2.9) shows the degree to which the body will respond to vibrations of any given frequency.

Together, *the vibrating element (string) and resonator (guitar body) combine to produce the spectrum of a given note on the guitar.* The string itself produces the fundamental musical pitch and additional harmonics, whose frequencies change in proportion to one another as different notes are played, thus retaining their harmonic relationship. The guitar body then determines to what degree each of these frequencies will be reinforced—providing extra reinforcement to those which fall within the peaks of the resonance curve. *The resulting spectrum gives the sound of a note played on a guitar its characteristic tonal quality,* traditionally referred to as its **timbre** (pronounced "tamber"). The timbre of an instrument's sound plays a vital role in allowing, for example, "E" played on a guitar to be heard as being different from the same note played on any other type of instrument (or another guitar whose own physical characteristics result in a slightly different spectrum).

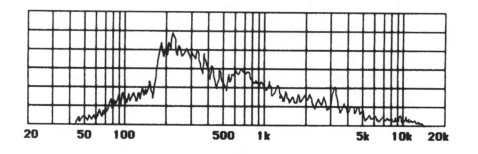

Fig. 2.9. A resonance "curve" such as this represents the degree to which each of the frequencies produced by a string, or other vibrating element, would be "amplified" by an instrument or other sound source. This characteristic is a primary aspect of what is modifyable by an EQ and/or microphone. (The plot shown would be roughly typical of an acoustic guitar or viola.)

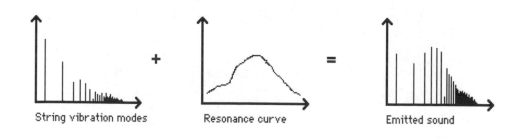

String vibration modes   Resonance curve   Emitted sound

In some instruments, such as woodwinds, a separate resonator is not used; a reed serves as a vibrating element and the notes themselves are determined by a player's control over the effective length of the air column in the instrument (roughly the equivalent of controlling the resonant note of a bottle or test tube by filling it with a certain amount of water). In other instruments, such as trumpets and trombones, the player's lips act as a vibrating element. In yet others, such as flutes and recorders, there is no physical vibrating element at all—the vibrations being created instead by a rapidly alternating airstream across the mouthpiece. In each case, the particular physical structure and manner of playing the instrument impart to the sound its own spectrum, and thus its tonal quality. *The difference between the concepts of vibrating element and resonator*, though, *are of some importance to an understanding of which aspects of a sound can be effectively controlled by a sound system, and which aspects cannot (see again Fig. 2.9).* This is discussed somewhat further in Chapters 6 and 17.

i) Phase and Interference.

An interesting and important characteristic of sine-wave motion is its close relationship to circular motion, This is the basis for the measurement of a wave's **phase**. The study of specific phase relationships among sound waves can in itself be highly complex, but for the purposes of this book it is necessary only to understand the basic idea.

Fig. 2.10 shows a sine wave graphed as a projection of a circle whose radius is equal to the peak amplitude of the wave. In this illustration, Point X_1 on the circle is assumed to rotate in its circular path at the same frequency as Point X_2 on the sine wave. If both start their motion simultaneously at zero degrees, their vertical displacements (amplitudes) will be identical at every point in their respective cycles.

When the cycle reaches 90 degrees, positive amplitude (compression) is at its peak value. At 180 degrees, amplitude is again zero; at 270 degrees negative amplitude (expansion) is at its peak value. At 360 degrees (the same as zero degrees), amplitude is once again zero and the next cycle begins.

When two or more waves interact with one another, their amplitudes are added algebraically. In a simplified example of this (Fig. 2.11), when two sine waves of the same frequency and amplitude are superimposed with both starting simultaneously at zero degrees (exactly **in-phase**), the result is a sine wave of twice their individual amplitude. The waves are said to **interfere constructively** with one another. If the same two waves are superimposed with one starting at zero degrees and the other at 180 degrees, their amplitude are then exactly oposite one another (180 degrees out-of-phase), and are said to **interfere destructively**, in this case cancelling one another out completely. If two waves of equal frequency and amplitude are superimposed with any other phase relationship with respect to one another, they will at times interfere constructively, and at other times interfere destructively. Another way of referring to this is as *partial or total reinforcement* (*constructive interference*) *or partial or total cancellation* (*destructive interference*). In the acoustic environment, waves seldom cancel each other entirely—mostly what we experience is partial cancellation. The same type of algebraic relationship holds for all interacting sound waves.

Sound waves from two different sources interact in a way that is comparable to the waves created by two separate disturbances on the surface of water (Fig. 2.11-B). Note that the alternate constructive and destructive interference does not alter the path of either series of waves. Their interference at any given point simply adds up to the degree of positive or negative amplitude necessary to pass the waves along on their outward journey. *A listener in any given position, though, will hear different frequencies to the degree that they are being accented or reduced at that particular listener's position.* This is important, since with systems involving more than one speaker location, we can expect the sound to vary somewhat throughout an audience, even when the sound is effctively dispersed by the speakers.

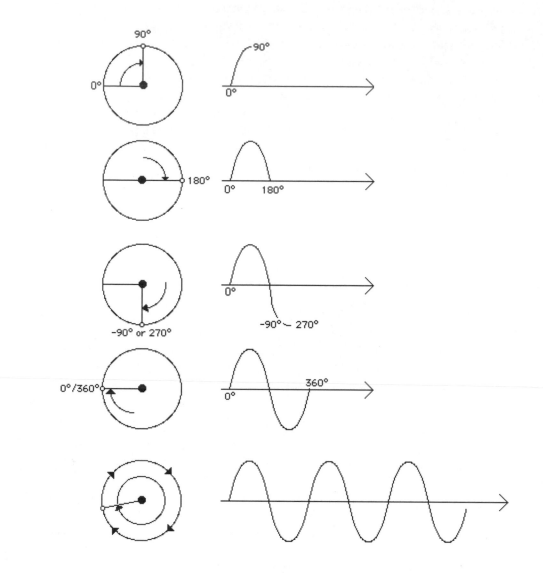

Fig. 2.10. The relationship of a circle to a wave's phase.
Sine waves (frequencies) are actually a form of circular motion extended outward along an axis, such as time or distance. Their close relationship to circular motion (from the standpoint of the physicist, the purest form of motion), accounts for why they tend to behave independently of one another, despite the fact that they combine in an infinite number of ways.

The notion of "phase" is of great importance to sound reinforcement. Phase is abbreviated "Ø". A common function on high quality mixers, some delay units and—rarely—crossovers allows phase inversion (also known as "reversed polarity") by 180°. This type of reversal can alo be accomplished by reversing the wires at one end of a balanced XLR-type cable as shown in Chapter 16.

Another important concern with regard to phase is that speakers be wired in the same polarity, especially if they are in the same enclosure or the same array of speakers, else they will tend to cancel one another's output, particularly at low frequencies. (Or in the worst case, blow out completely—see the explanation in Chapter 9 on "acoustic loading".)

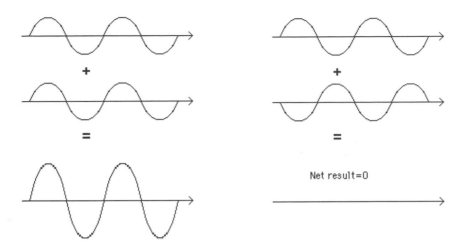

Fig. 2.11. Basic interactions of waves with one another. In their travels through the air or through the electrical realm, identical waves of identical phase double in intensity (+3 dB acoustically; sometimes +6 dB electrically, depending on the type of circuit). Identical waves of exactly opposite phase of-course cancel out completely.

When identical waves emanate from two separate sources, they normally intersect at a given listener's position in a variety of phase relationships in between these two extremes, either partially reinforcing or partially cancelling one another. (As well, there is typically substantial overlap with reflections from surrounding surfaces.)

Only when one is equally distant from the two sources (as below) do all frequencies reinforce. In any other position, some frequencies reinforce while others cancel. What this means for the system operator is that the sound can be expected to vary substantially from one point to another in an audience, even if being consistently spread by the speakers.

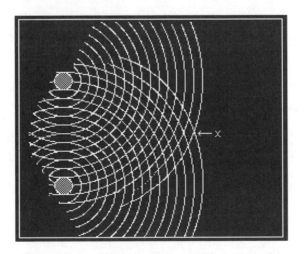

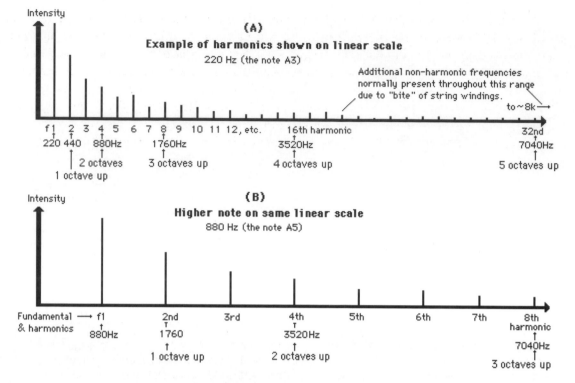

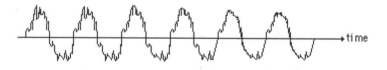

Fig. 2.12

A) Piano string harmonics shown on linear scale. This is a relatively low note, it's harmonics extending well up into the spectrum, in addition to perhaps other frequencies representing the "bite" of string windings against one another. (not shown). Notice how the overtones are more numerous with each successive octave on the scale. With a higher note (B) the harmonics are more widely spaced, so fewer frequencies are involved. As the notes get higher, the strings are usually also designed without windings, accounting for their characteristically "purer" sound.

C) Rough depiction of a complex waveform, resulting from the combination of frequencies involved. This would also represent the motion of a single speaker cone reproducing such a sound.

j) Complex Waveforms.

It was explained that each sound has its own spectrum of frequencies which the hearing process is capable of identifying as the special tonal quality of that sound. How, though, do the frequencies involved in each sound get simulaneously passed through the air? To answer this it seems appropriate to look at the loudspeaker piston again, in this case reproducing a complex waveform such as a note played on a piano.

Fig. 2.12 shows a typical spectrum of frequencies involved in the note "A", 220 Hz (one octave below Concert "A") played on a piano. (Incidentally, the seventh harmonic is minimal here because the striking point of hammer against string in this particular instance effectively eliminates this particular overtone). **When the fundamental and all its overtones are superimposed as described in the previous segment on phase and interference, they combine to produce a complex waveform** which might appear somewhat like that shown in Fig. 2.12-C. This waveform also would roughly represent the motion of a single speaker cone reproducing the same sound.

Actually, *it is possible for the waveform in the illustrated example to take on a large variety of shapes, all of which would sound very similar, if not the same*, to a listener. This occurs when the frequencies involved in the particular instrument's sound are reproduced by the loudspeaker in different phase relationships with respect to one another. Additionally, each frequency within a sound very commonly involves multiple sine waves of the same frequency combined in a variety of phase relationships. This is a result of the sound emanating from a broad area rather than from only one point, and adds a certain subtle fullness and naturalness to the sound. In practice, *the particular shape of a complex waveform, though, is not nearly as important as is the spectrum of frequencies it contains.*

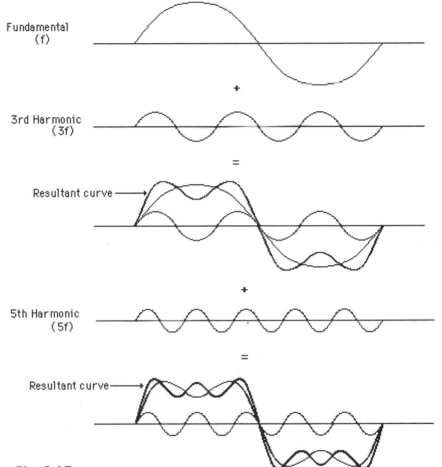

Fundamental
(f)

+

3rd Harmonic
(3f)

=

Resultant curve

+

5th Harmonic
(5f)

=

Resultant curve

Fig. 2.13

Note here that when odd-numbered harmonics are added in the proper phase and proportion, the sides get steeper and the top begins to flatten out. With a sufficient number of odd harmonics in the right proportions, a square wave is the result. A "perfect" square wave would have odd harmonics well beyond the upper end of the audio spectrum (to ∞). Below is shown the result up to the 29th harmonic.

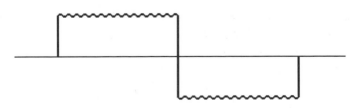

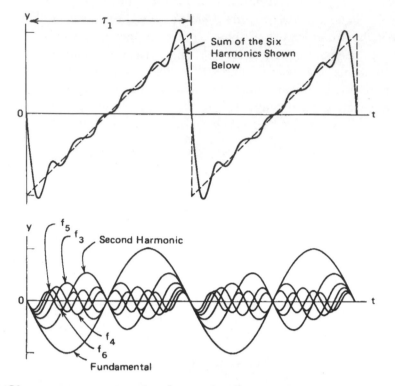

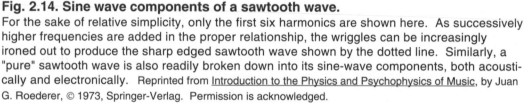

Fig. 2.14. Sine wave components of a sawtooth wave.
For the sake of relative simplicity, only the first six harmonics are shown here. As successively higher frequencies are added in the proper relationship, the wriggles can be increasingly ironed out to produce the sharp edged sawtooth wave shown by the dotted line. Similarly, a "pure" sawtooth wave is also readily broken down into its sine-wave components, both acoustically and electronically. Reprinted from Introduction to the Physics and Psychophysics of Music, by Juan G. Roederer, © 1973, Springer-Verlag. Permission is acknowledged.

Note that waveforms such as square waves, triangle waves and sawtooth waves are *not*, in actuality, simple. Square waves, widely used for lab testing of audio equipment, and other "simple" waveforms are readily generated by the most basic electronic systhesizers. While these waveforms *appear* simple and are fairly easy to electronically synthesize in their nearly exact forms, they also contain their own spectra of sine-wave components. A square wave, for example, actually consists of a fundamental and a succession of only odd-numbered harmonics (1st, 3rd, 5th, 7th, 9th, etc., as in Fig. 2.13). The sawtooth wave, as another example, is to some extent the theoretical model of a bowed string and the human vocal chords (though in real life they are far more complicated). Fig. 2.14 shows how a sawtooth wave can be broken down into its particular sine-wave components. Once they are generated, such "simple" waveforms actually behave according to the spectrum of frequencies (sine-wave components) involved, just as any other sound does.

It is now time to direct our attention to one of the most important—and perhaps the most widely neglected and misunderstood—aspect of sound reinforcement, that of the hearing process itself.

CHAPTER 3

HEARING AND BASIC PSYCHOACOUSTICS

A classic question, "If a tree fell in a forest and no one was present to hear it, was there a sound?," is often used to illustrate the double meaning of the word "sound." This question can be correctly answered with either a "yes" or a "no." The answer is "yes" if sound is considered to mean the physical creation of pressure waves in the surrounding air, ground, etc. If sound is considered to be the sensation created in the hearing process, the answer is of course "no."

In Chapter 2 we focused primarily on the physical nature of sound. This chapter discusses sound mainly from the standpoint of the human hearing process.

a) The Ear.

The function of the ear is sometimes likened to that of a microphone, since both the ear and the microphone convert sound waves into electrical signals. To the extent that this is true, the ear is a microphone of the most amazing sort. It actually serves as a "frequency analyzer", breaking down complex waveforms into their sine-wave-components, and sending separate sets of electrical impulses to the brain which represent each of the frequencies involved in the sounds it receives. It is also capable of hearing at intensity levels a trillion times greater than the softest audible sounds. That is a dynamic range many thousands of times greater than the available dynamic range of even the best currently available sound reinforcement systems. The ear, though, also has its own peculiarities and limitations, and an understanding of these can go a long way toward solving many common difficulties in designing and using systems.

First a brief description of how the ear works (see Fig. 3.1): Sounds which enter the outer ear are "funneled" through the ear canal, causing the eardrum, the thin diaphram of skin covering the end of the canal, to vibrate. Attached to the inside of the eardrum is the first of three very delicate bones which, by a lever action, transfer the vibrations to another much smaller opening (the *Oval Window*) leading to the inner ear. We've all heard this before. But what happens *beyond* the oval window undoubtedly makes the inner ear one of the incredible marvels of nature.

The inner ear is encased in an extremely small bony shell (the *cochlea*) rolled up in a shape closely resembling that of a snail. Inside the shell immersed in fluid, are numerous tiny hairlike cells on a membrane (the *basilar membrane*) running lengthwise along the inward spiral of the shell. The hairlike cells are responsible for converting the vibrations created in the fluid into electrical impulses. Each of the sine-wave-components (frequencies) in a sound causes maximum response at a special place along the length of the basilar membrane, which in turn causes impulses to be sent to the brain from that particular location on the membrane. In this way *the brain receives a separate series of impulses*

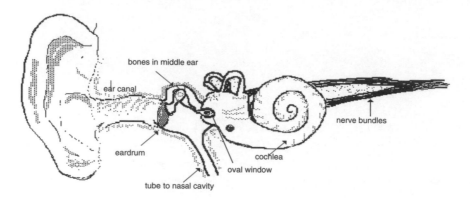

Fig. 3.1. Basic components of the ear. (Not to scale; the cochlea would be able to fit on the top of a fingernail.)

representing each of the frequencies involved in the sounds we hear, sorted out from the complex waveform received by the outer ear. In fact, in rare cases, with sufficient training it is possible for extremely astute listeners to pick out the specific pitch of various overtones when a musical note is played on an instrument. (Most of us simply integrate it into what we call "tonal quality".)

The lowest frequencies of the audio spectrum cause maximum response at one end of the basilar membrane, while the highest frequencies cause maximum response at the other. But the manner in which the membrane responds to frequencies between the extemes goes a long way toward explaining why we hear frequencies in a musical, or porportional, relationship to each other.

Note a fascinating thing about the ear's operation. Figure 3.2 shows a graph overlayed with a depiction of the cochlea, with the basilar membrane inside, "unrolled" to its full length. *Along the length of the cochlea, as on the graph, each doubling in frequency (octave) covers the same distance along the scale, regardless of its numerical value.* This is called a **logarithmic** relationship, by which any ratio can be represented on a special linear scale for easier handling. (In other words, *the ear is physically built to work logarithmically*.) The logarithmic relationship is useful not only in comparative measurements of frequency, but also in comparative measurements of intensity.

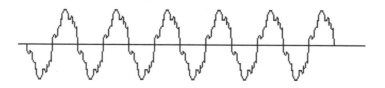

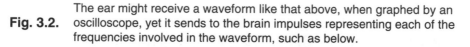

Fig. 3.2. The ear might receive a waveform like that above, when graphed by an oscilloscope, yet it sends to the brain impulses representing each of the frequencies involved in the waveform, such as below.

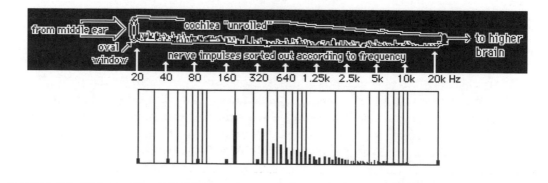

b) The Decibel.

Two very remarkable aspects of the perception of sound intensity make it appropriate to use the unit called the *decibel*.

Firstly, the 10,000,000,000,000-to-one range of acoustic power which the ear can hear would be extremely clumsy to work with in straightforward numerical values. Secondly and more importantly, the hearing process perceives intensity differences in a way that more closely resembles a logarithmic scale than it does a linear one.

Imagine a sound system reproducing a tone of steady intensity with a listener located nearby. Say the amplifier's measured output is 1 watt. If the measured level of the tone were to be doubled to 2 watts, the listener would not perceive the sound to be twice as loud. In fact, this order of difference is not much more than the minimum detectable difference by an average listener, and would normally be barely noticeable.

Imagine the same system again, reproducing the tone at a measured amplifier output of 5 watts. An identical tone at an amplifier output of 6 watts (also an increase of one watt, as in the previous example) would in general be significantly less than a noticeable difference. For the degree of increase in intensity to be judged as similar to the first example, the 5 watt tone would need to be roughly doubled, to about 10 watts. This doubling of intensity would also be, as in the first example, only slightly more than the minimum detectable difference to most listeners.

Like the musical octave and decade introduced previously, *the decibel is a relative quantity*, though it is *based upon ratios between sound intensities* rather than frequencies. The decibel is normally used in referring to audio signals at every point in their passage through the electronic realm as well, since they

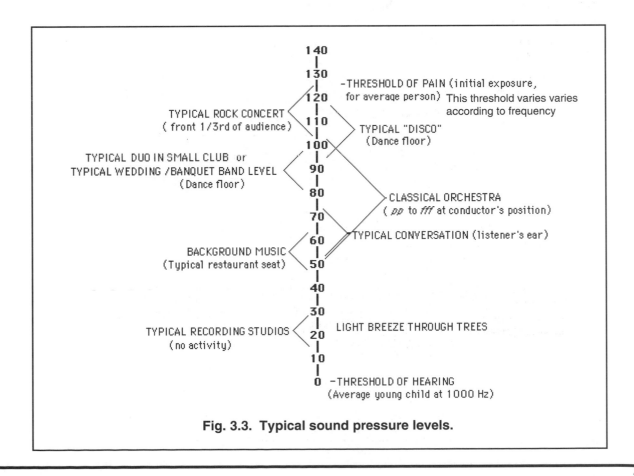

Fig. 3.3. Typical sound pressure levels.

represent signal strengths which ultimately are reproduced and passed into the acoustic realm. Practical use of decibel measurements will be introduced in Chapter Four. It should be noted here, though, that **every 3 dB increase of output level requires double the amplifier and speaker output power**. (In particular, see the power ratios in Fig. 4.7.)

Just as musical ratios among frequencies require a standard reference point (normally Concert "A", 440 Hz), so too does the decibel. *The accepted reference point for sound intensities is the minimum sound pressure (at 1 kHz) detectable by an average young child (.0002 dynes/sq. cm). This is considered to be 0 dB sound pressure level (0 dB SPL).* The upper end of the intensity range is generally considered to be around 140 dB SPL, though sounds do occur well beyond this—gunshots, jet engines and so forth. (This is well beyond the threshold of pain for nearly everyone, and a range in which serious damage to the hearing mechanism can occur—in some cases even with relatively brief exposure.) Fig. 3.3 shows typical measured sound pressure levels in some commonly encountered situations.

c) Frequency Response of the Ear.

An often seen (and usually quite exaggerated) statistic for audio equipment is: "Flat, from 20 Hz to 20 kHz." Even these types of exaggerations aside, it would be very convenient to compare electronic measurements to what a person hears if the ear's sensitivity to all frequencies were the same throughout the entire audio spectrum. This is, however, far from the case.

Hearing ability is much better in the high-midrange, and far less sensitive toward both the extremes. Taking into account individual differences, hearing is on the average most sensitive in the 2.5 kHz to 4kHz area, in large part because resonance in the ear and ear-canal amplifies the effect of this

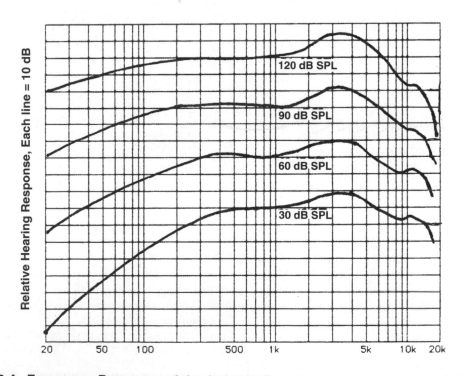

Fig. 3.4. Frequency Response of the Average Ear. Shown are hearing characteristics for an "average" person at 30dB, 60dB, 90dB and 120dB sound pressure level. Note how the curves tend to "flatten" substantially at higher levels in all but the highest portion of the spectrum. Interestingly, though, in the very high frequencies, response tends to be comparatively reduced at very high sound levels.

frequency range on the eardrum. (For adults this maximum sensitivity may be lower in frequency, for children it is often higher.)

The low-frequency limit can vary substantially from one person to another, and at the very lowest extreme it can be difficult to discern whether the sound is being heard or felt. In general, hearing acuity begins to drop off sharply below 100 Hz.

The high-frequency limit also differs from one person to another, and in addition, normally decreases with age. Very young children can sometimes hear to above 20 kHz, while extremely old persons commonly cannot hear above 5 kHz or so. In younger persons, long term overexposure to loud sounds most often results in a reduction of sensitivity to the higher frequencies, though damage to hearing ability can occur in any area of the audio spectrum, depending on the nature of the overexposure.

Not only is the ear's frequency response far from flat; it also changes substantially according to the intensity of the sound. Fig. 3.4 shows the frequency response curves of the average ear at a number of different intensity levels (remember that individual persons can vary widely from the average). Note that the reduction, or rolloff, in sensitivity below 1 kHz becomes less radical as intensity increases.

These hearing-response curves are often inverted to show what the frequency response of audio equipment, used at a given volume, must be in order for all frequencies to appear equally loud. When presented in this fashion, the curves are called *equal-loudness contours*. The equal-loudness contours show graphically that audio equipment with flat frequency response will tend to appear deficient in both the low frequencies and extremely high frequencies, and excessive in the midrange frequencies. *As the level of the system is increased*, this effect becomes gradually less predominant, and *the sound will appear*

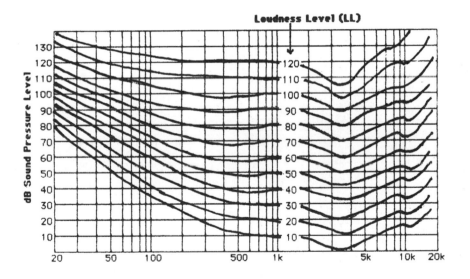

Figure 3.5. Equal Loudness Contours. These curves show what an "average" listener perceives as equally loud at different frequencies, according to actual measured sound pressure level.
Loudness Level can also be referred to in "phons". Example: 90 dB LL= 90 phons.

The 120 dB LL curve is generally considered to be the threshold of pain for an average person, though long term or repeated exposure at levels well below this can cause hearing damage. (How much exposure and at what levels varies from person to person, and is at-this-writing still being widely discussed and debated among audiologists, audio engineers and acousticians.) These curves are important. Note, for example, that in the 3kHz range, only 90 dB SPL is required to achieve 100 dB LL, while at 50 Hz, 110 dB SPL would be required. Note also that in this same frequency range hearing tends to reach its saturation point far more quickly than through the rest of the spectrum (usually the ear canal's resonance averages in the 2.5kHz to 3kHz range for adults).

significantly richer in both the low and high frequencies than it did when used at a lower volume. (The "loudness" switch on many home stereo systems is intended to roughly compensate for this characteristic at low volume levels, by boosting the low frequencies.)

At high levels, there are additionally important concerns. For example, *110 dB SPL at 50 Hz is very loud, but 110 dB SPL in the 2 kHz to 4 kHz range is beyond the threshold of pain for nearly everyone.* (See the curve in Fig. 3.5 for 120 dB Loudness Level, which is generally regarded as the limit of pain for the average person. Refer also to the discussion in section "e" of this chapter.)

d) The Time Line of Hearing.

Thus far the discussion has focused mostly on what can be termed a "microscopic" view of sound and hearing. One cycle of a simple or complex waveform within the audio spectrum occurs in less than .05 second (1/20th of a second), too small a time span, in most cases, for a listener to be consciously aware of a sound (except perhaps to wonder "what was that?"). In a sense, this is the "stop action" view of sound. Here we will attempt to put this microscopic view into a somewhat larger perspective.

It was explained earlier that the tonal quality of a sound—determined by the spectrum of frequencies it contains—is an important factor in allowing the hearing process to distinguish one sound from another. *Equally important to the essence of any sound, though, is the manner in which the waveform varies (or fails to) throughout the duration of a sound.* The importance of such changes in the recognition of a sound is readily shown by the difficulty we experience in attempting to recognize the various sounds on a tape recording played backwards.

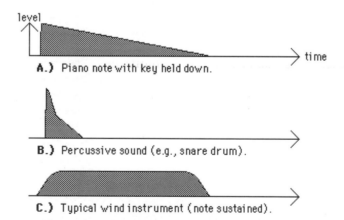

Fig. 3.6. Typical overall envelopes of several sounds. This type of graph is a simple way of expressing the overall dynamics of sounds, ranging from around 1/20th of a second to perhaps several seconds. Here the waves themselves are ignored, represented instead as simple lines indicating roughly the overall level measured or heard.

In addition to an overall envelope of this type, typical sounds vary according to frequency as well (see Fig. 3.7). Usually an acoustic-instrument sound involves greater high frequency content as its level increases, and less high frequency content as its level decreases.

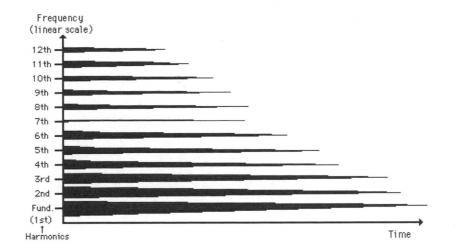

Fig. 3.7. Simplified spectral analysis of a note on an acoustic piano or guitar.
Notice that the higher harmonics decay more quickly than the lower ones. The presence of the higher harmonics is one of the cues the hearing process uses as an indicator of both intensity and closeness to the source. This is one of the reasons we are able to "compress" a musical sound to reduce wide dynamic variations and still allow an instrument or voice to sound "dynamic", so long as the relative intensity of the harmonics are left basically intact. (Compressors are introduced in Chapter 8.) An understanding of the importance of the harmonics' relative strength begins to hint to us that turning up an instrument's or voice's volume is not the only way to increase apparent intensity.

First, consider the relatively simple waveforms involved in musical sounds. The most obvious way in which most musical sounds vary is by their overall intensity. This is fairly easily shown by a graph appropriately referred to a a sound's *envelope*. Fig. 3.6 shows typical envelopes of sounds created by several musical instruments.

Basically, envelopes can be broken down into three aspects: *attack*, *sustain* and *decay*. "Attack" refers to the time it takes for a sound to reach its initial peak intensity. "Sustain" describes the maintenance of a relatively constant intensity level, while "decay" describes the manner in which a sound diminishes in intensity. These are often present in varying combinations—e.g., a fast attack and initial decay may be followed by a sustain and then a further decay, and so on.*

While the graph of a sound's envelope is helpful in showing the overall dynamics of a sound, it is nonetheless limited in that *all of the involved frequencies do not normally change in intensity in the same way*. These variations can be called the *internal dynamics* within the envelope. Fig. 3.7 shows a graph, called a *spectral analysis,* of a note played on a piano with the sustain pedal depressed. Spectral analyses can be presented in a number of formats—in this type of graph the intensity of each frequency present in a sound is indicated by the darkness of the line representing it. The higher overtones of the piano sound can be clearly seen to decay more quickly than the fundamental and lower overtones. *This type of pattern, in which the relative presence of the higher frequencies lessens as the overall intensity diminishes, holds true for most acoustic instruments.*

In some instances, though, nearly the opposite can be true. Two conspicuous examples are the sounds of a sitar and that of a gong. In both of these examples the maximum intensity of the higher

---

* On the control panels of electronic instruments, the terms "sustain" and "decay" sometimes are used to refer to slightly different functions than described here.

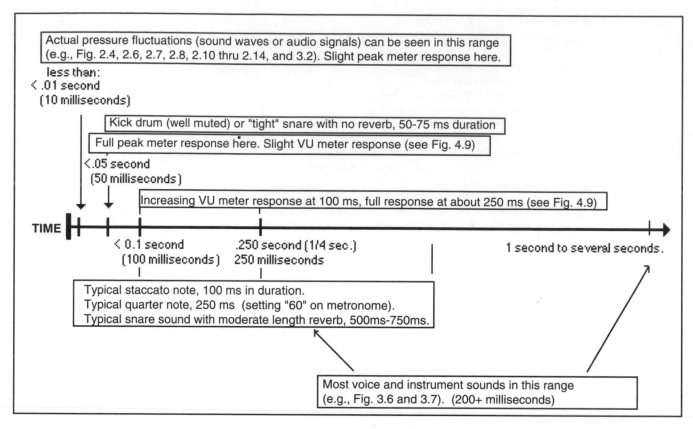

Fig. 3.8 The Time Line of Hearing

frequencies is delayed until well after the initial picking or striking action. It is this characteristic that accounts for the eccentric nature of their sounds. Similar juggling of the relationship between high frequency presence and overall intensity is commonly done with electronic synthesizers, and is one of the factors accounting for their often "unnatural" or characteristically "electronic" sound.

Vocal sounds are typically much more complex than musical instrument sounds, invloving many starts, stops and sweeps of pitch and resonance both upward and downward, which become the basis for the spoken language and for musical lyrics.

The ability of a sound reinforcement system to effectively pick up, reproduce and distribute to an audience the necessary spectrum of frequencies present in the sounds it handles, can in many cases be important not only for tonal quality, but also for dynamic quality. As an example, the contact sound (attack) of a drumstick against a drumhead involves a very different frequency range than does the vibrations of the drumhead itself. If, for a very basic instance, the frequencies involved in the contact sound are lacking in the output sound of the system, the percussive emphasis in the total drum sound can often suffer as a result.

e) The Perception of Intensity.

Firstly, and very importantly, ***the perception of intensity is very much time-dependent*** (i.e., on the duration of the sound). This is a characteristic fairly well represented by the standard VU meter (see Section 4.h and Fig. 4.9). Basically, rapid (transient) sounds are not perceived to be as loud as sustained sounds of identical level.

Beyond the issue of the sound's duration, the basic information on loudness for the "average" person is, as already mentioned, described by the equal-loudness contours (Figs. 3.4 and 3.5). These curves, however, do not by any means tell the whole story. The scale shown below in Fig. 3.9 is a standardized scale which roughly relates loudness levels to perceived intensity. As can be seen, every 10 dB increase in loudness level is on average perceived as a doubling of loudness (in the laboratory).

The scale in Fig. 3.9 serves as a very reasonable guide, but in real life the relationship often is not quite this direct in live reinforcement. An increase in the output level of a sound system at a low level is perceived differently than an equivalent increase of the same system reaching the listener at a higher sound pressure level. One obvious reason for this is that the system must get to a certain level over the sounds being reinforced before it's own level increases make much of a difference, beyond which minor adjustments become increasingly critical. But even accounting for this, a quick increase of overall level (stage volume and system volume combined) at a modest level (say from 85 dB LL to 90 dB LL) may not be as significant as a similar increase at an extremely high level (say from 105 dB LL to 110 dB LL), because the high level sounds are approaching a range where most persons' hearing becomes saturated.

What happens when the increase at the listeners' ears is at a high level such as, for example, 100 dB, 110 dB LL or more (not uncommon in high output music, where audiences often demand such levels)? Well, in the short term the ears adjust. The bones in the middle ear displace slightly to help protect the nerves from damage—this is known as a *temporary threshold shift*. (This displacement is possibly in-part why the very-high-frequency sensitivity tends to roll off more quickly at such high levels.) ***Over the long term, though (assuming a day-after-day or night-after-night schedule of performance, or frequent attendance at such events), permanent threshold shift (hearing loss) can easily result. Obviously, caution is in order in dealing with high-level systems on any regular basis.***

And in the short term, *running a system at extremely high levels in the audience position can produce listening fatigue among audience members and can actually be counterproductive to a strong musical performance or to effective speech.* Achieving a "strong" sound, in situations where "intensity" of performance is called for, does not require that the sound be "deafening". (This subject is dealt with in Chapter 17.) The human perception of intensity allows it to be simulated at relatively modest levels (what this means can of-course vary greatly depending on the audience and the type of music).

Constructive use of the equal loudness contours can go a long way toward this end. Another strong cue which the human hearing mechanism uses to judge intensity is related to the "edge" frequencies, which tend to be clustered in the 4kHz to 8kHz area. Creative use of these, discussed in the chapter titled "The Engineer as Artist" is another method of accomplishing an apparent increase in intensity. Use of an Aphex unit (introduced in Chapter 8) is yet another way to add "zip" or "sizzle" to a mix.

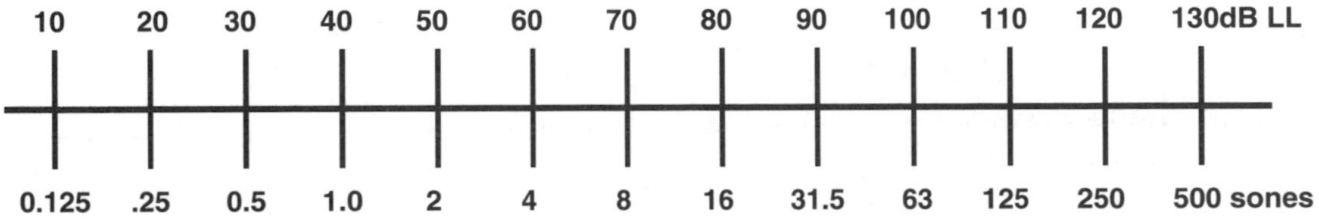

10	20	30	40	50	60	70	80	90	100	110	120	130dB LL
0.125	.25	0.5	1.0	2	4	8	16	31.5	63	125	250	500 sones

Fig. 3.9. Perceived loudness increases can also be represented as "sones". Sones are generally not an accepted unit of measurement in sound reinforcement, but serve well as a research tool for acousticians, and are shown here for purpose of illustration. In rough terms, system output must be increased tenfold (10dB) in order to achieve a doubling of perceived loudness to the average listener. (Loudness level follows the curves which were shown in Fig. 3.5.) In actual practice, perceived loudness of a sound system is also complicated by masking (shown in Fig. 3.10), and other psychoacoustic factors. A temporary threshold shift at high sound levels might also alter the perception of loudness increases. See the caution in the text above.

Certain types of distortion can also add to apparent intensity. This is of-course why electric guitar players use it so frequently. In part, this is due to that edge frequencies are increased in this type of distortion. One hears not only the normal harmonics in the "edge frequency" range, but also the distortion harmonics. (This, incidentally, is also largely why very melodic chords often don't sound right when played with strong distortion. The "good" distortion-chords tend to have large open musical intervals of 4ths and 5ths between the chord voicings—with more melodic chords the upper distortion harmonics tend to fall in dissonant spacings with respect to one another.) The other perhaps-obvious reason for percieving extra intensity due to distortion is that everyone in the modern world has heard a PA or stereo system distort, so the natural inclination is to perceive something as being overdriven. This author does not recommend distorting the PA system to achieve this effect. (Don't laugh too hard—it can be amazing how many system operators for rock and/or strong dance music are not satisfied until the PA is overdriven. This is a common trap, often caused in large part by temporary threshold shifts at high intensity levels. The ears having adjusted to one intensity level, the tendency is often to increase the system gain to the next notch, to which the ears adjust, and so forth.)

Another important factor concerning the perception of intensity is also very much frequency-dependent, but in a different way. For example, a 10,000 Hz tone along with a 500 Hz tone reproduced at a much lower level, and still clearly hear both tones. But if we simultaneously reproduce, say, a 600 Hz tone at a much higher level than the same 500 Hz tone, the tone which is lower in intensity becomes much more difficult to hear. This is largely due to the characteristic known as **_masking_**. Whenever two or more sounds are heard at the same time, the closer in frequency they are to one another, the less able we are to hear the one which is lower in intensity. _This characteristic is an important one to remember in "pulling together" an audio mix, since a sound heard by itself often sounds quite different when heard as part of the mix._ This is because certain frequency ranges are masked by other instruments or voices.

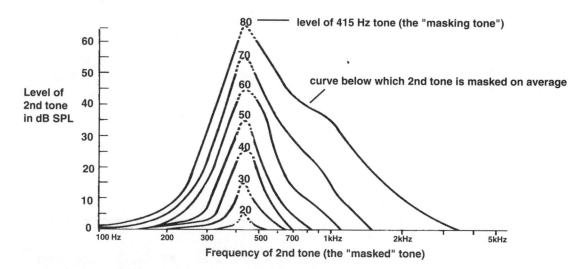

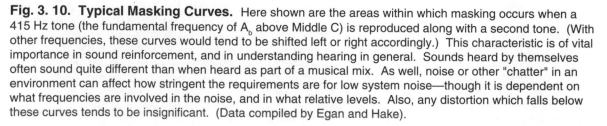

Fig. 3. 10. Typical Masking Curves. Here shown are the areas within which masking occurs when a 415 Hz tone (the fundamental frequency of A♭ above Middle C) is reproduced along with a second tone. (With other frequencies, these curves would tend to be shifted left or right accordingly.) This characteristic is of vital importance in sound reinforcement, and in understanding hearing in general. Sounds heard by themselves often sound quite different than when heard as part of a musical mix. As well, noise or other "chatter" in an environment can affect how stringent the requirements are for low system noise—though it is dependent on what frequencies are involved in the noise, and in what relative levels. Also, any distortion which falls below these curves tends to be insignificant. (Data compiled by Egan and Hake).

Masking also comes into play in numerous other ways. As an obvious example, system noise in a quiet environment is more readily heard than it is in a noisier environment. Masking is, though, a fairly complicated characteristic. For example, lower frequencies will tend to mask higher frequencies more effectively than the other way around.

f) The Perception of Direction.

The ability to perceive the direction from which the sound arriving is a result of the both the phase relationship and the relative intensity of the sound received by each ear. In the highest frequencies, the ear which is in the "shadow" of the sound receives a much lower intensity, since the wavelengths are unable to effectively bend around the head. In the mid-frequency range, there is a phase difference in the time of arrival at the ear, due to the extra split second it takes for the sound to bend around the head to the ear farther away. Combined with a slight difference in intensity between the two ears, this allows us to locate the approximate position of the source of midrange frequencies. Low frequencies, while one can often discern a general direction, tend to be nearly impossible to pinpoint because there is little difference in either phase or intensity for the hearing process to pick up. A 20'/6m wavelength (55 Hz), as an example, bends completely around the head with ease and also presents essentially no discernable phase difference to the two ears to be able to decipher (about 10° at most).

The average person's hearing is so finely tuned, well before pre-school age, that we are able to determine direction even in the vertical plane (i.e., the height of the source), where the phase and intensity differences between the two ears are much slighter. There is, however, one region where the hearing process has a bit of difficulty percieving the location of the sound source in the vertical (see Fig. 3.11). A sound coming in to the listener from the plane running directly in front of, over the head and behind tends to be more difficult to locate, vertically. This is known, among other terms, as the *plane of vertical indiscrimination.* (Ordinarily a very slight motion of the head identifies the vertical orientation if such a sound is encountered in day-to-day life, and having unconsciously noted the position we then "lock in on it".) This characteristic allows the designer of public address systems, especially in a permanent installation, an advantage in many cases. It allows one to install a speaker or cluster of speakers well above a podium, pulpit or lectern position, and still allow the partial illusion—enhanced by the visual image of and sound of the person speaking—that the sound is emanating from the podium position, rather than from the loudspeaker itself.

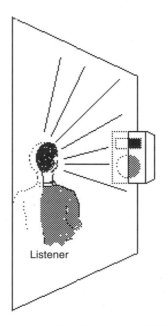

Fig. 3.11   Plane of Poor Sound Source Localization.
The height of a sound source anywhere in the plane shown in this figure (equally distant from the two ears) is comparatively difficult to discern. When combined with the visual image of the person speaking (assuming the loudspeaker is mounted within this plane), the result is the commonly perceived illusion that the sound is actually coming from from the talker him- or herself. This approach has proved to be extremely effective in permanent installations for speech reinforcement.

Listener

Another important characteristic related to the perception of direction, called the ***precedence effect***, has to do with the amount of time delay between the arrival of sound from two separate sources. This characteristic, introduced in section "k" of this chapter and also discussed in Chapter 12, comes strongly into play in distributed systems involving more than one speaker location.

g) Beats and Difference Tones.

An understanding of this section is important to a full understanding of section "h" of this chapter. Imagine an experimental setting in which two sine wave generators produce tones that are mixed together for a listener. If the tone generators are set for the same frequency and amplitude and mixed perfectly in-phase with one another, the result can be measured to be twice the amplitude of either tone individually. Since the hearing process "compresses" intensity differences, the doubling of amplitude is perceived (when heard at moderate intensity levels) as only a very slight increase (+3dB).

If the frequency of one of the tone generators is changed very slightly, *the waves will gradually fall in and out of phase with each other as shown in Fig. 3.12. This gives rise to alternating increases and decreases of volume known as **beats**.* The beats occur in cycles equal to the difference in frequency between the two tones. For example, if one tone is 440 Hz and the other is 442 Hz, the waves will fall in and out of phase with one another twice each second. This order of difference between frequencies is far too small for the hearing process to be able to separate them, so the combination is heard as one tone of varying intensity. The resulting beats are commonly used as an aid in tuning musical instruments, since the beating slows down as the two tones approach the same frequency, then finally stops when they are perfectly in tune with one another.

When, in the same experimental situation, the frequency of one tone is gradually moved farther and farther away from the frequency of the other, points are eventually reached at which they can, at first fuzzily and then more clearly, be heard as two distinctly separate tones. How large the interval between frequencies must be in order for the hearing process to clearly perceive them separately depends to some extent on the individual, and also varies depending upon what frequency range is involved. Generally it can be assumed to be roughly around 1/3 octave—more in the exremes of the spectrum, a bit less in the midrange frequencies. (This minimum detectable interval between pure sine waves (not to be confused with notes played on an instrument) has some important implications in sound reinforcement. Among other things, it means that minor variations in frequency response within 1/3-octave of each other have little impact on perceived sound quality. Here we are not talking about radical resonances and other excessively strong peaks of response, but rather variations of perhaps 3dB one way or the other. The fairly standard "plus-or-minus 3dB" tolerance often given in specifications is not entirely unrelated to this.)

As the tones are moved yet farther apart, another point is reached at which a third tone can be heard by the listener in addition to the two tones actually being synthesized. As already mentioned, the hearing process is relatively insensitive to the particular phase relationship of the frequencies it hears. This is why a complex waveform can take on a number of different configurations and still sound basically the same as long as the spectrum of frequencies it contains stays the same. The hearing process is, though, fairly sensitive to *changing* phase relationships.

When the two tones being heard are sufficiently far apart, the beats occur quickly enough for the hearing process to perceive the sine-wave-like phase changes as a separate tone (of substantially lower intensity than the two actual tones). This is called a *difference tone*. Normally the tones need to be separated by at least 40 Hz to 50 Hz for the difference tone to be "audible."

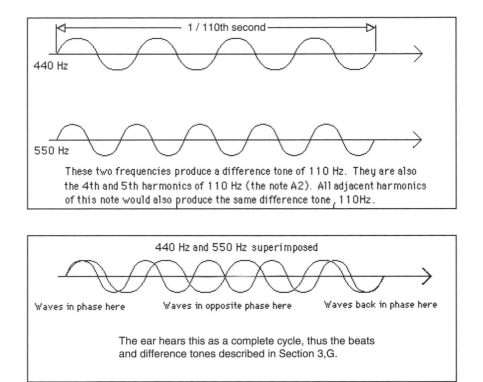

These two frequencies produce a difference tone of 110 Hz. They are also the 4th and 5th harmonics of 110 Hz (the note A2). All adjacent harmonics of this note would also produce the same difference tone, 110Hz.

440 Hz and 550 Hz superimposed

Waves in phase here   Waves in opposite phase here   Waves back in phase here

The ear hears this as a complete cycle, thus the beats and difference tones described in Section 3,G.

Fig. 3.12. Difference tones between harmonics provide the hearing process with an important cue about fundamental pitch (the actual musical "note"), even when the fundamental is below the frequency range of the system's capability. A system incapable of reproducing the fundamental does not ordinarily eliminate low notes. Only the tonal quality is affected. Understanding this gives us a reasonable basis to better understand the chart in Chapter 17 showing frequency ranges of various musical instruments.

h) The Missing Fundamental.

In Chapter Two it was shown that musical sounds have an overtone structure that is responsible for the tonal quality of a given note on a given instrument. For the vast majority of musical sounds, the overtones bear a harmonic relationship to the fundamental musical pitch of whatever note is being played; i.e., the overtones fall at frequencies that are whole-number-multiples of the fundamental. Thus, a note such as "A" 110 Hz would have overtones of 220 Hz, 330 Hz, 440 Hz, 550 Hz, 660 Hz, and so on upward. These frequencies would be the 2nd, 3rd, 4th, 5th, and 6th harmonics, or 2x, 3x, 4x, 5x, and 6x the fundamental frequency of 110 Hz.

*If pure tones (sine waves) of 220 Hz, 330 Hz, 440 Hz, 550 Hz, 660 Hz, etc., are produced simultaneously for a listener, they are heard as the note "A" 110 Hz, **even if the 110 Hz tone is absent!***
If the 110 Hz and 220 Hz tones are eliminated from the above series, the effect becomes slightly less distinct, but is still quite clearly identifiable by the listener as "A" 110 Hz. If the 330 Hz tone is eliminated, the effect becomes yet less distinct, and so on upward as successive harmonics are eliminated. In fact, ordinarily only after the first five or six harmonics are eliminated do most people begin to have difficulty recognizing the correct musical notes.

This effect is to some extent the net result of the difference tones between harmonically related frequencies (note that 110 Hz is also the difference between each successive tone in the above series). In fact, though, the fundamental musical note is heard by the listener at an intensity far greater than would be attributable to a difference tone. *The human brain/mind*, in acclimating itself to the natural ordering of its environment, *knows that any particular harmonic series belongs to a particular fundamental frequency, and "produces" that frequency as surely as if it were actually being received by the outer ear!*

The ability to hear the missing fundamental has important consequences in the audio field. This amazing aspect of human hearing is the reason we can clearly hear the correct notes being played by, for example, a guitar (whose fundamental frequencies can be as low as "E" 82 Hz) on a small radio whose frequency response does not go below, say, 250 Hz.

In sound reinforcement the same principle holds. A system that is incapable of reproducing the lowest extreme of the audio spectrum will not ordinarily eliminate low notes. What is sacrificed is depth of tonal quality. This is very important to a complete understanding of the frequency ranges of musical instruments or voices which are described in Part III. It is not necessarily the actual frequency ranges of each instrument or voice, but instead the particular distribution of energy along the audio spectrum which tends to be most important in providing pleasing sound. (On the whole, the distribution of energy tends to be as much a function of the resonator as of the vibrating element itself, as introduced in Chapter 2.) Each voice or instrument tends to have its own individual needs in this regard—this is why effective microphone choice and equalization can be so vitally important to the artistic aspects of live audio engineering.

i) The Frequency/Loudness Warp.

The sense of pitch, the ability to hear the highness or lowness of musical notes, corresponds closely with frequency. Interestingly, and of potential import to the operation of high-level sound reinforcement systems, this relationship is not an exact one.

Throughout most of the dynamic range of hearing, musical intervals can be heard as having a more or less direct relationship to frequency. For example, when played at a moderate level, "A" 110 Hz can be heard and easily recognized as one octave below "A" 220 Hz, two octaves below "A" 440 Hz, three octaves below "A" 880 Hz, etc.

At high intensity levels, though, the relationship between frequency and perceived pitch begins to degrade. In a sense, the low and high ends of the audio spectrum are stretched slightly outward when heard at very loud volumes. *At high levels*, then, *it is literally possible for a 110 Hz tone to sound like it is out-of-tune with its 220 Hz counterpart, and even farther out of tune with its 880 Hz counterpart* which is three octaves away. Most often, when listening to an overall musical mix, this type of "warp" is perceived as a slight increase in pitch when heard at very high levels.

Here is an example of how this aspect of hearing can come into play in actual practice. When using high level systems, performers onstage are commonly exposed to disproportionately high levels of low frequency sounds emanating from the system directed at the audience (for reasons explained in Chapter 9). If these sounds are of sufficient intensity, they can actually affect a performer's sense of pitch, and can cause that performer to be inclined to sing slightly off of the correct musical notes. In such a situation it becomes important that the performers adequately hear one or more of the treble instruments on-stage in order to have an effective pitch reference for their voices, rather than drawing their pitch reference from the bass notes. A well set-up stage, along with a well-designed and competently used stage monitor system, discussed in Chapter 15, can largely eliminate this particular problem.

j) The Listening Environment.

The acoustic environment, as is well known by soundpersons, experienced musicians and other perceptive listeners, can have a drastic impact on perceived sound quality. The study of acoustics indoors is a complicated discipline well beyond the intended scope of this book. But here we will take a brief look at what happens in a typical indoor environment of a size where sound reinforcement is normally required.

As mentioned in the previous chapter, audible resonances do exist in rooms, especially smaller rooms, which are due to the dimensions and shape of the room. These may tend to accentuate certain frequencies in certain locations within the room. Most often, low frequencies whose wavelength corresponds to the dimensions of the room tend to be accentuated. While resonances do occur in the midrange frequencies, these usually tend to be clustered so close together in frequency that no one of them ordinarily stands out above the others, at least not due to room resonance per se.

There are two very basic things concerning resonances which the operator of a sound system (not to even mention system installers) should regard as important. First: The apparent strength of any resonances will tend to change depending on the person's location within the particular room—in some locations resonant frequencies actually tend to cancel. (This fact makes all but the most blatant resonances difficult if not impossible to equalize.) And even those with the most astute listening abilities would not ordinarily be able to discern from only one position in a room what the resonant characteristics are in other positions. Since the effect of resonances will vary from one point to another, obviously the system operator should not draw her or his conclusions about resonances (or indeed about the sound in general) from only one location. Second: Listeners adjacent to walls or corners tend to be subjected to the maximum intensity of room resonance at many frequencies. This means, among other things, that *among the least desirable mixer positions from which to operate a sound system is backed up against a wall*, particularly if it is a highly reflective wall, and particularly if it is directly across the room from a loudspeaker (as opposed to at an angle). Even if the wall is highly absorbent (i.e., such as carpeted or draped—which helps),

Fig. 3.13. Basic room resonance. Resonances in rooms occur when a wave is reflected back and forth in such a way that they drastically reinforce each other in some positions of the room, and almost totally cancel each other out in other positions. Resonances occur at frequencies where the wavelength is equal to a particular physical dimension of the room, or any multiple thereof. These are also known as "standing waves" or "room modes". The more significant standing waves tend to occur in the lower frequencies.

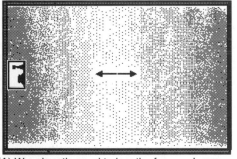

(A) Wavelength equal to length of room. Large standing wave can be excited by comparatively minimal sound at this frequency.

(B) Wavelength equal to 1/2, 1/3, 1/4, 1/5, etc. times the length of the room. Standing waves can occur between floor and ceiling or other surfaces as well. Light portions in Illustration are the null points in the room, the "nodes" of the standing wave.

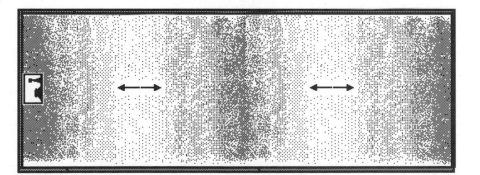

resonances in the low frequencies often will still tend to "collect" there. (Possibly the worst place from which to operate a sound system, incidentally, is tucked away in a booth with an open window—here the characteristics of the booth usually will tend to be drastically different than those in the audience area. A carefully equalized monitor system in such a booth can help, but would not duplicate the reverberation the audience hears, thereby putting the soundperson, and the performance, at a disadvantage.)

The next important aspect of room acoustics concerns what are generally called "early reflections". These are important in small to medium size listening environments, but may also come into play in large halls with a reflective canopy over the stage. Fig. 3.14 illustrates the development of the first few reflections heard by the listener. These are technically not regarded as reverberation (at least not from an acoustician's viewpoint), because they happen very quickly—a "snap of the fingers" in length, but they play a very important role in how we perceive sound in conjunction with the environment. Basically the hearing process integrates any reflections within the first 25 to 30 milliseconds (1/thousandths of a second) after hearing the direct sound, and essentially perceives them together with the direct sound itself. Sometimes these first reflections, in combination, are many dB louder than the direct sound from the source, and can play a major role in how loud the sound in general will be in a particular room.

The remainder of acoustical concerns, beyond resonances and "early reflections", tends to revolve around longer, more clearly perceptible, reverberation. Reverberation can of-course also vary widely from room to room, and it this which, in combination with resonances, gives us an intuitive idea of the environmental space and construction. While the specific aspects can be quite complicated and highly technical, there is, with relatively few exceptions, mainly only one concern relating to longer reverberation, which can be summed up with the question: "How long does it last?" Normally this is stated as *reverberation time*. Reverberation time in a particular room is accepted to be the length of time it takes

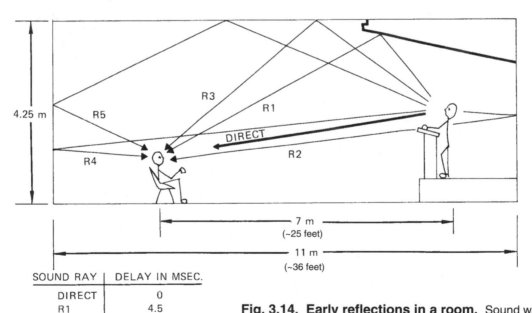

SOUND RAY	DELAY IN MSEC.
DIRECT	0
R1	4.5
R2	9.0
R3	13.0
R4	14.0
R5	18.0

Delay time here represents time difference between arrival of direct sound and arrival of reflected sound, at 13 & 1/2 inches per millisecond (round it off to a foot), or 0.34 Meter per millisecond (round it off to a meter every 3 msec).

Fig. 3.14. Early reflections in a room. Sound waves are depicted here as rays for the purpose of illustrating which waves are reflected to a given listener's position. Reflections arriving at the listeners ears within the first 25 milliseconds (0.025 second) or so, after the arrival of the direct sound, cannot be distinguished as separate by the hearing process, but play a major role in volume level and sound quality. Understanding this gives us an opportunity to understand the discussion in section "k" of this chapter. (illustration reprinted from Sound System Design Reference Manual, courtesy JBL Professional)

for the sound level in the room to drop by 60 dB, after the sound source has stopped emitting sound. This is defined primarily by two factors, the size of the room and how reflective the surfaces are *on average*. Obviously, in most cases, the longer the reverberation time is, the more the direct sound and early reflections will tend to be masked by the reverberation, and the more difficult the sound will be to understand and appreciate. For this reason, distributed systems with larger numbers of loudspeakers placed comparatively close to the audience are often used in environments with long reverberation times. Generally, there is much less tolerance for long reverberation in reinforcing speech than in reinforcing music, but there is a point at which music also becomes too cluttered by the reverberation to appreciate. Fortunately, there are some things which can be done to make this problem less severe, as illustrated in Fig. 3.15 and discussed in Chapter 9 and in Part Three.

Among the relatively few exceptions mentioned above is when there is a clearly defined echo off of a particular wall, which can be disastrous to sound quality. Sometimes all we can do here is "grin and bear it" and attempt to get through the event, or, we can stand our ground and insist that curtains or some

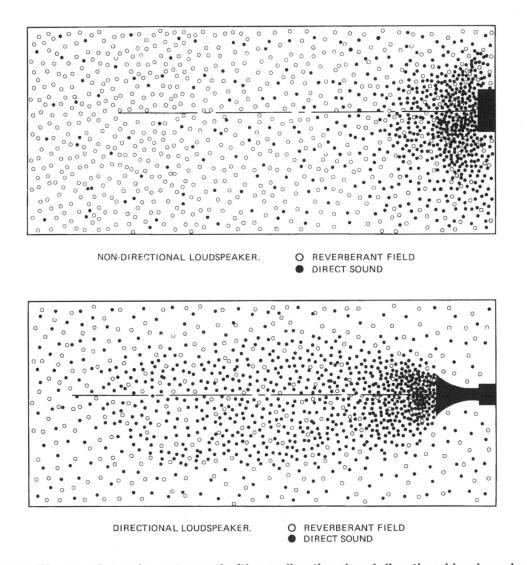

NON-DIRECTIONAL LOUDSPEAKER.   O REVERBERANT FIELD
                                    ● DIRECT SOUND

DIRECTIONAL LOUDSPEAKER.   O REVERBERANT FIELD
                                ● DIRECT SOUND

Fig. 3.15. Direct and reverberant sound with nondirectional and directional loudspeakers.
One way of dealing with highly reverberant environments involves effectively controlled coverage of a room with the loudspeaker(s), a topic reserved for Chapter 9. Note the different ratios of direct sound to reverberant sound in the two figures above. (Courtesy JBL Professional)

other form of absorptive material be put on the offending wall. Finally, beyond all of the just-introduced concerns, it should be obvious that shadowing of sound by large physical obstacles also will play a role in achieving effective coverage with a reinforcement system.

k) The Precedence Effect.

There is one vital aspect of the perception of direction that was not discussed in section "f", known as the *Precedence Effect,* or *Haas Effect,* after the researcher who first published effective data on the phenomenon. In the previous section it was briefly described that rapidly occuring reflections within the first 30 or-so milliseconds tend to be integrated into the direct sound itself. As mentioned, the combination of such reflections can often add up to many dB above the direct sound, particularly in a very small room. Yet the human hearing process learns very early in life to preserve the directional image of the sound based on the direction from which the direct sound arrives.

This can also be simulated with two loudspeakers. Fig. 3.16. depicts an experimental setup where two speakers reproducing the same sound are set up like a standard stereo system, except we have introduced the capability to delay one of the signals. Now, nearly everyone in the modern industrialized world is intuitively aware of how we "localize" a sound coming from two such speakers (or can learn it simply by fiddling around with a standard "balance" control on a stereo system). If the signal is identical in quality and intensity (i.e., in "mono") it appears to emanate from the center. However, *if we delay one of the identical sounds by between 5 and 25 milliseconds, the listener clearly perceives the sound as coming from the undelayed speaker.* Not only that, *we can actually **increase** the level of the delayed sound by a substantial amount (usually up to 4 or 6 dB), before the apparent sound image begins to move away from the speaker reproducing the earlier sound* (i.e., the "direct sound"). Only when the delayed sound reaches roughly 10 dB above the "original" sound, does the sound appear to emanate from center (beyond which the sound will move increasingly toward the delayed speaker). If we increase the delay beyond about 30 milliseconds, it begins to sound increasingly like a quick echo, and the effect ceases.

In sound reinforcement, the precedence effect allows a sound system to be arranged with supplementary loudspeakers to assist in improving sound quality, while still preserving the image that the sound is emanating from the front of the room (i.e., stage, lectern, etc.). This effect is so unbelievable that when it is experienced, people will "swear" the delayed speaker is off, yet in fact the sound from the delayed loudspeaker often is at least equally loud, and may be playing a major role in enhancing the sound quality at the listening position. (See also Chapter 12, Figs.12.13 and 12.15.)

Fig. 3.16. Precedence effect.

(A) Apparent source when right-hand speaker is delayed 5ms to 25ms. *Both speakers are fed an identical sound at the same level.*

(B) Apparent source when right-hand speaker is delayed 5ms to 25ms, and *increased by about 10 dB* above the left hand speaker.

CHAPTER 4

AUDIO MEASUREMENT TERMS AND CONCEPTS

Measuring sound and the electrical signals which represent it has, from the very beginning of the audio field, presented special challenges. The nonlinear and very personal nature of hearing makes the sharing of measurements of that aspect—even today—a difficult task at best. There are, though, generally accepted methods of exchanging data about sound, audio signals and hearing characteristics, which do a very respectable job of objectifying the flow of technical information in the field. This chapter focuses on a number of them, and also provides additional background material.

(We will try to be merciful. Some readers may wish to skip parts of this chapter, and use it instead to refer to later as needed.)

a) Frequency Response.

A component's ability to produce audio output within a particular frequency range (that is, to "respond" to those frequencies) is called *frequency response*. A graphed measurement of a component's output according to frequency, in comparison to the input signal, is, when presented as in Fig. 4.1, called a *frequency response curve*. This type of curve, when accurately represented, allows the user of the equipment to know in-advance approximately how the component will affect the tonal quality of the sounds or signals given to it.

When a component reproduces frequencies within a given range with equal emphasis, as compared to the intensity of the frequencies present in the input signal, the component's response curve is referred to as "flat" within that range (because the response curve within that range is directly horizontal, or "flat", on this type of graph). The sought-after "flat" response curve throughout the audio spectrum is most often characteristic only of amplifiers. Loudspeakers almost never achieve this to within very close tolerances (except within limited ranges). Fortunately, it is not absolutely necessary that they do. Some condenser microphones come close to this "ideal", but as already mentioned (Ch. 1), microphones usually do not need to have flat frequency response either.

Components such as mixers and other signal processing equipment would ideally display this characteristic throughout the whole audio spectrum, but in reality many such components change the tonal quality significantly, even when EQ controls are set in their flat position. (In other words, their response is not necessarily flat—though the highest quality mixers and other signal processing equipment tend to come extremely close.)

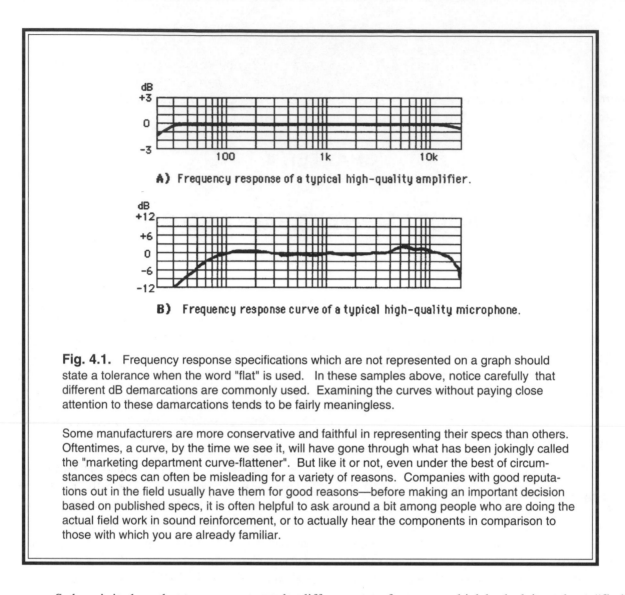

A) Frequency response of a typical high-quality amplifier.

B) Frequency response curve of a typical high-quality microphone.

Fig. 4.1. Frequency response specifications which are not represented on a graph should state a tolerance when the word "flat" is used. In these samples above, notice carefully that different dB demarcations are commonly used. Examining the curves without paying close attention to these damarcations tends to be fairly meaningless.

Some manufacturers are more conservative and faithful in representing their specs than others. Oftentimes, a curve, by the time we see it, will have gone through what has been jokingly called the "marketing department curve-flattener". But like it or not, even under the best of circumstances specs can often be misleading for a variety of reasons. Companies with good reputations out in the field usually have them for good reasons—before making an important decision based on published specs, it is often helpful to ask around a bit among people who are doing the actual field work in sound reinforcement, or to actually hear the components in comparison to those with which you are already familiar.

So how is it, then, that two components by different manufacturers, which both claim to have "flat" frequency response (and are in-turn inserted in an identical system with an appropriate electrical imedance match), in some cases sound very different from one another when they are given the same input signal? Most often the answer is, simply, they have different actual frequency response curves, no matter what the specs may claim. (And in some instances, most often in low budget components, the frequency response can change significantly as the signal level changes.)

Very basically, any frequency response specification not shown on the type of graph in Fig. 4.1 should at least state a tolerance, which for a speaker is most often ±3dB ("plus-or-minus 3dB"). The specification should also qualify the range throughout which the response is to be expected to remain within the stated tolerance limit. (With a "±3dB" spec, this would be a 6dB total swing within the quoted frequency range). In the case of a very-high-quality amplifier or signal-processing unit, stated tolerances might be more on the order of ±1dB throughout most of the audio spectrum.

With microphone and loudspeaker specifications, a more complicated set of issues comes into play. This is because response curves are generally measured directly on-axis. Off axis response can deviate very substantially from the published on-axis curve, even when those curves are accurately and honestly represented. This is dealt with somewhat further in Chapters 5 and 10. The basic forms of dB-related measurements are introduced later in this chapter.

●●

The reduction of sound intensity as the listener moves farther away from the source is due to two factors: (1) the geometric spreading of sound, and (2) losses due to friction between air particles. Over short distances the former (described by the inverse square law) tends to predominate. Over longer distances the latter (attenuation in air) becomes increasingly important.

b) Inverse Square Law.

Each doubling of distance from the sound source results in a fourfold reduction of sound power (equal to 6 dB). (More precisely, each proportional increase of distance from the source results in a decrease of sound level in inverse proportion to the square of the relative increase in distance.) This is illustrated in Fig. 4.2, and is known as the ***inverse square law***.

So, in an open area (with an absorbent ground surface), if one moves from 4' to 8' from a sound source, the level is reduced by 6 dB. If one moves again from 8' to 16', level is reduced by another 6dB (a total of 12 dB). If one moves again from 16' to 32' away, the combined reduction is of-course 18 dB, and so on. If one now moves from 32' to 64' away, the difference is (you figure it out).

Obviously, as one gets farther away from the source, moving a bit closer or farther away makes relatively little difference. (Incidentally, at around 1000'—roughly a fifth-of-a-mile, the reduction in intensity is still only 48 dB, which may give a perspective on why sound carries so far. Beyond the 48dB just mentioned, the sound would be somewhat further reduced, particularly in the higher frequencies, by the attenuation described in the following section.)

Indoors, as distance increases beyond a certain point, reflections from surrounding surfaces contribute to the overall intensity. So the combination of direct and reflected sound normally results in less and less of a reduction for each doubling of distance, as the reflected sound comes increasingly into play.

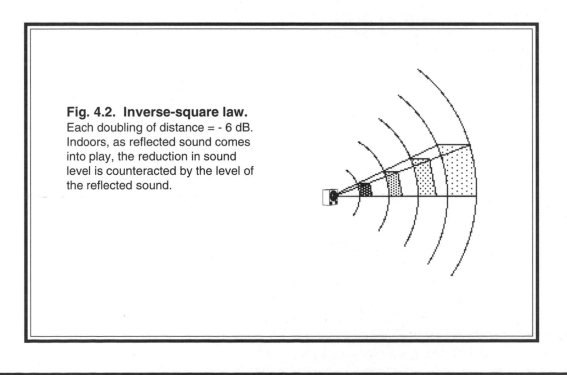

Fig. 4.2. Inverse-square law.
Each doubling of distance = - 6 dB.
Indoors, as reflected sound comes
into play, the reduction in sound
level is counteracted by the level of
the reflected sound.

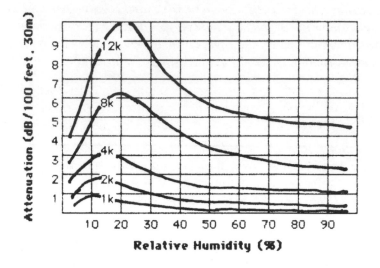

Fig. 4.3. Attenuation of sound in air per 100' (30m).

High frequency attenuation always needs to be considered in the operation of sound systems in very large environments. This kind of attenuation increases drastically in the highest frequencies. It is by far most substantial in the 10% to 25% range of relative humidity (less than this would only be found in the most arid climates). Notice, for example, that 12k is attenuated by as much as 10dB over as little as 100', depending on humidity. Interestingly, as the air gets more humid, the amount of attenuation actually decreases.

c) High Frequency Attenuation in Air.

Attenuation of higher frequencies is a particularly important factor in large environments. The higher the frequency is, the greater the loss is, so the more difficult it becomes to effectively project over a long distance. Stated simply, *low frequencies "carry" farther than high frequencies*. Fig. 4.3 shows approximate rates of loss, per unit of distance, for frequency ranges throughout the upper portion of the audio spectrum.

This type of loss, due to friction between air molecules, occurs in addition to the geometric spreading of sound described by the inverse square law. This energy is given up to heat. (The actual amount of heat is very small. It is estimated that the entire sound output of a football game in a crowded stadium involves roughly enough energy to warm a cup of tea.) *Attenuation occurs according to **unit** of distance, rather than by ratio of distance.*

This type of loss increases in severity as frequency increases because there more interactions between individual molecules as frequency increases. *The amount of high frequency attenuation also changes significantly according to humidity, as illustrated in Fig. 4.3.*

The practical effect of this type of attenuation is that, in very large environments such as outdoor stadiums and other large arenas, the more distant reaches of an audience will tend to receive a sound that is significantly lacking in "zip". A fairly common contemporary approach to resolving this issue (shown in Chapter 14) is to use supplementary high frequency components placed relatively close to the rear audience sections, with their output delayed so it is synchronized with the arrival of the sound from the main loudspeaker clusters.

d) Basic Electrical Measurement.

For the unfamiliar reader, here is a description of some very basic aspects of electricity. In Fig. 4.4, water propelled by a paddlewheel is used to provide power to a machine at the opposite end of its "circuit." In this way a continuous flow in one direction is created, by which force applied in one place is transferred to a device in another place. This is analogous to **_direct current (DC)_** electricity.

In Fig. 4.4-B, a paddle is repeatedly moved in alternating directions, first forward, then rearward, to provide power to a device designed to respond to such alternations. This is roughly comparable to **_alternating current (AC)_** electricity. The trough with its dual path roughly represents the cable with its two current carrying conductors, thus the term *circuit*.

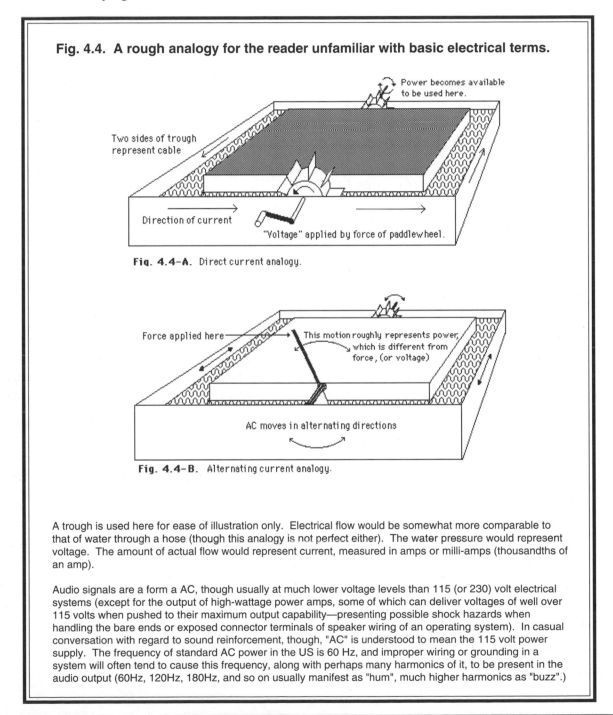

Fig. 4.4. A rough analogy for the reader unfamiliar with basic electrical terms.

Power becomes available to be used here.

Two sides of trough represent cable

Direction of current

"Voltage" applied by force of paddlewheel.

Fig. 4.4-A. Direct current analogy.

Force applied here

This motion roughly represents power, which is different from force, (or voltage)

AC moves in alternating directions

Fig. 4.4-B. Alternating current analogy.

A trough is used here for ease of illustration only. Electrical flow would be somewhat more comparable to that of water through a hose (though this analogy is not perfect either). The water pressure would represent voltage. The amount of actual flow would represent current, measured in amps or milli-amps (thousandths of an amp).

Audio signals are a form a AC, though usually at much lower voltage levels than 115 (or 230) volt electrical systems (except for the output of high-wattage power amps, some of which can deliver voltages of well over 115 volts when pushed to their maximum output capability—presenting possible shock hazards when handling the bare ends or exposed connector terminals of speaker wiring of an operating system). In casual conversation with regard to sound reinforcement, though, "AC" is understood to mean the 115 volt power supply. The frequency of standard AC power in the US is 60 Hz, and improper wiring or grounding in a system will often tend to cause this frequency, along with perhaps many harmonics of it, to be present in the audio output (60Hz, 120Hz, 180Hz, and so on usually manifest as "hum", much higher harmonics as "buzz".)

There is a fairly direct relationship between the force exerted by an electrical source, and the resulting flow of electrons through a circuit. This is described by the famous formula known as *Ohm's Law*:

$$V \div (R \text{ or } Z) = I$$

V = VOLTAGE (Electrical pressure, in **VOLTS**)
R or **Z** = RESISTANCE or IMPEDANCE (in **OHMS**, represented as "Ω")
I = INDUCED CURRENT (Electron flow, in **AMPERES**)

Here, the flow of electrons (current) is shown to be proportional to the generating force (voltage), and inversely proportional to the resistance or impedance in a circuit. By this "common-sense" formula, a doubling of voltage (electromotive force, or pressure) will cause also a doubling of current (the amount of electrons flowing through the circuit). A doubling of impedance (or resistance) will cut current flow by 1/2.

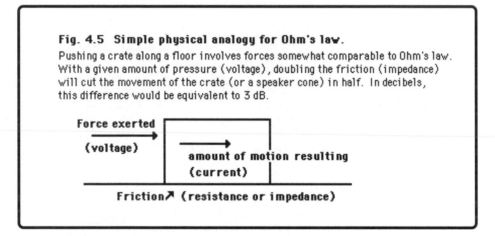

Fig. 4.5 Simple physical analogy for Ohm's law.
Pushing a crate along a floor involves forces somewhat comparable to Ohm's law. With a given amount of pressure (voltage), doubling the friction (impedance) will cut the movement of the crate (or a speaker cone) in half. In decibels, this difference would be equivalent to 3 dB.

Force exerted
(voltage)

amount of motion resulting
(current)

Friction↗ (resistance or impedance)

The term *resistance* applies to direct current. *Impedance* (represented by the letter "Z") applies to any kind of alternating current including audio signals. In a sense, impedance can be understood as a circuit's resistance to sine-wave-motion of a given frequency. It consists of DC resistance combined with a circuit's additional reactance to alternating currents. As a result, *impedance normally measures higher than resistance*.

While Ohm's Law describes the relationship between electrical pressure, impedance and the resulting flow of electrons, another basic formula is used to show the actual amount of power (which is very different from pressure) generated into an electrical circuit. *Power* is the ability to do some kind of work (such as move a speaker cone or drive an electronic circuit). This is shown by:

V-(voltage) x I-(current) = P-(power)

V IS MEASURED IN **VOLTS**
I IS MEASURED IN **AMPERES**
P IS MEASURED IN **WATTS**

This formula shows that *the amount of power actually dissipated ("used up") in a circuit—at a given time—is in proportion to both electrical pressure (voltage) and electron flow (current).* By this relationship, *a signal with relatively high-voltage/low-current can involve the same power level as a signal with relatively low-voltage/high-current. If the same amount of power is involved, they can both, when properly harnessed, do the same amount of work.*

A given amount of power can be transformed to change the relative amount of voltage and current. This kind of transforming is commonly done, for example, in distributed sound systems involving many low-to-moderate level speakers, as well as in many other aspects of audio work—particularly within electronic components.

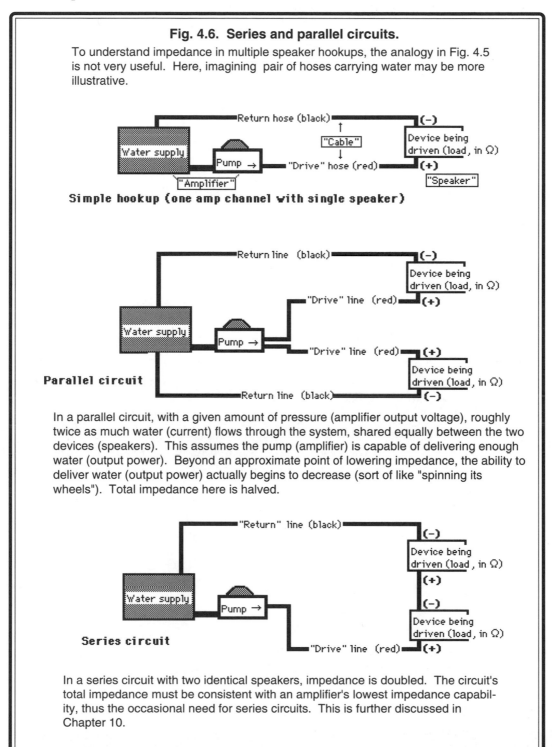

Fig. 4.6. Series and parallel circuits.

To understand impedance in multiple speaker hookups, the analogy in Fig. 4.5 is not very useful. Here, imagining pair of hoses carrying water may be more illustrative.

Simple hookup (one amp channel with single speaker)

Parallel circuit

In a parallel circuit, with a given amount of pressure (amplifier output voltage), roughly twice as much water (current) flows through the system, shared equally between the two devices (speakers). This assumes the pump (amplifier) is capable of delivering enough water (output power). Beyond an approximate point of lowering impedance, the ability to deliver water (output power) actually begins to decrease (sort of like "spinning its wheels"). Total impedance here is halved.

Series circuit

In a series circuit with two identical speakers, impedance is doubled. The circuit's total impedance must be consistent with an amplifier's lowest impedance capability, thus the occasional need for series circuits. This is further discussed in Chapter 10.

e) Pressure and Power.

For both sound waves and electrical signals (as well as for every other kind of motion) there is a basic relationship between the amount of force (pressure) applied in a given direction and the measurement of the actual power (ability to produce electrical or acoustical motion) which results.

For electicity this can be shown by combining Ohm's Law with the above introduced formula for computing power. Ohm's Law shows that if the voltage is changed by a certain amount, it will cause the resulting current to change in direct proportion to that amount. For example, if voltage is doubled, current is also doubled. And by the formula $P=ExI$, voltage is then multiplied by current to figure the increase in power, in this case an increase by a factor of four.

In other words, all else being equal, **power is related to the square of pressure.** By the same method of computing, an increase in voltage by a factor of 3 would cause a ninefold increase in power (3^2); an increase in voltage by a factor of 4 would cause a sixteenfold increase in power (4^2); an increase in voltage by a factor of 10 would cause a hundredfold increase in power (10^2), etc. (this of course assumes that the impedance remains constant).

Sound power is similarly related to the square of sound pressure. Power is not measured directly. It is normally derived by measuring the pressure and then using a version of the above arithmetic.

The decibel is basically oriented around power ratios. *Every ten decibels (one **bel**) is equivalent to a ratio of one order of magnitude (a 10-to-1 power ratio.)*

For pressure ratios, the scale must be adjusted. *The beauty of the decibel* (as with any logarithmic scale) *is that it can be used to deal with pressure ratios simply by doubling the number of decibels.* The squared relationship of pressure to power is thus automatically taken into account. This is illustrated in Fig. 4.7.

When the decibel is used to describe voltages in an audio system, it is done with the assumption that a power ratio is exactly related to the square of the voltage ratio. *The relationship, it should be carefully noted, is not always exact.* It is usually fairly close, though, except when a component is nearing its maximum operating limits. An increase in the flow of electricity can cause a rise in impedance—especially when high power levels are involved, due to added heat. (This is one of a number of factors which can detract from the efficiency of speakers used at high levels.) Situations like these reduce the resulting power ratio to less than an exact squared relationship. In addition, impedance commonly varies very drastically according to frequency (this is discussed further in Chapter 9 and 10).

There can also be variations in *acoustical impedance*, similar in principle to electrical impedance. These variations are a natural occurance in and around horns and speaker enclosures, and also when sound encounters any obstacle, including the surrounding physical structure of its source. (On the whole, though, decibel values derived from sound pressure ratios are reasonably accurate for sound waves in open air.)

f) Output (Source) Impedance and Input (Load) Impedance.

The impedance in a circuit is a result of the combination of the impedances of both components and the cable in-between. In speaker lines the impedance of the cable can be significant, since it rises with higher output voltage. In low-level circuits, the cable impedance tends to be fairly insignificant unless one of the connections or the cable itself is faulty.

Source, or output impedance originates in the component output. *Load, or input impedance* is

Fig. 4.7

Scale of linear to logarithmic values.

Notice the squared relationship of pressure to power here. This is accounted for in decibels by simply doubling the number of decibels-per-given-ratio, as shown in the chart below.

The squared relationship of pressure to power breaks down substantially at, or near, the limits of a component's or system's normal effective capability. When a component approaches its effective operating limits, increased pressure (or voltage) results in less and less of an increase of power and usually in increasing distortion.

Ordinarily, it is not necessary to know the voltage ratios, except when dealing with fairly intricate aspects of component operation and/or system design (though they can come into play when using multiple louspeakers, particularly in the lower frequencies).

The power ratios, though, are very significant to our purposes in this book. For example, a 6dB increase in the output requirements of a system involves 4x the amount of amplifier and loudspeaker output, and so forth according to the chart on the left.

POWER			**PRESSURE or VOLTAGE**		
RATIO BETWEEN: ACOUSTIC or AMPLIFIER POWER LEVELS		DIFFERENCE: in decibels (dBm or dB SPL)	RATIO OF: VOLTAGES or PRESSURES		DIFFERENCE in decibels (dBV, dBu)
1.25-to-1	=	1.0 dB	1.25-to-1	=	2.0 dB
1.6-to-1	=	2.0 dB	1.6-to-1	=	4.0 dB
Double 2-to-1	=	3.0 dB	2-to-1	=	6.0 dB
Triple 3-to-1	=	4.8 dB	3-to-1	=	9.5 dB
Quad. 4-to-1	=	6.0 dB	4-to-1	=	12.0 dB
Etc. 5-to-1	=	7.0 dB	5-to-1	=	14.0 dB
" 6-to-1	=	7.8 dB	6-to-1	=	15.6 dB
" 7-to-1	=	8.5 dB	7-to-1	=	16.9 dB
" 8-to-1	=	9.0 dB	8-to-1	=	18.0 dB
" 9-to-1	=	9.5 dB	9-to-1	=	19.1 dB
10-to-1	=	10. dB	10-to-1	=	20. dB
100-to-1	=	20. dB	100-to-1	=	40. dB
1000-to-1	=	30. dB	1000-to-1	=	60. dB
10,000-to-1	=	40. dB	10,000-to-1	=	80. dB

Note: The term "Sound Pressure Level" often is a confusing one here for the less-than-highly-technical person, even at the higher levels of the business of sound reinforcement. Any of the dB-based measurements used in the field apply, in some sense, to both scales above. For example, with dB SPL measurements, if the linear measurement is made in acoustic watts (a power measurement), the scale on the left would apply; if the linear measurement is made in dynes per square centimeter (pressure), the scale on right would be used.

Additional note: When two identical speaker components operating in the same frequency range are placed in close proximity to one another, the pressure scale on the right may apply. This happens at frequencies which have wavelengths much greater than the distance between the two identical components. Often the resulting increase in SPL will fall somewhere between the two scales, a subject reserved for Chapters 9, 13 and 14.

encountered at the input stage of the component to which the signal is being sent. Generally, the load impedance should be very substantially larger than the source impedance. **A load-to-source impedance ratio of 10-1 or more is usually considered optimal between components in a system**. Some of the more specific aspects of effective impedance matching between components are dealt with in Parts Two and Three.

As indicated, speaker lines are almost a separate story. Since high power levels (meaning lots of current) are involved, additional load is added by small guage cable in speaker lines. (This is an example of how the squared relationship of voltage-to-power can degrade as impedance rises with power. It is somewhat like trying to force a lot of water through a narrow hose—turn up the pressure all you like, but it gets harder and harder to squeeze more and more water through it.) Some of the actual power output is lost in this circumstance, given up to heat. (Chapter 16 includes a chart of power losses according to speaker-wire guage.) The load-to-source impedance ratio of a speaker to a power amplifier is the exception the 10-to-1 guideline just given. Here the ratios ideally are on the order of 100-to-1 or much more, depending on frequency (this is specified as "damping factor" in power amplifier specifications).

g) RMS Values

To identify the rapidly changing amplitudes of a wave as being of a particular intensity, an average value is used. A simple averaging of positive and negative amplitudes in a wave normally would produce a net result of zero. What is required is a method of averaging that provides a meaningful assessment of amplitude, whether positive or negative. The *root mean square (RMS)* method of computation uses the equivalent intensity of DC electricity, over a full cycle or more, to describe the average strength of a wave (see Fig. 4.8).

The RMS value of a sine wave is approximately 0.7 x the peak amplitude of the wave. While the relationship between RMS and peak value is always the same for pure sine waves, the peak value of a complex waveform can vary widely in comparison to its RMS value. As a result, the peak value can be an extremely misleading indicator of the voltage or power a component is capable of delivering on a continuous basis. The RMS figure tends to be a more objective assessment of intensity level.

Still, RMS ratings that are not further qualified can be misleading, because a brief tone burst withstood by a component, and measured by its RMS value, might not accurately reflect what that component is capable of withstanding on a long-term basis.

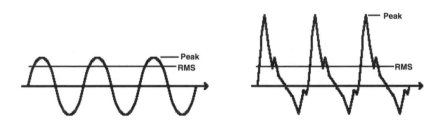

Fig. 4.8. Instantaneous Peak vs. RMS. The instantaneous peak value of a sine wave is always 1.4 x the RMS value. However, the highest instantaneous peak of a complex waveform can value widely in comparison to the RMS value. At its most basic, this is why RMS values are used in quoting audio signal levels. For example, using a peak value such as at right would allow for easy exaggeration of a component's capability. But the existence of waveforms such as at right is one of the important reasons for having system headroom as depicted in Fig. 4.12. The term "instantaneous peak" should not be confused with "peak RMS power" (also called "peak program"). "Peak RMS power" refers to transient peaks as depicted in Fig. 3.6-B.

Understanding the difference between RMS and "Program" or "Continuous Program" ratings involves a different concern. For many years manufacturers have understood that a swept-frequency sine wave or continuous sine wave provided a reasonable basis for assessing the likely power handling capability of a speaker out in the field. Experience has taught that "compressed" mixes on a recording have much less severe peaks than do typical live amplifying situations. Thus the much higher "program" ratings also quoted by most manufacturers of sound reinforcement speaker components.

h) Volume Units.

Volume units are based upon the hearing process's tendency to compress intensity differences, and to ignore or downplay very rapid (transient) peaks. The scale is adjusted to display decibel values in roughly the way we tend to hear intensity differences. By using a compromise between continuous and peak value, the ear's tendency to ignore peaks is roughly accounted for. Abbreviated *VU*, this is the unit of reference used for VU meters.

The VU meter allows a visual indication of the signal level at one or more points in the circuitry of audio equipment. While +4 dBm is the standard for 0 VU, meters are normally calibrated to the appropriate operating levels of the equipment into which they are built.

On the whole a very workable compromise, *this method of measurement has as one of its disadvantages the fact that very rapid peaks—which by themselves tend to be bypassed in the hearing process—can sometimes cause momentary distortion* which might be more easily noticed as a change in the quality of the sound of, for instance, a drum. For this reason, VU meters are commonly supplemented by a peak level indicator, commonly known as a *Peak Program Meter (PPM)*.

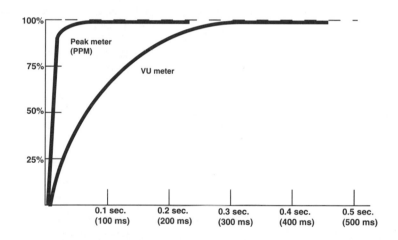

Fig. 4.9. VU and Peak Meter response. Note above why transient sounds such as drums do not fully register on VU meters. The VU response roughly represents the human perception of loudness according to the duration of a given sound. (The term "peak-program" has a significantly different meaning than the "instantaneous peak" as shown in the previous figure. If needed refer back to accompanying caption for the previous figure.)

i) Loudness Level.

This method of measurement is based on the equal-loudness contours for average hearing. Loudness levels are measured in *phons*. While difficult to measure exactly (because the equal-loudness contours are not precise measurements), loudness levels serve as a reasonable guideline in exchanging information about the perception of intensity at different frequencies (Fig. 4.10).

Sound-level meters are commonly designed to weight their scales in a rough approximation of loudness levels. Typical weightings use curves based on the equal-loudness contours for *40 phons ("A" weighting), 70 phons ("B" weighting) and 100 phons ("C" weighting)* as depicted in Fig. 4.10. While loudness levels are far more representative of human hearing than straightforward SPL measurements, it is worth remembering that they are approximations based on statistical averages, so they are not necessarily accurate for a given person. They are, though, a very useful guideline.

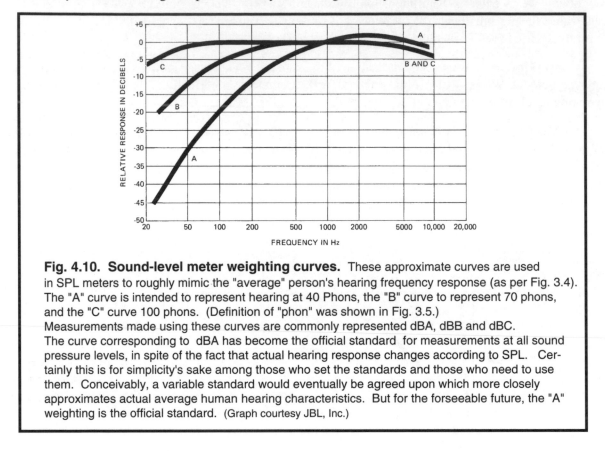

Fig. 4.10. Sound-level meter weighting curves. These approximate curves are used in SPL meters to roughly mimic the "average" person's hearing frequency response (as per Fig. 3.4). The "A" curve is intended to represent hearing at 40 Phons, the "B" curve to represent 70 phons, and the "C" curve 100 phons. (Definition of "phon" was shown in Fig. 3.5.)
Measurements made using these curves are commonly represented dBA, dBB and dBC.
The curve corresponding to dBA has become the official standard for measurements at all sound pressure levels, in spite of the fact that actual hearing response changes according to SPL. Certainly this is for simplicity's sake among those who set the standards and those who need to use them. Conceivably, a variable standard would eventually be agreed upon which more closely approximates actual average human hearing characteristics. But for the forseeable future, the "A" weighting is the official standard. (Graph courtesy JBL, Inc.)

j) dB.

As explained in Chapter 3, the decibel is a relative quantity. *Technically, the use of measurements in decibels (dB), with no other qualifications, is simply a comparison of two intensity levels on a logarithmic scale.*

Often, though, the term is understood to refer to one of the scales introduced in the following sections. For example, the statement "The system's output was approximately 100 dB at 10 feet" would normally be assumed by an engineer to refer to "dB SPL at 10 feet". Similarly, the statement "The mixer's nominal output is +4dB" would normally be assumed to mean "+4dBu" (or its equivalent).

k) dB SPL.

The previously introduced scale of sound pressure levels uses a standardized reference point from which measurements can be made and readily shared. This has been established to be .0002 dynes per square centimeter, the average young child's threshold of hearing at 1 kHz. The power level at this threshold is on the order of 10^{-16} acoustic watts/cm^2 (in the ten millionths, of a millionth, of a millionth of a watt per square centimeter) of acoustic power. The threshold of feeling, the approximate average level at which hearing is saturated, is on the order of 2000 dynes/cm^2, equivalent to an acoustic power of about one thousandth of an acoustic watt per square centimeter, or 1/10 acoustic watt per square meter (not to be confused with electrical watts). Measurements on this scale are normally identified by the abbreviation *dB SPL.*

The following sections on dBu, dBm, dBV and dBv introduce the most commonly used standards for defining signal levels in sound systems. If it seems like gobbledygook, don't be too discouraged—it has been testy to some of the best engineers in the field.

Much of the confusion exists because different organizations orignally worked independently of one another, and each produced their own guidelines for measuring signal strengths in their particular type of work. Also, as technology changed, the methods of measurement needed to change too, in order to be more meaningful to the engineers using the equipment. Naturally, some of the earlier measurement methods are carried over from the past, and are occasionally still quoted when the manufacturer decides they are appropriate. As well, many older units and specifications continue to be found out in the field.

But the confusion is not quite as deep as it sometimes seems. *Ordinarily, unless the equipment is mismatched to other components in the system, or unless the specs are "fudged" to hide flaws in the design of equipment or to exaggerate their capabilities, the different forms of specifications equate fairly well*. For, example, a unit which has a stated output capability of, say, +4 dBm, or +4 dBu, or +4 dBv (with a given amount of headroom) will tend to have similar available output level (to the ear, at least). And the difference between these and dBV (note the capital "V"), is under typical circumstances only 2.2 dB.

In practice, what tends to be most important is that the impedances between components are appropriately matched, and that the mixer, outboard EQ and/or crossover outputs are sufficient to adequately drive the power amplifiers to the needed levels. Most modern professional sound reinforcement components (as opposed to hi-fi, home-stereo-type components) are generally able to interface fairly well with one another. Radical impedance mismatches between modern components are rare, and even then the result is usually inaudible. The need to use an impedance-matching device is usually only necessary when using an older vacuum tube device or a device with an output labeled "high-impedance" somewhere in the signal chain—an extremely unusual circumstance today. Thus the primary concern tends to be effective gain staging, (or gain structuring) among the components within a system, discussed in Section "o" of this chapter, and in Section 7.h.

l) dBu

The unit *dBu* is a measurement based upon *voltage,* used to quote normal operating levels and maximum capabilities of components. This is a fairly modern term which is *most useful in dealing with moderately-to-extremely-high-impedance line inputs of around 2000 ohms and upward* (which covers most currently manufactured sound reinforcement equipment). 0 dBu is equal to 0.775 volts RMS.

m) dBm.

Measurements based on the unit dBm are most useful in expressing power capabilities in a low-impedance circuit.

The unit *dBm* is based upon a computation of *power.* 0 dBm = 1 milliwatt (.001 watt) RMS. This figure is equivalent to 0.775 volts RMS in a circuit with an impedance of 600 ohms. The figure 600 ohms is a generally accepted reference point for low-impedance circuits, though actual 600-ohm circuits are rarely used any longer except in some extremely large sound reinforcement systems and in certain aspects of broadcast work. For many years the term dBm served as the industry standard, and has recently been increasingly replaced by dBu, which tends to be a more appropriate measurement of signal strength with the somewhat higher impedances generally used today. (This should not be confused with the term "high impedance" used to describe unbalanced microphones used in many small, inexpensive PA systems. See the explanation in Chapter 5, section "J" and "K".)

n) dBV, and dBv

The unit *dBV* is based upon a measurement of *voltage*, referenced to 1 volt RMS (0 dBV). This expresses an electrical pressure, independently of circuit impedance. This unit is today most often used by manufacturers of hi-fi, home-stereo-type equipment, and is generally not an agreed-upon reference for professional sound reinforcement equipment (though it may occasionally still be found in specs for somewhat older equipment).

The unit *dBv* (note the small, lower case "v") is also a measurement of *voltage*, but is referenced to .775 volts RMS. This measurement is another way of expressing dBu, i. e. the translation is exact under all circumstances ("dBv" was an earlier transitional usage that has been replaced by the current standard "dBu").

The difference between dBv (or dBu), and dBV, is 2.2 dB. In other words, a measurement of 0 dBV is equal to 2.2 dBu or 2.2 dBv. How these relate to dBm depends very strongly on the actual impedance into which the circuit was terminated ("hooked-up" to) when the measurement was taken. As mentioned before, so long as the impedance requirements of the equipment are properly matched, the different forms of specification tend to equate fairly well—*if* the manufacturer has been faithful in quoting the levels at which the equipment is capable of operating.

o) Basic Gain Structures.

Audio signal strengths can be grouped into three basic intensity ranges: (1) *mic level*, (2) *line level* and (3) *power amplifier output* or *speaker level*.

Microphone output levels are generally measured in millivolts (mV= thousandth of a volt). Mics tend to have output levels in the area of -70 dBu to -30 dBu.

Line levels are considered to be between 1 and 2 volts RMS (+2 dBu to +8 dBu) in professional equipment. This refers to *nominal*, or recommended average operating level at inputs and outputs; peak levels may extend to over 10 volts RMS (+22 dBu). The accepted standard for sound reinforcement equipment is +4 dBu. Unfortunately, many lower-budget components fall short of these levels, so we may need to "baby" their level, and find another source for the signal strength necessary to drive the power amplifiers, such as at the crossover. We may encounter an outboard unit (say, an EQ) designed for "hi-fi" home stereo use, where the accepted standard for nominal operating level is roughly 15 dB lower (generally -10dBV, equivalent to about -8dBu). In such situations the difference in operating levels requires a lower level at both input and output for the outboard unit, thus possibly compromising the signal-to-noise ratio. This is discussed below.

Power amplifier output levels depend on the requirements of the output transducers used. These levels can extend upwards to 1,000 watts (about 90 volts into 8 ohms) or even more for each power amplifier, but depend highly on the application and the required intensity level.

The organization of an appropriate gain structure in a sound reinforcement system (a process sometimes referred to as *gain staging*), is vital to its effective operation. Put simply, *if the gain levels in one or more of the components are too low, the system noise may be heard in the output sound during quieter portions of the audio program; if the gain are too strong, one or more points in the system circuitry may produce audible distortion when a strong signal is present.* Thus the task is to attempt to drive each component's input with an adequately strong signal to be well above the component's electronic noise level (also known as the noise "floor"), while leaving enough "headroom" for rapid peaks and the strongest signals likely to be encountered by each particular channel of a component at a given event. This process is important, because electronic system noise is cumulative through a system. Plus, the overall dynamic range of a system is never better than its weakest link. Fig. 4.11 illustrates a typical basic gain structure for a reinforcement system.

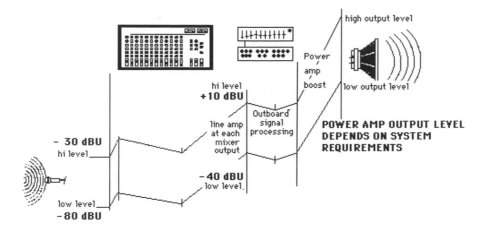

Fig. 4.11. Typical basic gain structure in a simple reinforcement system.

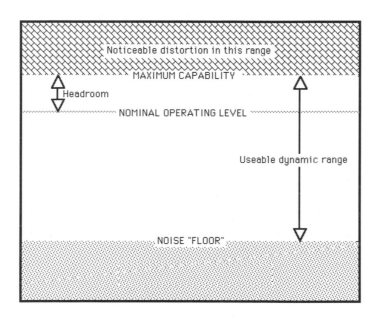

Fig. 4.12. Usable dynamic range of an audio component. The amount of headroom afforded above the nominal operating level (or "average" operating level quoted by the manufacturer) among other things reflects the ability of the component to handle transient peaks, such as drum sounds, without noticeable distortion. Most often, the nominal operating level is represented as "0 dB" on the unit's meters. A nominal operating level of +4 dBu, with perhaps 20 dB of headroom, is generally considered optimal for modern sound reinforcement equipment, though many modest-budget components fall short of these levels (or sacrifice headroom above their stated nominal level). When encountering components with this type of limitation, we may need to "baby" them by reducing the amount of signal fed to them from the previous component in the signal chain, then make up the difference at a place such as the main outboard EQ or electronic crossover.

p) Distortion.

Audio signal distortion can take on a number of forms, arising out of any of a number of causes in an audio system. Strictly speaking, variations of any kind between an input signal and an output signal or sound is a form of distortion. From a practical standpoint, though, distortion refers to any alteration which adds frequencies not present in the original sound or changes the duration of any of those frequencies, or any other characteristic that changes the nature of a sound in an undesirable way.

Harmonic distortion is the addition of frequencies not present in the original waveform, which bear a harmonic relationship to the frequencies in the input waveform. Harmonic distortion is commonly associated with overloading of circuits, although it can occur at levels well below the maximum limits of circuits too.

When a circuit is severely overloaded the peaks of a waveform are limited in a radical way as shown in Fig. 4.13. This is commonly called *clipping*, since the top of a waveform is literally clipped off in a graph of the output signal. Clipping results in the addition of additional harmonic frequencies not present in the input waveform. At levels below complete overloading both harmonic and *subharmonic* distortion also commonly occur in loudspeakers. The occurrence of these is accepted as natural, but keeping them to a reasonable minimum is a basic objective of sensible loudspeaker design.

Transient distortion is the inability of a component to effectively reproduce rapid changes in the intensity of a signal. This type of distortion results from a delay in the time the output waveform takes to accomplish an intensity change equivalent to that of the input waveform. Since no component is perfect, some degree of transient distortion occurs at every stage. Usually, in low level components, transient distortion is negligible.

While transient distortion can occur in any component, it is a characteristic which tends to occur most noticeably in power amplifiers and transducers, usually most severely in loudspeakers. Because of the relatively large physical mass of the vibrating element, particularly in cone-driven speakers, the momentum of the cone can cause it to take extra time to "catch up" to radical changes in the intensity of the input waveform. This type of distortion can also result from structural faults or resonances in a horn or speaker enclosure. Having been set into motion, they can continue for a brief period even after the driver stops moving.

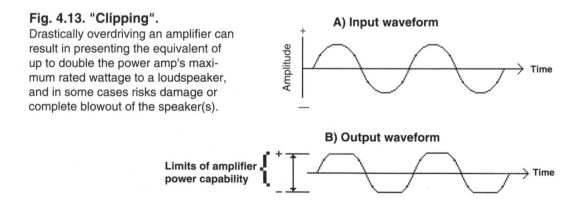

Fig. 4.13. "Clipping".
Drastically overdriving an amplifier can result in presenting the equivalent of up to double the power amp's maximum rated wattage to a loudspeaker, and in some cases risks damage or complete blowout of the speaker(s).

A) Input waveform

B) Output waveform

Limits of amplifier power capability

Note: If the addition of distortion harmonics in "B" is unclear, refer to Fig. 2.13 and 2.14

Since it is historically assumed that some degree of transient distortion is unavoidable, it is most commonly measured as "Transient Response". *A **higher** degree of transient response means there is **lower** transient distortion.* Lack of good transient response can also occur to a sometimes notable extent in moving coil microphones, and in relatively low budget power amplifiers. In power amplifiers, transient response is measured as "slew rate". Basically, the greater the power capability of a power amplifier is, the higher its slew rate should be.

Intermodulation distortion occurs as a result of widely different frequencies being produced simultaneously, and usually occurs in amplifiers and loudspeakers. When IM distortion occurs in speakers, it is commonly a result of the ***Doppler effect*** (sometimes doppler distortion is regarded as a completely different form of distortion, though technically it is a form of IM distortion). When IM distortion occurs in amplifiers, it is a result of the basic difficulty involved in producing widely varied frequencies simultaneously at high power output levels, and causes new non-harmonically-related frequencies to be created.

Phase distortion is any alteration of the phase relationship of frequencies by a component. Phase distortion is possibly the least insidious of all the forms of distortion. This type of distortion is possible in any component, but tends to be most characteristic of electronic crossovers, which commonly shift the phase of their output. The result is sometimes heard as a slight reduction of response in the range around the crossover points. When phase distortion occurs in amplifiers or equalizers, the effect is generally not noticeable and tends to be minimal, especially when compared to the phase shifts that are a natural part of a typical acoustic environment.

Distortion levels are normally measured as a percentage of the overall signal level, and need to be referenced to a particular operating level in order to be meaningful.

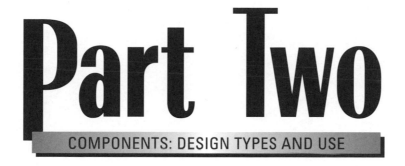

Part Two

COMPONENTS: DESIGN TYPES AND USE

CHAPTER 5

MICROPHONES

Of all the classes of components in audio systems, the development of the transducers—microphones and speakers—has probably been the most cumbersome. The development of the loudspeaker has, at many stages in its respective evolution, taken some wild turns—many of which have resulted in dead ends. The development of the microphone, though, has at times been truly bizarre. The history of microphones in their early evolution includes hydraulic and liquid-cooled microphones, "microphones" the size of washing machines, microphones that—like a miniature coal bin—needed to be regularly replenished with new carbon granules, and "microphones" with output power so strong that measurements were given in horsepower.

Today most of the basic design obstacles have been overcome (and who knows what improvements the future might hold). While there are still compromises and limitations involved in both design and use, the well-designed-and-utilized contemporary microphone is eminently capable of delivering clear, high-quality sound through the electronic realm and ultimately to an audience. An understanding of the limitations and compromises, though, can in many cases be vitally important to their effective use.

a) Design Types.

The transduction of sound waves into audio signals can be accomplished in a number of basic ways.

Dynamic microphones involve a magnetic structure and a vibrating element which generates a voltage in response to sound waves. Dynamic microphones are, to date, the most widely manufactured and commonly used microphone types for sound reinforcement applications. Most often used is a *moving-coil* propelled by a thin diaphram as shown in Fig. 5.1, essentially the same principle as a conventional loudspeaker in reverse-miniature. Moving-coil microphones can be very durable and cost effective, and are marketed in designs capable of handling almost all sound reinforcement situations. They range from low-budget, marginal quality mics to fairly expensive mics of almost incredible quality. In recent years, new magnetic materials such as neodymium have resulted in extremely lightweight designs, often with superb audio quality.

Condenser microphones work on the electrostatic principle described in Fig. 5.2. By and large, they are capable of extremely high-quality output, and are particularly noted for the relative accuracy and strength of their very-high-frequency response. In exchange for the high quality, there is a slight inconvenience. Condenser mics require a power supply for the mic. In some designs, the power supply needs to be provided-for in the mixer design or by a unit inserted along the path of the microphone cable as shown in Fig. 5.2-B. This is known as *remote power,* or *phantom power.* Other condenser designs

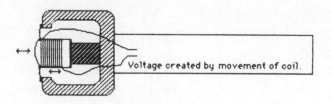

Figure 5.1. Basic dynamic (moving-coil) microphone.

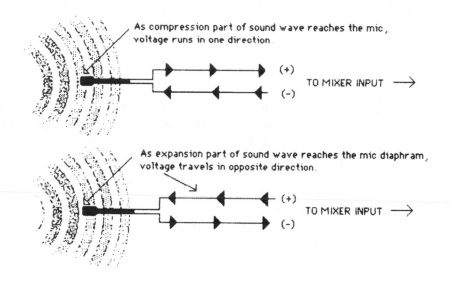

Fig. 5.2. Basic condenser mic hookup.

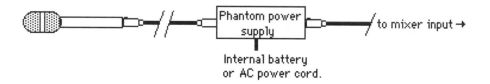

Operating a condenser microphone requires a power supply. Remote powering, also known as "phantom" power, allows a standard mic cable to carry the power to the mic (in mics so designed). Some designs allow the option of using either; a few designs allow the option of using either battery or phantom power. High quality mixers commonly provide phantom power, eliminating the need for an intermediary unit as above.

A note of caution here: If an in-line transformer/adaptor or attenuator is used, it cannot be inserted between the power supply and the mic, or the mic will not function.

use a replaceable battery in the microphone body. Some designs allow the option to use either a battery or phantom power. This is described further in the segment of this chapter on "circuit considerations".

Ribbon microphones utilize a thin electrically conductive ribbon which vibrates within a magnetic field to initiate the audio signal. Technically, they are another form of dynamic microphone. Ribbon microphones use the same electromagnetic principle as moving-coil microphones (actually electro-*dynamic*, hence the term "dynamic"), but in substantially different configurations (Fig. 5.3). While they are capable of providing excellent sound quality, ribbon mics can be very sensitive to physical shock, and in many designs, care is warranted to avoid breaking the ribbon by dropping the mic or overloading it with excessively loud sounds.

Piezo-electric microphones (and contact pickups) involve the use of a substance which, when twisted or otherwise deformed by a force—such as the pressure provided by a passing sound wave—generates a voltage (called a piezoelectric voltage). *Crystal* and *ceramic* microphones both utilize this principle. Traditionally they are strong utility microphones of poor sound quality (they are commonly used in telephones, for example). *A large number of piezoelectric contact-pickup designs with very high audio quality are marketed and are very useful for sound reinforcement, whenever it is possible to fasten the pickup to a vibrating plate (particularly a wooden one).* This type of pickup is commonly installed in acoustic guitars by their manufacturers, and is also often useful with other stringed instruments.

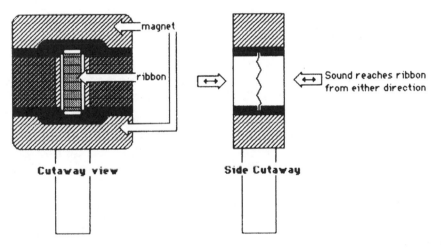

A. Representation of a bi-directional ribbon mic.

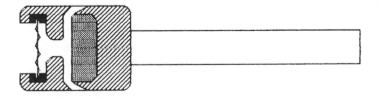

B. Cutaway representation of a contemporary ribbon mic

Fig. 5.3. Ribbon mics. (A) The basic directional characteristic of the traditional bi-directional ribbon microphone is of importance to the discussion in Section "b" of the text. (B) A unidirectional ribbon mic.

b) Basic Directional Patterns.

Directional pickup of sound is vital for minimizing pickup of ambient (or distant) sounds and room reverberation, for reducing acoustic feedback, and for separating the pickup of different sound sources to allow better control over an audio mix. Because certain very basic mic designs tend to exhibit certain very basic directional pickup patterns, it seems useful here to describe in-brief some very basic microphone mechanics, that of the original moving-coil and ribbon microphones.

In the basic moving-coil microphone shown in 5.1-A, the structure of the magnet and surrounding assembly does not allow waves to affect the rear of the diaphram. Remember that a wave of a given frequency will tend to easily bend around obstacles much smaller or thinner than its length. For an object as thin as a contemporary microphone, this would usually include most of the audio spectrum (a 10 kHz wave, to illustrate, has a length of about 34 mm, or $1\text{-}^{1}/2"$, roughly the diameter of a typical mic). So, frequencies throughout all but the highest portion of the audio spectrum, when coming from the sides and rear of this type of microphone, will act on the diaphram about the same as when they are coming from the front—this is because no cancelling or overriding forces are able to act on the back of the diaphram.

As a result, such a microphone tends to be equally sensitive to sounds coming from every direction. This is called an *omni-directional* pickup pattern. (The smaller the microphone barrel is, the higher would be the frequencies up to which it would tend to remain omnidirectional. An infinitely small microphone of this type would be omni at all frequencies. Above 4 or 5 kHz is a typical range around which the pattern of an omnidirectional microphone begins to degrade, as the wavelengths approaching from the rear become less than about 2-or-3-times the diameter of the mic, and thus have increasing difficulty in fully bending around its structure.)

The other basic design, the original "classic" ribbon mic, placed the ribbon within a magnetic gap as shown in Fig. 5.3-A. Of course any sound approaching it from either the front or back would cause the ribbon to vibrate in-sync with the sound. The phase relationship of the microphone's output (+ or -) is dependent on from which side the sound approaches. Sounds approaching the ribbon from anywhere in the plane across its middle would tend to encounter the ribbon with equal effect on both sides, causing little or no motion of the ribbon, and hence little or no electrical output (i.e., they cancel one-another out fairly completely). The result is a figure-eight pattern as illustrated in Fig. 5.4, 5.5 and 5.7B, called a *bi-directional* pattern.

In the bidirectional microphone, sound waves do in-fact quite readily bend around the mic as well, (except for the highest frequencies). But the rearward influence is delayed by a small fraction of a second and reduced in intensity ever so slightly—just enough to allow the ribbon to be set into motion by the oncoming waves (i.e., they do not quite cancel out). As sounds approach from directions closer and closer to the sides, though, these forces become more nearly equal in both intensity and time of arrival, tending to cancel each other out to form the null areas in the bidirectional pattern. This kind of cancellation provides the basis for microphones of various *uni-directional* patterns. *By combining a bidirectional pattern with an omnidirectional pattern in appropriate proportions, unidirectional patterns are obtained.* (Since the rear sensitivity of the bidirectional pattern is of directly opposite phase to that of the front, it destructively interferes with the rear part of the omnidirectional pattern, which is of the same phase for sounds approaching from every direction (see Fig. 5.5).

There are a number of specific ways this can be done. Originally a ribbon and a moving-coil element were sometimes actually used in tandem and their outputs mixed together. Other early designs involved large and often clumsy systems of many tubes and ports to gather waves of varying frequencies, and divert them to the diaphram in the necessary phase and amplitude. These types of early designs had substantial practical and acoustical drawbacks.

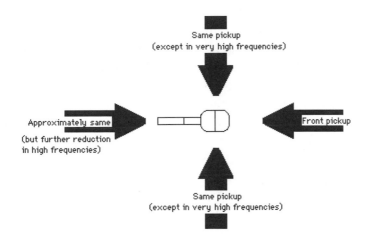

Same pickup
(except in very high frequencies)

Approximately same
(but further reduction
in high frequencies)

Front pickup

Same pickup
(except in very high frequencies)

**Fig. 5.4
Basic microphone directional
response.**

OMNIDIRECTIONAL

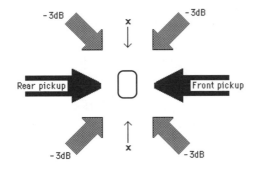

-3dB

-3dB

Rear pickup

Front pickup

-3dB

-3dB

BI-DIRECTIONAL (FIGURE-8)

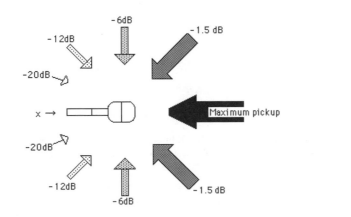

-6dB

-1.5 dB

-12dB

-20dB

x →

Maximum pickup

-20dB

-12dB

-1.5 dB

-6dB

CARDIOID

Among modern designs, some use twin diaphrams placed back-to-back, with an electrical network to provide the necessary phase and amplitude relationships—but these tend to be very expensive, and are mainly used in the recording studio (with rare exceptions). Most of the modern designs use the same basic principle incorporated within the microphone housing, in the form of miniature channels with openings toward the rear of the mic element (these are the mics most often used in sound reinforcement). These miniature channels are designed to allow adequate entry for waves coming from the rear so they cancel out the arrival of those same waves at the front of the diaphram, while still allowing the waves from the front to encounter the diaphram without complete cancellation in the other direction, a design principle known as *pressure gradient*. (This feat of basic mic design is remarkable because in order to have the proper amount of interference, the right delay through these channels and the right balance of force on the diaphram is required for each frequency continuously throughout most or all of the spectrum.) **No matter what the method of design, though, the resulting pattern of a basic mic design always roughly manifests itself as some form of combination of bidirectional and omnidirectional** (see Fig. 5.7).

When the manufacturer combines an omni and bi component in aproximately equal proportions as shown in Fig. 5.5, the result is the basic unidirectional pattern whose name is derived from its heart-like shape—the *cardioid* pattern. Cardioids ideally have their maximum rejection at 180 degrees-off-axis (directly to the rear).

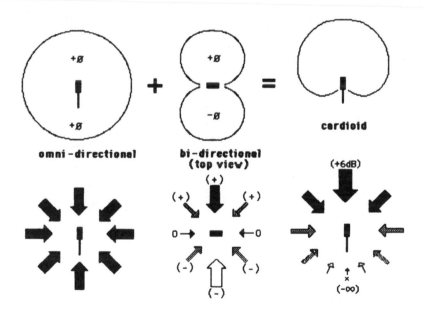

Fig. 5.5 How a cardioid pattern is created at the design stage.

From a technical standpoint, a standard cardioid pattern is a combination of omni- and bi-directional influences in equal proportions. Supercardioid and hypercardioid patterns involve somewhat stronger bi-directional influence in their design. So in any pattern narrower than cardioid, some pickup around the direct rear is unavoidable.

Adding a stronger bidirectional component results in a pickup pattern slightly narrower than cardioid, usually called *supercardioid*. When an even stronger bidirectional influence is added, the pattern becomes narrower yet, and is normally called *hypercardioid*. There is a tradeoff when this is done. **As the pickup pattern becomes narrower, the beginnings of the bidirectional pattern re-emerge directly to the rear.** The narrower the pattern becomes, the stronger and wider this rear sensitivity becomes. As well, the narrower the pattern becomes, the narrower the useful working angles of the mic are. Is the rear pickup of a supercardioid or hypercardioid pattern necessarily a disadvantage? Not at all—in fact they can be an advantage, *if* the mic is used effectively. Generally, this means keeping the user as close as possible to the center axis of the mic (directly in front). Among the basic mic patterns, a hypercardioid pattern is capable of providing the most reduction of overall off-axis pickup (see Fig. 5.11). (The notable exception to this discussion is the line gradient, or "shotgun" microphone, shown later. These tend to be physically long and financially very expensive, and are not intended for close-up use).

Overall directional patterns are usually represented on the type of graphs shown in Fig. 5.7, called *polar patterns* . *This type of graph depicts directional pickup that is actually three dimensional, so if one were to rotate the mic without changing its proper front-to-back orientation (as in Fig. 5.7.B), the pattern would normally remain the same.*

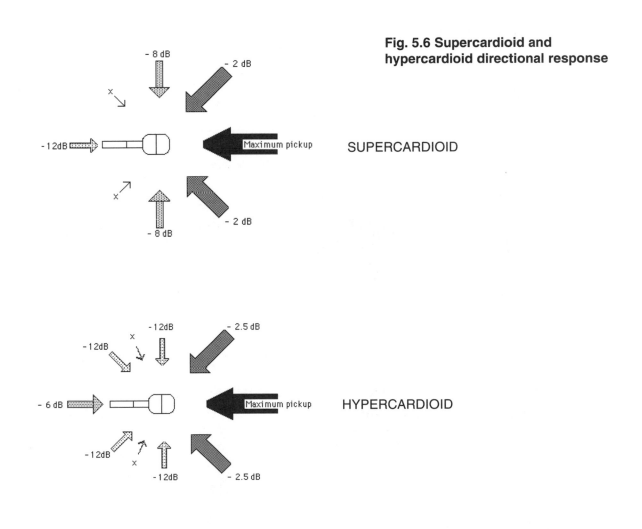

Fig. 5.6 Supercardioid and hypercardioid directional response

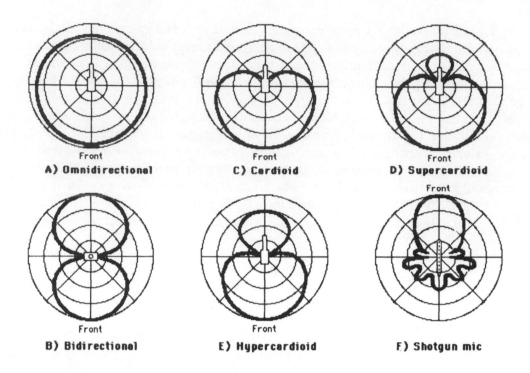

Fig. 5.7. Basic microphone polar patterns

In this type of basic graph, the closer the response curve is to the center, the less sensitive the mic is to sounds arriving from a given angle. In the real world, each of these patterns often deviate from the theoretical models, and the manufacturer will call the mic whichever pattern most closely describes the mic. Usually, a simple understanding of the basic patterns is adequate to be able to use them effectively.

(Omnidirectional pattern shown is for 5 kHz on a typical omni. "Shotgun" pattern depends strongly on the design.) See the comparisons in Fig. 5.10 to make a rough assessment of the maximum side-to-side working angles of a given pattern. These, of course, represent three dimensional patterns, as below.

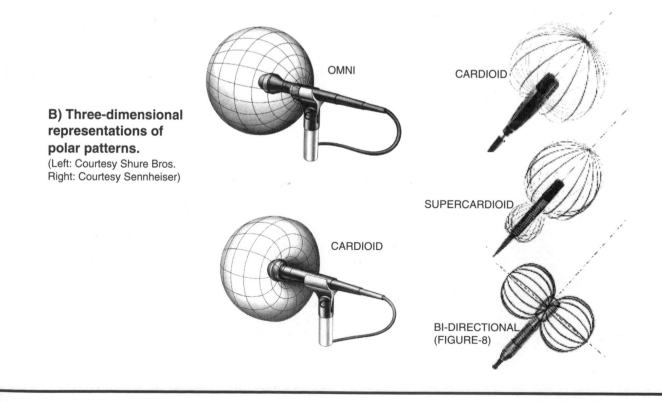

B) Three-dimensional representations of polar patterns.
(Left: Courtesy Shure Bros. Right: Courtesy Sennheiser)

The theoretically ideal unidirectional microphone would exhibit a polar pattern identical at all frequencies. In practice this does not occur (though a few designs come close). Polar patterns such as the ones shown in Fig. 5.8 show the directional characteristics of a microphone at a number of different frequencies throughout the spectrum. This type of graph allows the user to get an approximate idea of how the response may be expected to change at different angles off-axis. It is thus possible to make an asessment of the useful working angles of the mic in highly critical applications, in terms of both pickup of the desired sound source and rejection of unwanted sound.

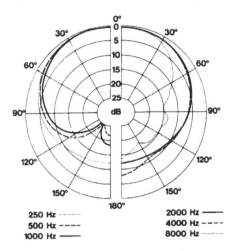

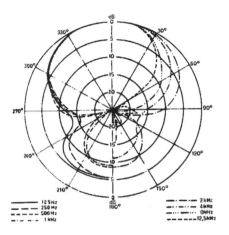

(A) Sennheiser MD 421 (Cardioid)　　　　　　　　　**(B)** Beyer TGX-580 (Hypercardioid)

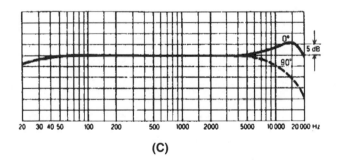

(C)

Fig. 5.8. Examples of pickup pattern variations by frequency.

Shown in A and B are polar patterns at different frequencies of two high quality microphones, courtesy of the manufacturers. In this type of graph, only half is used to illustrate the pattern at any given frequency, since it is assumed the pattern is symmetrical, i.e., the other half will be a mirror image at a given frequency. (The MD-421 is one of the most recognized mics worldwide—a standard for rack toms, sometimes bass drum, and brass in concert sound reinforcement, in addition to finding international use for speech reinforcment. The TGX-580 is one of a new class of hypercardioids finding increasing vocal use in high-sound-level concert situations.) Note how the pattern narrows at very high frequencies—this is normal in a standard-size microphone. Shown in "C" is how this "high frequency beaming" looks on a frequency response graph (Courtesy Sennheiser). Notice again that the very high frequency response is reduced at angles well off-axis. This is another important reason for keeping the sound source as close as possible to the center axis.

c) Proximity Effect.

A related aspect of cardioid and bidirectional microphones is the boosting of low-frequency response in comparison to high-frequency response as the sound source gets closer to the mic. This effect is most often called *proximity effect*, *bass-boost*, *bass tip-up* or *close-talking effect*. This change in frequency response with respect to distance between microphone and sound source is a natural byproduct of directional microphone design. (It is, though, correctible through the use of certain types of additional design features. A number of unidirectional microphones are manufactured which do not exhibit the proximity effect to any noticeable degree.)

The proximity effect is nonexistent in the basic omni pattern, gradually increases in prominence as the patterns move through cardioid, supercardioid and hypercardioid, and is most severe in the basic bidirectional pattern. (So, without the additional compensating design feature just mentioned above, a supercardioid would exhibit this characteristic more noticeably than a cardioid, a hypercardioid more than a supercardioid, etc..)

Proximity effect typically becomes audible at distances of less than about a half-meter (about 20") whenever the source-to-mic distance is changed by any significant proportion. It is most noticeable at very short distances. For example, moving from 100mm (4") to 25mm (1") would in a basic cardioid, supercardioid, or hypercardioid design cause a substantial deepening of tonal quality. Moving from, say 100mm to 300mm (about a foot), would normally cause a noticeable thinning of tonal quality.

Fig. 5.9. Typical proximity effect.
Proximity effect has both advantages and drawbacks, as discussed in Section "c".
The bass-boost due to proximity effect is always strongest when the source is directly on-axis, and weakest at the angle where the response is down 6dB from the on-axis response (90° off-axis for a cardioid, 70° to 80° off-axis for a supercardioid or hypercardioid).
(A) Courtesy Audio Technica, ATM-41 vocal microphone curve shown;
(B) Courtesy Sennheiser, MD 416 curve shown.

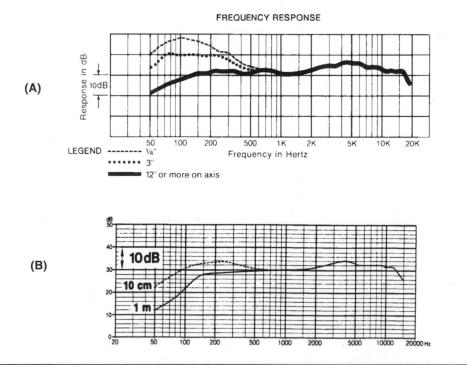

The proximity effect has both advantages and disadvantages. *Proximity effect can add fullness to a sound, but in excess it can also contribute to muddiness or boominess of sound quality in close-up miking.* Too, it can be responsible for wide variations in voice quality when a vocalist or instrumentalist moves farther-from or closer-to the microphone. As mentioned above, unidirectional microphones are marketed which do not exhibit proximity effect. A microphone of this kind is sometimes well suited to some applications where the source-to-microphone distance varies substantially. If necessary, the varying signal level can to a large extent be automatically compensated with the use of a compressor on that particular channel, (introduced in Chapter 8). The compromise here would be significantly reduced gain-before-feedback.

Despite the disadvantages, *proximity effect can definitely be a great asset.* In close-up miking it allows the low frequencies to be cut at the mixer or at the mic (in microphones so designed), allowing sufficient fullness of vocal or instrumental sound for the up-close user while reducing the amount of pickup

Figure 5.10

Proximity effect can also be either enhanced or virtually eliminated by the manufacturer, depending on the uses for which the mic is designed. Pictured in A, B and C are commercial designs which make effective use of the proximity effect by enhancing it.

(A) Crown CM-310 "Differoid" cardioid vocal mic. Here the diaphram is positioned extremely close to the front of the protective screen, as compared to a typical mic. This positioning allows an extremely close source-to-mic distance on-axis, increasing proximity effect when the lips are touching the mic. As well, because of the inverse-square law (introduced in Chaper 4), this close-to-the-windscreen positioning of the diaphram allows increased pickup of the intended source in comparison to that of the surrounding environment or output of stage monitors. But don't move away from this type of mic, or bye-bye sound.

(B) Beyer TGX-580 hypercardioid (the polar pattern of which was shown in Figure 5.8). This type of mic uses a similar principle to that in"A", though with a somewhat narrower pickup pattern.

(C) AKG D-558B, "noise-cancelling/differential" mic. a hypercardioid announcement microphone utilizing a similar principle, but taken to an extreme. In this type of mic, proximity effect is extended greatly upward in frequency, providing extreme discrimination against sounds originating farther away, in favor of the up-close user.

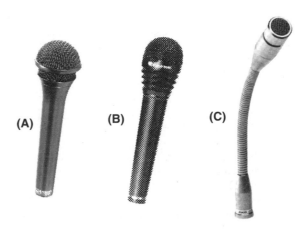

Proximity effect can also be reduced or eliminated in unidirectional mics. Two methods are commonly used.

(D) Electrovoice RE-20 (also marketed as PL-20). This mic, a favorite for bass drum and saxophone (as well as broadcast announcement), uses the added porting system along the length of the mic barrel to elminate proximity effect. This is one of a group of microphones without proximity effect, marketed by this manufacturer as "Variable-D". Do not cover these ports with a hand, or the "Variable-D" principle is degraded, along with the directional pattern.

(E) AKG D-202E cardioid. Here two diaphrams are used, one behind the other, along with a crossover. A dynamic cardioid mic with little or no audible proximity effect, this mic has been an internationally favored podium microphone.

(E) AKG D-224E cardioid. Same principle as "E".

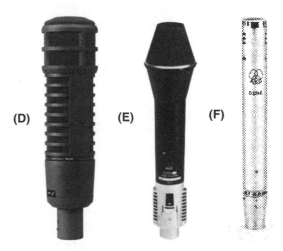

of more distant sound sources (system output, reverberant sound and other ambient noise). Some microphones, described later in this chapter and in Part III, are intentionally designed to make maximum use of this principle, in conjunction with their directional pattern, to reduce pickup of ambient sound in noisy environments. Also, proximity effect has become part of the "stock-in-trade" of many vocalists, and personal mic technique is often built around this characteristic. Generally, the vast majority of vocal mics designed for hand-held use will exhibit the proximity effect.

d) Practical Use of Directional Patterns.

The effective use of a microphone's directional pattern can provide an important advantage towards the overall effectiveness of the system in which it is used. Obviously it can be used to help minimize the pickup of sound from sources other than the designated source—this is of-course the reason for directional mics in the first place. The difference in pickup of off-axis sounds between an omni and a unidirectional mic, for example, is normally about 4dB to 6 dB overall when referenced to the on-axis response. Between 90 and 180 degrees, the general direction from which most of the direct and reflected system output normally approaches a microphone, the average difference between an omni and a cardioid is about 12 dB. Thus, the advantage gained in protection against feedback can be much greater if the angles of maximum rejection are well aligned with the positions of the loudspeakers, and/or the main angles from which reflected sound comes.

But this is not the only factor involved. *The proximity effect of directional mics, as mentioned in the previous section, can further assist in isolating the sound of a close-up sound source from that of more distant sources.* (This is, of course, only a factor with designs in which the proximity effect has not been eliminated.) The advantage gained by the proximity effect is generally very significant in the lows, moderately significant in the lower mids, and negligible in the high frequencies, where we need to rely mostly on the directional pattern itself to reduce pickup of more distant sounds.

The best sound-source isolation and protection against feedback is obtained by minimizing the distance from the sound source and maximizing the distance from the speakers (a basic formula for this is given in Part III). The directional pattern and proximity effect are perhaps best seen as supplementary aids in minimizing pickup of unwanted sounds from the surrounding environment. But they can be very substantial aids (see Fig. 5.10 and 5.11).

How about the difference between the basic directional patterns thus far introduced in this chapter? Often, cardioid, supercardioid or hypercardioid microphones can be used in roughly the same way. But supercardioid or hypercardioid patterns may be a more appropriate choice than cardioids in certain situations, such as when extremely high system output levels are required, or when the source-to-mic distance needs to be increased, but does not involve wide side-to-side swings of the sound source. Though the effective side-to-side working angle is somewhat reduced, rejection of sounds approaching from the direct sides and the wider angles to the rear is more effective (see Fig. 5.10-B). As indicated earlier, a potential tradeoff with supercardioids and hypercardioids is their ability to pick up sounds from the angles close to the direct rear (150-180 degrees off-axis). But oftentimes the effect of the rear pickup is not that substantial, in comparison to the potential benefit of reduced overall off-axis pickup (see Fig. 5.10-A, "Ambient sound sensitivity".

Since basic supercardioids and hypercardioids have proximity effect in greater abundance than cardioids, the relative pickup of more distant sources—no matter from which direction they come—is further reduced when used up-close, particularly in the range below about 500 Hz.. As an example, the hypercardioid "noise cancelling/differential" microphone illustrated in Fig. 5.10 relies very heavily on this effect, using it in conjunction with its directional pattern to drastically reduce the relative effect of ambient sound. This approach can be helpful in very-high-level close miking—several designs are marketed with specifically this intent. This type of mic can also be very useful as an announcement

	OMNI-DIRECTIONAL	CARDIOID	SUPER-CARDIOID	HYPER-CARDIOID	BI-DIRECTIONAL
POLAR RESPONSE PATTERN					
COVERAGE ANGLE (-3dB)	360°	131°	115°	105°	90°
ANGLE OF MAXIMUM REJECTION (NULL ANGLE)	—	180°	126°	110°	90°
AMBIENT SOUND SENSITIVITY (RELATIVE TO OMNI)	—	- 4.8dB	- 5.5dB	- 6dB	- 4.8 dB
DISTANCE FACTOR (RELATIVE TO OMNI)	1	1.7	1.9	2	1.7

A) Microphone characteristics by basic polar pattern.
(Courtesy Shure Bros., Tim Vear)

B) Typical coverage angle (down to -3dB below on-axis response).

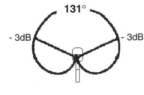
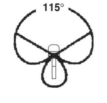
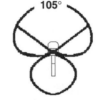

131°   -3dB   -3dB   115°   105°

CARDIOID   SUPERCARDIOID   HYPERCARDIOID

FIG. 5.11

C) Distance factor on-axis, relative to omnidirectional pickup. Note here that with a unidirectional design we can achieve one of two basic objectives (or some combination of the two). (1) With a cardioid, supercardioid or hypercardioid mic (as compared to an omni), the distance between the sound source and the microphone can be increased by up to a factor of two before an equivalent level of feedback or ambient sound pickup is reached (as illustrated below). (2) At a given source-to-mic distance, with a unidirectional mic the pickup of sound from the surrounding environment can be *decreased* by up to a factor of two, making the cardioid family important tools in avoiding feedback and other unwanted pickup, particularly when used up-close.

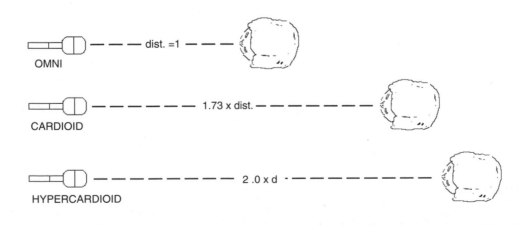

OMNI — — — dist. =1 — — —

CARDIOID — — — — 1.73 x dist. — — — — —

HYPERCARDIOID — — — — — 2.0 x d · — — — — — —

microphone in noisy environments (factories, certain types of sports events, transportation centers, etc.).

Interestingly, when a supercardioid or hypercardioid mic is used very close-up for high level performances, the pickup from the direct rear not only becomes less significant, but also actually can be an advantage at some frequencies (normally in the upper midrange and treble). This is because a certain amount of sound "bounces off of" the face of the person speaking or singing close-up, particularly when a stage monitor is pointed at that position from behind the mic (it is actually partly reflection and partly resonance). Because the rear pickup is of opposite phase, it literally can help to cancel out some of the reflected sound from the face. The tradeoff with close-up use of a hypercardioid (i.e., one in which proximity effect is not eliminated in the design) is that changing the source-to-mic distance, or moving significantly off to the side, can drastically change the pickup of the intended sound sourceb, both in terms of level and tonal quality—*so here the close-up on-axis position should be fairly diligently maintained.* As well, some method of effectively cutting low frequency response is often required (this depends on the frequency response in the lows), in order to avoid an excess of low frequency output. This can involve additional expense, either in the cost of a microphone with built-in low-cut switch, or in the cost of more versatile EQ capability.

Highly directional "shotgun" microphones (as in Fig. 5.12) can in some instances be useful in sound reinforcement, for example, to aid voice projection of actors in a theater. These are of more complicated construction than the cardioid family, and are not intended for close up use. "Shotgun" mics are also sometimes used (with varying degrees of effectiveness) to pick up the voice of an audience questioner and reinforce it so it can be heard by the rest of the audience and the talker on-stage. As an example, two such microphones are used in the White House Press Room with a monitor-speaker positioned near the podium. A potentially strong drawback in this type of application is its extreme dependence on the skill and alertness of the person pointing the microphone.

Bidirectional (figure-"8") mics continue to find effective, if limited, use for close-up miking of bass instruments (including bass drums), since they have the strongest low frequency proximity effect of the basic patterns. Favored mics for bass instruments, though, run the whole gamut from omni through bidirectional.

So how does this all stack up in terms of advantages and disadvantages? Well, the more directional the mic is, the more effective it is capable of being in terms of avoiding feedback and isolating the intended sound source—*if it is used effectively.* In terms of moving the sound source closer or farther away, or farther off-axis, an omni of-course provides the most flexiblity—this is largely why they are so often used for news gathering and and other situations where feedback tends not to come into play. With an omni, the primary consideration is the distance from the sound sources, and proximity effect is not a factor (though remember that high frequencies are reduced somewhat at wide angles off-axis).

Cardioids fall between the two extremes. Here there is still a fairly large degree of flexibility when the sound source moves off to the sides, upwards or downwards from the center axis. But the degree of flexibility is reduced somewhat more with supercardioids, and decreases somewhat further with hypercardioids.

So, at the risk of overstating the obvious, *the narrower the pattern is, the more carefully the pointing of the mic needs to be considered in order to profit from the potential benefits of the narrower pattern.* As well, *the stronger the proximity effect is, the more able we are to reduce pickup of lower and middle frequencies from the surrounding environment.* The tradeoff: *the stronger the proximity effect is, the more evident will be the changes in tonal quality when the source-to-mic distance is altered, so the more important it becomes that a reasonably consistent distance be maintained when used up-close.* (Remember that the strongest proximity effect is found in a bidirectional mic, and that it gradually decreases with hypercardioid, supercardioid, cardioid and semicardioid mics, with no proximity effect at all in an omni mic.)

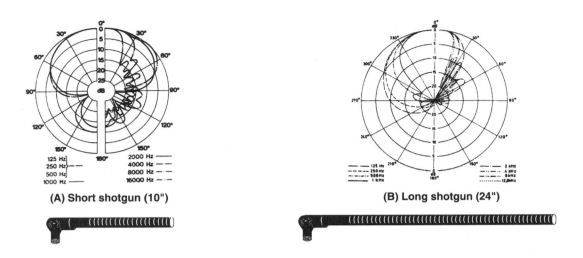

Fig. 5.12. Line gradient (shotgun) mics.

In this type of mic, designed for highly directional pickup at a distance, note how the pattern depends strongly on the length of the mic. The longer the mic, the lower the frequency at which the "shotgun" pattern tends to be maintained. At lower frequencies, each of these mics behaves as if it were a member of the cardioid family. (A: Sennheiser MKH 416 pattern, supercardioid below about 2 kHz. B: Beyer MC-737, cardioid below about 300 Hz or so.)

e) Frequency Range and Response Curves.

The required frequency range and response curves of a microphone depend on the applications for which it is used, as well as on personal taste.

Under the vast majority of circumstances it is not necessary for a microphone to be able to cover the entire audio spectrum, nor for it to have flat frequency response throughout its entire range. In fact, in many cases these characteristics can actually be counterproductive.

First off, in all but very rare instances, it is not a requirement to cover the lowest octave of the audio spectrum (20 Hz-40 Hz), because a typical full-range audio mix does not involve substantial energy in this range. Moreover, this is a range in which low-frequency speaker components become severely stretched by practical design limitations. Further reductions in a mic's low frequency capability can in many instances be an advantage, particularly for vocals and treble instruments. To fulfill this need, many microphone designs offer the ability to cut the microphone's response in the lower frequencies simply by moving a built-in switch.

A typical full-range audio mix also does not involve any substantial energy in the highest 1/2-octave of the spectrum (about 14k-20k). Normally only the very highest overtones of thin cymbals and certain types of bells are present in this range. Electronic instruments sometimes have significant energy in this range, but they do not require miking, and the very-high-frequency energy is almost always a superfluous and unnecessary side-effect of their method of synthesis. It is also worth noting that most of this highest 1/2 octave is not withing the hearing range of most adult listeners.

An extended frequency range beyond the approximate extremes just described, though, can be an indication that a microphone is capable of reaching them with reasonable effectiveness, since response curves taper off at their extremes. The response at the outer reaches of a mic's range can sometimes also be quite erratic—this is a characteristic often present in moving-coil mics at their high-frequency extreme (and not always shown in published response curves). As a result the "frequency range" specification given by the manufacturer tends not to be the most important concern. Obviously the mic should be able to respond to the needed frequency range, but it is the response curve in between the low and high frequency limits which tends to be most important.

What about the frequency response between the extremes? This depends on the way the sound needs to be shaped, and should be assessed on a case-by-case basis. If a sound source needs to be accurately represented with no appreciable adjustments in tonal quality, a mic with fairly flat response can be advantageous. Very commonly, though, a change in tonal quality imparted by a microphone is considered to be preferable to the sound of a flat response. Again, this is very much a matter of personal taste. As well, in any given system the response curves of microphones *relative to one another* plays an important role in the overall mix which will result. For this reason, in music reinforcement different mics tend to be used which will tend to impart the tonal changes we wish to have on each type of instrument. We may use one type of mic on vocals, one type on kick drum, another on snare, yet another on brass, etc.

In general, though, what is important is that the frequency response curves have relatively smooth transitions along the spectrum, which remain reasonably consistent to the ear throughout its required off-axis working angles. Strong resonant peaks and very sharp dropoffs in response—especially in the lower and middle frequencies—can in some instances be obstacles to high-quality sound and, when they occur, are extremely difficult to correct through equalization.

For example, a reasonably gradual rise and fall in response from, say 125 Hz through 1 kHz, will affect the tonal quality of a voice or instrument in a certain way. But generally it will not tend to misrepresent the relative level of musical notes, nor will it misrepresent formants (natural resonances) that are vital to an instrument's characteristic sound. Serious aberrations in the mic's response in this range, though, can fairly easily cause noticeable changes in apparent volume level and/or tonal quality as the fundamentals and lower overtones pass in and out of the affected frequencies when different notes are played or sung. Fortunately, this is ordinarily a problem only with very-low-budget microphones. These types of disproportionate peaks in response are usually more of an issue in assessing speakers than in assessing microphones.

In the high frequencies, though, a somewhat different set of considerations is involved. It is common for a microphone to have certain combinations of peaks and dips in high-frequency response to assist in imparting its own characteristic sibilance or "edge," especially to vocals. While this type of trait carries its own set of potential obstacles (a strong peak of this kind can reduce gain before feedback and in some cases may be difficult to equalize), it is often considered by users and listeners to be a desirable effect. Also, to a large extent it is the response characteristics of this kind—in the range from about 1k upward—that allow a mic to retain its characteristic "sound" in spite of variations due to proximity effect.

For vocal applications, strong response below about 150 Hz or so is simply not necessary, and can in fact be a problem at times (here we are not talking about *overall* response range quoted by the manufacturer—we are talking about overly strong response). Firstly, mic stand thump is picked up most severely in the low frequencies. Secondly, wind noise—particularly the sudden releases of breath associated with the consonants "P", "K", and "T"—is also picked up most severely in the lows. (This type of noise can have repercussions into higher ranges too, but is more prevalent in the lows). While difficult to completely eliminate without a bulky external windscreen, the problem can be drastically reduced by a combination of low-frequency cut and a reasonably adequate internal windscreen—commonly built into microphones marketed for vocal use. Finally, when used close-up, the proximity effect can cause cause substantial boost of this range to the point where it can hinder an effective sound—this can take the form of obscuring bass instruments or simply of "muddying" the sound.

Perhaps not surprisingly, the highest quality microphones often (though not necessarily) have very broad frequency ranges extending well into the low end. Does this make such mics unacceptable for vocals? Absolutely not—in fact, many favored vocal mics fall into this category. But it should be kept in mind that in up-close use the lows may need to be cut, sometimes radically, and in some cases this might involve additional cost. Many mic designs have a low-cut switch intended largely for this purpose. The response can also be cut at the mixer or by an additional outboard EQ, if necessary. (If the speakers do not have strong response in this low frequency range, this may not be necessary, though in some cases system power can be wasted in dealing with unneccesary low frequencies picked up by the mic.)

Instrument microphone needs can vary widely, and are discussed further in Part III. Perhaps obviously, mics for kick drum, low toms, and acoustic bass instruments should tend to have relatively strong very-low-frequency response.

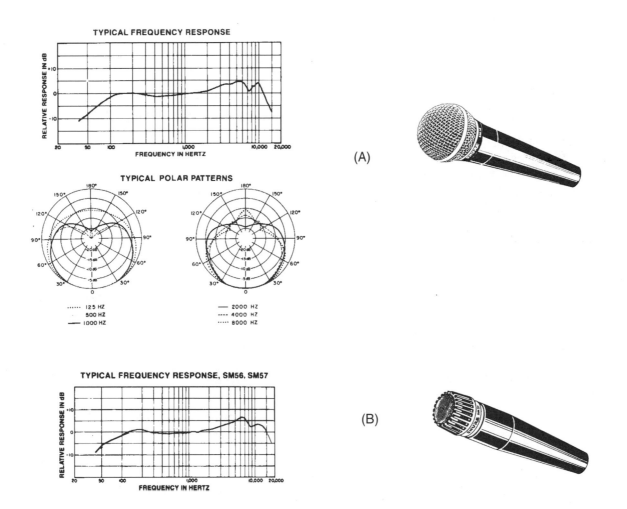

Fig. 5.13 (A) This is possibly the most recognizable micophone in the industry, originally marketed under the trade description "Unisphere". The Shure SM-58 is widely regarded as the classic vocal microhone, and remains a staple in the industry for applications from the modest-budget to the high-quality application. (Close proximity response not shown here.) (B) The Shure SM-57 is a multipurpose mic with somewhat broader frequency response. (Close proximity response not shown.)

Note the subtle difference in the response curves at the low and high frequency extremes. If these two mics were to be used in the same system, the most likely combination would be to use the "58" for vocals, and the "57" for instruments which require better low frequency pickup, such as on drums. Due to its comparatively wide frequency range, the 57 is a good "all purpose" mic.

f) General Use of Microphones.

To sum up the discussion of the previous several sections, effective use of microphones generally involves the following:

1) Minimize the distance from the intended sound source, and/or maximize the distance from the loudspeakers to the best reasonably possible extent.

2) Make effective use of the directional pattern by keeping the sound source reasonably within the useful working angles of the mic shown in Fig. 5.10-B (ideally, directly on-axis).

3) Try to keep the loudspeakers reasonably close to the angles of minimum pickup (generally at least 90° or more off-axis).

4) Attempt to keep the distance between the sound source and mic reasonably consistent.

5) In close-up miking, the proximity effect can assist in further reducing pickup of more distant sound sources, sometimes offsetting deficiencies in following guideline 3. But here the close-up use must be diligently maintained. (As well, EQ cut of the low frequencies may be required to offset the increased up-close pickup of those frequencies.)

6) To the best possible extent, follow the 3-1 guideline described in Fig. 5.15.

Some additional guidelines:

Wherever very high sound levels are required, an extremely close working distance is usually also required. A cardioid, supercardioid or hypercardioid mic positioned close-to or touching the lips on-axis can assist in allowing a high signal level for stage monitors and main loudspeakers (this is often called "eating the mic"). Even if the mic is hand-held, this practice can usually allow sufficient sound level at

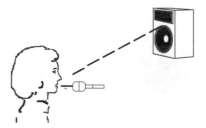

ACCEPTABLE FOR STAGE
MONITOR OR PODIUM MONITOR

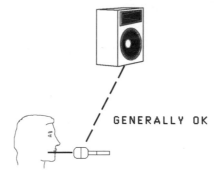

GENERALLY OK

Fig. 5.14. General microphone guidelines.

•**Keep the distance to the sound source as small as reasonably possible, and keep the distance to the speakers as large as reasonably possible .**
•**Keep the sound source on-axis and the speakers off axis to the best extent possible.**
•**And/or, keep the mic as far as reasonably possible out of the dispersion angles of high level speakers.**
(See also Fig. 5.20.)

GENERALLY A PROBLEM

the mic diaphram to counteract the effect of pointing the microphone in various directions—though caution may still need to be exercised in close range of stage monitors or if walking in front of the main speakers.

Situations requiring more distant miking (e.g., lecterns and pulpits) may present an incentive to use two mics as shown in Fig. 5.15-A and B. This approach can reduce fluctuations in intensity when the talker faces left and right or physically shifts from side to side. As well, it may encourage the talker to maintain a reasonably consistent source-to-microphone distance by setting an imaginary arc within which to work—outlined by the two mic positions. The disadvantages of this practice can sometimes outweigh the advantages, however, due to the phasing problems that occur when two mics are used in this fashion. The tradeoff is poorer frequency response *which changes as the talker moves position* (see again Fig. 5.15). Whether or not this tradeoff is too much depends in large part on the acoustics of the room. If the reverberance of the room causes sound clarity and articulation in the audience to be a problem, it may be necessary to have this factor in your favor and simply use one mic. Clear instructions to the talker(s) about microphone technique might be in order in such a case.

Where a moderate range of movement is required, one method of maintaining a consistent source-to-mic distance is the use of a *lavalier* or clip-on microphone. This type of microphone is most often omnidirectional, and is often designed to impart a significant boost of the very-high-frequency range to compensate for the somewhat limited dispersion angles of these frequencies from the mouth.

Wireless microphones can of-course provide a practically limitless range of movement for a public speaker or vocalist, though they also tend to involve more work to set up and more opportunities for failure during an event than do standard wired mics. While to-date still somewhat costly, wireless microphones are manufactured in designs which, properly used, are capable of virtually eliminating signal dropouts and radio-frequency interference—common obstacles in earlier designs. Lavalier mics are commonly combined with a wireless "belt-pack", as in Fig. 5.18. Wireless units are outlined in section "o" of this chapter.

No matter what approach is used, it is important to remember that as the source begins to approach the wider extreme of the useful working angle (the "coverage angle" as in Fig. 5.11-B) of a directional mic, the mic's response approaches 3dB down as compared to the on-axis response. *This means not only that the pickup of the intended sound source is reduced, but also that the pickup of other sounds from the environment is, by comparison, increased.* When the response angle reaches -6dB, we could do just as well or better by using an omnidirectional mic. (If necessary, refer again to figures 1.3, 5.4, 5.6.and 5.11.) Best results are normally achieved by keeping the source as reasonably close as possible to the axis of maximum pickup.

Off-axis colorations (differences in frequency response) can sometimes also play a notable role in miking. Typical off-axis response tends to involve somewhat of a reduction in the extreme highs, but may occasionally involve other areas of the spectrum as well, particularly as the source moves to angles very far off-axis.

This type of coloration can, for example, also be a noticeable consequence of using one microphone to cover three singers up-close with a relatively high-level system. Since the two singers on the sides are approaching from an angle (say 90°off-axis) where the high frequency response is reduced, their voices may be lacking some of the highs as compared to the center vocalist. (As well, they of-course need to move closer to the mic to obtain an equivalent level of pickup.) While not as effective as one closeup microphone per vocalist, mics are sometimes shared for performance reasons with reasonably acceptable results. The main tradeoff with this practice is in the reduced gain-before-feedback, as compared to the available gain with the vocalist's mouth close-up on-axis.

Fig. 5.15 Multiple microphones

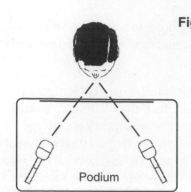

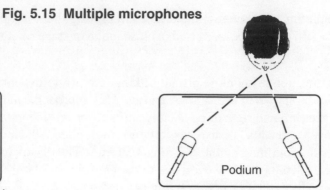

Two mics combined in-phase when source is equally distant from both

(A)

Two mics combined when source is off-center

(B)

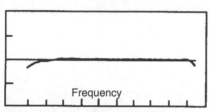

Resulting Response (assuming flat response of each mic individually

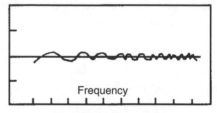

Resulting Response

•**Use as few mics as are necessary to get the job done, and follow the 3-to-1 rule to the best possible extent.**

Notice in C what happends to the frequency response when two identical signals are combined with a slight delay between them (from about .1 millisecond up to about 10 milliseconds). This is the famous "comb-filter" effect. When the delay is varied the result is a characteristic "swishing" sound which is the basis for "phasing" and "flanging" effects commonly used on electric guitar and other instruments. (This effect assumes the signals are identical in intensity.) In actual practice, when two microphones are used as in A and B, there is a partial comb filtering when the source moves off center, as shown in the resulting frequency response in B. The slight delay between the time it takes the sound to arrive at the more distant mic causes some cancellation at the "comb-filter" frequencies. The cancellation is somewhat offset by the fact that the latter signal is slightly lower in intensity due to the extra distance it must travel, but still leaves aberrations in the combined frequency response as in B. (Which frequencies are involved depends on the delay time, and also on the distance between the mics. The "comb-filter effect" tends to be most audible with very widely spaced mics when the source moves from side to side.) The optimal solution to this dilemma is expressed by "Burrough's 3-to-1 rule". At this relative distance, the sound received by a second mic is sufficiently lower in intensity to make the comb-filtering negligible, and the response curve becomes, for all practical purposes, accurate again.

(Illustrations C and D courtesy Shure Bros.)

(See also the discussions in Chapter 12, Fig. 12.4 and Ch. 13, Fig. 13.1.)

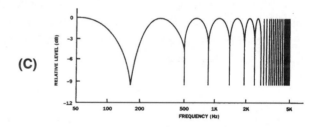

(C)

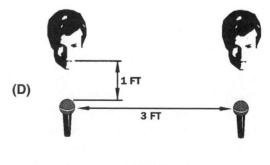

(D)

The 3-to-1 Rule.

g) Balanced and Unbalanced Mic Circuits.

Microphone cables carry the audio signal to its destination in either of two basic ways. *Unbalanced* circuits use one of the signal-carrying conductors as a shield against electrostatic interference, as illustrated in Fig. 5.16. *Balanced* circuits use matched signal carrying conductors as pictured in Fig. 5.16.B, with a third conductor surrounding it as a shield.

Unbalanced mic cables are reasonably effective over short distances. There are, though, two basic disadvantages. Firstly, unbalanced microphone lines are typically terminated into an extremely high impedance. The higher the impedance of a mic circuit is, the more susceptible it will tend to be to electrostatic interference. (Electrostatic interference originates in sources such as flourescent lights, appliances and some electric motors, and can manifest as an audible buzz in the output sound.)

Secondly, electrical properties which are a natural result of this basic cable design can cause a noticeable deterioration of high-frequency response--which becomes increasingly worse as cable length increases. This can be compounded by the high-frequency buzz to which this type of circuit is already susceptible, since equalizing to make up for the reduced high-frequency response also raises the level of foreign high-frequency noise. Low microphone output—whether due to microphone design or manner of use—can further allow the noise to predominate. (*Unbalanced line level* cables, incidentally, are a different story—these are commonly used for distances at least up to 50m (150') or so with very reasonable signal-to-noise ratio, as discussed in Chapter 16).

A reasonable rule of thumb would allow the use of unbalanced mic-level cables—in most normal environmental conditions—with cable lengths of not longer than 6m (20'). Unusually high-interference environments might require a reassessment of this guideline. High mic-output levels, minimal sound-quality requirements or other factors might perhaps allow it to be stretched somewhat.

Balanced circuits typically (though not necessarily) involve a somewhat lower impedance than do unbalanced circuits. Balanced lines are designed to allow the shield to drain electrostatically induced currents (which are not as severe in a low-impedance circuit), independently of the signal-carrying conductors. This separation of tasks is helpful, but the main advantage of balanced circuits is that electro*magnetic* fields (these are not deterred by a shield) encounter identical conductors that are twisted into a spiral inside the shield. The twisting causes the electromagnetic field to be continually reversed with each full twist, largely preventing it's influence from traveling along with the mic signal. Any remaining electromagnetic "hum", to the extent that it is common to both 180-degree-out-of-phase conductors, is automatically cancelled out by the balanced input of the mixer, thus virtually eliminating this type of interference.

This is not the case with unbalanced lines, in which the two signal-carrying conductors are not twisted. Also, the unbalanced conductors are of different configurations (one a small solid conductor, the other a relatively larger hollow cylinder coupled electrically to the frame of the mixer) and thus have different electrical properties than one another. Thus they are unable to cancel out electromagnetic interference to any reasonable extent.

Balanced, "low-impedance" lines have been found to be an excellent compromise, and are currently the standard configuration in mic lines for high quality audio applications. This type of circuit typically allows for high-quality signal flow at lengths of up to at least 100 meters under typical conditions (see Fig. 14.3, regarding very long cable runs). Yet another advantage of balanced circuits is that they readily allow the shield ground to be disconnected ("lifted") at one end in order to avoid ground loops (Chapter 15 and 16).

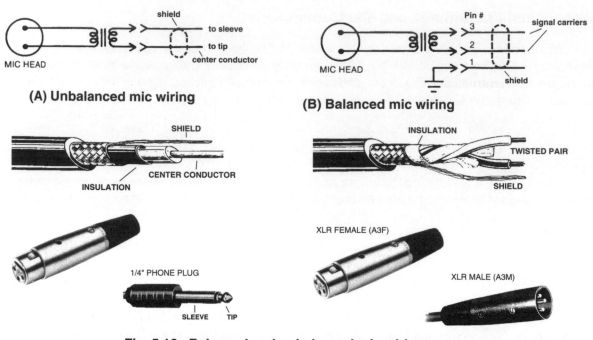

Fig. 5.16. Balanced and unbalanced mic wiring.
(Top: courtesy Audio Technica. Center: courtesy Canare Cable, Inc. Bottom: courtesy Switchcraft)

h) Microphone Impedance.

Mic cables need to terminate into a device whose input impedance is reasonably consistent with the microphone's designated impedance range, or be adapted with an impedance-matching device so the electrical requirements of microphone and mixer are compatable. As explained in Chapter 4, the actual input (load) impedance of the mixer should be at least about 5 times the actual output impedance (source impedance) of the microphone itself, or signal degradation can sometimes result.

The following approximate ranges for microphone impedances have prevailed in the audio industry.

High-impedance *mics* (~5,000-ohms-or-more output impedance) typically terminate into mixer inputs in the 25,000-ohm-and-up range.

Low-impedance *mics* (~150-400Ω output impedance) typically terminate into mixer inputs in the 1,500-5,000Ω range.

Very-low-impedance *mics* (~20-75 ohms)(originally used mainly in broadcast systems and recording studios, and rarely used today) are designed to terminate into input impedances of 150-600 ohms. This type of mic is also fully capable of terminating into standard modern balanced inputs, though there may be low signal level at the input stage of the mixer—generally this would be a matter of simply adjusting the input gain accordingly.

Normally, microphones rated in these ways will operate properly when plugged into mixer inputs similarly classified.

In most cases, high impedance inputs use phone plug input jacks for an unbalanced cable. Low impedance inputs normally provide XLR input jacks (Fig. 5.18-B) with a balanced termination (pins 2 and 3 are signal carriers; pin 1 to shield), Balanced inputs sometimes use the TRS phone plug configuration shown in Chapter 7 and 16, though this is not a normal design for microphone inputs.

i) Other Circuit Considerations (Condenser Mics).

Condenser microphones designed to accomodate remote power (phantom power) typically accept voltages from 9 VDC to 52 VDC which is sent to the microphone along the signal carrying conductors (pins 2 and 3) and returned along the shield. Since the voltage is common to the matched pair of 180-degree-out-of-phase conductors, it is "ignored" by the balanced input in the mixer circuit. Also, since the voltage is common to the two signal carriers, no current flows between them. Therefore, standard dynamic mics can safely operate with phantom power on (though sometimes a "pop" is heard when plugging the mic cable in).

Normally the standard 48 Volt phantom power provided by many high quality mixers will allow such a mic to operate. Occasionally, though, a condenser mic will be designed to have a specific preamp and/or powering requirement, so if in doubt, check the specs or consult the manufacturer. Ordinarily, a lower voltage power supply (such as a battery-powered supply) will still allow the mic to operate, but with reduced gain.

Electret (permanently polarized) condenser mics do not require a polarizing-voltage source, so their power requirements are limited to a small low-voltage internal battery to power a built-in impedance-converter/amplifier designed to transform the high-impedance, low-power audio signal of the condenser output to a sufficiently strong low-impedance output. Many electret designs also allow the use of phantom power rather than an internal battery.

j) Sensitivity.

The level of a microphone's output at a given level of sound pressure is often called its sensitivity. Sensitivity is generally not a very useful parameter for assessing the quality of a microphone, but can be important in assesing the amount of gain adjustment required at the mixer. High sensitivity can sometimes help increase signal-to-noise ratio somewhat, though it is not by any means the main consideration in reducing noise.

Most commonly, sensitivity is measured at 1000 Hz, and is most commonly quoted in dBu or dBm of output per pascal (1 Pa=10 dynes per square centimeter, equivalent to *94 dB SPL*). Sometimes also used, though, are measurements given in dBu or dBm per dyne/sq. cm., which is equivalent to *74 dB SPL*, in which case we would need to add 20 dB to compare it with a mic sensitivity quoted in the first specification method. Specifications given in other methods of measurement (which is very rare) can be converted along the guidelines given in Chapter 4. Typical mic sensitivities range from -65 dBu/Pa (fairly low output) to -40 dBu/Pa (a very "hot" mic).

k) Distortion.

Total harmonic distortion levels of under 1% at 1000 Hz are normally considered acceptable for a high-quality microphone (1% is generally not at all audible). Maximum sound pressure level statistics for mics are normally referenced to this percentage of THD, thus usually allowing some flexibility beyond the stated maximum SPL (though this specification is not always published).

Transient response can be a significant factor in sound quality, as explained in Chapter 4. Transient distortion (or lack of good transient response) can be a notable consideration in many (though not all) moving-coil microphones, due to the mass of the diaphram/coil assembly. Condenser mics, ribbon mics and most neodymium-magnet designs tend to reduce transient distortion substantially, as compared to many "traditional" moving-coil designs.

Somewhat related to transient distortion, is *dynamic compression*, which is the inability of a mic to provide accurate output in response to high lound levels. Sometimes as much as 3dB or-more of output is lost at high levels. This can be signicant in high-sound-level performances, such as where a vocalist is singing very loudly into a mic, and where maximum possible output is desired. This is another nonlinearity which modern neodymium magnets and new diaphram materials have helped to reduce.

I) Wireless Microphone Considerations.

Wireless mics obviously require a transmitter, electrically connected to the microphone, and a receiver, electrically connected to the mixer. With a handheld design, the transmitter is normally included in the microhone body itself. With a lavalier (or clip-on) mic, the transmitter is likely to be in the form of a battery powered "body-pack", or "belt-pack".

Receivers are of two basic design configurations, single antenna, and dual antenna. The dual antenna design is generally called a ***diversity*** receiver, and is normally designed with internal circuitry which essentially allows the receiver to "choose" the antenna receiving the strongest signal at any given moment. The advantages of a diversity design are illustrated in Fig. 5.17.

The transmitting radio-frequency and receiving radio-frequency (known as the *carrier frequency*) must of-course be properly matched. This is invariably done by the manufacturer, though some systems offer the option to select one of several available frequencies provided in the manufacturing stage, in which case both transmitter and receiver must be appropriately switched by the user. Potentially serious concerns can arise in selecting the appropriate radio-frequency range for an application. Here there tends to be a compromise in terms of cost vs. the system's ability to operate without interference from other sources of radio-frequency emission. Overall, the considerations which can come into play here are fairly complicated, and deserve consulting directly with the respective manufacturer.

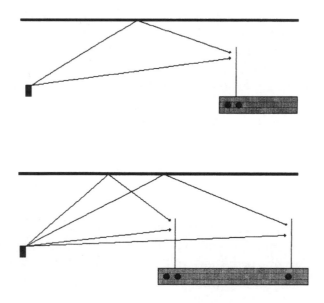

Fig. 5.17. Diversity vs. non-diversity wireless-mic receivers.
The dual-antenna "diversity" receiver chooses between the two antennas to reduce the likelihood of "dropout" due to phase cancellation of direct and reflected carrier-frequency signals.

The radio-frequency ranges used in wireless designs can be divided roughly as follows. (The manufacurer's literature should in each case be consulted to ensure that there are no FCC rules involved which could possibly be transgressed by the particular units.)

VHF-low-band systems are generally available at the most modest cost, though this range is also shared by cordless telephones and other "home-use" wireless systems.

VHF-high-band systems (150-216 MegaHertz) are currently the most commonly encountered wireless designs. This range is shared in part by TV channels 7-13. Here, selection of the appropriate operating channels first involves ensuring that the chosen channel(s) for the wireless mics do not match TV channels operating in the same geographic location. As well, other commercial radio services operate in this area. If a VHF-high-band system is to be taken on the road, a selectable-frequency system probably should be chosen to allow switching to unused radio-frequencies in a given location.

UHF-low-band (450-600MHz) and *UHF-high-band* (806-950MHz) tend to be somewhat more costly, but also tend to be significantly more interference-free.

Fig. 5.18. Typical lavalier "clip-on" mic (courtesy Shure Bros.).

to wireless "body-pack" or "belt-pack"
(or directly to mixer via appropriate adaptor)

Fig. 5.19. An additional microphone design of importance. In certain cases it is important to have a microphone flush-mounted on a flat surface. This illustration depicts the primary advantage of a "boundary micrphone"—eliminating cancellations due to reflections from a hard surface. Such a microphone also commonly finds use on stage aprons and underneath closed piano tops. (This particular type of mic, a high-quality omnidirectional condenser design marketed as a "Pressure-Zone Microphone" (PZM), was developed by Crown International.) Boundary microphones in-general are marketed by several manufacturers in both omnidirectional and unidirectional designs. (illustration courtesy Crown)

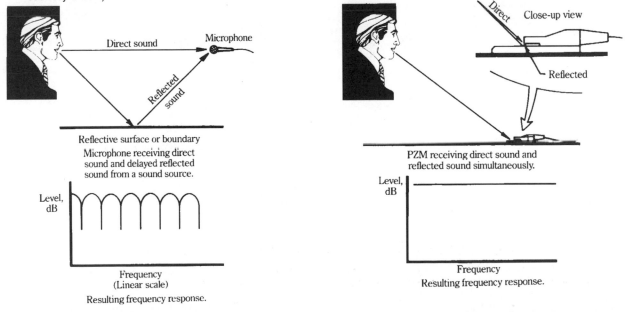

Fig. 5.20. Additional mic guidelines.

Top: When audible feedback occurs, the first instinct is often to cover the mic. This radically degrades the directional pattern and also creates a resonant cavity, making the problem far worse. Go immediately for the level control instead. If in doubt as to which channel is responsible, calmly reduce the master level control until the problem stops. (Occasionally we can move the mic itself and/or use the human body to put the mic in a "shadow", then send someone else to reduce the level control.)

Bottom: Cupping a unidirectional mic as illustrated tends to turn the mic into an omnidirectional mic, actually reducing the mic's ability to reject sounds from the rear. (If this is confusing, refer again to section B of this chapter). Unnessessary feedback is often the result.

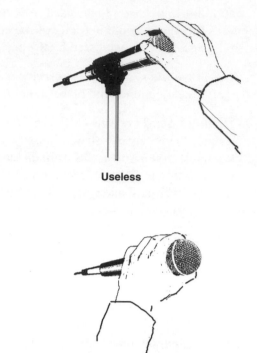

Useless

Sometimes a problem

Fig. 5.21. Reduction of available system gain with multiple mics.
Each time we double the number of "open" mics at a given gain level, all else being equal, we allow double the amount of system output to recirculate through the system, reducing available gain-before-feedback by 3 dB. This can be of great importance, for example, in theater productions, reinforcement of large orchestras and conferences with multiple mic positions.

One mic at given maximum available gain before audible feedback

2 "open" mics: 3 dB less gain before audible feedback

4 "open" mics: 6 dB less gain before audible feedback

8 "open" mics: 9 dB less gain before audible feedback

CHAPTER 6

EQUALIZERS

The art of equalization is regarded by many audio engineers as the height of the art of audio engineering. Beyond being a highly important practical tool for controlling feedback and compensating for acoustical problems in a listening environment, the EQ allows the engineer to alter the "colors and hues" of the sounds that will be blended by the mixer, then finely tailor the final product for presentation to an audience.

a) Basic Design Types.

EQ circuits are technically referred to as "filters" or "filter sets". In a typical EQ the circuitry which does the work of each band is designed to filter out frequencies other than those it is meant to affect. It is this aspect of the design of equalizers which closely confines the influence of a particular control to its designated frequency range. The filter outputs are then recombined to produce a full-range output.

From an operational standpoint, most equalizers can be categorized into one of these basic types:

A *fixed* equalizer is a filter or set of filters designed to accomplish a very specific purpose, such as altering a signal to accomodate a particular type of loudspeaker or a particular acoustical situation in a permanent system. This type of equalizing circuit does not generally allow for on-site adjustment.

Cut-only EQ filters allow an operator to cut the system's response at any of a number of preset points throughout the audio spectrum. This type of equalizer design is extremely useful for feedback control, but is generally not suitable for effective tone control. Changes in tonal quality initiated by this kind of equalizer come only as a byproduct of its primary function—to prevent feedback loops or reduce the effect of strong resonances. To be technical, this type of filter set is not an equalizer (because it is not capable of boosting any frequency ranges, except relative to those frequencies at which a cut is induced) but for convenience it is usually lumped into this category nevertheless. A more versatile version of the cut-only type of EQ, often called a *tunable notch-filter set*, allows the operator to tune very narrow bands of cut to fairly specific frequencies, in order to "notch out" resonances or feedback points without unduly affecting tonal quality.

Fixed frequency EQ filters allow the operator to variably decrease or increase sensitivity in preset areas of the spectrum. Often referred to as *variable cut-and-boost*, *this is the most commonly used category—the format used for tone control in many audio mixers as well as in the standard design of graphic equalizer.*

Sweepable, or *variable frequency* filters allow the operator to move the range(s) of emphasis of the desired cut or boost to any point along a continuous frequency range, as in Fig. 6.2. This type of EQ is sometimes referred to as *quasi-parametric* or *semi-parametric*.

A much less flexible version of sweepable EQ allows the operator to switch the center frequency to one of two-or-more preset points along the spectrum. This is usually referred to simply as *switchable* between center points (and should not be confused with a switchable cut, as in Fig. 6.3.) This is sometimes called a "click-stop" EQ.

Parametric EQ's allow the operator to select not only the points of emphasis for cut or boost along the spectrum, but also the *bandwidth*, or range of emphasis to the sides of the chosen center point. As the name implies, this type of EQ allows adjustment of the guidelines (parameters) within which cut or boost will occur. Oftentimes EQ's of this type are referred to as *fully* parametric, to distinguish them from sweepable EQ's.

b) Shelving EQ.

Shelving EQ controls affects all frequencies either above or below a particular point in the spectrum as illustrated in Fig. 6.1. Standard bass and treble controls normally belong in this category. Note in Fig. 6.1 that the response characteristics gradually become stronger according to frequency as it progresses toward the outer reaches of the spectrum, until a certain approximate point is reached. Beyond this point, all frequencies should be about equally affected by an adjustment of that control knob. (This is the "*shelving region*", so named because it lifts or lowers the frequency response of that region as if on a shelf.) The approximate frequency at which the curves level off is normally quoted as the "shelving frequency". As indicated, frequencies farther in toward the center of the audio spectrum are also affected, but to a smaller and smaller degree as the frequencies get farther away from the extremes of the spectrum.

c) Peak/Dip EQ.

When an EQ control has *center* points at particular frequencies, at-and-around-which frequency response can be adjusted, it can be referred to as having a *peak/dip EQ characteristic*, or simply as *peaking EQ*. This would be characteristic of a midrange tone control, or each band of a typical graphic equalizer.

With a peaking-type EQ filter, how far outward the effect of the EQ's control extends (from the center frequency) depends on the filter's *bandwidth*, often described as *"Q"*. (In general terms, *the higher the "Q" is, the narrower the bandwidth is, i.e., the sharper the focus of the filter on the center frequency.*)

d) Switchable Cut / High Pass and Low Pass.

Often a mixer or other component will include the capability to cut frequencies at either extreme of the spectrum. Most often, this takes the form of a "*low-cut*" switch designed to reduce very low frequency response. Such a switch is actually engaging a *high pass* filter, so named because it passes only frequencies above a certain approximate point in the audio spectrum. Perhaps the most common use for the low-cut switch is to eliminate unneccesary low frequencies from the input channels being used for vocals and treble instruments. Also occasionally encountered for EQ-related purposes are "*high-cut*" switches, which are technically a *low pass* filter.

The frequency of the cut is normally quoted as the point at which the slope reaches -3dB. Typical slopes would be 12 dB, 18dB or 24dB of cut for every octave below the filter frequency (written 12dB/Octave, 18dB/Octave or 24dB/oct.).

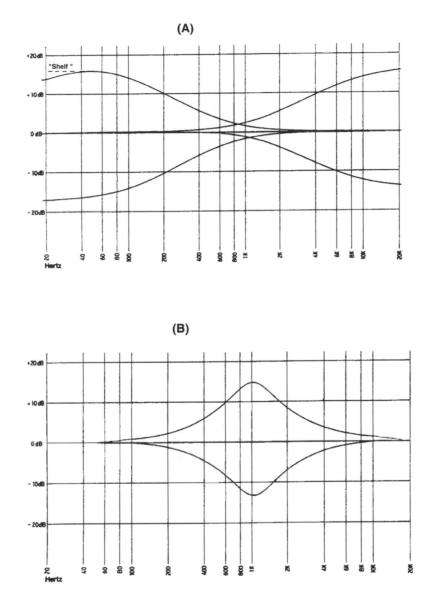

Fig. 6.1. Typical curves for onboard EQ controls set at maximum cut or boost
(courtesy Soundcraft). (A) Low and high frequency "shelving" type. The shelving frequencies
here are 60Hz LF and 10kHz HF. In theory, the "shelf" would be flat, though in practice the
graphed response can vary slightly. For practical purposes, though, we can regard it as a
"shelf" extended to the extreme of the audio spectrum. Note how adjustment of the control
also affects, to a lesser extent, frequencies over a broad range towards the middle of the
spectrum. For an example, turning up the low frequency control also somewhat affects
frequencies higher up in the mid-bass, so (to take the example one step farther) it would not
necessarily be contradictory to engage a 100 Hz high-pass filter as well as boost a 60 Hz LF
shelving control.
(B) Mid-frequency "peak/dip" or "peaking"-type EQ.

e) Typical 2,3,4 way EQs.

Fixed-frequency tone controls on mixers or other signal processing devices. These of-course represent the manufacturer's assessment of which center frequencies and bandwidths are likely to be most useful on average.

A typical two-band EQ might have 125 Hz L.F. shelving and perhaps 5 kHz H.F. shelving.

A typical three-band EQ might have 100 Hz shelving, 1 kHz or 2 kHz peaking (peak/dip) EQ, and perhaps 8 kHz shelving.

A typical four-band EQ might have 70 Hz shelving, 400 Hz and 2 kHz peaking EQ—each over about a one-and-a-half-octave span, and perhaps 10 kHz shelving.

f) Switchable Frequency and Sweepable Frequency EQs.

Switchable frequency EQ allows some choice in deciding what areas of the spectrum to affect. A switchable-frequency EQ reflects the designer's assessment of what center points are most likely to be useful in the field. A few examples: A midrange control, switchable between, say 500Hz and 2kHz; a bass control, switchable between 60Hz and 150Hz; a treble control, switchable bewteen 5kHz and 10kHz.

On mixers where a sweepable EQ is provided, it is most often used for the midrange tone controls. Fig. 7.2 shows a four-way on-board EQ with sweepable upper and lower midrange, which has been a high-level industry standard for many years.

g) Graphic EQs and Other Multiband Filter Sets.

The International Standards Organization (ISO) has established standard center frequencies for multiband EQs of 10 bands or more.

A typical 1-Octave EQ has 10 bands, the center frequencies of which can be seen at the end of section 6(i) in the description of frequency-related subjective qualities(they are the ones underlined in the description). A typical 2/3-Octave EQ has 15 bands, which are centered at every second band of the 1/3-octave configuration (they are the ones with a dash).

Typical 1/3-Octave EQs take the form of 27-band, 30-band and 31-band configurations. In the 27-band configuration, the octave with the lowest three bands of the spectrum (20, 25, and 32 Hz) are not included in the design. In practice this is seldom a disadvantage. Some models include a high-pass (low cut) option for the purpose of reducing very low frequencies. Other designs include some method of variable frequency high-pass.

h) Parametric EQ.

Fig. 6.3 shows the response curves of a typical *parametric* EQ. As can be seen, this type of EQ provides maximum flexibility of control over frequency response, with relatively few controls (as opposed to, for example a graphic EQ, which can in some cases be impractical—especially for input channels). *Paragraphic EQ* is a parametric or sweepable EQ designed with sliders for cut and boost, rather than rotary controls.

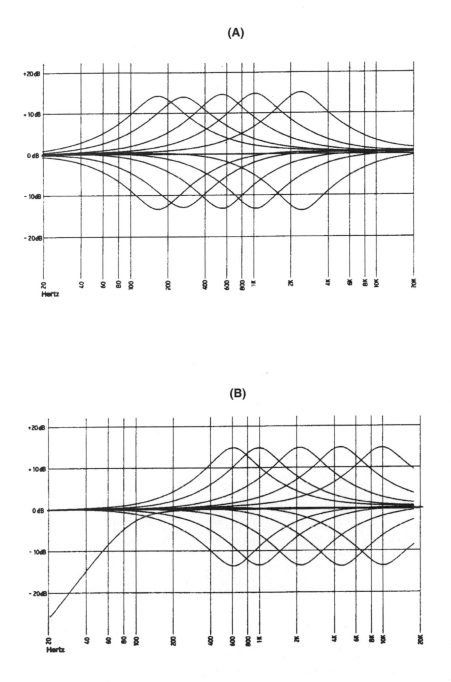

Fig. 6.2. Typical sweepable EQ curves. (A) Low-mid EQ curves on the Soundcraft 800 series input channel, with continuously variable center frequencies from 150 Hz to 2.4 kHz. Curves are shown for maximum cut and boost at several frequencies throughout the sweepable range. (B) High-mid EQ curves for the same mixer, continuously variable center frequencies from 600 Hz to 10 kHz (100 Hz low-cut (high-pass) curve also shown). (C) Visual layout of the same input channel EQ section (courtesy of the manufacturer). The use of the low-cut switch is fairly standard when reinforcing vocals and any instruments where very-low-frequency reproduction is either unneccesary or a hindrance.

i) General Use of EQs for tone control.

Which aspects of the tonal quality of sound can and which aspects cannot be controlled by an equalizer? In Chapter 2 it was briefly explained that the majority of sounds involve two basic aspects: the function of the vibrating element and that of the resonator. While this is a very simplistic description of the makeup of a sound, it serves as a helplful guide in understanding what can and cannot be controlled by an EQ. An EQ has relatively little control of pitch or harmonic structure, which are set up in large part by the vibrating element of the sound source, which is in turn also affected by the manner of picking, striking, or otherwise setting it in motion. To give several illustrations:

• If someone is singing or playing out of tune, obviously there is little or nothing an EQ (or any other device, at this writing) can do to effectively compensate.

• If the overtones created by an instrument are inharmonic or out of tune with the fundamental (common, for example, with poorly tuned drums) an EQ certainly cannot change this. (though with a drum, a good flexible EQ can serve to reduce the response in the frequency range of the overtones).

• If, for some reason, the resonance characteristics radically change from one note to another (this more-than-occasionally happens with voices), there is relatively little practical effect an EQ can have in compensating. All we can do is seek a reasonable "average" setting.

• An EQ obviously cannot compensate for non-frequency-related issues, such as excessive sustain or other dynamic problems. (Dynamic problems are sometimes correctible with compressors and noise gates, discussed in the following chapter.) Nor, it should also be said, can an EQ change reverberation characteristics or alter room resonances, though an EQ can be used to de-emphasize the frequencies at which they occur most blatantly. This would of-course fall under the category of system equalization.

What an EQ *can* do, with regard to tone control, is:

• Adjust, or in some cases completely change, the perceived tonal characteristics of the "resonator" (e.g., guitar body, drum shell, clarinet bell, etc.) as differentiated from the "vibrating element" (e.g., string, drumhead, reed, etc). The resonant characteristics of an instrument come into play mainly in the low-to-midrange frequencies. For a simple example, if the sound is generally too "thin", we can "thicken" it, and vice-versa;

• Reduce resonances that cause certain notes to stand out above others (this may require the insertion of a notch filter or other flexible outboard EQ);

• On instruments such as drums (which have only one fundamental pitch each, excepting Roto-toms and the like) an EQ can bring out or subtract from the fundamental and low overtones (normally in the low frequencies up to about 250 Hz, to add or subtract depth. We can also reduce the higher overtones here if they are "ringing", this comes into play in the lower midrange, usually from about 300 to 600 Hz. In the upper midrange and highs it is more the stick-meeting-drumhead sound which we encounter, and of course an EQ has substantial control over this aspect of the sound.

• An EQ can add or subtract "edge" frequencies, which are heard as, for example, the "bite" of a guitar or string bass, the type of "snap" of a drum sound, the "edges" and/or sibilances of a voice. This comes into play in the high frequencies. This is where the role of the vibrating element usually comes into play indpendently of the resonator, since most musical instruments have comparatively little "resonance" in the highs. But again, if there are problems with the vibrating element(s), for example, a string which "buzzes", an EQ can minimize them, but the normal "edge" or "bite" of the instrument's sound would need to be sacrificed.

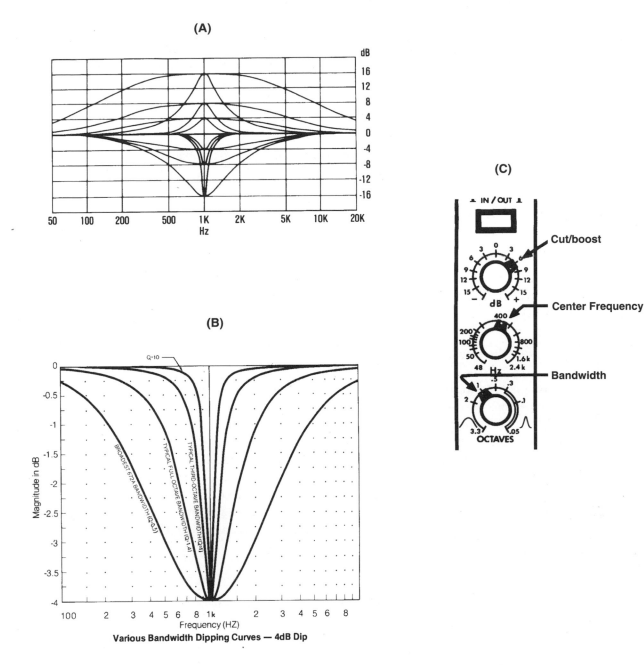

Fig. 6.3. Typical parametric EQ curves. (A) Response curves at widest and narrowest bandwidth settings. Curves shown are for the Orban model 622. Note in "A" how the "cut" curves differ from the "boost" curves. This is fairly standard. The reason for this design approach is that deep cuts are generally used mainly for the purpose of reducing feedback prone frequencies or excessive resonances. Almost never would a boost be initiated over such a narrow range. In "B", the "cut" curves for the Orban 672 A are shown. This particular design involves what are known as "reciprocal curves", where the "boost" characteristic is a mirror image of the "cut" characteristic. Here we would generally need to be cautious of initiating a very narrow boost in most live applications. (C) Typical face-panel controls of a parametric EQ (only one band shown).

(A and B courtesy Orban/ Parasound. C: courtesy Ashly Audio.)

•••••••••••••••••••••••••••••••••••••••

Below are the main ranges of emphasis which can be heard with several common vocal sounds (approximate, when whispered). These are intended as a very broad guideline for understanding roughly where some commonly heard sounds fit into the spectrum (it is not generally advisable to do this exercise in public):

"ooh" (whispered)	around 125-300 Hz, with smaller amounts of energy higher up
"uh" (whispered)	around 160-400 Hz, " " " " "
"aahh" (whispered)	around 200-500 Hz " " " " "
"K" (no vowel)	around 500-2k, with smaller amounts above and below
"CH" (no vowel)	around 2k-6k, with smaller amounts of energy lower in frequency
"S" (no vowel)	around 4k-12k, " " " " "

•••••••••••••••••••••••••••••••••••••••

Below are *associations* which can be made with some of the basic vowel sounds (related to the main range of resonant emphasis in the mouth cavity—not vocal chord pitch). Listen carefully and note how these basic resonant sounds rise in frequency as presented here. Note: this is an approximate idea of how a number of persons in an informal study describe these frequency ranges when they are allowed to "ring", or feed back continuously. In actual speech, the articulation of the vowels in the mouth is usually confined to a somewhat narrower pitch range (of fundamentals, at least) and is really more complicated, with upward and downward sweeps of pitch and changes of resonance and harmonic content, interspersed with consonants. So these are only associations to help the person early in the learning process in gaining an initial feel for the frequency ranges on an EQ. (If you *whisper* and sustain each of the sounds below, you may be able to hear the actual resonance of your mouth increasing in pitch as you move through the sounds as listed here. This may give you an idea of how these associations are subconsciously developed.)

"OOOH","deep U"	around 100-250 Hz
"O"	around 200-400 Hz
"AHH"	around 300-600 Hz
"A"	around 500-1000 Hz
"E"	around 800 Hz-2kHz
"eeee"(chipmunky)	around 1.6k and up

As can be seen, there is significant overlap between the approximate ranges of pitch associations, mainly because these vowel sounds are not hard-and-fast categories, and are rarely articulated by themselves. They and other vowel sounds are normally combined with one another and with consonants in a way that is recognizable as a word or syllable, all of which involve much more complex changes of pitch and mouth resonance.

•••••••••••••••••••••••••••••••••••••••

(A)

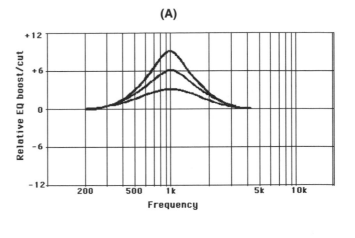

Fig. 6.4. Typical response curves of a 1-octave (10-band) EQ at 3dB, 6 dB and 9 dB of boost, with resulting shift in phase response shown in "B". The shift in phase caused by a cut or boost is standard, and is characteristic of all currently available EQ circuits. Is this a problem? Absolutely not, unless a very critical electronic testing situation is involved. Variations in phase relationships among frequencies are a natural part of the normal acoustic environment. Variations much greater than these often result from acts as simple as moving a microphone a bit in comparison to the position of the sound source. As well, sounds emanating from the source, as mentioned in Chapter 2, commonly combine in various combinations. The EQ is there for a reason—if it needs to be used, use it. Listeners are far more sensitive to tonal quality than relative phase.

(B)

Typical Phase Shift at 3dB, 6dB and 9 dB boost

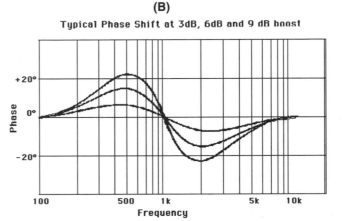

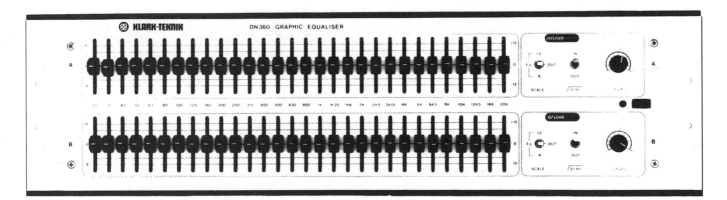

Fig. 6.5. Typical face panel of a dual 1/3-octave EQ. (coutesy Klark-Teknik)
Note the select switch (labeled "Scale") allowing a choice between between 6dB and 12 dB maximum cut/boost. The 6dB setting would allow finer control of the effect of the sliders when a major cut or boost is not required. Technically, even a 1/3-octave or 1/6-octave EQ is known as a "broadband" equalizer, despite the comparatively narrow slices of the audio spectrum covered by each band. A true narrowband EQ might cover a frequency range of only 3 or 4 Hz for each band, and would be used only to deemphasize blatant resonances in a system or particular room.

As a practical exercise in becoming more familiar with frequency ranges within the spectrum, it may be helpful to do one or both of the following:

(1) Set up a system with a microphone, EQ (preferably a 1/3-octave EQ), amplifier and full-range speaker (preferably a very small system with a limiter, to avoid the possiblility of damage to any part of the system and/or hearing overexposure). Start with all of the EQ sliders controls cut as far as the EQ will allow. Pick one EQ slider (start with one somewhere in the midrange) and boost it as far as it can go. Turn the system gain up to the point where it feeds back, and note the pitch. Now start at the bottom (around 40 or 50 Hz, or at the lowest frequency at which the system will enable you to get enough gain to allow noticeable feedback) and repeat the procedure, leaving all other sliders at their minimum. Repeat the procedure with successively higher sliders throughout the entire spectrum, while attempting to memorize the pitches heard (if necessary, hum, sing or—best of all—whistle, the ones you can).

(2) In a reasonably quiet environment, set up a noise generator (or, lacking this, use the system noise by itself) with an EQ, amplifier and a full-range speaker. Follow the above procedure, paying special attention to the pitch heard with each band of the EQ. Repeat the procedure, moving the sliders in various combinations from lowest to highest and in-between, noting the changes as you go.

•••••••••••••••••••••••••••••••••••••••

As another exercise in becoming more familiar with ranges within the spectrum, try also the following:

(1) Set up a tape, record or CD player with a contemporary recording, or other familiar music, a 10-band (1-octave) EQ, amp, and full-range speaker(s). Follow the above procedure of boosting one band at a time, to get an idea of the changes in the sound of the recordings you are familiar with. (Refer to the section showing frequency-related subjective qualities. Become aware of the general changes in tonal quality related to the range controlled by each band of the EQ.

(2) Repeat the procedure in (1) with the EQ sliders at their middle, or "flat" positions. One at a time, drop each of the faders gradually to their maximum cut, again noting the changes in tonal quality.

(3) Repeat the above (1) and (2), moving the sliders in groups: for examples, move two, three, four or five sliders at a time in both directions throughout the whole spectrum. Note the changes in tonal quality.

(4) Repeat the above procedure with a 2/3-octave, 1/2-octave or 1/3-octave EQ to become familiar with yet finer aspects of tone control.

(5) If possible, construct a similar setup as above with individual voices or musical instruments directly in-line with the EQ, noting the changes in tonal quality as different sliders or groups of sliders are boosted or cut.

(6) Finally, if at all possible, do the same as above—with a voice or instrument mixed in with a recorded program. Change the EQ of the voice or instrument as above, in comparison with the rest of the mix, noting the changes in tonal quality throughout the spectrum.

•••••••••••••••••••••••••••••••••••••••

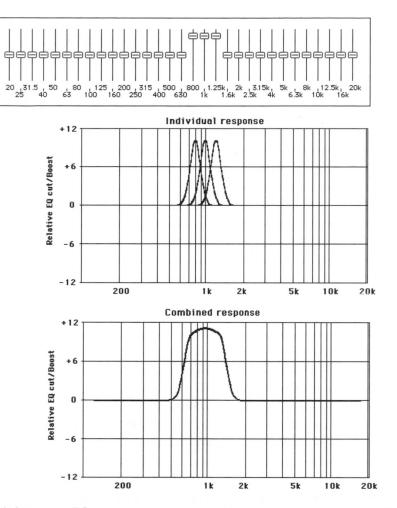

Fig. 6.6. **Combining-type EQ curves.** Three adjacent bands of a combining-type EQ are boosted here for purpose of illustration. Note that the adjacent bands act together to form a broader overall curve. This is not the case with a "non-combining" EQ, which would leave notches in the combined curve. The majority of commercially available graphic EQs today are of the combining type. Still, it is generally the safest practice to "average-out" an EQ curve so the average position of the sliders is in the center, as illustrated below.

More commonly encountered than "non-combining" EQs are equalizers in which the bands overlap excessively—this is often characteristic of low budget 2/3-octave and 1/3-octave EQs (basically a result of inexpensive filters). Here it is sometimes necessary to slightly compensate in the opposite direction with an adjacent band. (The emphasis should be on *slightly*, radical movements of adjacent bands in opposite directions should seldom, if ever, be done. The exception to this would generally be only when we are intentionally cutting the response in the extreme of the spectrum, a subject reserved for Chapters 9 and 17.)

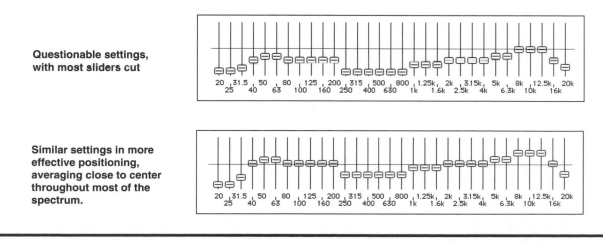

Questionable settings, with most sliders cut

Similar settings in more effective positioning, averaging close to center throughout most of the spectrum.

Below are some general factors to consider with regard to equalizing, which are further discussed in Chapter 17.

• The overall frequency response is caused by the combination of the frequency response curves throughout the system, from the sound source to the microphones right through the system to the loudspeakers, and beyond into the acoustical realm of the audience.

• All equalization changes in individual voices or instruments will be heard in comparison to the tonal qualities of the other input signals being mixed. (In other words, changes in the EQ of the *overall* mix can often solve many tonal problems. But the *individual* changes made on input signals or subgroups will change the sounds mainly in comparison to other sounds within the mix—this is also discussed in Chapter 17.) Examples: Reducing the sibilance of the vocals may actually allow the cymbals to be better heard; increasing the midrange of vocals and instruments may cause the midrange of the drum sounds to be masked, etc.

• An adjustment of an EQ control will often have effects well beyond the center frequencies or shelving frequencies (how far depends on the particular EQ). For example, boost of an 80Hz shelving control may also be affecting response upwards of 250 Hz or more. Boost of a 2k peaking control to increase clarity of a voice, for another example, may also be boosting 4k sufficiently to also cause some degree of harshness, and so forth. To a lesser degree this also applies to graphic and other outboard EQ's.

• Since the response curves of different mic designs can vary widely, the EQ needs can change widely from one mic to another. Oftentimes better results are obtained substituting a microphone with a more suitable response curve. In many cases the desired sound can be more closely achieved simply by altering the microphone positioning to obtain a more suitable sampling of the sound source.

• Different vocal qualities often require widely different kinds of adjustments, different drums often require widely different adjustments compared to one another, and so forth. For example, ordinarily, we require a low end boost to bring out the depth of , say, a bass drum or floor tom, but depending on the overall system response, mic response, and the actual sound of the drum, the lows on the on-board EQ might actually need to be cut in some instances. So there are no hard-and-fast rules which will always hold in every circumstance—only general rules of thumb.

•••••••••••••••••••••••••••••••••••••••

Below are some examples of frequency-related subjective qualities as described in an informal study conducted by the author, and which generally agree with the author's experience. Because they are subjective, they are of-course readily subject to debate. They are intended only as a guide:

31.5 Hz   A typical extended-range musical program has little or no energy in the 20-32 Hz range—generally this range is only necesary for special effects. Extremely difficult for most loudspeaker systems to effectively
40—   reproduce at substantial levels, especially in sound reinforcement applications.

50   Too much energy in the 40-100 Hz range: "murky", muddy, or around 80 to 100 Hz, "boomy"

63 Hz—
   Too little energy in the 40-100 Hz range: kick drum lacking "thump", bass
80   lacking depth or "guts" in lower notes.

100—

125 Hz

160—   Too much energy in the 100-250 Hz range: boomy, muddy, muffled, or too "thick".

200   Too little energy in the 100-250 Hz range: treble instrument, voice or snare is lacking depth or thickness.
   Too little around 200 Hz or so: bass guitar or string-bass lacks "roundness"
250 Hz—

315

400—
   Too much energy in the 250 Hz-630 Hz range: "cloudy", "boxy" or opaque.
500 Hz   Too much energy in a narrow band between 500 and 800 Hz, "megaphone-like"

630—   Too little energy through the 250-630Hz range:"empty", lacking fullness, substance or breadth, or (towards 800 Hz) lacking "solidness".
800
   Too much energy in the 630-1200 range: "honky", excessively hard, or
1 kHz—   (in the extreme)"telephone-like"
   Too little energy in the 630-1200 Hz range: lacking fullness or adequate solidness.
1.25k

1.6k—
   Too much energy in the 1 kHz to 2 kHz range: excessively hard or (~2k) "blary".
2 kHz
   Too little energy in the 1 kHz to 2 kHz range: lack of clarity or adequate hardness
2.5k—
   Too much energy in the 2 kHz to 4 kHz range: "blary", "tinny", "trebly" or "brash"
3.15k
   Too little energy in the 2 kHz to 4 kHz range: lack of clarity or (around 4k) "bite"
4 kHz—
   Too much energy in the 4 kHz to 6 kHz range: excessively harsh, sharp or brash
5k
   Too little energy in the 4 kHz to 6 kHz range: lack of distinctive edge, sometimes heard
6.3k—   as lack of clarity or "bite".

8 kHz   Too much energy in the 6.3 kHz-and-above range: excessive or annoying sibilance.

10k—   Too little energy in the 6.3 kHz-and-above range: inaudible sibilants ("S", "Z", "T" sounds), lack of "zip" or sweetness.(for "zip", around 6.3-8k; for sweetness, or "sizzle", normally 8kHz and above).
12.5k

16kHz—   This is usually the extreme limit of hearing for an adult with very good hearing.

j) General use of EQs for Feedback Control.

The procedure of equalizing a sound system to eliminate feedback is usually referred to as **ringing-out**, because the objective is to reduce the system response at the most sensitive frequencies which "ring". The objective of ringing-out a system is (believe it or not) to get as many frequencies as possible to ring at the same time as the system goes past its gain-before-feedback limit. When a system rings at many frequencies simultaneously, it is an indication that no one or two frequencies stand out well above the others in the system's total response.

A way of approaching the setup of a system which is feedback-prone is to ring out the system first, then adjust the tonal quality and volume level to taste. This approach would be especially appropriate for a monitor system, where the speakers are usually pointed more-or- less directly at the microphone positions—and would also be useful wherever else high output levels or high gain is required. (Ideally, this procedure should be done with a limiter in the system, which should be set with a relatively low threshold so that no damage occurs to any component in the system. Limiters are described in Ch. 8.)

One approach to "ringing out" the system—to be done with no audience present:

(1) With the EQ sliders set in their flat position, gradually raise the system gain until it begins to slightly ring at one frequency.

(2) Find the slider closest to the frequency of the ring, and gradually reduce the slider level just far enough for the ringing to stop. (If finding the appropriate slider is difficult, arrange several opportunities to try the exercise described in section "i" of this chapter. A good live-engineer should ordinarily be able to find the nearest slider on a 1/3-octave EQ on the first or second try.)

(3) Increase the overall level of the system further, until one or more additional frequencies ring.

(4) Gradually reduce the sliders at those frequencies until the ringing stops.

(5) Repeat the procedure until the system rings simultaneously at as many frequencies as is reasonably possible.

(6) If necessary, adjust the tonal quality until it is reasonably satisfactory to the ears.

(7) If new rings have been created, reduce the gain, or repeat steps 2 through 6 until a reasonable combination of feedback control and acceptable sound have been achieved. This may require a compromise, so a judgement call is in order at this point as to which is more important—maximum possible gain, or pleasant sound (oftentimes, "flat" is not considered the most pleasant by those making the decisions).

(8) Finally, and perhaps most importantly, back the system off a bit from the point where ringing begins (i.e., reduce the gain). How much the system should be backed off depends on the sound quality requirements and also on the environment. Generally, the more the reverberation in the room is a problem—especially in a small reverberant room—the more the gain should be reduced below the point of feedback. In a reverberant room, where clarity is commonly hard to achieve, the optimum reduction might be as much as 6 dB or-more below the point where ringing occurs. In a very "dry" room, as little as 3 dB might be more than adequate. (See also Fig. 6.8.)

Note: If the mics will be used close-up by the talker or performer, the mics normally need to be double-checked with a person standing with mouth next-to or touching the front of each of the mics. This is due to reflection and resonance involving the up-close user, which can add to feedback potential.

Equalizing a large sound system or a permanent installation is a normally a significantly more complicated procedure involving the use of a noise generator and a spectrum analyzer, in conjunction with critical analysis of what proportion of the overall sound is direct, and what proportion is reverberant sound. Such a procedure is also likely to involve adjustment of the crossover levels as well, as discussed in Chapter 9.

Fig. 6.7. Feedback control with a graphic EQ. (courtesy Yamaha Corp.)
For simplicity of illustration, a 1-octave EQ is presumed here. The area above what is designated 0dB here is the point above which continuous feedback occurs.

(A) In this example, when the system gain is increased, the first feedback ring we hear is in the neighborhood of 1kHz.

(B) The 1k slider is reduced (as illustrated by the dipped dotted line) just sufficiently to alow us to bring the system gain up another 2 or 3 dB.

(C) The next rings we hear as the system gain is further increased happen to be correctible with slight adjustments of the 125 Hz, 500 Hz and 2k sliders. This allows us to bring up the gain somewhat further yet.

(D) Finally, in this hypothetical example, we find that we are able to increase the 63 Hz, 8k and 16k sliders slightly without feedback. This, in rough terms, is our maximum gain before feedback.

Adjustment of other factors such as the source-to-mic distance, the pointing of the mics, and the positioning and directional characteristics of the speakers may allow us to further increase gain. Often, we may wish to sacrifice some degree of maximum gain in favor of trying to achieve a particular tonal quality we desire, particularly in a music reinforcement system.

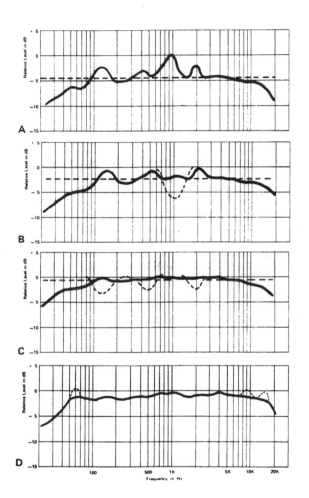

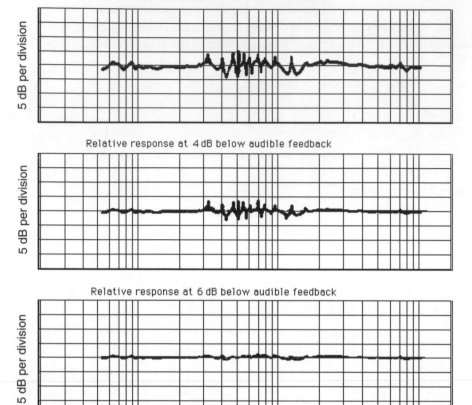

Fig. 6.8. Typical aberrations of frequency response when system gain is near continuous feedback. This illustration points to the need of keeping a slight "safety margin" below the point where we hear continuous feedback, even after the system has been "rung out". Along with frequency response, transient response is also degraded as system gain nears the point of continuous feedback.

CHAPTER 7

MIXERS

The term "mixer" describes a class of components as wide as the entire audio field. Variously also referred to as board, sound board, mixing console and mixing desk*, the mixer's basic purpose is, of course, to mix, control, process and effectively route the signals fed into it. In all but the most basic systems, the mixer is the main practical tool of any sound system operator. It is in a sense the canvas on which the artistry of the audio engineer is brought to life.

a) Basic Mixer Functions.

Audio mixers can be designed to perform a fairly wide variety of signal processing/routing functions. Most of the functions of a typical mixer can be described in two basic categories: those associated with an input channel and those associated with a master, or output channel.

A typical input channel, from an operator's standpoint, will have two level controls, a tone control (EQ) section, and one or more auxiliary controls allowing signal copies to be sent to separate outputs.

Mixers for all but the most basic applications are designed to allow the signal strength to be controlled in several stages. This allows the operator to make optimum use of the system's circuitry (to allow adequate headroom and best possible signal-to-noise ratio). The first stage, *input attenuation*, allows the incoming signal to be regulated before entering the remaining circuitry of that channel, to allow adequate signal strength without overloading the channel. It also allows the fader to be positioned within a convenient working range for the operator. The *fader* is normally placed at the bottom of the channel (or closest to the operator), and is usually configured as a slider rather than a rotary control. The fader regulates the amount of signal sent to the output section (or submaster) of the mixer.

From the standpoint of the operator, the function of any level control can be roughly compared to a simple valve that can reduce the signal strength, or stop the flow altogether. (The emphasis here is on the word "roughly"; actually what is controlled is the amount of *gain*—i.e., the degree of amplification) This is accomplished by a *potentiometer*, usually called a *pot*, for short. Pots allow adjustment, on a gradual basis, of the intensity of any function on a mixer for which a simple switch would be inadequate.

---

* Generally the term "desk" is used mainly in the UK. Ordinarily, any mixer 12 channels or larger which sits flat can reasonably be referred to as a "board", while any mixer 30 channels or larger can reasonably be called a "console".

Input channels normally allow individual equalization for each channel (*on-board EQ*). The type of on-board EQ included in the mixer design depends of-course on both the applications for which the mixer is designed, as well as (very heavily) on cost factors. The more versatile mixers, not surprisingly, tend to be designed to have more flexible and intricate on-board EQ. The effectiveness of a versatile on-board EQ such as one with sweepable filters or parametric filters obviously depends in-large-part on the skill-level of the operator. In many mixer designs, as mentioned, a low-cut switch is also included to allow the operator to cut the low frequency response for voices and treble instruments.

A typical input channel also will provide two or more *auxiliary sends*, whose signal arrives at separate auxiliary outputs. These allow the operator to separately adjust the amount of signal that will be sent to devices other than the main amplifiers and speakers, such as to monitor-amplifiers or sound effects units.

When the pot of an auxiliary send is turned up, the signal is fed into a *buss* wire inside the mixer. A buss, as the name implies, is a way of carrying a group of individual signals along a common route. Here the destination is a combining amp, also known as a *summing amp* (or simply, a *sum amp*). The sum amp inside the mixer puts out a signal which represents the combination of all the signals fed into that buss—in this case an aux. buss. An aux. master control then determines the overall output gain of the auxiliary mix. Similarly, all of the channel faders feed their signal into a main mixing buss (a.k.a., program mixing buss) which is summed up and then arrives at a main output of the mixer after control by the main fader.

The master section of a mixer can, in addition to the output fader(s) and auxiliary master controls, include controls for the return signal from effects units for inclusion into the main mix, as well as access-for and control-of auxiliary input signals from sources such as tape machines, or signals from the output of an additional mixer (used in this way, the additional mixer would be called a "submixer").

A common design in more versatile mixers involves the use of *submasters*, or *subgroups*. Submasters allow the operator to control groups of input channels in categories, for example voices, drums, etc., by using the appropriate switches on the input channels. Certainly this is helpful to the mixing process when many input signals of varying kinds are involved. A more involved design called a *matrix* allows the operator to provide multiple outputs and send each of the submixes to each of the matrix outputs in variable degrees, thereby setting up a separate mix at each matrix output. Typical uses of a matrix would be for on-site multitrack recording and/or as a method of providing several monitor mixes from the main mixer.

Mixer designs for basic applications often do not include many of the above features, but might include additional on-board EQ for the mixed signal, as well as perhaps an internal power amplifier with speaker level outputs. (This, for the benefit of those not previously exposed, would usually be called a "mixer/amplifier", "powered mixer" or "PA head".)

Figure 7.1.

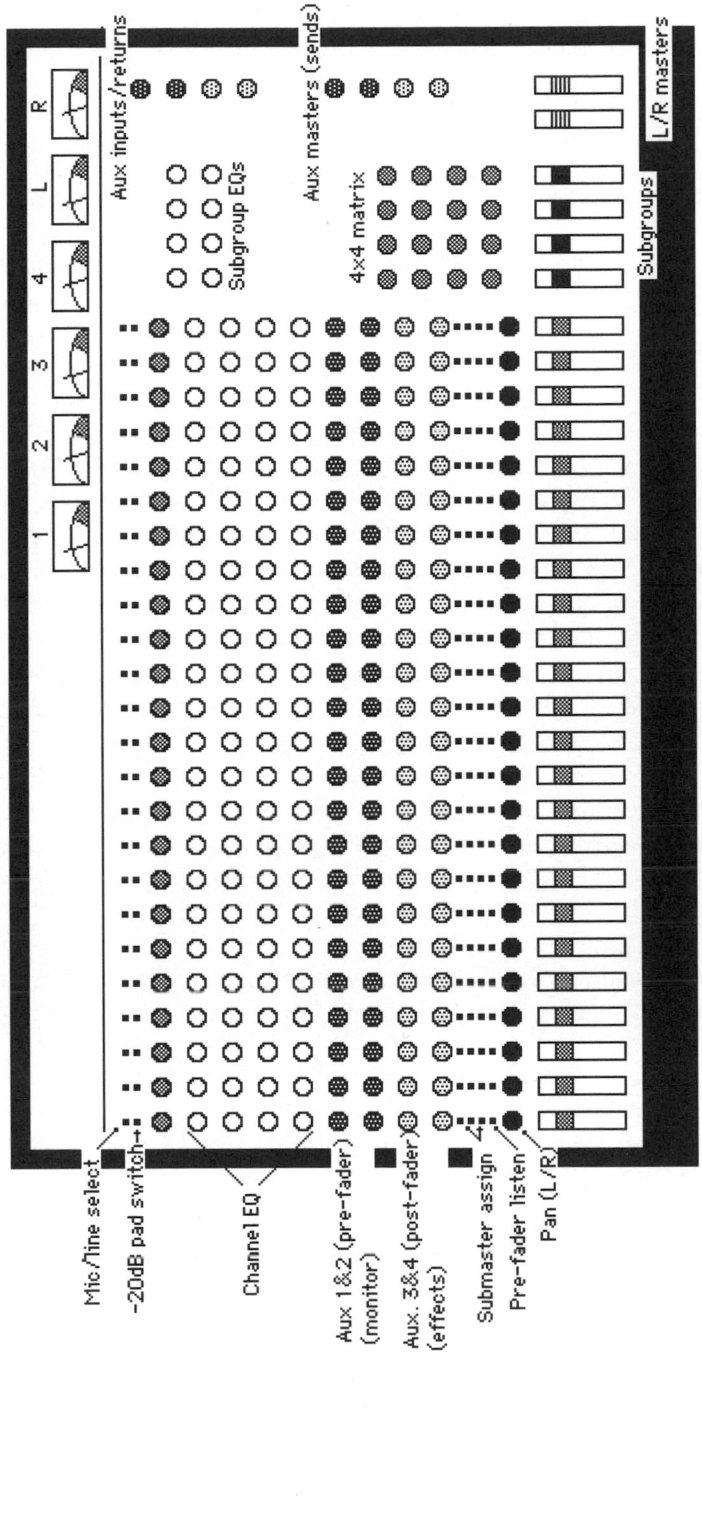

Typical 24 Channel Mixer Configuration (with 4x4 matrix).

b) Input Attenuation.

The input attenuator, as mentioned, allows the operator to adjust the incoming signal level on an input channel. This function is also variously called *input level, gain, input gain, pad* or *trim*.

This may be supplemented by an additional switch, usually referred to as *pad*, which further reduces the input signal level if necessary to prevent overloading. The additional pad switch—if provided—can also be useful at levels somewhat below channel overload, in order to bring the input attenuator back into a more workable range if it begins to approach its own limit of level reduction.

c) On-board EQ.

As mentioned, on-board EQ varies widely according to the design of the mixer. Two, three, and four-way fixed-frequency EQs, and to some extent anything less than a fully parametric EQ each have their own limitations in terms of how they are able to affect the character of the sounds they are supposed to "control".

Interestingly, these varying characteristics can even have an effect on which microphones are used to most effectively achieve the desired sound. Why? For just one of many possible examples, say the snare drum is not "fat" enough for our taste. A typical four-band fixed-frequency EQ will provide low frequency cut-or-boost usually in the area of 60 Hz or 80 Hz shelving, and a low-mid control most often centered around 400 Hz or so. The "fatness" of a snare usually tends to be found in the 160-250 Hz area. So we boost the lows, but now the snare is too "boomy" in the range below 160Hz. Try rolling off the low end? Now the "fatness" is completely gone, and the lower mid control is too far up in frequency to be of much help. So now a different mic, if available, may need to be chosen in order to more closely approximate the desired sound. If we had an EQ with a sweepable lower mid, we could move the low-mid EQ down to the needed 200 Hz-or-so range, and have our adjustment where it was needed. This kind of situation is fairly common, and is certainly not limited to any one instrument or type of voice. (It would perhaps be ideal if one could simply choose the right mics for each application and leave the EQ untouched. But, most experienced engineers would agree that quite often the mic by itself—no matter which one is chosen or how it is used—is not adequate to get the job done quite right without effective EQ capability to supplement it.)

The point is this. Certainly, a simple EQ is less likely to get an inexperienced operator into much trouble. But the importance of a reasonably flexible on-board EQ to an experienced operator with a good ear cannot be overstated.

d) Auxiliary Outputs (Sends).

There is no hard-and-fast rule as to where—in the signal path through a channel's circuits—the signal copy for an auxiliary send will be made. Most often, the following guidelines are used by manufacturers.

As a rule-of-thumb, a *monitor* or *foldback* send will draw its copy *before* the on-board EQ and fader (i.e., adjustments of these will not affect the tonal quality or the intensity of the signal from that bus). This is referred to as *pre-EQ/pre-fader*. The purpose of separating the function of the monitor send from the movement of the channel fader is to allow the operator to adjust individual levels given without needing to be concerned with boosting the monitor level of that channel to the point where feedback occurs, nor with reducing it to the point where it cannot be heard onstage. In most cases the audience considerations differ from the onstage considerations.

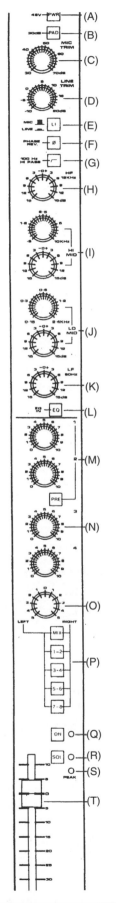

Fig. 7.2 Sample input channel controls for a 24 x 8 mixer.
(courtesy Soundcraft)

(A) 48v phantom power on/off, allows remote powering of most condenser mics via the mic cable.

(B) 30 dB pad in/out, allows additional attenuation of high-level input signals, for situations where "C" and/or "D" are inadequate.

(C)(D) Mic Trim and Line Trim. In this mixer design, separate variable attenuators are provided for the XLR input and the 1/4" phone input.

(E) MIC/LINE seclect. Chooses whether input channel receives signal from XLR or 1/4" line input.

(F) Phase Reverse. Allows polarity to be reversed when necessary. An example of this would be the optional bottom mic of a snare drum.

(G) High Pass Filter. This cuts low frequencies, for example, for vocals or other instruments not requiring strong low end reproduction.

(H) High Frequency EQ control with shelving cut/boost.

(I) Hi-mid EQ with peaking, or "bell" characteristic. Upper control selects center frequency, lower control varies the amount of cut or boost. (On some mixers by other manufacturers the position of these two knobs is reversed. On a few designs, it is coaxial, i.e. one inside the other.)

(J) Lo-mid EQ with peaking, or "bell" characteristic. Same as Hi-mid, except different range of center frequencies.

(K) Low Frequency EQ control with shelving cut/boost.

(L) EQ in/out, disengages EQ section when necessary—most often used when the operator wishes to sample the signal without any EQ, rather than centering all of the EQ knobs.

(M) Auxiliary sends 1 and 2 in this design are normally post-fader, with switch to allow pre-fader operation if needed.

(N) Auxiliary sends 3 and 4 are in this design wired permanently post-fader. Ordinarily these are effects sends.

(O) PAN, routes channel output on a variable basis to left or right, left to odd-numbered submasters, right to even numbered submasters.

(P) Submaster assign switches, used in conjunction with PAN.

(Q) Channel on/off switch, allows channel to be disengaged when not needed.

(R) Solo (PFL), allows pre-fader monitoring of the channel through head-phones, or level check in the master VU meters.

(S) Peak overload LED, lights as channel nears clipping.

(T) Fader

Sometimes a monitor send will draw its signal *after the Channel EQ*, in which case it would be referred to as ***post-EQ/pre-fader*** (i.e., adjustments of the channel's EQ would cause a similar change in the tonal quality of the monitor signal as well, but movements of the fader would not affect it).

Traditionally, only studio mixers tie input-channel-EQ adjustments into the monitor signal (on these boards the monitor function is most often referred to as "cue"). Some boards are designed with both studio *and* live mixing purposes in mind—this is where this configuration is most often encountered in live mixing. Some operators actually prefer this design in live applications where the monitors are mixed from the house (main) mixer.

There are good arguments both for and against using a mixer with post-EQ monitor sends in live sound reinforcement. Generally, it is often preferable to have adjustments of tonal quality of voices and instruments reflected in monitors. This is because when two or more vocalists or instrumentalists are singing or playing together, the operator makes tonal adjustments to bring their individual tonal qualities into better alignment with one another. If these adjustments are done effectively, the performers can often benefit from having the adjustments reflected in the monitor sound. (In other words, well-considered and effective adjustments of voices or instruments harmonizing with one another help to create a better mix, whether in the house mix or the monitor mix. The emaphasis here is on "effective"—even the most experienced system operators are sometimes caught off-guard, since they are not always in a position to hear the onstage results. Errors here can sometimes actually be disconcerting to performers.)

But the main disadvantage with a post-EQ monitor send in a live application is that feedback is more likely to occur in the frequency ranges where boost is initiated in the main mix. If, for example, an EQ boost is created at different frequency ranges for different vocalists (which is very common), the overall gain-before-feedback of the monitor system tends to be *reduced* (in other words, the likelihood of feedback is *increased*). This is because boosts initiated by the on-board EQ will increase the effective frequency response in those areas of the spectrum in which boost is initiated. As a result, peaks can be created which go above the point at which feedback occurs. For this reason, "monitor" sends are generally wired pre-EQ.

An ***effects send*** is almost always ***post-fader***, so any adjustment of the EQ and/or the channel fader will also affect the signal from that send. This is because the normal expectation is that effects units will receive a signal similar to that sent to the main mix, and return the modified version accordingly. (An example: If the operator cuts the high frequencies of the channel EQ, we would normally expect the highs on an echo to be similarly reduced, else the echo would simply sound out of character with the original signal. The same principle usually holds for the overall level of the fader.)

Sometimes manufacturers specifically label these sends "reverb" and/or "echo", since these are the most common uses for an effects loop. (These designations are generally used only on small-to-moderate-size mixers of 12 channels or less. In the case of "reverb" sends, oftentimes the manufacturer has included in the mixer design a basic spring-type reverb unit within the mixer itself—on newer units this may be a digital reverb or multi-effects processor.

Very commonly an input channel will have one or more sends (sometimes all of them) that the manufacturer has simply labeled "aux." These may be qualified by the labels "pre" or "post"—if not, the operator may need to consult the manufacturers literature or do some trial-and-error experimenting with it to determine what to expect when the mixer is used for an actual event. Many high quality mixers allow the operator to decide between "pre" or "post" by providing a switch which changes the sampling point for the particular aux. send on its respective channel.

Fig. 7.3. Key input-channel functions which should be double-checked before beginning a performance or event.

(A) Mic/line select and Channel on/off switches (if applicable). On mixers which do not have an on/off switch, the mic/line select switch often is used to switch a channel in or out when needed. Such an instance would be when a wireless mic is switched on or off, or being changed from one person to another onstage. Obviously attention should be paid to the switch's status.

(B) Phantom power, Input pad and Gain. The phantom power switch (in this case labeled 48VDC), if left on, would not under normal circumstances cause any damage to a standard dynamic mic. But, whenever this switch is "on" a loud pop is sometimes heard through the system if a mic cable is plugged in after the system is powered up. Obviously, if a remotely powered direct box or mic is used, this needs to be in the on position.
The additional pad switch is occasionally an issue. If it is engaged during a check, or in a pinch when encountering an unexpectedly high signal during an event, it should be engaged during a lull in the event. In the meantime, back the variable gain off as far as it will go and use the fader instead—unless it is an emergency and you are hearing radical distortion as a result of the excessive signal. When disengaging the pad switch, back off a bit on the variable input gain knob before doing so, to avoid a potentially unpleasant overly strong signal. Then, if need be, bring the gain or fader back up gradually until the appropriate levels are found.

(C) Aux pre- or post-fader select, if applicable. For monitors controlled from the main house mixer, this should be in the "pre" position.

(D) Pan/Submaster assigns, if applicable . Obviously, these need to double- checked to ensure that each signal is being sent through the appropriate bus. Pan left to odd-numbered submasters; pan right to even-numbered submasters.

(E) When using any PFL/Solo to monitor that channel's level in the main meter(s), care needs to be exersized that there is only one PFL switch engaged, else there would be a combined reading along with another channel. (Of course, if using headphones, such an error is likely to be recognized. But even with head-phones, there is sometimes enough cross-pickup between mics in live performance that such an error is possible.)

(F) Start the sound check with faders and/or input gains at or near their lowest setting, then gradually work up to a comfortable average setting. The optimal average postion for faders varies from one mixer to another. Most often it is about 3/4 of the way up, allowing adequate room to boost for lead voice/instrument parts or to compensate for varying signal level. Most mixers will have a visual demarcation of some kind for the recommended optimal average position, but there is no hard-and-fast rule. Ultimately, of course, do what needs to be done to effectively accomplish any particular job.

Last but not least, when first starting out a sound check, generally it is preferred to set all EQ controls (not illustrated here) in their "flat" position. Of course, when beginning the actual event, double check to be sure all settings are as they were left during the check.

(A)

(B)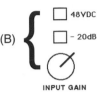

(C)

(D)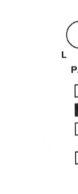

(E)

(F)

e) Auxiliary Inputs, Effects Returns.

The terms "aux. loop" and "effects loop", as mentioned earlier, refer to a signal route involving both a send and return line. The return signal, in its modified form, is then available to be included in the mix as desired.

Ordinarily, in controlling the return signal from effects units, it is preferable to use a standard input channel, for the simple reason that it offers more control of the return signal. When too many of the input channels are tied up for lines coming from the stage, the auxiliary returns can be used instead. Most mixers do not give equal priority to the design of these extra inputs, in many cases using only a rotary pot for control. This can sometimes put the operator at a disadvantage in controlling the effects return signal, since there would be no control over the EQ of the return signal, and also because the rotary pot on the master section is generally less convenient to use than the linear fader of a standard input channel.

f) Panning and Submaster Assignments.

Many mixers are designed to produce stereo output (which, by the way, does not make them inappropriate for mono use). To determine how much of a particular channel's signal will be directed to each of the two main output channels ("left" and "right"), a "pan-pot" is included in the mixer design. Short for "panoramic potentiometer" , this function is usually labeled simply "pan".

Very commonly pan-pots are designed to be used in combination with submaster assignment switches. In these cases (Fig. 7.2, 7.3), panning to the left would route the signal to an odd-numbered submaster; panning to the right would route the signal to an even-numbered submaster.

g) Meters, PFL, Solo.

There are a number of common ways of providing visual indication of the signal levels in a mixer.

Some mixers provide no metering at all, though this tends to be true of only the most basic and/or lowest budget mixers. Normally, any contemporary mixer will provide at least a single overload indicator light. The sampling point for this type of on/off overload indicator is often referenced to the output level, though many designs have multiple sampling points, any one of which, when overloaded, will cause the overload light to go on. This type of indicator may or may not have a sampling point at the actual channel inputs, so in some cases the operator may need to consider the possibility that an input signal is too strong for the input stage of the channels. In such a case, the input line may require an in-line attenuator as shown in Chapter 16.

When a single meter is provided, it is usually referenced to the actual output level.

More versatile mixers, generally those of 12 channels and upward, commonly provide multiple meters. Several formats are common. Typically, mixers are designed with one meter for each main output channel and for each submaster channel. Many mixers provide one or more meters with switchable sampling points. Mixers with this kind of option normally allow the metering of aux. levels and/or individual channels before the channel fader (a function usually referred to as ***Pre-fader listen (PFL),*** or ***solo***.) The use of the PFL function also sends the signal of that channel to the headphone output, so it can be listened to independently (thus the terms PFL and "solo", originally coined in the recording studio).

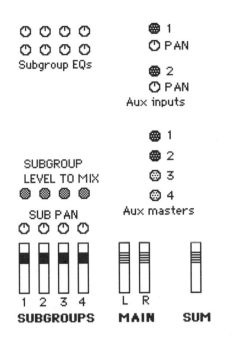

Fig. 7.4. Sample master section.

The most common design in mixers equipped with subgroups is to split each submaster output into stereo, which feed the left and right main outputs according to how the "pan" is set. For the majority of live applications in venues smaller than, say, a large concert hall, a mono mix is used. In mixers which do not have a "sum" output, whenever a mono mix is used we would simply choose between left or right, and designate it as our "main". (Additional guidelines are presented in Chapter 13 for alternate uses of this configuration.)

The Aux. masters of-course control the level which is sent to the Aux. outputs, whether used for stage monitor or effects. The Aux. inputs (sometimes labeled "Aux. return") are provided for situations where an effects return is required. Ordinarily, though, most operators prefer to use a standard input channel for effects returns. The advantages of using a standard input channel are that it allows easier control of the level in the mix, that additional EQing of the return signal is possible, and that it is possible to use the effects return to feed yet another effects unit when desired. For these reasons, manufacturers of high-quality mixers today are increasingly inclined to design the effects returns to act very much like a standard input channel.

The "Sum" is, of course, the combined mix from Left and Right masters.

Fig. 7.5. Typical matrix.

A matrix design (in this case 4 x 4) allows control over separate outputs, to which the operator can send the submixes in any desired combination independently of the main mix. A typical use of a matrix would be to feed additional stage monitor mixes, or to feed a multi-channel tape recorder with the expectation of later remixing. Below is shown a sample combination.

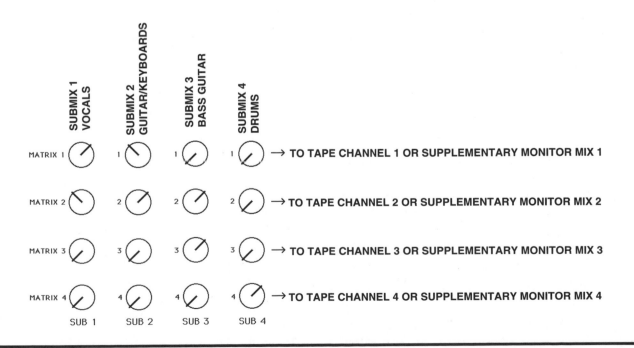

Most meters use the VU method of measurement described in Chapter 4. Rapid peaks can sometimes cause momentary distortion—particularly with drums and percussion instruments—that do not fully register as an overload on the meter scale, so extra caution might be necessary here. Often, mixers offer an additional red "peak LED" light (with needle-type meters this is often included on the actual meter). Oftentimes mixers with LED ladders (the graduated scale with usually green, yellow and red LED lights) offer the option to display the peak level on the ladder by the use of a switch or button.

h) Achieving a Workable Gain Structure.

The already introduced concept of gain structures (Chapter 4) is an extremely important one to keep in mind when operating any but the most basic mixers. In addition to the gain structure among the component stages of a system, a typical mixer of 12 channels and upward normally has at least three stages of gain control available to the operator.

An effective gain structure in a mixer normally involves the following: (1)The available controls are adjusted for a given event to allow reasonable ease of moment-to-moment operation. (2) A reasonable compromise is found between: (a) the softest sounds or weakest input signals needing to be greatly amplified (where the amount of system noise and ambient noise, and the potential for feedback howls, are the main factors), and (b) the loudest on-stage sounds and strongest signals likely to be encountered (where avoiding distortion is the main concern). A balance of these factors and some common working sense can usually allow flexibility of adjustment of the controls while also keeping the mixer within its useful limits.

A way to set up a workable gain structure is while conducting a sound check prior to an event, using the loudest sounds likely to be encountered as a guide in setting the input attenuator of each channel. (Example: if a vocalist is expected to talk or sing loudly, it seems sensible to try to anticipate this during the sound check. Ideally, the operator should request the particular singer or talker to demonstrate their individual style by showing their maximum level, and set the controls appropriately in order to avoid distorion at the mixer stage). If the mixer provides PFL metering capability, the operator can readily judge an appropriate maximum setting for the input attenuators simply by referencing each channel to the PFL meter (remember that boosting the channel's EQ controls will often increase the pre-fader level, which may require compensation by further reducing the input level).

Once the levels have been set so that no channels are overloaded, the operator is in a position to gradually reduce the input attenuators on those channels which are too loud in the main mix when the faders are positioned at the chosen reference point. Generally, the channels with signals which will be loudest in the mix will be the ones whose pre-fader levels will remain at-or-near their maximum level on the meter. (The highest levels of a typical musical mix, for example, might tend to be lead vocalists, and perhaps certain drums, most commonly kick and snare.) The input attenuators on the rest of the channels can then be adjusted downward to allow the faders to be brought into a reasonable working range, so they do not end up at the very bottom of their throw.

Most often, pots are most useful when set in their middle ranges—between 1/2 and 3/4 of their full range—because this allows the most flexibility should that function need adjustment upward or downward. (This can vary from one design to another, according to the pots and/or faders used by the manufacturer, so each design should be taken individually for its own characteristics. Some designs of pots can be very touchy in the lowest or highest extreme of their range, where a slight movement can sometimes have a major result. Others may have "hot spots" somewhere in their middle ranges.)

Adjustment of the variable input attenuator, as mentioned, should be used to bring the fader into a workable area in its total length. Usually the manufacturer will provide guide marks along the throw of the fader to indicate an "ideal" reference point, or average setting, for the operator. (Remember that re-adjusting the input-attenuator level will also affect the signal level at the aux. sends, so they may need to be readjusted as well.)

Similarly, if the strength of the signal at the master fader(s) is so strong that they need to be very near the bottom of their range to get the desired level for the whole mix, then the average setting on the faders and/or the individual settings on the input attenuators can be reduced to allow the operator to bring the master(s) into a more workable range. We could also reduce the overall system gain at an outboard EQ or other signal processor, such as at the crossover input-level control.

If submasters are used, check the PFL at the submasters and the main faders, and attempt to find a reasonable balance of gains at each stage as shown on the PFL meter. Finally, check the main output meter(s) to ensure these are not indicating overload at the loudest program levels. If overload is occurring at any stage along the signal path, further reduce the input levels until an appropriate balance of fader positions is found. In well designed mixers, the above procedure would normally ensure that no overloading of circuits is taking place at the mixer stage.

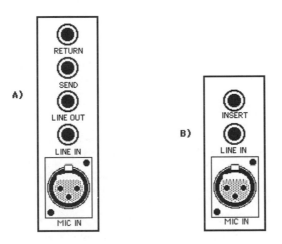

Fig. 7.6. Sample input channel connections.
In both the examples here, the line input would generally be somewhat less sensitive (and of a somewhat higher impedance) than the "mic" input, allowing standard line levels to be handled. Most often this is simply a standard two conductor "guitar-type" jack, though on some mixers the "Line-In" is a "TRS" balanced configuration. An unbalanced phone plug as introduced in Chapter 5 (the standard "guitar-type" plug) can be plugged into such a jack in all cases. But a TRS balanced plug would not function unless the "Line In" jack is also balanced. (These wiring configurations are further described in Chapter 16.)

The "Line Out" in example "A" would allow us to receive the individual channel's output post fader, most often for multichannel recording purposes.

For patching purposes, e.g. for a limiter or supplementary EQ, the insert is provided. In example "A" two separate unbalanced lines are used, most often labeled "Send" and "Return". In example "B" a TRS jack is used, with the tip and ring serving as separate lines as shown in Fig. 7.8. Careful here, some mixers use the tip as the send, others use the tip as the return.

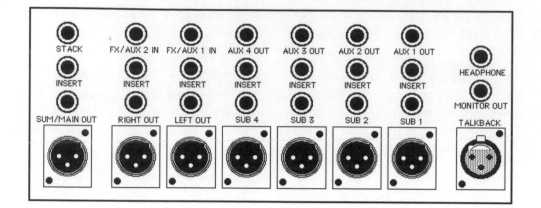

Fig. 7.7. Sample master section, rear panel connections of a 16x4x2 mixer.

Often mixers are encountered without immediate access to an operator's manual. This sample hypothetical output panel is a composite which includes several common sources of confusion for the inexperienced user.

Stack: This would ordinarily be an input, designated to receive signal from a supplementary mixer to be included in the main output.

Inserts: Here we can assume that the insert is a TRS format as shown in Fig. 7.8. If unsure as to whether the tip is the send or the return, some brief trial-and-error tests should establish the format for the entire mixer. Since the inserts are not labeled according to channel, each clearly corresponds to the particular output directly below it (in this case four subgroups, L/R out and sum out).

Outputs: Here it would ordinarily be the case that each XLR output is balanced, each 1/4" output unbalanced. Note that since there is no labeling below the XLR outputs, the manufacturer would in this hypothetical case be presuming an understanding of these standard formats on the part of the person using the mixer. Ordinarily, the Subgroup outputs 1 through 4 would only be used for taping purposes.

FX/Aux In 1&2: Here two returns are provided for effects loops, which should be adjustable by similarly labeled controls on the front panel. The normal assumption here would be that only two of the four aux outputs would be used for effects. The other two, normally the pre-fader auxes, would most often be used for stage monitor sends, so they would not normally require returns.

Monitor Out: In this case we can reasonably assume that the output labeled "Monitor Out" does not refer to a stage monitor send, for two reasons: Firstly, the fact that the four auxes are labeled as Aux. 1 through 4, would tend to indicate that the term "monitor" in this case refers to a different function than it would on mixers with aux. outputs labeled "effects" and "monitor". Secondly, its positioning, along with the headphone output and talkback-mic input, indicates a format which would allow the mixer to double as a recording mixer, with a monitor in the control room. This type of output would most often be a line-level version of the same signal sent to the headphone output.

Talkback: This would generally be a standard balanced mic input, designated to the pre-fader aux(s) and controllable by a similarly labeled control on the master section of the mixer.

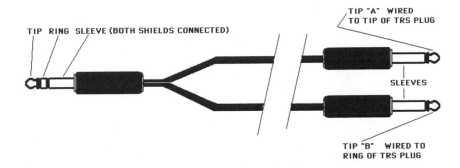

Fig. 7.8. "TRS" patch (insert) configuration.

The tip-ring-sleeve 1/4" connector is used here to handle two unbalanced lines, (much like a standard stereo headphone connection). (This is a format which is not compatible with TRS balanced lines as described in Chapter 16.) As mentioned earlier, if the operating manual is not handy, a trial-and-error determination needs to be made for a given mixer design as to which is the send and which is the return.

CHAPTER 8

OTHER SIGNAL PROCESSING and EFFECTS

This chapter introduces the basic kinds of additional outboard and/or optional equipment which can facilitate the goals of sound reinforcement.

a) Compressors and Limiters.

The basic purpose of a *compressor* and/or *limiter* circuit is to assist in keeping the signal level within a workable dynamic range, whether for the ear or to accomodate the limits of the system. What this type of circuit actually does is proportionately reduce the amount of additional gain beyond a given signal level, or "threshold".

The term which technically describes the compression/limiting function is *gain reduction*. *A gain reduction circuit reduces the amount af additional gain above the threshold setting by a certain ratio* (see Fig. 8.1). Most currently designed compressor/limiter circuits allow variable or switchable gain reduction ratios.

The objective of any compressor/ limiter circuit is to ensure that the signal level does not go beyond a certain approximate level, or to reduce the severity of level increases beyond a given threshold setting. Basically, the functions of compressors and limiters are the same. The only difference is in the amount of gain reduction they assert beyond the threshold—i.e., the severity of the "cap" that is put on the signal level. Ordinarily, any ratio of gain reduction above about 10-to-1 would fall in the category of "limiting" (though commercial descriptions may differ, so it is sensible to know the ratio specifications for a particular component). Traditionally, the limiting function has also been referred to as "leveling" and "peak limiting".

Limiting is extremely useful for system protection, to avoid actual damage to power amplifiers and/ or speakers, or to avoid distortion which would be caused by overloading other parts of the system such as a power amplifier. Limiters for system protection can be placed prior to the crossover, with the crossover set so that when the limiter is engaged, the system gain does not produce output which would be unsafe for the amplifiers or loudspeakers. The best protection method for loudpeakers in a system with an electronic crossover is to separately limit each crossover output. Here, each limiter should of-course be individually set so it engages before the power limits of either the amplifier or speaker component are reached.

To reduce unpleasant dynamic peaks or to keep a vocal or instrumental signal within a relatively limited dynamic range, a somewhat lower gain reduction ratio is normally used. As mentioned, the ratio of gain reduction can, in most units, be adjusted. With a variable ratio setting, the operator can adjust, to taste, the amount of "resistance" to level increases above the threshold setting. Typically between 2-to-1 and 4-to-1 compression ratios are adequate for this purpose, though some applications may call for higher ratios.

Using an excessive amount of compression at too high a ratio can cause an unnatural and usually unpleasant occurence known as "breathing" or "pumping". This is caused by relatively quick and radical engaging and disengaging of the compressor/limiter circuit, especially when used on an entire mixed program. Excessive compression on a mixed program can also cause a component of the mix, say a voice, to "push down" other components of the mix. Another disadvantage of using excessive amounts of compression is that feedback can occur much more easily after the signal ceases and the unit brings the gain back to normal. This can be avoided by choosing a sufficiently high threshold so that an adequate amount of uncompressed gain can be achieved to meet the needs of the application. (Use of compressor/limiters for facilitating a musical mix is discussed further in Chapters 13 and 17.)

There are two basic methods of adjusting the threshold setting. One design-method used by some manufacturers is to provide a set threshold level, with a variable gain control at the input stage. The input gain control allows the operator to bring the signal level up to the provided threshold setting. An output level control allows adjustment of signal level leaving the unit. The other method provides a variable threshold level, which allows the operator to "back-up" the threshold to the level of the input signal. The latter method is slightly more expensive to manufacture, but tends to be much easier to use.

Variable (or switchable) **attack**-time and **release**-time (or attack- and release-rate) settings are also commonly provided by manufacturers. Bascially, *fast attack and release times are used for speaker protection and percussive instruments such as drums*. Too fast an attack and release time, though, can actually "clip" the tops off of lower frequencies, usually causing an unpleasant form of distortion—so some degree of judgement is in order here to find a balance between effective limiting and this type of clipping. Fortunately, most manufacturers today design their units in such a way as to eliminate this type of distortion no matter what setting is used.

For compression of vocal and other instrumental sounds, more moderate attack and release times are usually most appropriate. Good judgement needs to be exercised here as well. Generally, the slower release time tends to be most important, providing for a generally smoother program dynamics and helping to avoid the "pumping" effect. *Too* slow a release time, though, can cause the unit to linger excessively long before it is completely disengaged. This can have the effect of continuing to reduce moderate-level passages following a strong surge of intensity. Too slow an attack time can fail to engage the signal quickly enough to be completely effective, and might also sound a bit unnatural.

Some manufacturers provide for a gradual transition into the gain-reduction range. This feature was first marketed by DBX, Inc. as "Over-easy" compression, and avoids a sudden onset of compression—particularly helpful when a relatively high compression or limiting ratio is used.

Most manufacturers provide additional jacks to allow for a "control loop". These jacks give access to the detector circuit which engages the compressor/limiter (in some cases this might be one jack with a TRS configuration introduced in the previous chapter). This feature, among other possibilities, allows insertion of an outboard EQ which can be used to alter the frequency ranges which reach the threshold first. As an example, if insufficient high-frequency limiting is occurring in a given application, the upper EQ sliders of the control-loop EQ can be boosted to "tell" the limiter to respond more readily to the highs.

Fig. 8.1. Compressor-limiter, gain reduction characteristics.
Graphed in "A" are gain reduction ratios of 4-1, 8-1 and 20-1. A ratio between 2-1 and 4-1 is typical in compressing voices and musical instruments. The 8-1 and higher ratios would generally fall under the category of limiting for protection of speaker components and/or elimination of amplifier clipping. In casual conversation in the field, though, the term "limiter" is sometimes used to describe a unit which accomplishes both compression and limiting as described here.
(B) Using two stages of "soft compression" in series is one of several methods to reduce wide level fluctuations subtly, while keeping a stronger "cap" on signal level at its highest.

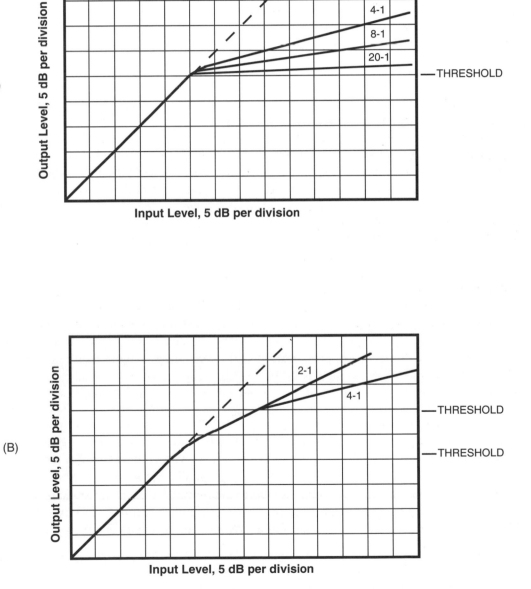

De-esser cricuits are designed with an internal control loop—usually involving a bandpass filter which causes only the extreme high frequencies to engage the gain reduction circuit, independently of the low, low-mid and high-mid frequencies. The purpose of this type of unit is to allow a boost of the high frequencies to increase the "zip" or "sizzle" of a vocal (or instrumental) sound, without radical amounts of high-frequency energy being included in the mix—particularly with the "s" sound.

A brief additional note: The "ideal" compressor/limiter would operate fairly independently with respect to each frequency in a program. In practice, the VCA's ("voltage-controlled amplifiers", the control circuit in the design) affect frequency ranges other than the ones which are reaching the threshold. So, as an example, a vocal signal pushing above the threshold can "stomp on" or "push down" the rest of the mix, perhaps including for-example some of the low end of the drums and bass guitar. This points to the advantage of using separate compressor/limiters on key components of a musical mix, discussed in Chapter 13.

Multi-band compressor/limiters provide another way of separating the action of compression upon different aspects of a musical mix. This type of unit breaks the spectrum into segments—not unlike a crossover—and allows them to be limited separately. The unit then recombines the separate bands into a full-range output.

b) Noise Gates and Downward Expanders.

At the low range of a sound source's or system's dynamic range, the main concern tends to be the amount of noise which is present. In many cases it is an advantage to eliminate hiss or hum from a stage amplifier, ambient noise or "crosstalk" from the stage or platform environment, or any other kind of background or system noise. *The function of a **noise gate** or **downward expander** is to reduce the amount of gain below a certain threshold*, thus reducing or eliminating the noise when there is no program signal, but allowing the desired signal to pass when it presents itself as a sufficiently strong signal.

The difference between a downward expander and a noise gate is similar to that between a compressor and a limiter. The main difference is in the ratio of gain reduction beyond the threshold, in this case below the threshold, rather than above. Often in the case of a noise gate the ratio is infinite or nearly infinite, acting more like an on/off switch. Thus, a true hard-and-fast noise gate is designed to turn off the signal entirely when signal level is below the threshold. A downward expander is designed to reduce the signal by a much lower proportion (ratio) when the signal level falls below the threshold—so such a unit is capable of serving as a "soft" noise gate. Any noise gate with adjustable attack/release parameters, however, is capable of being adjusted to function in a way which sounds similar to a downward expander, by virtue of being able to reduce the quickness of the "ons" and "offs".

"Attack" and "release" (release is sometimes called "hold") settings in this type of unit function similarly to the same functions on a compressor/limiter. As with compressor/limiters, the attack-time determines how quickly the unit will respond to a signal which reaches or exceeds the threshold. The release-time setting determines how long the unit remains engaged after the signal recedes below the threshold. Excessively high threshold settings with a noise gate or downward expander can cause a "jumping" or "pumping" of the signal, as the unit engages and disengages during the quieter portions of the program dynamics.

A common and very useful application for noise gates is in systems with multiple microphones used for voice. Gating each microphone individually allows substantially more gain-before-feedback than would be allowed without gating. (With two mics, this would be 3dB more; with four mics, 6dB more; with eight mics, 9dB more, etc.)

Fig. 8.2. Typical action of a compressor to reduce wide dynamic variations.
Recall from Chapter 3 that as long as the relative intensity of the "edge" frequencies is left unaffected, a gain reduction unit can keep an individual signal within bounds, without unduly sacrificing its perceived intensity. Compressors can allow the engineer some degree of freedom from worrying constantly about any particular voice or instrument unexpectedly "jumping out in front of" the rest of the musical mix. Where we run into a stickier issue is when one compressor is used on an entire mix. When budget allows, one compressor should be used for at least each category of voice/instrument, e.g., drums, electronic keyboards, guitars, background voices, etc. (this of course assumes submasters are available).

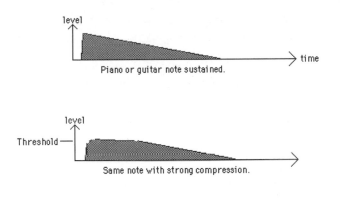

Fig. 8.3. The effect of a noise-gate on output gain.

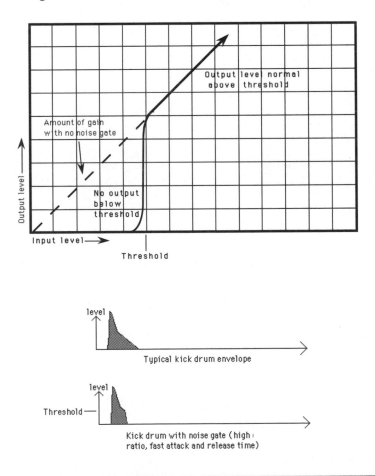

Fig. 8.4. Commercial examples of noise gates.
(A) Symetrix 564-E 4-channel Expander/Gate (courtesy Symetrix).
(B) BSS DPR-504 4-channel noise gate (courtesy AKG Acoustics).

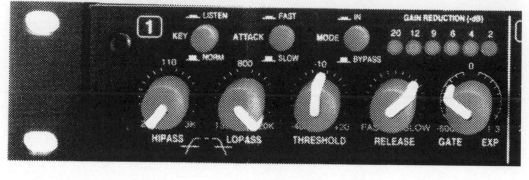

(A)

One of four channels is shown here. In this instance the control on far right chooses between a subtle downward expansion or a comparatively stronger gating action, depending on which direction it is rotated. The farther to the left this knob is set, the greater the gain reduction whenever the input-signal strength falls below the chosen threshold. Setting this knob to the right of 0 would reduce gain not by a set amount, but instead in expanded proportion to how far the input signal falls below the threshold.

Note the keying filter on this type of unit. This function is adjusted with the hi-pass and lo-pass controls. This allows us to tune in a relatively specific frequency range to trigger the gate, usually eliminating the need for a separate control loop. For example, the pedal beater sound of a kick drum (typically from about 1k-4k) could be used to trigger the gate for the kick drum channel, reducing the likelihood that cross leakage from other onstage sounds would inadvertantly cause the gate to open. The "Key listen" function would allow us to listen to the range into which we are attempting to tune. Obviously this "listen" function should be used only during a soundcheck, and should be returned to the "normal" position for actual operation.

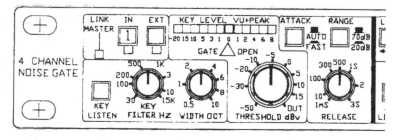

(B)

One of four channels is shown. Here the gain reduction "range" below the chosen threshold is set by a simple switch (-20dB or -70dB). This amounts to a choice between relatively subtle gating, e.g., for reduction of pickup of background noise for vocal or musical instrument mics, and relatively strong gating (-70dB), as might be used for drum channels. The keying function in this unit is a tunable filter with a bandwidth adjustment, another method of accomplishing the same goal as the keying filter in "A" above. The "link master" allows the channel to be linked to the adjacent channel for stereo use.

Gating of drum channels is another common and extremely helpful application. This can greatly assist in "tightening-up" the sound of a drum kit by removing the ringing sustain after a drum is struck.

If used for a mixed program, a downward expander with a modest downward expansion ("DEX") ratio (say 3-to-1 or 4-to-1) and relatively slow attack and release times can assist in taming system hiss and background stage noise in between speeches and songs in an event. A higher threshold setting would be possible here, since this approach does not involve the relatively abrupt starts and stops that are characteristic of a simple noise gate. The optimum insertion point in the signal flow for this type of application would usually be immediately before the crossover input.

Perhaps obviously, when the unwanted noise is of a level approaching or equalling the lowest level of the desired signal, there is a bit of a conflict. A relatively low DEX ratio with a reasonably slow attack and release rate can be helpful here. Another technique which can be of assistance here is the insertion of an EQ in a control loop, described below.

Similarly to compressor/limiters, manufacturers of DEX's and noise gates usually provide access to the detector circuit. This type of patch, known as a "control loop", allows the use of a different signal source to trigger the gate. The control loop also allows downward expansion to be frequency dependent, allowing, for example, noise with emphasis in different frequency ranges than the strongest ranges of the desired signal, to be somewhat "separated out" from one-another. This approach would involve inserting an EQ as illustrated in Chapter 13 (Fig. 13.23), and cutting the main ranges of emphasis of the noise (for example, the high frequency "rushing" sound sometimes encountered with guitar processing systems that are using a high degree of signal compression) while boosting the frequency ranges where the instrument itself tends to be stronger.

c) Expanders.

The function of an expander is the opposite of that of a compressor.

True full-range expanders (not to be confused with downward expanders as described in the previous section, which only perform gain reduction) are seldom used in live sound reinforcement. Their usual purpose is in decoding specially compressed signals for the purpose of noise reduction in taping systems and wireless microphone systems (called "companding"). In many wireless systems, companding serves to compress the dynamics into a smaller overall range to accomodate the limits of the transmitter/receiver circuits, then retreive the full dynamic range at the receiver end.

An expander can be used to bring out some of the missing dynamics in compressed recorded programs, but the key here is moderation. An expansion ratio of 1.3-to-1 would be a typical ratio used to bring stronger dynamic expression to a recorded program being played back. A ratio of 1.5-to-1 would be a very strong ratio. This degree of expansion, and anything beyond it, would usually be in serious risk of causing unpleasant and unnatural dynamics, as a result of radically different expansion charactersitics than were used at the original compression stage. (These would be a result of having different frequency-dependent compression and expansion, as well as the use of different compression characteristics for different components of the mix, e.g., for drums as compared to vocals, etc.)

The attack and release time settings, if provided by the manufacturer, can assist in bringing percussive sounds a bit more out-front in a recorded program. Here, a relatively fast attack and release would be used. A control loop EQ can further assist in determining which drum ranges are most emphasized. As an example, boosting 100Hz and below would tend to emphasize the kick drum by causing its lower ranges to reach the expansion threshold first (careful here—if , for example, the bass guitar is engaged at the threshold, it would also jump out and may sound quite unnatural). Overall, this type of operation is fairly obscure—it should be done *very cautiously* and with only a very slight expansion ratio. Most recorded programs are just fine as they are and are usually best left alone.

A repeat caution is in order here: some manufacturers use the term "expander" to refer to what is described in the previous section as a "downward expander". This is a very important difference, because a downward expander causes expansion *only below* the threshold, acting similarly to a noise gate. Other expanders provide expansion throughout the whole dynamic range, in which case the threshold setting, if provided, is fairly arbitrary (i.e., very flexible—somewhere in the middle of the program's dynamic range is usually recommended). Because of these differences in expander designs it is important to know the specifications of the unit in use, to avoid the potential for an inappropriate purchase and/or a very nasty surprise (or even damage to the speaker system).

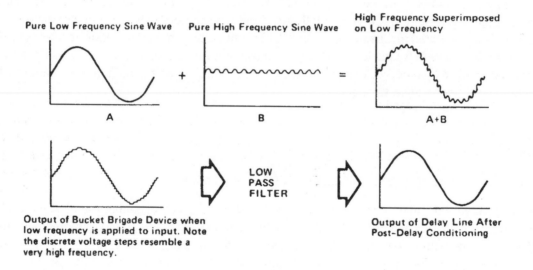

Fig. 8.5. Description of a digital-to-analog converter (DAC).
(Courtesy Yamaha Corp.)
See section "D" of this chapter for a basic description of digital effects units.

d) Delay/Echo and Reverb Units.

The basic principle of a delay and/or reverb unit is to store a copy of the input signal for a certain length of time, then reproduce the signal (or a modified version of it) as needed. The manner in which this is done differs according to the purpose(s) for which the unit is designed.

A *delay* unit will, in essence, store a signal and return a copy of it to its output at specific time intervals, the length of which are determined by the operator. From a design standpoint, there are currently three basic ways of accomplishing this, normally referred to as *tape-delay, analog delay* and *digital delay lines* (*DDL* 's for short). A description of the general design idea of each of these can be found farther below in this section.

Delay units normally serve one of two basic purposes. One type of delay system serves the need to reproduce a signal for loudspeaker clusters farther into an audience, so the output of these clusters is timed with the arrival of the sound coming from the primary clusters at the stage or platform (this signal is of-course fed to the power amplifiers for the supplementary clusters). Today, this type of system is exclusively of the digital design—units are marketed by a number of companies specifically for this purpose. The more common purpose of a delay system is to provide an audio effect. This type of unit is manufactured and marketed in both analog and digital designs (tape-delay units are essentially an outdated design, having been replaced since the late 1970's by the more compact and effective analog and digital units). For sound reinforcement purposes the digital format is fairly standard, and generally much more versatile.

A delay unit for effects use allows the operator to adjust the number of repeats, or more specifically, the degree of their decay beyond the first repeat. This control is usually labeled "feedback", since it controls the amount of delay signal which—within the unit—is fed back to be delayed again, thus determining the amount of repeats. Each successive repeat is of-course lower in intensity than the previous one. However, an excessively high setting of this control usually results in an effect which, as it develops, increasingly becomes an uncontrolled feedback loop—an occasionally interesting, but usually undesirable, effect. Many digital units provide a "hold" or "∞ repeat" switch which allows repeats to be heard ad-nausium until the operator disengages the switch. Joking aside, this feature can occasionally be useful in allowing the operator to end the repeating effect when desired, by reducing the aux-return level on the mixer.

Typical digital units provide programmable delay-time presets which can be recalled on demand. Most digital delay units also have an additional oscillator intended to provide the "flanging" effect described in the following section of this chapter.

One particularly helpful design-approach seems to deserve mention here. Several units to-date have incorporated a feature which allows a standard foot-pedal to be used to set the delay time. Here the unit monitors the interval between successive "taps" on the pedal, eliminating the need to "zero in" on the desired delay time with the manual controls on the face of the unit. This approach can be very useful for an operator in setting delay times while occupied with other setting changes commonly required in the transition from one song to another.

A *reverb* unit is designed to return the input signal numerous times, at very closely spaced intervals. Originally, this was specifically intended to approximate the kind of reverberation heard in very reflective environments, to add some degree of richness, subtle sustain and apparent spacial depth for musical voices and instruments. Today, as most readers should be aware, many off-beat and sometimes almost spectacular variations of this same principle are available.

Most of the early reverb devices designed for sound reinforcement purposes used one or more internal springs, an approach still occasionally found today. Generically known as a *spring reverb*, this approach uses a transducer at both the input and output stage, to convert the electronic signal into mechanical vibrations in the spring, and then back again into an electrical output at the other end of the spring. The sensor at the output end picks up reflections of the signal from one end of the spring(s) to the other. This type of unit certainly has the advantage of being very inexpensive. But, besides having a certain readily recognizable artificial sound, these units tend to be inflexible in adjusting the length of the reverb and other characteristics that are important in varying the character of the reverb sound. (Several high-quality spring-type reverb units used mechanical methods for varying the length of the decay, providing a relatively limited degree of flexibility.) Other obstacles with this type of unit include mechanical pickup of vibrations and a very limited ability to handle strong transients from percussive instruments.

With the digital format briefly described below, very high quality and realistic reverberation effects are possible. As well, digital reverb units allow a number of additional reverb-type effects not found in any natural environment. Examples of this are "gated" reverb, which proceeds for a given amount of time, then fairly suddenly "shuts off", and reverse reverb, which *increases* in intensity, then fairly suddenly stops.

The parameters of control afforded by digital reverb units can vary significantly from one design to another. A number of preset reverb programs are included with almost all commercial units, with control over the length of the reverb decay. Presets can be handy because they do not require additional setup time prior-to or during an event. Typically, a high quality digital reverb unit will enable the operator to create and store customized programs. A variable pre-delay before the onset of the reverb sound is another useful feature often provided. Some units allow a degree of control over the timing and intensity of the early stronger echoes after the initial signal. Other adjustable paramaters include variable frequency low-pass (high-cut) and high-pass (low-cut) filters, and perhaps programmable EQ settings for the reverb sound. Creative use of reverb effects is discussed in Chapter 17.

Here is a brief description of the basic design methods used in delay units. *Tape-delay* units use a continuous-loop tape with two heads, a recording head and one or more playback heads. The heads are spaced so that the playback occurs a certain interval after the input signal is recorded on the tape. To allow control over the delay time, some designs allow the spacing between the heads to be varied; other designs allow the tape speed to be varied as well.

Among more contemporary designs, the analog and digital approaches prevail, with the digital delay being the standard for sound reinforcement (analog designs at this writing are marketed primarily for musical instrument effects). Both approaches break the input waveform down into thousands of individual samples per second.

In ***analog delay*** units, usually in the range of 25,000-or-so samples-per-second of the input signal are taken. The numerous samples, represented within the unit as individual voltage values, are passed from one storage stage to another in what is known as an electronic "bucket-brigade device", or "BBD". The variable delay-time control of the unit affects how quickly the signal is passed through the BBD. The tiny steps in the waveform (somewhat like stairs on a graph of the waveform) end up being the equivalent of very-high-frequency square waves, so these must be smoothed out by using a very steep low-pass (high-cut) filter.

Fig. 8.6. Commercial example of a DDL primarily designed for effects purposes.
(Courtesy Roland Corp.)

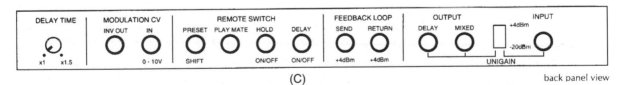

(A)

The SDE-1000, the original programmable DDL by this manufacturer, is a good example of a first generation programmable unit. This unit involves programmable presets for delay time, feedback (simply on/off), phase reverse (on/off) and modulation (also simply on/off). The remainder of the controls are adjusted with rotary pots on the face panel of the unit. The "feedback" setting adjusts the number of repeats. The modulation settings are intended for "flanging" and "chorusing" effects with very short delay times. For "flanging" the delay time would normally be between .005 and .015 sec. (5 to 15 milliseconds) with strong "depth" setting. For "chorusing" the delay time would most often be between .020 and .050 sec., with relatively slight "depth" setting.

(B)

The SDE-3000 is at this writing the newest descendant of the unit in "A". Note that all of the functions are programmable. The primary advantage of this approach in live sound is that customized presets can be called upon (choice of 8 changable presets available in the unit itself) simply by choosing among #'s 1 through 4 and Bank A or B. The only disadvantage here is that it often takes a bit longer to change the feedback setting, and/or the modulation settings for various chorusing and flanging effects when they are not already programmed into a preset (i.e., when it needs to be done on-the-spot on a song-to-song basis). (Many live engineers still prefer the "old-fashioned knob", particularly for the "feedback" setting. Future generation production units will possibly improve on this limitation, perhaps allowing for both preset *and* manual adjustment.) Unlike the recording studio, the flanging and "phase shifting" effects are seldom needed for live sound reinforcement, most often being accomplished by the individual musician with his/her onstage equipment.

(C)   back panel view

Back panel view of the SDE-3000. For sound reinforcement use, the "delay" output would be used for an effects loop; the "mixed" output would be ignored. The level setting for a typical sound reinforcement system (labeled "unigain") would most often be +4 dBm. The "playmate" function is designed for a proprietary footswitch which allows the delay time to be reset from song to song, simply by tapping in the appropriate tempo with the music being handled. The importance of effectively synchronizing an echo time is further discussed in Chapter 17. On this particular unit the additional delay-time setting on the rear panel allows the maximum delay time to be increased when necessary.

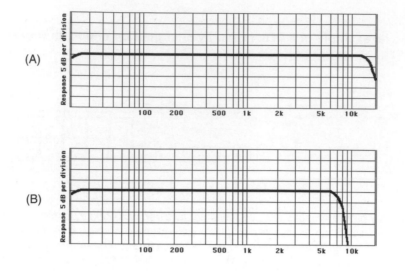

Fig. 8.7. Typical requency response limitation when using a (x2) delay-time setting.
A highly useful function found on many delay units allows the delay-time setting to be increased by
a factor of 2 with a simple switch. (Typical use of this function is discussed in Chapter 17.) Shown
in "A" is a typical response curve of a delay unit output with standard settings. When the "x2"
function is engaged, the available digital memory is stretched, and the resulting frequency response is limited to about one octave less, as in "B". For effects use this is not ordinarily a
problem, though such a response curve as "B" would be unacceptable for feeding a delayed
cluster as in Chapter 12 and 14. High quality DDL's are manufactured specifically for the purpose
of feeding delayed speakers, without the various accessories normally associated with use as an
effects unit.

With *digital delay (DDL)* units, usually on the order of 30,000 to 50,000 samples per second are
taken of the input waveform. An analog-to-digital converter ("ADC") converts each sample to a
numerical value, which enters the digital memory system within the unit. Like a digital version of a BBD
involving thousands of successive stages in the memory, the samples are passed from one stage to
another, at a speed determined by the delay-time setting. At the final stage, the sample values enter a
digital-to-analog converter ("DAC") and are passed to the output stage of the unit.

Some performers (as of this writing) still prefer the sound of analog delays, since the analog units
generally tend to sound somewhat warmer. This appears to be mainly because analog delays are usually
designed without strong high-frequency response—mostly a result of their relatively slow sampling rate.
Similar warmth can, in practice, be readily achieved with digital delays with appropriate equalization
to take the high-frequency "edge" off of the delayed sound.

Today, the low cost of digital processing systems, the accuracy of their delayed signal, as well as
the increased flexibility of parameters of DDLs, has allowed the digital delay to overwhelmingly
predominate as the industry standard for sound reinforcement.

Digital reverb units use similar technology to that of DDLs, but with very substantially more
complex programs which read the stored waveforms and send the successive repeats (representative of
the "reverberations") to the DAC numerous times per second. Prior to reaching the DAC, the reverb
"reflections" are selectively altered in terms of their energy distribution (frequency content) and their
intensity. (Special programs called "algorithms" determine the patterns of these alterations, which are

arranged in such a way as to convincingly provide the reverberation effect. In a basic reverb program, each closely spaced repeat is slightly lower in intensity than the previous one, and has slightly less high frequencies, since in the majority of natural environments, the high frequencies normally decay the most quickly.

Fig. 8.8. Commercial examples of digital reverb units. (Courtesy Yamaha Corp.)

(A)

Face plate layout for the SPX-1000. This unit is a direct descendant of the classic SPX-90. Here, as is typical of many newer digital effects designs, the "recall" function activates the setting which is seen in the readout window. This allows a new setting to be created while the unit is still in operation, then "recalled" at the moment the new setting is actually needed. A digital high-pass and low-pass filter is an additional function in this type of unit, allowing the reverb sound to be tailored, for example, to eliminate excessive low frequency cluttering of the reverb sound. This can be of extremely important assistance in fine tuning a typical mix, since the reverb is often not desired throughout the entire frequency range.

(B)

Yamaha REV-5, a direct descendant of the classic REV-7, both of which have been staples on the professional concert tour. Aside from somewhat higher quality processing, conspicuous functions here include a full numerical keypad for preset select, a timesaver when changing preset rpograms. Note the optional "quick pick" presets (labeled REV1 through REV4). These allow the user to choose, from among the 99 presets, the ones which are likely to be needed most, then recall any of them as necessary with a touch of a single button. Note also the ability to call up several major parameters ("level", "initial delay", "1st reflection", etc.) with a touch of the appropriate button, rather than scrolling through all of the parameters. This particular unit also provides additional onboard EQ capability.

e) Aural exciters.

A useful and very intriguing type of signal modification is accomplished by circuitry currently under patent by Aphex Systems, Ltd. With this proprietary circuitry the signal is modified in such a way as to achieve an increase in apparent loudness in the high frequencies well beyond what would be measurable by any electronic measuring devices currently available. In addition to an increase in apparent loudness through the selected HF range, the subjective effect is normally heard as an increase in "zip", "bite" and/or "sizzle".

The "Aphex", as these units are casually referred to in the field, involves a variable high pass filter, which within the unit "splits off" frequencies above a given selected point in the spectrum, most often between about 2k and 10k or so. (The frequency of the high-pass filter is determined by the setting on the control labeled "tune" on the faceplate.) The selected high frequency range is passed through a harmonics generator, then recombined with the "main" signal as in Fig. 8.9. Continuing refinements in the original patented circuitry have included sensing circuits designed to track level changes, and respond to increases in overall signal level with equivalent increases in the output of the harmonics generator. (At its most basic, this approach could be considered a "distortion box" which only affects the very high frequencies. But in fact the circuitry is somewhat more complex, accentuating primarily the even-numbered harmonics of the frequencies passed through the harmonics generator and shifting their phase relationship by a certain amount.)

The exact mechanism in the hearing process that accounts for the apparent increase in loudness beyond what is measurable as amplifier output or loudspeaker output is not fully understood today—it is basically related to the way the hearing process perceives frequencies combined in certain multiple phase relationships. But suffice it to say that this can be useful in conserving very high frequency power capability of compression drivers as described in the following chapter, and when used in moderation is regarded as a pleasant effect by the vast majority of people. (The use of Aphex units has become widespread practice in the recording industry.)

Fig. 8.9

AURAL EXCITER BLOCK DIAGRAM

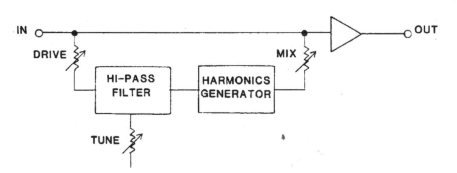

CHAPTER 9

SPEAKERS AND CROSSOVERS

Loudspeakers capable of delivering a clear and potent sound have been on the market for at least a few decades as of this writing, and the advancements still continue to pour forth. As the "business end" of the system, the loudspeakers are of-course also responsible for delivering the output sound over a pattern which (ideally) will reach most, or all, of the audience with reasonably consistent quality. Only in recent years—with the advent of readily usable powerful computers—have midrange and high-frequency components been designed which can do this with precision through most-or-all of their range. Discussed later in this chapter, these newer designs have greatly aided the goals of sound reinforcement.

a) Basic Design.

Speaker components can be classified under two basic design approaches: direct radiators and acoustic horns, or some combination of the two. Though loudpeaker designs can take on an extremely wide variety of forms, nearly all can be described as utilizing one, or both, of these basic approaches.

All speaker components involve a ***driver***, which accomplishes the actual transduction of electrical signals into sound waves. A ***direct radiator*** uses a relatively large vibrating element—usually a conventional piston-action, cone/voice coil speaker assembly (as in Fig. 9.1). The rear side of the driver is coupled with an enclosed or semi-enclosed cabinet that plays an integral role in properly developing the sound waves.

A ***horn/driver*** assembly involves the use of a driver with usually a comparatively small vibrating element, operating in tandem with an appropriately designed horn, as depicted in Fig. 9.3. (In more casual conversation out in the field, such an assembly is usually referred to simply as a "horn"—which presumes an understanding that a driver is also involved.) The advantages of a horn include increased efficiency of conversion from electrical to acoustical energy, and better potential control of the directional characteristics of the output sound.

*In both horn designs and enclosure designs there is a basic relationship between the driver and its horn or enclosure, based on the principle of acoustic **loading** .* (Technically, the currently popular use of the term "loading", as in "unloaded speaker cabinet" or "cabinet loaded with Brand X speaker" is a widespread mistake—albeit an understandable one.) Usually, in about the lower two-thirds or so of a driver's intended frequency range, the speaker cone or diaphram requires an extra amount of acoustical impedance (or load) to keep its motion "under control". A well designed direct radiator enclosure balances the mechanical characteristics of the speaker with the air volume within the enclosure, in order to produce a reasonably smooth frequency response curve throughout its range. A well designed horn/ driver assembly provides a similarly balanced acoustic impedance for the driver diaphram throughout its designated range. The horn also serves to properly expand the waves, which is further explained in the sections on "Basic Horns" and "Mid/High Horn Designs".

Practical loudspeaker component design involves some necessary compromises among a number of factors: dispersion and pattern control, frequency range of the components, size, smoothness of frequency response curves, maximum output, efficiency, and of-course, cost. As one example, the wider the bandwidth a component is asked to handle, the more the frequency response throughout its designated pattern will tend to develop irregularities, and the more difficult it becomes to maintain a consistent directional pattern. For a second example, the smaller a component needs to be, the more its low frequency response and effective directional pattern control will tend to be compromised. As another perhaps-obvious example, the clearer, more powerful and consistently dispersed the output of a horn/driver combination is, the more financially expensive it tends to be.

Generally, most of the audio spectrum can be fairly well covered, with reasonably consistent directional dispersion, by three properly-designed-and-chosen components. Four-way and five-way systems today tend to be offshoots of this basic approach An example of this is a typical 3-way system with a supplementary subwoofer as shown later in this chapter. This approach in high-output systems is currently a fairly standard one in the industry.

Compact 2-way and 3-way cabinets usually have directional patterns which often make them most appropriate for "near-field" applications (i.e., relatively close up).

Fig. 9.1

Typical compact 2-way enclosure with direct radiator and high-frequency horn.

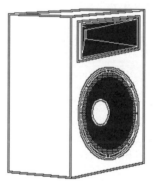

A well-designed unit of this basic type can be highly useful in reinforcement of voice and musical instruments (not including low-bass and low-pitched drums) for small-to-modest-size audiences, as well as for many "sidefill" stage-monitor applications. The optimal crossover frequency for such a unit would depend strongly on the driver designs as well as upon a number of other factors discussed in this chapter, and might be as low as 500 Hz or as high as 4 kHz or so.

b) Basic Enclosures.

The most essential reason for having an enclosure of some kind surrounding the back of a driver is that in all but the highest frequencies of its particular operating range, the rear energy bends right around the speaker and largely cancels out (destructively interferes with) the energy emanating from the front. (For readers who as yet do not have a grasp of why it is that this happens, the explanation in the "Pattern Control" section of this chapter may be helpful.) This is perhaps the most basic idea relating to speaker enclosure design, in which the basic sealed enclosure is called an *infinite baffle*. Originally, in the very early development of loudspeakers, back radiation from the speaker was isolated from the front radiation by the use of a simple baffle, or plate, with the speaker mounted in the center. The enclosure, from this standpoint, serves as a baffle infinitely high and wide, since no back radiation crosses over the boundaries of the box to interfere with the front radiation—thus the term "infinite" baffle. Today, this type of box is most often simply called a *sealed enclosure* .

Beyond this, as mentioned, *the limited size of the enclosure also serves to help keep the driver from flopping out of control at lower frequencies* (due to the amount of acoustical load). With the enclosure assisting in this way, it is mechanically much more reasonable to design drivers to cover a reasonably broad range with reasonable efficiency. Over the years a fairly standard method has evolved for computing the size of the enclosure needed to provide frequency response down to a given range, with a given driver size and specification.

It is possible to reduce the enclosure size and still gain extra low frequency response by adding a **vent** or **port** to the enclosure. There is a tradeoff, though. *Below the extra low frequency range gained by the port (Fig. 9.2) the frequency response drops off radically*, and the speaker cone's excursion increases dramatically. When the speaker is asked to reproduce significant amounts of energy below the resonant frequency, the speaker "unloads" and begins to be drastically more inclined to push beyond its normal excursion limits, which at best sounds bad, and at worst risks driver failure (i.e., a blown speaker).

A port can be designed to bring the usable response of the enclosure lower yet with the use of a tube, or **duct**, which further lowers the resonant frequency of the air mass in the enclosure—this is pretty-much standard procedure today. More complicated internal baffles can further reduce the size of the enclosure,

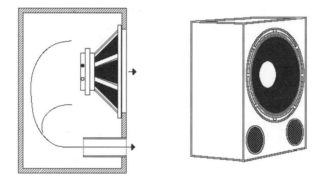

Fig. 9.2 Ported (ducted) enclosure. In the half-octave or-so around the "resonant frequency" of the enclosure, back energy serves to reinforce front radiation in a well designed unit. Here the "resonance" is used to compensate for the reduced response in the low frequencies. Because cone motion at the resonant frequency is relatively slight compared to port output, and because of a very slight delay in the port output, cancellation does not occur. Below the resonant frequency, though, the cone and port output are in more-or-less opposite phase, so they tend to cancel and response drops off radically, along with the danger of cone overexcursion. (Do not attempt to compensate for this dropoff with an EQ. With any ported design, the speaker should not be asked to reproduce any substantial amount of sound below the point at which response drops off. If an EQ is used to increase the low frequency response, it should be boosted only at or above the port's "resonance". Frequencies below port resonance should generally be cut with an EQ or, ideally, a high pass (i.e. "low cut") filter.)

Below: Typical response curves for sealed and ported enclosures of equivalent size.

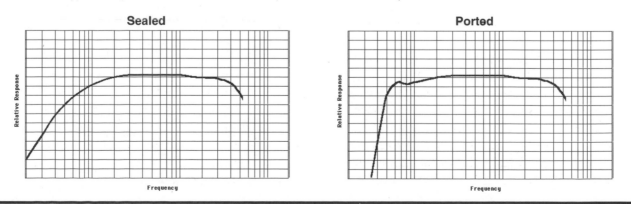

while still allowing the rear of the speaker to "see" a much larger enclosure and behave accordingly.

A number of today's more high-level processor-controlled systems take a different approach to achieve relative compactness, compensating with increased response at the processor stage—really a form of equalization. (The tradeoff is that significantly more power is required to produce the same output level in the lower frequencies. But it allows the size of the enclosure to be reduced very substantially.)

Certainly the capabilities of the driver (briefly discussed later) are a major factor in the quality and quantity of the sound, as is the construction of the enclosure. The primary characteristic of a good enclosure, beyond its basic design, is its sturdiness. A good quality speaker enclosure needs to remain rigid, with little or no flex in the enclosure walls or looseness in the joints. Flexing of the walls creates unneessary resonances, reduces efficiency and maximum output, degrades the principle of the infinite baffle, and can also degrade transient response (the enclosure keeps vibrating briefly after the driver has stopped moving).

c) Basic Horns.

Horns are useful for two basic reasons: (1) they are generally more efficient than direct radiators, and (2) they afford better control of the directional pattern of the output sound, particularly in the mids and highs.

The basic function of the horn is to allow the vibrating element (driver diaphram or cone) to be much smaller and move within a smaller excursion—allowing a more accurate reproduction of the waveform, while still providing substantial output. A well designed horn provides a form of broad-band "resonance" (to greatly stretch the normal use of the term), thus amplifying the sound over a broad frequency range.

A horn provides a form of "impedance matching". It is designed to present a relatively high acoustical impedance to the driver. A horn serves to develop a wave of relatively high pressure, low air particle movement (the equivalent of higher voltage/lower "current"), into a wave of greater volume at the mouth of the horn where it encounters the normal acoustical impedance in the open air. This is somewhat comparable to what an electrical transformer does. (In other words, by comparison to a horn loaded driver, *the direct radiator has to move more—i.e., over a greater excursion range—to cause a certain amount of volume. The horn-loaded driver moves less, but pushes and pulls harder to do it.* The horn does the transforming.)

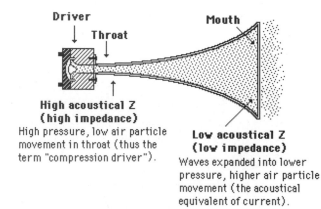

Driver
Throat
Mouth

**High acoustical Z
(high impedance)**
High pressure, low air particle movement in throat (thus the term "compression driver").

**Low acoustical Z
(low impedance)**
Waves expanded into lower pressure, higher air particle movement (the acoustical equivalent of current).

Fig. 9.3. Typical high frequency horn: side cutaway. The primary purpose of a horn is to allow the driver's vibrating element (diaphram) to move over a smaller distance (excursion), allowing an increase in efficiency and accuracy of sound reproduction. An almost equally important reason for the use of a horn is that it can be designed to control the directional pattern of the output sound far more effecitvely than any arrangement of direct radiators.

Specific factors such as driver size, throat size, mouth size and expansion rate (flare rate) determine the basic frequency-related characteristics of the horn. Certainly the driver has at least as important an influence on the sound as does the horn, since they work as a team. There are other factors as well, discussed later in the section on "More on Mid and High Freq. Horns"

Fig. 9.8-B illustrates a typical horn design intended for use in the mids. Some midrange horn designs make use of cone drivers, while other designs utilize midrange compression drivers.

d) Low Frequency Horns.

Low-frequency horns ideally need to be extremely large, so practical considerations normally require some kind of compromise for high-level reproduction of the low end of the spectrum. Horns can be, and commonly are, folded to fit a given horn length into a smaller space. The effective higher-frequency (mid-bass) range of the unit is compromised as a result. For low frequency folded horns this compromise is not a serious disadvantage, since folded horns tend to be used in a comparatively narrow range—normally up to about 2 octaves (as compared to, for example, a traditional re-entrant paging horn, which does get used over a wide range higher up in the spectrum, without good sound quality).

Folded horns are shown in several different forms in Fig. 9.4. Three of the designs shown are commonly referred to as *"W-bins"*. In addition to limited frequency range, there is another compromise with folded horns, which is that the smoothness of frequency response often tends to suffer somewhat (published specs usually smooth out the wriggles in the curves). It is often accepted to be worth the price, though, in order to obtain the relatively compact size the "W" configuration allows.

The idea of a folded horn can be taken a step farther toward better efficiency and smoothness of the response curve, by using curved surfaces within the internal flare of the bass horn. This eliminates the "step transitions" of a conventional folded horn, but is also much more expensive to manufacture.

A variety of additional approaches are also used in order to achieve relative compactness or extra lower-frequency response in low frequency horns.

Low frequency horns, both straight and folded, are commonly supplemented with one or more ports, or other avenue of partial escape for the back radiation of the driver, in order to extend their low frequency response. Similarly to ported enclosures, the extension of low frequency response comes at the expense of a more severe dropoff of response below the "resonant frequency" of the ported air mass within the enclosure.

Fig. 9.5 shows three basic enclosure designs involving both a horn and one or more vents. An enclosure of this type is most often put to use as the low-frequency component of a 2-way system, or the low-mid, or mid-bass component of a 4-way system. The design in Fig. 9.5-A is sometimes referred to as a *horn/reflex* enclosure, "reflex" referring to the idea of using the back radiation of the driver to extend the low frequency response of a relatively very short horn. This approach (in 9.5-A) provides substantially more energy somewhat higher in the bass region than the designs shown in Fig. 9.5-B and 9.5-C (why this is so is discussed briefly in section K of this chapter). As with any enclosure, when one or more ports are included in the design, energy is increased around the "resonant" frequency range—but below this range, output capability drops off very radically and driver excursion increases dramatically.

Two common designs both popularly referred to as a *"scoop"* take on two slightly different forms. One involves a bent horn similar to the design in Fig. 9.7. The other is a direct radiator enclosure which couples the rear radiation to a fairly long folded horn in a (relatively) compact cabinet as in Fig. 9.4-D.

Among the more efficient and compact low-frequency horn designs using a standard cone/voice-coil driver, manufactured as of this writing is is somewhat similar to the design shown in Fig. 9.7, first widely marketed under the trade-name "Turbobass". This is a low frequency design with a bent horn which well balances the acoustical impedance of both the horn and the enclosed air mass behind it. The advantage of this basic approach is to allow a relatively small enclosure, while still producing excellent low-frequency response without the disadvantage of the quick dropoff in response which a port whould cause.

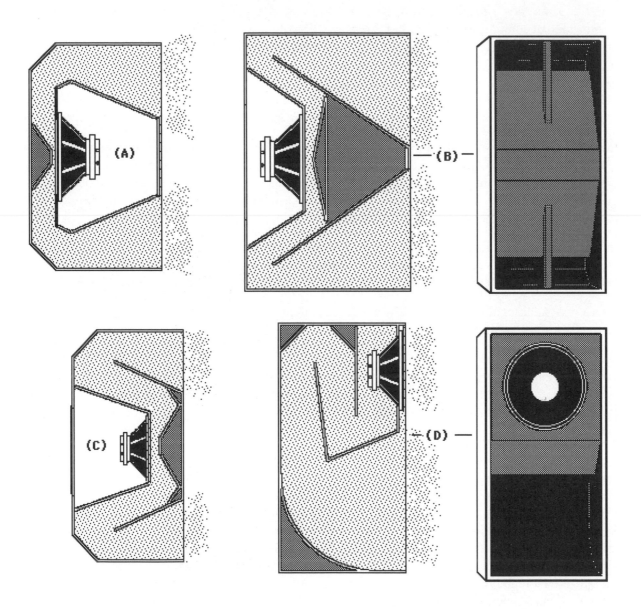

Fig. 9.4. Several classic designs of low frequency folded horns. Examples A, B, and C are commonly called "W-bins", though B and C truly fit this informal name. Example D, often referred to as a "scoop", combines the principle of a long folded horn (for very low frequency response) with that of a direct radiator (for extended response above 125 Hz or so).

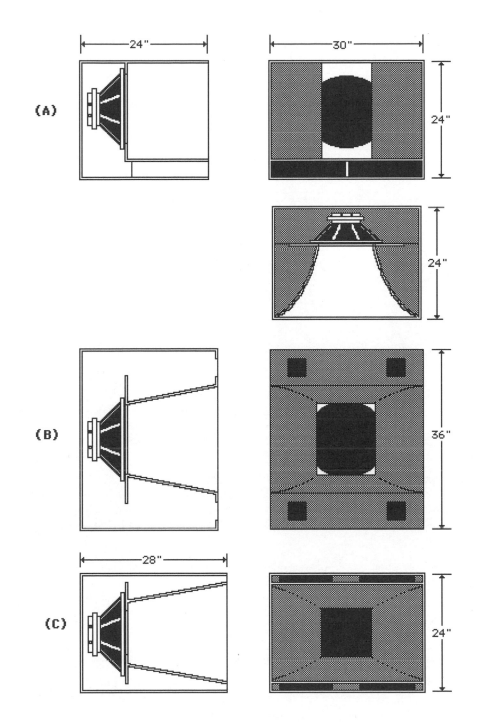

Fig. 9.5. Several classic ported low-frequency horn designs. (A) Altec 816 (mini-"Voice of the Theater"), dating back to the 1960's, and still often encountered out in the field; (B) JBL 4560, widely known as a "Perkins Bin"; (C) Forsythe (EAW) single 15".

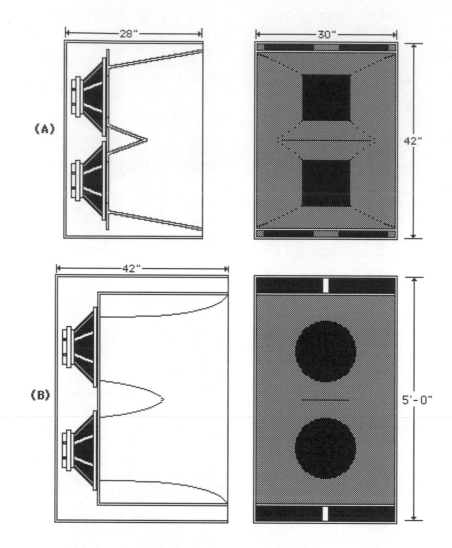

Fig. 9.6. Two examples of double-driver low/low-mid horns.
(A) Double 15" "Forsythe". This was among the first "portable" double-driver LF horns, widely marketed in the early 1970's. Previous much larger designs (such as the Altec A-4 and 815, and JBL 4550) were more suited for permanent installations, and similar large formats are still marketed today.

(B) Community "Boxer series" low-frequency unit. This particular unit accomodates either 15" or 18" drivers. The cabinet incorporates a fiberglass horn within a wooden enclosure. The horn itself gradually tapers from a round throat to a rectangular mouth, resulting in a substantial increase in efficiency for this type of design. The greater depth and lower flare rate extends response to a somewhat lower frequency in comparison to other designs of this type (see also Fig. 9.11).

Another highly effective and compact high-level approach, depicted in Fig. 9.33 and first marketed under the trade description "Manifold Technology", uses long folded paths within the enclosure, combined with "front" radiation. Since this design uses four drivers, it requires a significant amount of power amplifier capability to drive to its maximum potential. The reward, though, is big low end in a relatively compact size.

Certainly the most effective currently manufactured very-low-frequency design uses relatively standard, though well-designed low-freq. horns, "W" bins and sealed enclosures, adapted for a unique servo-driven driver—introduced in the section on "Other Approaches".

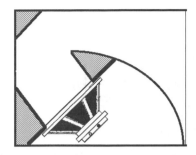

Fig. 9.7. "Bent" low frequency horns.
(Above) Cross section of a bent horn similar to the "Turbo-bass"® design. (Right) Another basic design sometimes referred to as a scoop, involving a shorter horn than the design shown in 9.4-D.

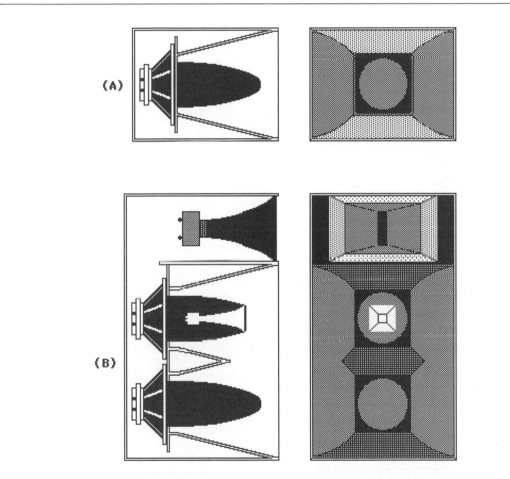

Fig. 9.8. Phasing "plugs". The phasing plug provides better coherence of the developing wavefront in the upper frequencies of a horn's designated operating range and better loading of the drivers. (A) Midrange horn with phasing plug (12"/300mm, 10"/250mm, and 8"/200mm are the most commonly used driver sizes). A potential tradeoff when used as illustrated here is somewhat narrower dispersion in the upper frequencies of the operating range. (B) Dual low/low-mid drivers with VHF unit in phasing plug. High-mid unit in the illustration is commonly included in this type of "full range" enclosure. This type of enclosure would generally involve an optional "subwoofer" to enhance the lows below its effective range. The subwoofer would generally take over below an 80-160 Hz crossover point, depending on the design. As excellent example of this approach is the Community RS-220/660/880 design (which has slightly different driver alignment than shown here.

e) Crossover Basics.

The frequency dividing network, or crossover, is a fundamentally important aspect of loudspeaker design and operation. As mentioned in Chapter 1, the crossover can take on two basic forms. Passive (high-level) crossovers are designed to operate at power amplifier output levels, and are often integrated into the design of speaker enclosures. (Check the manufacturer's specs—normally, if there are only one or two unlabeled jacks on a "full-range" enclosure with two or more components in it, it usually can be assumed that the passive crossover network is included in the design).

Active, or electronic (low-level) crossovers, are inserted in the signal path prior to the power amplifiers, with each of the outputs feeding separate power amplier channels. The choice between active or passive crossovers often comes down to the following: *Active crossovers are generally more efficient and flexible. In low-level or moderate-level systems, passive crossovers are generally less costly and easier to use.*

Compact full-range 2-way and 3-way speakers most often are marketed with built-in passive crossovers. Some provide the option to bypass the passive network and separately feed each of the drivers. The quality and power-handling capability of the passive crossover plays an important role in the overall sound. It is often possible to get a higher quality sound with modest-quality drivers and a high quality crossover more easily than the other way around (excellent drivers with a cheap crossover). As well, some passiver crossovers can saturate long before the power handling capabilities of the drivers themselves are reached. A passive crossover with very high power handling capability usually tends to be fairly large and heavy.

Ordinarily, to produce high levels of high-quality full-range sound, an active crossover and multiple power amplifiers are required. Systems can be designed so an active crossover handles every crossover point, or some of them.

In a high-output system, passive crossovers are generally most useful in the transition into the hi-freq. horn or supertweeter. In such a case (as in Fig. 1.7), the active crossover would be used for the low-to-midrange or low-to-lower-mid crossover point.

A crossover unit involves two or more filters, which determine the frequency ranges to be reproduced by each speaker component. Each crossover point involves both a low-pass and high-pass network which work together to confine to a particular range the signal sent to each output.

The idea of a crossover band which stops at a particular frequency, and simply doesn't allow anything beyond that frequency to pass, is often referred to as a "brick wall filter". Audio engineers though the years have had many a chuckle over the notion of the brick wall filter, a theoretical "ideal" unachievable in the real world—though some modern circuits have come amazingly close.

Fig. 9.9. Basic Crossover Characteristics.

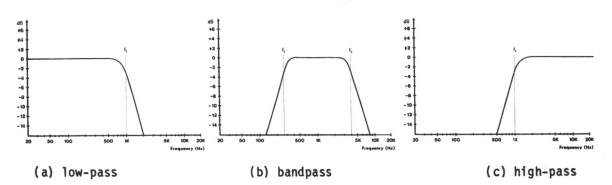

(a) low-pass   **(b) bandpass**   **(c) high-pass**

(Above: courtesy Ashly Audio) The three basic filter types above would correspond to low, mid and hi outputs of a 3-way crossover. The actual frequencies would vary from one system to another, depending on the types of components used. Manufacturer's minimum recommended crossover frequencies should always be heeded.   The slopes would vary according to the crossover used, as below. In the idealized system, the acoustic outputs of the components combine to fill in the 3dB "notch" at the crossover point.

6 dB per octave

12 dB per octave

24 dB per octave

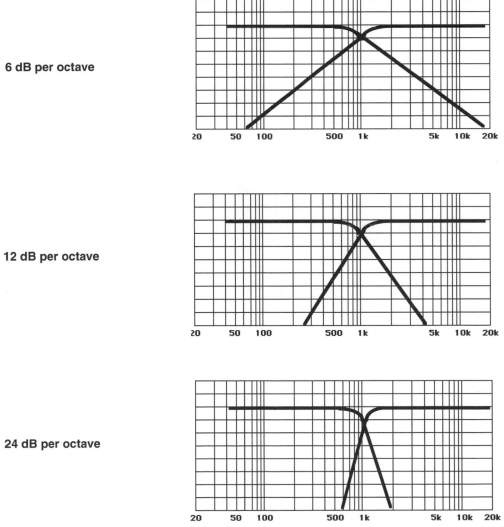

The slope of a crossover is always a gradual one, the steepness of which is determined by the circuitry, and which comes in 6 dB intervals. Common crossover slopes are 6dB/octave, 12dB/octave, 18dB/octave, 24dB/octave, or 1st-order, 2nd-order, 3rd-order and 4th-order, respectively. A 6dB/oct. passive crossover involves a simple capacitor and inductor (coil) of values appropriate to the crossover frequency and the impedance of the drivers. Higher orders involve increasingly complex circuitry. Special filter circuits are designed to have as high as 10th order (60dB/oct.) filters—even higher orders are sometimes used (these are most commonly used in conjunction with digital-to-analog converters used for effects units and delay lines).

But rarely are filters beyond 24dB/octave used for crossovers today. What the future holds—who knows? Digital crossovers at this writing are beginning to be marketed with upwards of 90 dB/octave slopes (kind of a tilted brick wall), and it is still being widely debated as to whether or not these radically higher slopes are a significant advantage (though the high frequency drivers certainly love it).

The higher the slope of the crossover filters, the less the overlap in the crossover region. Several practical factors are involved here. The lower the slope, the less protection there is for drivers in their low range—where they are most prone to overstress, and the more overlap there will be in the range between adjacent components. In the overlap region, which is sometimes as wide as several octaves, the two components in many cases may be interfering with one-another's jobs. On the other hand, the higher the slope is, the more phase shift there tends to be in the output signals of adjacent bands and in the crossover region. (To make matters more complicated, the amount of phase shift changes according to frequency.)

Typical crossover slopes for sound reinforcement purposes are between 12 db/oct. and 24 dB/oct. Among these commonly used crossover slopes, 24dB/octave provides the best protection for drivers used at high levels, and is generally the current standard for high-level reinforcement. (6dB/oct. is usually inadequate for all but the most elementary low-budget sound reinforcement systems, and in many cases fails to offer adequate protection for high-frequency drivers.) Another advantage of a steep slope is that it can be used to protect low- and low-mid-freq. drivers in ported enclosures around the point where the response drops off in their lowest usable range. Though the 24 dB/oct. slope is at this writing regarded as the standard for most high-level, high quality systems, 12dB and 18dB/oct. units are also used for a variety of purposes, often with equally acceptable results to the ears of most (and occasionally better). A main factor involved in why this is so, the relative alignment of the drivers, is briefly dealt with in the discussions accompanying Figs. 9.43 through 9.45.

Processor-controlled crossovers, available from a number of manufacturers at comparatively high cost, use "floating" crossover points designed to adapt on a nearly instantaneous basis to dynamic changes of the program, whenever the system nears its maximum capability. These are somewhat further described in chapter 14.

f) Basic Use of Crossovers.

The basic crossover frequencies chosen for use in a given application vary quite widely, and are sometimes also a matter of personal taste. *Effective choice of electronic crossover points involves several considerations.*

(1) *The frequency response curves of each component, and the practical low and high frequency limits of the components (which is normally much narrower than their quoted overall frequency response range.* Normally, the lowest recommended crossover frequency (quoted by the manufacturers of mid- and high-frequency components) determines the absolutely lowest crossover points which should be used. Commonly, though, it is sensible to use much higher crossover points, for the reasons in (2) and (3) below.

(2) *The required output level.* As the crossover frequency at the low end of each component's bandwidth is raised, its output capability tends to increase—up to a point. This is discussed in Fig. 9.19 and in the section of this chapter on "The Crossover Regions".

(3) *The dispersion pattern.* Commonly, as the low-to-mid and mid-to-high crossover points are raised in frequency, projection of the crossover-frequency ranges into the farther reaches of an audience will tend to increase somewhat. (There may, though, be compromises in sound quality here beyond a certain point. This can be a somewhat complicated matter, and can vary substantially with different component designs. This consideration is discussed further in "Dispersion and Pattern Control", "Mid and High Freq. Directional Patterns" and "Practical Use of Component Directional Patterns".)

The selected crossover points in any system of-course depend very heavily on the design of the components. ***It is important to know the manufacturers' recommendations for crossover frequency. Normally, one can safely move higher in frequency than their recommendations, but almost never lower***. (See, for example, Figs. 9.19, 9.30 and 9.40.)

Most active crossover designs (and many passive ones) have variable level controls for each band. These are useful for equalizing a system to adjust for different power amplifier gains, for differences in speaker component efficiency, and also for tuning a system to taste. In practical terms, these controls act as a form of shelving EQ. (An important note of caution is in order here. If a limiter is used in the signal path prior to the crossover for loudspeaker protection, these controls can serve to defeat its effectiveness. Limiter thresholds should be set (or re-set) with this in mind. Ideally, limiters for system protection should be installed on each crossover output.)

See also the last several illustrations of this chapter.

g) Dispersion and Directional Pattern Control.

Dispersion refers to the ability of a component to spread out the sound to a certain (hopefully consistent) angle.* **Pattern control** refers to the ability to keep the output within the bounds of certain angles, i.e., to also prevent it from spreading *too* far out. While the terms are often used interchangeably, there is a subtle-but-significant difference, as will be explained below.

Why is it desireable to attempt to provide even dispersion and to control the pattern?

(1) *So there is consistency of sound quality through the designated angles of the equipment.*

(2) *To assist in avoiding feedback.*

(3) *To assist in reducing excessive reverberation from the side walls and ceiling.*

It might be helpful to know about the basic factors that are involved here. An understanding of them can assist in choosing the appropriate equipment, and in positioning it in the best possible way. The following somewhat lengthy explanation may be helpful to readers who are attempting to get a grasp of roughly how the directional patterns of sound waves develop.

The speed of sound's outward spread (~340m/sec., 1130'/sec.) is the approximate rate at which air particles respond to changes in pressure from their neighbors on the microscopic level. (This is due to the air's elasticity and density, the two factors which determine the speed of sound in any substance— you pick the substance.) In a "fluid" substance like air, individual particles will always do their best to seek some kind of equilibrium, or balance of forces among one another.

Remember that different frequencies basically behave individually even when the cone or diaphram is vibrating in a complex waveform (Chapter 2). In other words, each frequency being reproduced evolves into its own separate pattern. In the development of a wave immediately around the sound source, successively farther-out sets of particles have increasing opportunities to adjust the direction in which the pressure changes are spread, within the limits set by the surrounding physical structure. *Beyond about a wavelength outward from the physical stucture, the waves will tend to continue following the pattern that has been established for each particular frequency.*

Take, as an example, a direct radiator in a modest-size enclosure. In the low frequencies, the direction of the pressure transfers among air particles has an opportunity to bend completely around the breadth of the physical structure, which is much smaller than the wavelength being created. By the time the direction of the speaker cone is reversed, the farthest-out air particles, still experiencing the first half of the cycle, have already spread their pattern out pretty-much uniformly. This is why *low frequencies tend to become omnidirectional—the waves of pressure transfers going out in every direction.*

---

* Many manufacturers quite reasonably use the term "dispersion" to refer to the nominal coverage angles of components or full-range speakers. The term "nominal" essentially means "what we choose to name it".

In the high frequencies, the pressure from the neighboring particles to the sides impedes the sideways spread, forcing most of the back-and-forth energy to go more-or-less directly outward along the axis. This is because the farthest out point of the first wavelength is relatively close to the speaker. Each particle has plenty of neighboring particles to the side (left, right, top and bottom), which are also trying to adjust to the pressure changes. Long before those particles have a chance to collectively pass their energy outward to the sides, they have been sucked back in the second half (the expansion phase) of the cycle. So they tend to keep each other headed in the same direction—except around the outer fringes, which is many dB below—and pass their energy fairly directly on-axis. Roughly explained, this is why *high-frequency "beaming"* occurs (Fig. 9.15). With something like a simple direct radiator, *the higher the frequency is, the narrower the pattern will be.*

So, in rough terms, *the lower frequencies of a component's range tend to spread out too widely, while the highest frequencies of a component's range tend to spread out not far enough.*

The challenge, then, is to have neither excessive spread of the sound nor high-frequency beaming. (This is of-course in addition to the fundamental challenge of achiveing pleasant and accurate sound reproduction.) So, the basic compromise here revolves around the need to confine the outward spread at the lower range of the component's designated bandwidth, while creating sufficient dispersion at the highest frequencies of the bandwidth. This involves wavelengths over about a 20-to-1 ratio with typical two-way systems—in some cases as much as 40-to-1 (a very hefty range). With three-way systems, effective pattern control in the mids and highs is still something of an engineering challenge, but over a 10-to-1 ratio of wavelengths in the mids and highs it is a manageable proposition, well handled by a number of manufacturers today.

In the very low frequency range of the audio spectrum, it is usually useless to even try to control the pattern, since it would require a low frequency component (or a stack of low frequency components) some 30-or-so feet (8 or 9 meters) in both height and width. So this is usually accepted as something which just needs to happen. But around the low-midrange, it becomes a much more reasonable proposition to try to gain the advantages of effective pattern control (see also Figs. 9.16 and 9.34).

Now, consider each midrange and high frequency horn to have an effective frequency range of roughly 10-1 (example: ~300Hz-3kHz). From a physical design standpoint, the need to keep the relatively lower frequencies of the component's designated band from spreading out too far is accomplished by the larger outer structure of the horn.

The need to disperse the highest frequencies of the component's band—i.e., to avoid beaming— is accomplished, depending on the design, by the smaller curves, fins or slot farther in towards the throat. For these frequencies, once their pattern is set, they tend to be less affected by the larger stucture of the horn, except in the outer edges of the pattern, where they are reflected back into the designated angles by the larger internal surfaces of the horn.

Through the middle of the component's frequency range, the curves are designed to control the pattern in the most consistent way possible (this also involves some engineering compromises). No horn is perfect, but many current designs have dispersion patterns that are remarkably consistent throughout their designated range.

Still, with a typical well-designed mid or high horn of the compact type used in many portable systems, there are variations of the pattern which the user should be aware of. *In a typical 2-way or 3-way system, there usually is a substantial compromise of directional pattern made at the crossover point(s).* Perhaps the most important way this affects the operator of most systems is in the crossover region leading up to the highs, explained later.

Fig. 9.12 introduces two methods of presenting a component's directional characteristics on a graph. *The main difference between a "near-field" 2-way or 3-way speaker (such as in Fig. 9.1), and one designed for a larger room or more projection, is in the directional pattern of the mids and highs.* In terms of projection in a typical portable system, *this difference tends to be most important in the vertical plane* (see Fig. 9.10).

In almost all applications, a vertical pattern of about 30°-40° would be more then adequate to cover the entire audience, as illustrated in Fig. 9.10 (in many cases 20° would be more than adequate). Beyond about 30-40°, the additional vertical spread tends to be projected up towards the ceiling and down into the front audience sections—subjecting them to an excessive amount of those ranges, and/or failing to project those ranges sufficiently deep into the farther reaches of the audience. So in the "ideal" portable system the vertical pattern might be in the neighborhood of 30° or 40°, with the horizontal pattern most often between 60° and 90°, depending on the design. This amount of consistent *horizontal* dispersion (and more) is today readily achievable from an engineering standpoint. But it requires a fairly tall stack of midrange and high components to accomplish the "ideal" *vertical* pattern control, so some kind of compromise is generally made. These types of compromises are dealt with somewhat further in this chapter in the caption accompanying Fig. 9.38.

The generally accepted guideline in quoting specifications of directional patterns at specific frequencies is to use the angle at which the response drops 6 dB below the on-axis response. Oftentimes in published specs, manufacturers will average these out to come up with a "nominal" directional pattern, for the sake of simplicity of marketing and use.

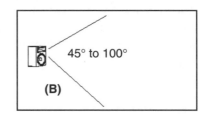

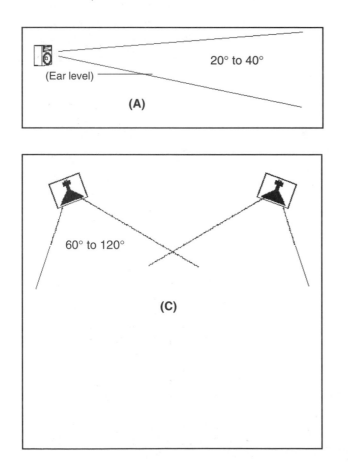

Fig. 9.10.
Typical dispersion requirements.
(A) Side view of typical performance room, where the vertical coverage needs to be only about 15° to 30° (unless there is a sloped seating arrangement or the speakers are suspended high overhead).
(B) Side view of a "nearfield" dispersion pattern, where a broader vertical pattern is used intentionally.
(C) Typical room , top view.
Here the horizontal dispersion most often needs to be between about 60° and 120° overall, depending on the room.
Note: the idea of a "long throw" speaker system, as discussed in the above section "g" of the text, is strictly a matter of how narrowly the system design is able to channel the available energy of the drivers in a given direction, *both* horizontally and vertically. The lower the frequency at which we expect a high degree of "throw", the larger the particular component must be.

h) Mid/High Horn Designs.

The basic horn configuration, in wide practical use for the past half-century or so, is that of an *exponential* horn. Fig. 9.2 shows the essential curve this type of horn follows.

Fig. 9.11 shows a depiction of a *round exponential* horn. This design finds use primarily as a high frequency horn. This type of horn emits a roughly cone-shaped pattern. The conical pattern with this type of horn is sometimes extremely wide around the crossover point (usually 800Hz-3kHz) and normally gets narrower with frequency, tending to exhibit a severe amount of high-frequency beaming. This type of horn perhaps finds use in stage monitors for stationary microphone positions. By increasing the expansion rate and using a wider mouth, as in Fig. 9.11-B and D, the pattern variation can be reduced substantially, though this also reduces the loading on the driver, requiring a higher crossover point for a given driver (and slight VHF beaming still is exhibited here as well). An excellent example of this approach is found in the Meyer UM-1 shown in Fig. 9.11, in which the driver is crossed over almost two octaves above the driver's minimum usable frequency. (A bit of middle-aged audio history here: The first widely used fiberglass horn was also an exponential round horn, introduced by Community Light and Sound in the late 1960's to cover the midrange gap left by the 2-way systems commonly used in concert sound reinforcement prior to that time.)

Commonly, high-frequency round horns are supplemented with an acoustic *lens* to assist in developing a somewhat more consistent pattern. A variation of this form of horn involves an eliptical mouth, also designed primarily for use with a lens. Acoustic lenses generally take the form of stacked louvers mounted in front of the horn or perforated plates mounted within the horn.

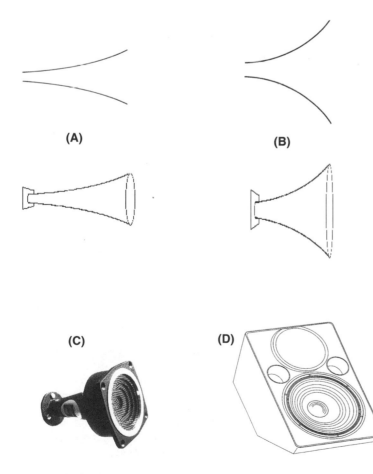

(A)

(B)

(C)

(D)

Fig. 9.11. Basic horn flares.

(A) low flare rate.
(B) high flare rate.
For a given size horn, the lower the flare rate, the lower the minimum usable frequency tends to be. This basic principle applies to low frequency, midrange and high frequency horns, within their respective category of size. A horn with low flare rate and small mouth size (as "A"), though, tends to exhibit wider pattern variations.

Bottom: Two commercial examples of round exponential horns.
(C) JBL 2305 "potato masher", which uses an acoustic lens design called a "perforated plate" to assist in dispersion of the VHF range. This horn uses a comparatively low flare rate for a compact high-frequency design.
(D) Meyer UM-1, which uses a HF horn with a comparatively high flare rate.

Both of these horns exhibit a pattern which at any given frequency would be roughly cone-shaped.

Straight exponential horns, as depicted in Fig. 9.12 -A, tend to have a directional pattern more closely approaching a rectangular one. A horn of this type can remain fairly consistent in the horizontal pattern through all but the high ranges of the horns designated band, up to about 60° (straight horns with "side walls" angled wider than 60° tend not to have consistent patterns). Depending on the dimensions of the horn, however, the vertical pattern may vary widely according to frequency. Another obstacle with this design is that high frequency beaming still occurs well before the upper ranges of most drivers are reached. (This of-course depends on the driver; usually a HF horn of this kind will tend to display the beaming characteristic above about 5k-8k, depending on the horn.) This type of horn finds fairly wide use as a midrange or upper-midrange horn, and occasionally for controlled-pattern paging applications.

A much wider and somewhat more complicated set of pattern variations occurs in the type of compact straight exponential horn shown shown in Fig. 9.12-B, which has a relatively narrow vertical opening at the mouth. The exponential flare is on the sides with this design. The type of horn shown in 9.12-B exhibits significant VHF beaming, with a very wide vertical pattern below 4kHz (commonly in excess of 120° below 1kHz). This type of horn perhaps finds its best use in a nearfield device, such as a stage monitor.

Fig. 9.12.

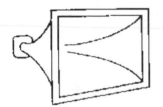

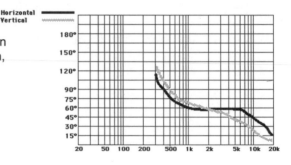

(A) Straight exponential horn with flare on top and bottom, straight sidewalls angled at 60°. Typical dispersion at right.

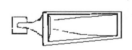

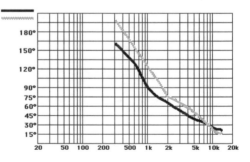

(B) Typical straight compact exponential horn with flare on sides, straight wall on top and bottom. Note the extremely wide pattern variation with this type of horn.

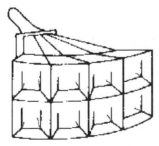

(C) Typical multicell horn. Horizontal pattern at right is for 8 kHz. Note the VHF lobing characteristic of this basic design approach.

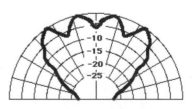

Multi-cell horns, as depicted in Fig. 9.12-C, are capable of providing fairly effective pattern control in the upper mids and highs, if they are sufficiently large at the mouth. This type of horn consists of a series of exponential horns arranged in the multicell configuration, with a common throat leading from the driver. This type of horn, which due to its usual size has traditionally been used mainly in permanent installations, also partially solves the high frequency beaming issue. The compromise, as illustrated in the accompanying graph, is what is called "lobing". This type of VHF lobing is actually the result of the beaming characteristic exhibited by each of the cells.

Radial horns, as depicted in Fig. 9.13, involve an exponential curve rotated through a given horizontal angle. These traditionally were sometimes referred to as *sectoral* horns, because the sidewalls define a certain sector, or angle, within which the horn is meant to disperse its output sound. The exponential curve in most radial designs (except for some of the earlier or more recent low-budget ones) is modified so the highest frequencies are spread outward somewhat (it is technically possible to do this and still retain the basic exponential flare rate). This design, numerous versions of which have been in very wide use since the early 1950's, still leaves two disadvantages.

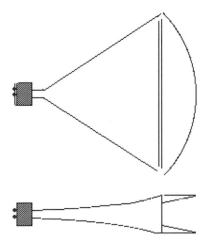

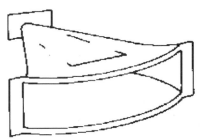

Fig. 9.13. Radial (sectoral) horn.
This type of horn can also be set back behind a flat front, as shown at right. As well, the horn can be "chopped" to achieve a flat front before the end of the flare, as shown below right. Typical dispersion shown below. (Perspective view courtesy Community Light and Sound.)

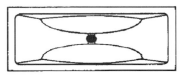

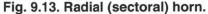
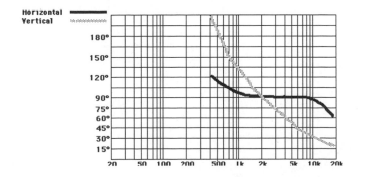

Firstly, even the best of the larger designs (2" throat HF horns and 10"-12" cone-driven mid horns), tend to exhibit the beaming characteristic in the highest frequencies. (The engineering compromise which made this unavoidable is briefly described in the section of this chapter on "Mid/high Output Capabilities".)   Secondly, while the horizontal pattern is fairly consistent in all but the highest frequencies, the vertical pattern varies very widely—in some designs well over 100° around 800 Hz, and less than 20° above 10k.

To help disperse the extreme highs, several horn designs combined the multicell idea with the radial flare. One basic design, the classic Altec 811 and 511 "Voice of the Theater" horns which first came into wide use in the 1950's, used vertical fins in the outer flare (near the mouth) of the horn to assist in despersion as well as phase alignment. Another of the various approaches to dispersing the extreme highs came in the form of multiple slots in the throat of the horn. This horn, marketed by Northwest Audio, was a fairly popular design for a good number of years following the mid-1970's (also in large part for the horn's generally pleasing sound quality—mostly a function of the materials used). This approach still has as a disadvantage a sometimes noticeable amount of lobing in the extreme high end (similar to the pattern shown in Fig. 9.12-C), along with the vertical pattern variations mentioned above.

Within the past two decades, the two problems of vertical pattern variation and high-frequency beaming have been drastically reduced—in some cases virtually eliminated—with newer design appraches. Horns which tend not to have these problems to a severe extent are most commonly called *constant-directivity* horns, (*CD* horns, for short). This basic approach was first marketed in the US by Electro-Voice beginning in the mid 1970's. Some versions of CD horns use step transitions to approximate an exponential "flare" in both the vertical and horizontal directions (as in Fig. 9.14). While this approach may compromise the accuracy of the directional pattern slightly, many people prefer the subtle difference in sound quality of these designs (in well constructed models of this type, the lower and middle frequencies of the horn's bandwidth get "amplified" somewhat less). Other versions use radial flares expanded in both the vertical and horizontal planes.

Fig. 9.14. Typical contemporary "constant-directivity" ("CD") horn.

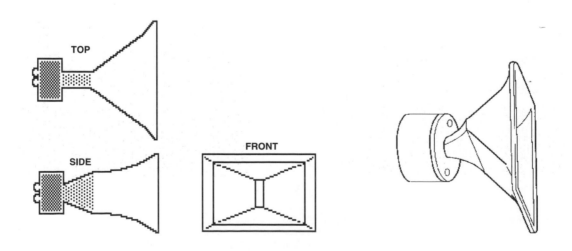

The quest to resolve the issue of very-high-frequency beaming achieved another major breakthrough in the 1980's with a complete change in the method of attempting to disperse the extreme highs. This was achieved by further refinements in the shape of the throat. Several approaches have been used. One is to expand the waves first along a vertical shaft. A severe step- transition into the radial segment of the horn allows the outer radial flares to serve the lower and middle frequencies of the horn's range, while allowing the slot to disperse the extreme highs (see Fig. 9.14 and 9.15). This development was somewhat like integrating, into the horn design, the principle of a VHF horn popularly known as a "slot tweeter" (shown in the section on VHF components). Another common approach is simply to use a short throat with a severe step transition, as above. Yet another more recent approach, now under patent by ElectoVoice, Inc., is to use vertical wave guides in the throat.

Another form of CD horn, marketed by JBL under the trade name *Bi-radial*, first arrived in production form in the mid-1980's. This development was aided by computer programs permitting ready computation of the proper flares—in both the vertical and horizontal planes—that were required to achieve extemely consistent patterns through the sought-after 10-to-1 ratio of wavelengths, and well beyond. Combined with the "slot" principle mentioned above, this approach was another major breakthrough.

The issue of size, however, has not gone away. A constant directivity horn designed to be crossed over around 600 Hz, for example, still needs to be roughly 30" in height to maintain a reasonably tight vertical pattern control around that crossover point. Many compact versions of CD or Biradial designs have been marketed for use in portable systems, which, as mentioned before, still involve major compromises of the vertical pattern in the lower frequencies of their operating range. The section on "Practical Use of Directional Patterns" is intended to present an outline of how these compromises come into play in many practical applications.

Fig. 9.15. Diffraction principle. Waves in a fishtank can be used to illustrate what happens at the step-transition from the throat to the outer horn flare of a constant-directivity horn. At left, note the relatively straight-ahead pattern when the wavelength is much smaller than the "slot". At right, note the extremely wide pattern when the wavelength is larger than the "slot". The outer flares of the horn then serve to keep the dispersion roughly within the designated angles.

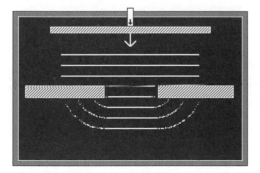 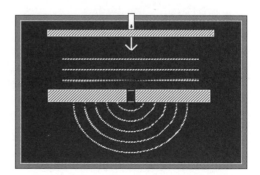

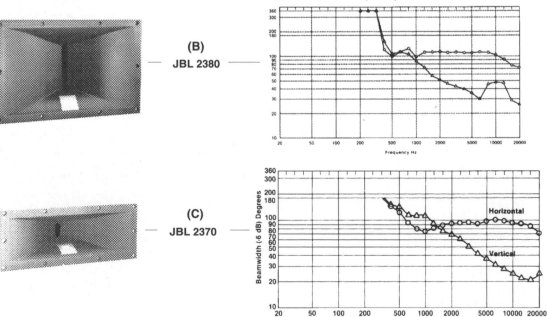

Fig. 9.16.
Vertical pattern variations in CD horns.
Shown are three HF horns by JBL, Inc., courtesy of the manufacturer, in their approximate size as compared to a 15" LF driver. As is fairly standard in the industry, the graphs shown at-right trace the angles at which the response reaches -6dB below the on-axis response. Note that all three have a very consistent horizontal pattern in the 90° to 110° range throughout most of their intended range.

The vertical pattern, though, is very much dependent on their height. As can be seen, it takes a larger horn to achieve more "throw" at a given frequency. (See also the chart of approximate wavelengths in Fig. 9.34.) Obviously, we must make a compromise between size and the amount of "throw", or narrowness of pattern, we need to have at a given frequency. The horn at top-left measures about 30" (.75 m) in height, the 2380 (center) is about 11" high, the 2370 (bottom) is less than 6" high.

(A) Model 2360A
Beamwidth vs Frequency

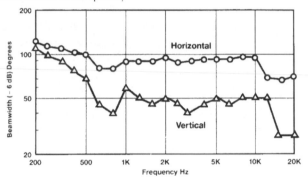

Beamwidth vs Frequency

(B)
JBL 2380

(C)
JBL 2370

i) Mid/High Freq. Response Curves and Output Capability.

High frequency drivers are most commonly available with throat outlets in the following sizes: 1", 1.4" and 2" drivers, or 25mm, 35mm, and 50mm.

Midrange compression drivers are generally available in designs with 1"(25mm), 1.4"(35mm), 2"(50mm), 2.4"(70mm), 3"(75mm) and 4"(100mm) throats.

Frequency range and response curves differ very widely among designs in any of the above throat sizes. The primary difference between a 1" and 2" HF driver, for example, is most likely to be its maximum output capability. Frequency range and frequency response curves in a well designed driver tend to be mostly a function of the material(s) of which the diaphram is constructed, as well as the design of the diaphram suspension.

There is some difference in the frequency response of different sized drivers at the high end of their range. A good 2"-throat driver (with an aluminum or titanium diaphram), for example, might have usable response up to, say 16kHz, while its 1" counterpart might typically have usable response to 18kHz. The main difference in frequency range, though, is more often the low frequency limit, where the larger drivers usually are capable of going two-thirds of an octave to one octave lower. (Many other concerns are involved as well, a thorough discussion of which would be well beyond the scope of this text. In the balance of this section we will ignore 1" to 2"-throat drivers with "phenolic" diaphrams meant mainly for upper midrange and paging applications. These often work well in the midrange but generally lack significant clean HF output. In critical high quality applications, a driver of this type usually requires a VHF unit above about 5kHz or so. (The term "phenolic" refers to a diaphram constructed of a resin-coated fiber composite, usually brown in color.))

Combining drivers with horns on a customized basis can be a fairly complicated matter, oftentimes coming down to personal taste. Since the horn and driver work together, the characteristics of both will affect the overall sound.

For example, a driver with strong output around 1.6k-3k might sound awful on a horn which accentuates that range severely, but might sound quite acceptable on a horn which minimizes it, and vice-versa. (It is not at all uncommon for a horn and driver to both be strong in the above montioned range, which is compounded by the ear's extra sensitivity in this range. A reduction of response in such a range with an EQ is a fairly common practice when this problem is encountered in the field.)

The effective frequency range of the driver generally should also be reasonably consistent with the ability of the horn to provide a directional pattern which works for the application. Example: A horn which "beams" above 6k might not be put to its best use with a driver that provides strong energy well above 12k (unless it is meant for a low-qualtity paging application, for a monitor directed at a stationary mic position, or when it is crossed over into a VHF unit on-top to appropriately spread the highs).

The absolute lowest safe crossover frequency is almost always a function of the horn's cutoff frequency, determined by the flare rate of the horn (check the manufacturer's specs). This minimum crossover frequency might be higher if the driver is not designed to be used to as low a frequency as the horn. But it should never be lower, because the driver loses its cushioning acoustic load and can very easily overextend its excursion limits. The slope of the crossover plays a role in this too. Most manufacturers quote both a lowest recommended crossover frequency and a crossover slope for that frequency. The slope should be plotted to ensure that no significant amount of power is given to the driver in the range below the cutoff frequency.

Fig. 9.17. Typical HF driver response curves.

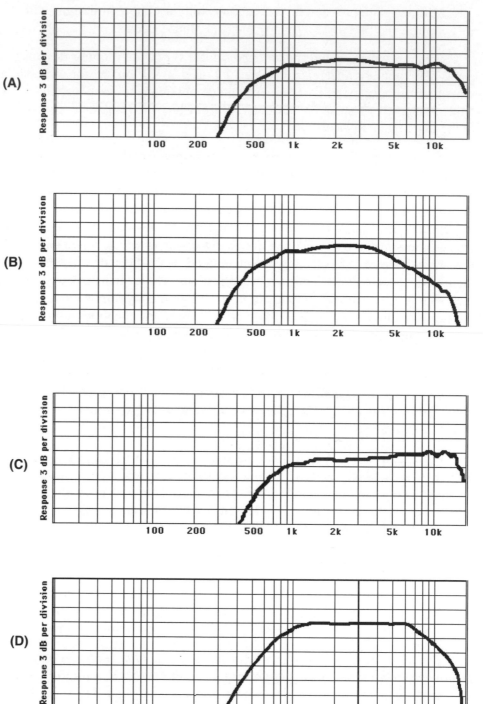

(A) Typical 2" throat driver with aluminum or titanium diaphram, on straight exponential horn (as in Fig. 9.12-A), measured on axis.

(B) Same driver as "A", on constant-directivity horn (as in Fig. 9.14), measured on axis. Note that because the CD horn tends to lack the "beaming" characteristic of straight exponential horns, the highs roll off. This is because they are dispersed over a wider, more consistent angle. This ordinarily requires compensating equalization above about 5k or 6k.

(C) Typical 1" throat driver with aluminum or titanium diaphram, mounted on a compact straight exponential horn (as in Fig. 9.12-B), measured on axis.

(D) Same driver as "C", measured when mounted on a larger constant-directivity horn (as in Fig. 9.14). Note two things here: the lack of HF beaming results in a a rolloff of the highs on axis, because they are being spread over a consistent angle; and also slightly stronger frequency response in the lower range, because the larger horn projects better.

Generally, the power handling capacity of a driver increases substantially as the lower crossover point is moved upward in frequency, up to about 2 octaves above the low frequency limit of the driver. This is because in the driver's lower ranges, its main limitation is mechanical stress on the diaphram suspension, and its maximum excursion limits. As the danger of "bottoming out" or jumping out of the voice coil gap is removed (Fig. 9.19), its ability to handle power is increased.

Beyond about two octaves above the lowest recommended crossover point of a typical driver, the main limitation in power handling tends to become the amount of power the voice coil itself is capable of withstanding. Within this limitation, the apparent output of a driver can often be increased somewhat further by increasing the crossover point further, allowing the available power capacity to be used within a smaller, higher range (hence allowing that range to be kicked into a slightly "higher gear", if you will, but over a narrower frequency range). The just-mentioned technique of narrowing the high-frequency driver's bandwidth is sometimes useful if a system needs to be stretched slightly beyond its normal maximum output level. There may be a compromise in both sound quality and directional pattern here, since this requires the component in the next lowest band needs to cover a higher range, which may be beyond *its* effective capabilities. As an example, we can get a typical 2"-throat HF driver to "scream" in the range from say 3k or 4k up to around 10k or so, but if using 12" cone drivers in the mids, a very significant gap is left below the crossover point where the 12s cannot cover very effectively, at least not at angles off-axis. (Simlarly, we can often get very high output from a typical 1"-throat HF driver in the range above, say, 5 or 7kHz, but the component below it must be able to effectively cover up to this crossover point, or a gap will be left at angles off-axis. Remember that the pattern of a cone driver keeps narrowing as frequency gets higher.)

Fig. 9.18. Typical on and off-axis CD horn response curves with and without equalization.
(Curves for 2445 driver on 2380A horn, courtesy JBL.)

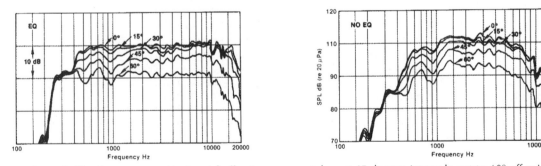

Horizontal off-axis response. Horizontal off-axis response taken at 15 degree intervals out to 60° off axis. Both normalized (equalized flat on axis) and unequalized responses are shown.

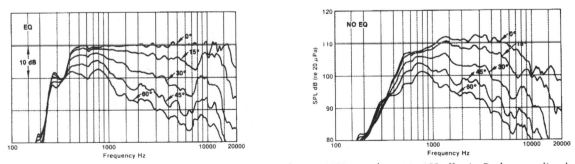

Vertical off-axis response. Vertical off-axis response taken at 15° intervals out to 60° off axis. Both normalized (equalized flat on axis) and unequalized responses are shown.

As indicated before, *the difference between drivers of different throat sizes, while definitely frequency related, is often mainly the maximum output capability*. For example, 2" drivers tend to handle more power and are often also somewhat more sensitive (efficient) than 1" drivers. From a practical standpoint, the main difference between the two is in the size of the diaphram, phase plug entrance and exit area, and throat. These differences in size alone would (assuming an equivalently stronger magnet, and equivalently larger and stronger diaphram and voice coil) allow a 2" throat driver to deliver nearly 4x the output of an equivalent 1" driver (6dB more). (In practice, this difference is considerably less than 6dB, and is also dependent on frequency. And as might be expected, the larger drivers in-general tend to perform far better when asked to reproduce lower frequencies.) An equivalent 1.4" throat driver would fall about halfway between the two sizes just mentioned, providing slightly more than half (almost 3dB less) the output of a 2" throat driver, and nearly twice (+3dB) that of a 1" throat driver.

Fig. 9.19. Typical HF driver capability according to frequency. These curves, while not intended to represent any particular driver, are roughly typical of a 2"-throat HF driver with an aluminum or titanium diaphram.. With a typical 1" throat driver, the curves would tend to be moved upwards in frequency.

In "A", note that the ability to handle power is limited in the lower ranges by the physical excursion limits of the diaphram itself. Of course, the lower the frequency, the greater the excursion, thus the more readily the diaphram would tend to exceed its excursion limits, and therefore the less power it could handle without potential damage.
At some point, the excursion limits of the diaphram no longer come into play, and the only remaining limitation is the amount of electrical power the driver is capable of withstanding.

In "B", the maximum output capability of the same hypothetical horn/driver combination is shown, according to frequency. A constant directivity horn is assumed here. The rapid dropoff below 400 Hz in this case represents what happens below the cutoff frequency of the horn (this is essentially a useless range for this particular setup). Above the horn's cutoff frequency, the output capability increases at roughly 6dB per octave as the frequency is raised, then briefly levels off. Above a certain frequency, though, as response (efficiency) drops off, so does its maximum output capability. The driver can usually be fed the same amount of amplifier power in the VHF range, but the maximum acoustical output decreases. (There are, though, some instances where the diaphram is not rigid enough or durable enough to withstand anywhere near full power above 8k or 10k without substantial distortion, or in extreme cases, complete breakup of the diaphram—this could somewhat further reduce maximum output capability in the VHF range.)

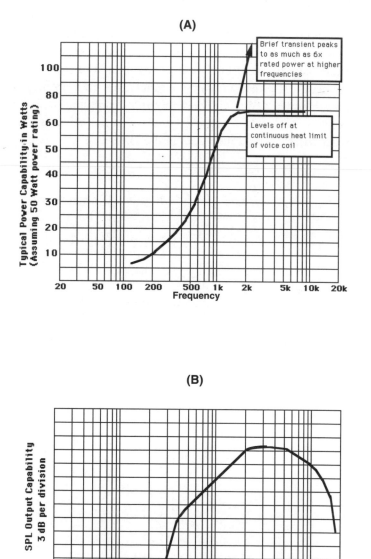

There is another important consideration having to do with the throat size. Throat distortion occurs at high levels—a function of excessive pressure within the throat. Compromises need to be made at the design stage between type of throat required to provide very high frequency dispersion, and the size of the throat required to minimize distortion to the best possible extent. Interestingly, this is one of the areas where the 2" throat format can offer an additional advantage, since throat distortion increases as the throat gets smaller. But the diaphram must be able to remain rigid and be also be lightweight enough to handle the VHF range, which involves yet another engineering compromise. Some manufacturers of horns and drivers have this compromise fairly well in hand—others still are grappling with it.

The vast majority of 2"-throat drivers, though, still become substantially less efficient above about 4k to 6k. (Remember that most published frequency response specs are measured on an exponential horn which exhibits the beaming characteristic already discussed. If we put the same driver on a constant-directivity horn, the highs tend to roll off, since the energy is distributed over a broader angle.) This generally means we have a choice. We can boost the EQ in the range where efficiency falls off for the particular driver (and/or cut the EQ in the range where it is most efficient). The tradeoff is that the driver is now used at less than its full output capability. (For many application this is fine, since there still tends to be fairly strong maximum output even at 10 or 12k for most 2" drivers. A reasonably strong 10k can sound mighty sweet, even if the response rolls off quickly above that. Many high quality systems work wonderfully with 2" drivers handling the highest frequency range of the system.) However, if we wish to use a typical 2"-throat driver to its full capability in the range where it is more efficient, we need to add one or more VHF units. Typically, the VHF unit would take over above about the 5kHz to 10kHz range, depending on the type and quantity of the units used. A 1"-throat horn with appropriate VHF response, or units of the kind shown in Figs. 9.23 through 9.25 are good candidates for this purpose.

Fig. 9.20. Comparative response curves of several commonly encountered drivers.
Here several 2"/50mm throat drivers mounted on a radial horn are measured on-axis (response on a CD horn would tend to be different, as per Fig. 9.17). The JBL 2440 was generally regarded as having a very "sweet" sound— the upward peak around 9-10kHz accounts for this. The JBL 2441 used a different diaphram design which extended the VHF response, but which requires an EQ boost to bring out the "sweetness". The JBL 2445, not shown, would have a similar curve to that of the 2441, with somewhat higher response above 6 kHz due to the titanium diaphram used in the 2445. The Gauss HF 4000 series, not shown, woiuld have somewhat higher response in the 4kHz-5kHz range. (Illustration reprinted from Handbook of Sound System Design, by John Eargle. Courtesy Elar Publishing.)

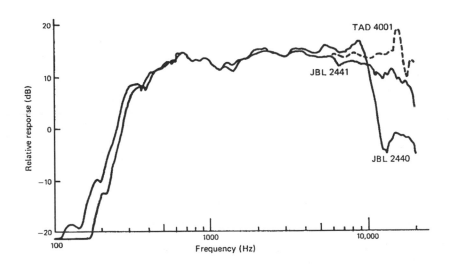

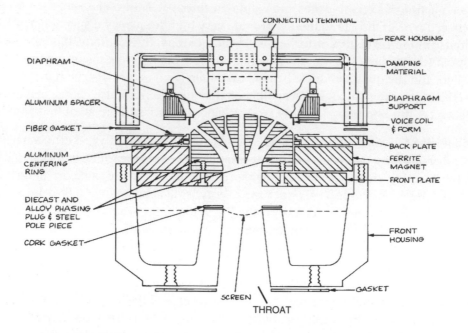

Fig. 9.21. Cross section of typical high-frequency driver.
(Courtesy Yamaha.)

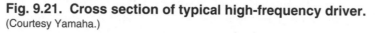

Fig. 9.22. Cross section of a midrange compression driver.
This design involves a 4" diameter throat. The Community M-4, introduced in 1981, represented a ar breakthrough in effective reproduction of midrange frequencies from 300Hz to 3 kHz, and at this writing remains the consummate midrange compression driver. (Courtesy Community .)

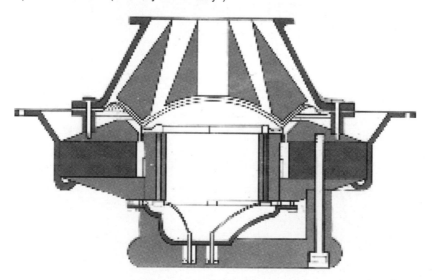

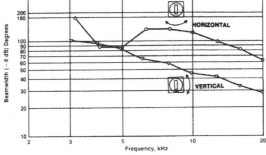

Beamwidth vs. Frequency

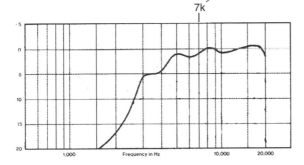

mimimum recommended x-over freq @ 12 dB/oct.

7k

Polar response of the 2405H in the horizontal plane, measured with ⅓-octave band pink noise in a free-field environment.

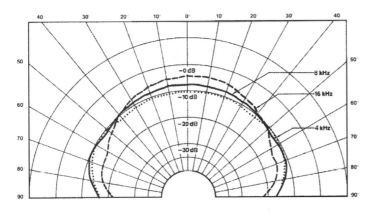

Fig. 9.23. Diffraction-type VHF unit.
(Courtesy JBL)

Widely known as a "slot" tweeter, this design mates well as the VHF complement to a 90° to 110° horn. Horizontal dispersion is *perpendicular* to the direction of the "slot". If crossed over at its 7k minimum recommended crossover point, two such units would provide excellent supplement to a typical 2" throat driver. If two or more are used together, ordinarily they should be placed one atop the other. If crossed over at 10k or so, one such unit would ordinarily keep up with a typical 2"-throat driver.

(Note: Similar designs by other manufacturers may have lower minimum crossover frequencies due to different diaphram construction or other differences in design.

Vertical dispersion of the 2405H.

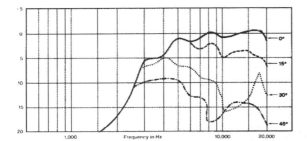

Polar response of the 2405H in the horizontal plane, measured with ⅓-octave band pink noise in a free-field environment.

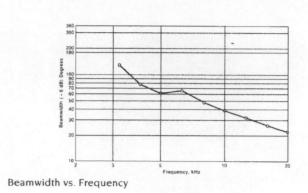

Beamwidth vs. Frequency

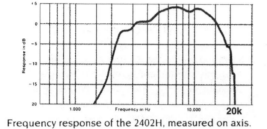

Frequency response of the 2402H, measured on axis.

Fig. 9.24. "Bullet" tweeter.

(Courtesy JBL)
This design displays a conical pattern. Here the minimum recommended crossover frequency is 2.5k. Two to four such units arranged side-by-side in a semicircular array can form an effective VHF complement for a typical 2"-throat driver, if crossed over around 5k to 8k.

The pattern of this type of unit tends to be very narrow above 8k or so. In rough terms, we could average out the pattern above 8k to about 30° or 40°, as shown in the beamwidth plot above.

(Note: Similar designs by other manufacturers may have different frequency response and minimum-crossover-frequency requirements.)

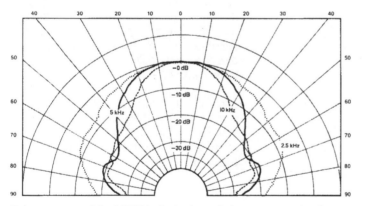

Polar response of the 2402H in the horizontal plane, measured with ⅓-octave band pink noise in a free-field environment. The curves were traced by an automatic recorder. Power fed to the 2402H was adjusted to provide the same 0 dB reference for each curve.

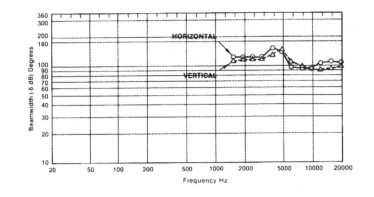

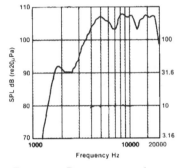

Frequency Response on-axis

Fig. 9.25. JBL Biradial® VHF unit.
Displaying a remarkably consistent 100°
pattern in both the horizontal and vertical, this
type of unit is an excellent call for nearfield
use, in conjunction with a 90° or 100° horn. A
typical crossover point for this unit would be
between 4k and 8k (Courtesy of the manufacturer)

j) Low Frequency and Low-mid-Freq. Cone Drivers.

Several basic factors in the design of cone drivers tend to be most relevant in selecting an appropriate match for a low- or mid-frequency horn or enclosure. Most often, the manufacturer's recommendations are the easiest and most effective route to follow here. However, since low frequency drivers are often "transplanted" from one type of enclosure or horn to another, and because older specs are often hard to locate, the following are offered as general factors to consider. (The relevant considerations are technically and very accurately described by the Thiele/Small parameters currently used in effective low frequency loudspeaker design—and almost always quoted today by manufacturers. The following are intended only as a rough guide).

(1) *The stiffness of its suspension.* Drivers with relatively stiff suspensions (this is usually called the *surround* or the *compliance*—the flexible outer portion which allows the cone itself to move) usually require a relatively large sealed enclosure, or a relatively long horn or duct to produce equivalent very-low-frequency response. (Carefully note the difference between the two basic suspension types in Fig. 9.27.) This factor is more closely described by Q_{ts} of the Thiele/Small specifications. Along with f_s (resonant frequency) and V_{as} (enclosure volume), Q_{ts} combines to determine performance in a sealed or ported enclosure. A higher Q_{ts} value usually means deeper bass in a given enclosure size.)

All else being equal, drivers with a relatively stiff compliance (which normally have lower Q_{ts}) tend to operate best in a somewhat higher bass frequency range, often making them good candidates for the mid-bass in a 4-way system, or the LF driver in a two way system. With practice one can learn to roughly estimate this by tapping gently on the cone (never the center dome) of speakers while they are out of their enclosures, then relating it to how these drivers sound in various enclosures. Over a period of time, a general familiarity with this characteristic can be developed, and can be helpful when when one needs to take a quick guess without access to the specs.

And at its most basic, when a driver is transplanted into a ported enclosure, the free-air resonance should closely coincide with the port tuning. When both of these specs are available, this basic match should be accomplished in order for the combination to work well. (There are ways of testing to determine these measurements effectively, but these are beyond our scope in this book. For any critical high-quality application, the job should be referred to a qualified person able to accomplish this task.)

(2) *Its maximum excursion capabilities.* Generally (though not necessarily), speakers which find their best use as low-frequency direct radiators also have a comparatively long excursion capability, in comparison to equivalent designs meant to be horn loaded. (Perhaps the most commonly encountered exception to this rule of thumb is shown in Fig. 9.4-D, involving a direct radiator with a long horn designed to exploit its rear radiation.)

(3) *Its cone rigidity.* A horn loaded LF driver coupled to a high throat impedance generally needs to have a somewhat stiffer cone, in order to avoid flexing in the face of the throat's impedance (remember that the horn loaded driver needs to push and pull harder, but over a somewhat shorter excursion). This is a completely different concern than the stiffness of the suspension mentioned in (1) above. Many loudspeaker designs today are still made of paper-based material, and some of them flex substantially. (This is often because they have been made relatively thin to enable them to be of lighter weight to better reproduce frequencies higher up—these are often marketed as "musical instrument" or "full-range" speakers. Some of the polymer and metallic cones, though, are able to both remain rigid and have extended range relatively effectively. The ribs often designed into low frequency drivers are a feature intended to reduce flexing—i.e., distortion—of the cone itself when under high stress.) A cone design capable of remaining relatively rigid under high stress is not at all a disadvantage in use as a direct

Fig. 9.26. Typical low-frequency driver. Top: cross-section. (courtesy JBL)
Center: basic parts identification. (courtesy Yamaha)
Bottom: most common causes of failure or overstress. (courtesy Yamaha)

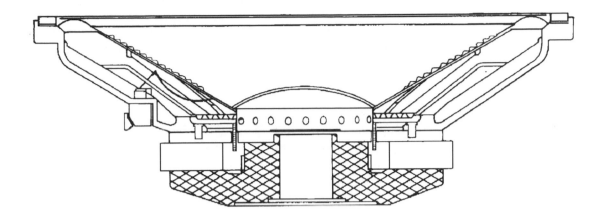

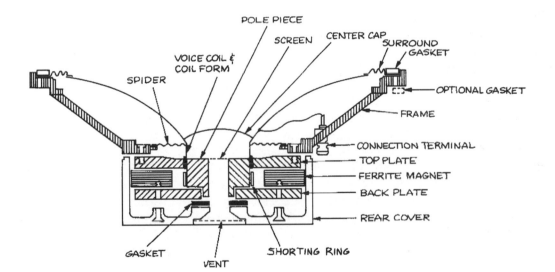

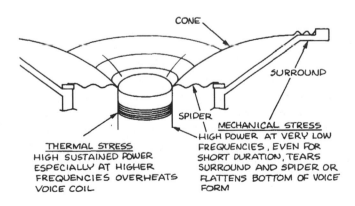

radiator. But a cone which flexes to any notable extent can be a significant disadvantage in a long horn with a relatively low flare rate. This might be of some extra concern, for example, in horns of the type shown in Fig. 9.4-D, 9.6-B and 9.8, or any long folded horn.

Note: low frequency drivers coupled to a short horn/reflex or short horn with ports as in Fig. 9.5, or short folded horn as in Fig. 9.4-A, fall between the two extremes (direct radiator vs. very long horn— either straight or folded). Many manufacturers market drivers intended primarily for this purpose, and since they fall between the two extremes these are also often marketed as all-purpose drivers.

The frequency response curve of a cone driver is usually plotted with the driver installed in a sealed enclosure, whose size should be quoted by the manufacturer as V_{as}, in order to roughly assess how the driver will behave in a given enclosure. (A specific discussion of the Thiele/Small parameters, with which one can accurately predict this, is somewhat beyond the scope of this text.)

A large variety of other concerns and compromises are involved in designing and manufacturing cone-drivers—far too much to discuss in any detail here. Below is a basic description of some of the additional factors involved in speaker design, which can affect the output sound.

Perhaps it should be said first that a cheap speaker is, well, a cheap speaker—no matter what compromises are made. Having said this, a high-quality speaker tends to have a well-braced and sturdy frame, a relatively large voice coil (at least $2^{1}/2"$-4" diameter), minimal distortion, and reasonable efficiency and/or maximum output. (A number of companies who manufacture high-quality speakers have very good reputations in the field—usually for good reasons, so ask around a bit.)

Normally there is a compromise between high sensitivity (efficiency) and maximum power handling. After this compromise is made, a high-power speaker may require much more power (i.e., it is not quite as sensitive, or efficient), but its maximum output level will tend to be higher. Obviously, the tradeoff here is that a higher power amp output level, and thus a more expensive power amplifier, is required to drive it to its maximum output level.

There is also a compromise made among maximum excursion capability, sensitivity and accuracy. This is because a deeper voice coil is required to accurately produce a very long excursion. Since much of a deep voice coil is not in the strongest part of the magnetic field at any given time, power is "wasted". Hence, as mentioned above, a speaker with a relatively long excursion capability cannot push and pull quite as forcefully as an equally high-quality design meant to have a shorter excursion (mentioned in #2 above). This is why this type of speaker (with comparatively long excursion capability) is often better suited as a direct radiator or short-horn driver than as a driver for a very long LF horn. It should perhaps be said here that several manufacturers today market drivers which have both long excursion capability and amazing strength—both in terms of cone rigidity and strength of compression and rarefaction, so such a driver might function quite well in a long horn with high acoustical impedance. But still, with a given level of construction quality the same just-mentioned compromise holds true.

Fig. 9.27 and 9.28 further describe the compromises introduced in the previous two paragraphs.

Fig. 9.27. Basic suspension types in LF drivers. (Courtesy Cetec/Gauss) See explanation in Fig. 9.28.

4580: double roll surround, closeup at right (with aluminum dome).

4582: double roll surround (with "paper" dome, actually a compressed cardboard composite).

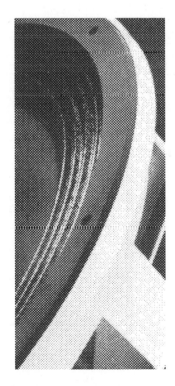

4583: triple-folded surround, closeup at right.

4580/4560

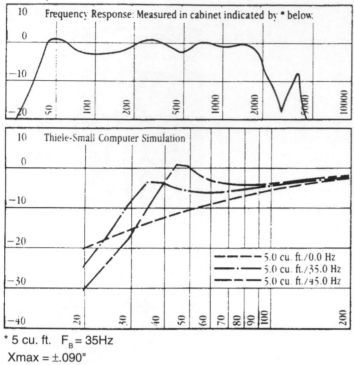

* 5 cu. ft. F_B = 35Hz
Xmax = ±.090"

4582

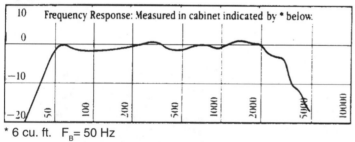

* 6 cu. ft. F_B = 50 Hz
Xmax = ±.040"

4583A

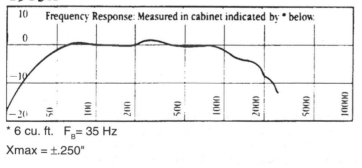

* 6 cu. ft. F_B = 35 Hz
Xmax = ±.250"

Fig. 9.28.
Partial data ("simplified") for 15" designs shown in Fig. 9.27.
These three drivers are typical of a high quality selection of "woofers" for sound reinforcement. Note that the frequency response presented by the manufacturer can change depending on the enclosure in which it is installed when the measurements are taken. The capability of the driver to accurately reproduce very low frequencies at high levels is not represented by the response curve, but by the Xmax specification.

Top: Gauss 4580. The curve labeled 5.0cu. ft./0.0Hz is a sealed enclosure with 5ft.³ internal volume. The other two curves represent the computed low frequency response in enclosures with two different ducted port tunings. The peak in the response curve around 3k to 4k is typical of the aluminum dome. This speaker could be characterized as a multipurpose LF driver, with a maximum linear excursion (Xmax) of plus/minus .090". (The maximum *peak-to-peak* excursion, incidentally, is much greater, and would be shown as a separate specification.)

Center: Gauss 4582. This design is meant primarily for horn loading, and has a shorter voice coil (not to be confused with the voice coil diameter). As a result, the maximum linear excursion capability is relatively short. This is represented as an Xmax of plus/mimus .040". The shorter voice coil depth, though, is more efficient, and allows for more power and accuracy in the face of the comparatively high acoustical impedance of horn loading. (Response is shown for a 6 cubic ft. enclosure with a port tuning (F_B) of 50Hz. An enclosure is used here because this is a standard way of presenting a response graph for any cone driver.)

Bottom: The model 4583 has an Xmax of plus/minus .250", so such a design is able to have much larger excursions, and therefore more output capability at very low frequencies. The compromise here is that this design is 3dB less sensitive (efficient), and might not be as effective in a bass horn as the 4580 or 4582. *Note again that this capability for more excursion at very low frequencies is not reflected in the response curve, but in the Xmax specification.* The triple-folded-type surround shown in Fig. 9.27 allows the greater excursion to fulfill this need.

A few other considerations here:

The best contemporary cone drivers are designed to have accurate symmetry of compression and rarefaction. (They are able to push and pull with equal effectiveness.) Traditionally, the failure to do this accurately—due to the basic design of the magnetic gap—has resulted in a subtle, but nevertheless significant, nonlinearity. (The compression stage would be slightly more powerful than the rarefaction stage.)

Also, what is known as "power compression" can result in decreased efficiency as the power level rises. There are two causes for this, a feature which every cone driver displays to one extent or another. One cause is heating of the voice coil after the speaker has been in use for a time—typically between a few seconds and several minutes, depending on the design and the amount of power being handled. This is one reason why high-quality cone-drivers are designed with effective venting and heat dispersion capability (the other perhaps-more-important reason is simply to help prevent possible heat-related damage to the voice coil and related assembly).

Another occasional cause of power compression is the mechanical resistance of the compliance/suspension. (This kind of limitation is another reason why a driver designed for a relatively short excursion—usually with relatively stiff compliance and comparatively high free-air resonant frequency, or f_S of the specifications—is oftentimes not put to its best use as a LF direct radiator or short-horn driver, unless it is used higher up in the mid-bass.) Sometimes, power compression can also be caused by a very long LF horn, due to the high acoustical impedance, which can increase as the power level rises.

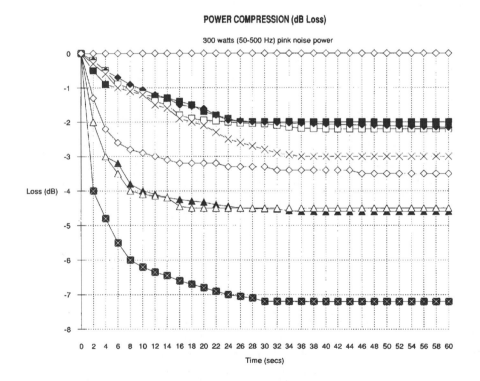

Fig. 9.29. Power compression due to voice-coil heating.
(Reprinted from JBL Technical Notes Volume 1, Number 18, courtesy JBL.) Data is shown for 8 competitive 15" LF driver designs.   Power compression has both advantages and disadvantages. On the one hand, it can help to protect drivers from failure when steadily pushed close to their power-handling capacity, by reducing the amount of power drawn from the amplifier. On the other hand, a much stronger power amplifier is now required to drive it to it's capacity, and the actual system gain is altered in the frequency range being affected (usually lows).

k) More on Low Frequency Horns and Enclosures.

Low frequency horns tend to follow a standard exponential flare—the slower the expansion rate is, the lower the cutoff frequency is. Often this type of flare is expanded in two dimensions. Usually, with this type of design, such as was shown in Fig. 9.5, significant pattern narrowing tends to occur above about 500Hz or so. A folded horn most often approximates the exponential flare in a series of "step transitions" as was shown in Fig. 9.4.

With any low frequency horn, there are two primary factors which affect the usable low-frequency response: (1) the flare rate and (2) the length of the horn. These factors, along with the additional load of the air mass behind the driver, determine the frequency response characteristics of the horn, as well as its cutoff frequency—below which the driver will tend to "unload".

When compactness is desired in a low frequency enclosure or horn, there is a compromise in efficiency in the low ranges. This means compensating equalization might be necessary (not necessarily a disadvantage), and also means more amplifier power is required to achieve an equivalent response.

There is also an important difference between low frequency response and maximum output capability as roughly depicted in Fig. 9.30. Strong low frequency response indicates that a driver requires comparatively little power to achive a given level of output at certain frequencies in a given type of enclosure. But its maximum output capability is a function of the total surface area of the driver's cone and the maximum excursion it is capable of achieving without objectionable distortion. (Almost needless to say—what is "objectionable" is very much a judgement call, and standard specification criteria for peak-to-peak excursion capability are, at this writing, not as yet agreed upon in the field).

Fig. 9.31 shows a configuration known as a "Helmholtz resonator", which is the theoretical basis for the resonance of the type of air mass found in a ported speaker enclosure.

A well designed low-frequency ducted enclosure serves to produce output at the ducted ports which compliments the direct radiation of the driver around the frequency of the port's resonance. The phase relationship at the port's resonance is actually somewhat out of phase (about 90°, at which relative phase angle no cancellation is caused.) Because of the strength of the resonant output from the port(s), though, the port's contribution to the overall output is overwhelmingly predominant at this frequency. At frequencies well above the port's resonant frequency, there are certain frequencies at which the cone and port output are of more-or-less opposite phase, but because the port's contribution at these frequencies is minimal it has very little impact on the overall output. An effective design method for an enclosure of this kind is well in hand by most manufacturers, but we still need to heed the potential for a poorly matched driver/enclosure combination wherever the original driver has been replaced. If you suspect the possibility of such a mismatch, the job is usually best referred to a person with a working knowledge of the Thiele-Small parameters, which allow for very effective matching of LF drivers to both sealed and ported enclosures. Most ported enclosures are readily modified to change the port tuning if necessary.

As noted in Figure 9.2 and 9.31, *below the port's resonant frequency, the output of direct radiator and port are increasingly of opposite phase, and response drops off radically.* Should we boost these frequencies with an equalizer to compensate? ***Absolutely not!*** Below the port's resonant frequency the cone loses its acoustic loading and there is the risk of overexcursion at any significant power level. Therefore, if anything, we should reduce any graphic EQ sliders below this frequency, or use a high-pass (low-cut) filter, or both. Obviously it is helpful to know what this frequency is for a given enclosure design, so check the specs if possible. If operating a sound system at relatively high output levels without access to any specs, pay attention for a "flopping" sound which is characteristic of a cone overextending itself at very low frequencies (though this type of sound could also be caused by other factors, such as by loose joints in the enclosure).

Fig. 9.30. Typical maximum output capability of low frequency components.

At high power levels, very-low-frequency output can be limited by the mechanical excursion limits of the drivers. The audible result of this type of limitation would be a change in the tonal quality of, for example, a bass drum, when pushing a system to its limit. It would simply have less of the very low frequencies, and much higher amounts of 2nd harmonic and 3rd harmonic distortion. If we drasically exceed this maximum capability at very low frequencies, there is ordinarily a characteristic sound which results from the cone overextending itself. Any operator of high-level systems not protected by an appropriate limiter would do well to learn to listen for and recognize this sound, and if-necessary correct the situation either by reducing the very low end, or reducing the overall system level. The actual frequency at which the rolloff of output capability occurs can vary from one design to another.

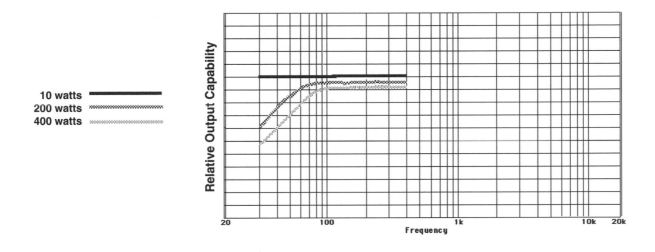

Fig. 9.31.

A Helmholtz resonator (left), involving an enclosed air mass, with a ducted port, is the theoretical basis for a ported enclosure. An effectively designed enclosure/driver combination will allow the cone to "coast" a bit around the frequency of maximum port output, increasing its capability in that range. (In order to be a well matched enclosure/driver combination, the reduction in cone motion shown below must coincide with the enclosure tuning. This reduction also coincides with an impedance rise as shown in the following chapter, Fig. 10.4.)

Note again that below the approximate frequency of maximum port output, the total output becomes increasingly useless, since cone and port output below this frequency are of essentially opposite phase. If the system is to be used at high levels, the range well below port tuning should ideally be cut with an EQ or high-pass filter, to reduce the potential for wasted power and/or cone overexcursion.

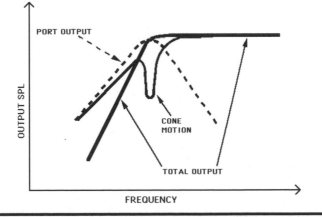

Fig. 9.32

The pre-eminent low frequency driver at this writing involves a special servo-motor, literally an electric motor in the sense most people normally think of it. Belts link the motor to the dual cone drivers. A notable limitation is that its upper frequency limit is 125 Hz (12 dB/oct.). But power compression is *under 1dB at maximum rated power* (refer back to Fig. 9.29). Shown at right is a cutaway view of the Servo-drive SDL-5, with very conservatively rated maximum output of over 135dBSPL @1 meter, from 34 Hz to 125 Hz. The enclosure configuration is a specially designed "W-bin". (courtesy Intersonics, Inc.)

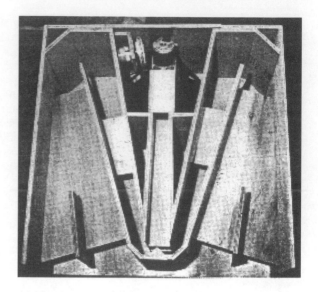

Fig. 9.33. Two additional approaches to LF reproduction.

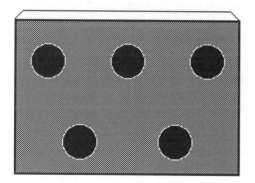

(A) Low frequency enclosure with ducted outlets only.

An enclosure of this type has relatively little output above typically 250 Hz or so, depending on the design. A notable characteristic of this approach is a major reduction in apparent distortion, even when the drivers or power amps are distorting. Above the "cutoff" frequency range, distortion harmonics are reduced along with all other energy in the range above the ports' effective output capability.

(B) 4 x 18" "Manifold" Unit.

EV MTL-4 is an interesting and effective unit. Here the "fronts" of the drivers are focused into fairly long, narrow folded paths, the outlets of which can be seen at each of the corners. The "back" of the drivers here serve to produce fairly direct radiation— almost the opposite of the traditional approach. A 2x 18" version of this unit is also manufactured.

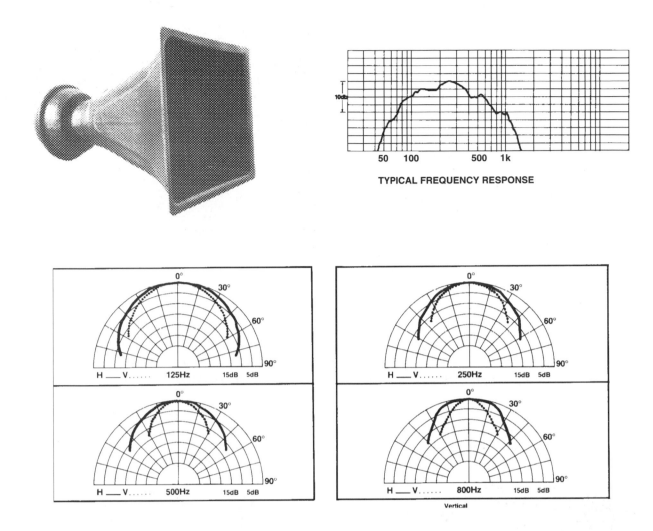

TYPICAL FREQUENCY RESPONSE

Fig. 9.34. Mid-bass horn designed for effective pattern control.
(courtesy Community Light and Sound)

Shown is the Community CB 594. Frequency response curve at top-right is fairly typical of a non-folded bass horn with no ports. To achieve extended low frequency range, we might expect to need a subwoofer below about 80 Hz (or an array of several such units). Designed to allow a choice of 15" or 18" driver, the mouth of the horn measures approximately 44" high by 54" wide, well illustrating the dimensions needed for pattern control in the lower-mids and mid-bass frequencies.

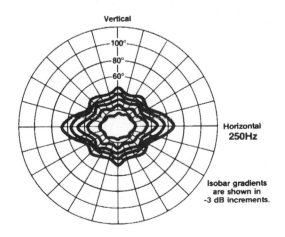

I) Practical Use of Component Directional Patterns.

In the theoretically "ideal" high-quality system, the directional pattern would be relatively constant throughout the entire frequency range of the system. In the real world there are significant variations in any component's directional pattern which may need to be understood and dealt with in high-quality applications where consistency of sound quality throughout the audience is important. This section is an attempt to convey some of the basic compromises commonly made along these lines.

As mentioned earlier, with rare exceptions, it needs to be accepted that very low frequencies will tend to be fairly omnidirectional. With very large arrays it may be possible to reduce this somewhat by arranging the subwoofers into a separate array. (There is another motivation for doing this as well, which is to couple the low frequency components' outputs—discussed in this chapter under "Speaker Arrays".) Also, some manufacturers market low frequency horns specifically designed to assist in pattern control in the low frequencies. These horns, as with mid- and high-frequency horns, display directional patterns which radically widen when the wavelength exceeds the size of the mouth in either the vertical or horizontal, or both.

Below is a description of how various component designs tend to behave in terms of their basic directional patterns. Many manufacturers publish detailed specifications of their components' patterns at various frequencies, and these can be of valuable assistance to the process. Hopefully, since many systems are put together "piecemeal" by soundpersons and/or musical bands, the information presented in this section and in Part III is helpful to an understanding of what kinds of components will tend to exhibit directional patterns which work well together.)

Midrange direct radiators have a conical pattern which typically varies by frequency as in Fig. 9.35. With any direct radiator, the -6dB point will become less than approximately 75° when the diameter of the driver equals the wavelength (this may vary somewhat, depending on the geometry of the cone).

Using the diagrams in Fig. 9.35 and substituting the size of the cone (not the nominal speaker diameter) for "D", we can see the following. With a single 12" direct radiator (~10" cone) a typical driver size for midrange reproduction, the pattern would typically begin to go below 90°-or-so in the neighborhood of 700 Hz. Typically, with a 12" speaker, the pattern reduces to less than 75° around 1.2k-1.6k, and begins to go below 60° around 2k. With a 10" speaker (~8.5" cone) the 60° pattern @-6dB would usually be reached slightly above 2k. In the case of a specially designed midrange direct radiator often found in "nearfield" speakers, typically in the 5"-8" range, the 60° pattern might be reached in the neighborhood of 3k-5k (again, as always, this may vary slightly, depending on the size and shape of the cone itself, as distinguished from the nominal speaker diameter). At around 200 Hz (a typical low-to-midrange crossover point) we might typically expect the pattern to be as much as 180° (perhaps much wider with a very compact enclosure). These basic patterns of direct radiators would hold true in *both* the horizontal and vertical plane, since the pattern is conical.

When direct radiators are arranged in a line-array, as depicted in Fig. 9.36, the pattern in the direction of the line-array (usually vertical) will more closely resemble the pattern of a driver whose size is roughly equal to the length of the array. The horizontal pattern would tend to remain approximately the same as it would be for a single driver.

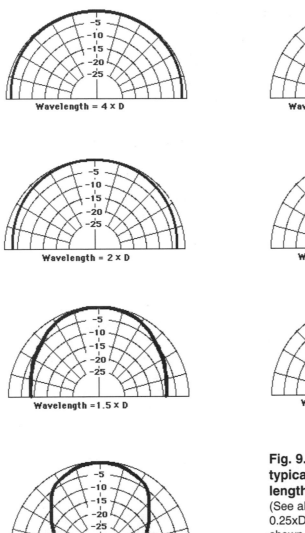

Wavelength = 4 x D

Wavelength = 2 x D

Wavelength = 1.5 X D

Wavelength = D

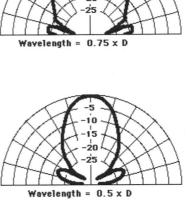

Wavelength = 0.75 x D

Wavelength = 0.5 x D

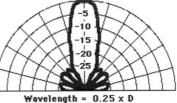

Wavelength = 0.25 x D

Fig. 9.35. Directional pattern of typical direct radiators as wavelength compares to cone diameter. (See also Fig. 9.37.) The pattern for 0.25xD, incidentally, is roughly what is shown in Chapter 2, Fig. 2.2. These patterns also depend somewhat on the shape of the cone.

Fig. 9.36 Line array ("column").
Such an array, when aligned vertically, assists in narrowing the vertical dispersion. In the horizontal plane, such an array behaves roughly as if it were a single driver, as graphed in Fig. 9.35.
In the vertical plane, though, such an array behaves approximately as a driver equal to the height of the whole array (in this case roughly 4 x D). Above the frequency at which the wavelength is roughly equal to the diameter of a single driver, though, the usefulness of such an array is diminished, requiring either a supplementary high frequency horn or specialized tapering of the array. (With 10" speakers for example, this would be about 2k, above which the advantage of the array would tend to be lost.)

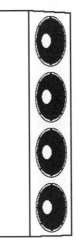

The basic pattern of a horn in its lower ranges, as mentioned, will depend heavily on the size of the horn's mouth, as well as on the design of the horn. The chart of approximate wavelengths throughout the spectrum given below may be helpful here. (Rule of thumb: wavelengths larger than the mouth=wider than 60°.)

With straight exponential (both mid and high) horns, the tendency of the pattern to narrow in either the horizontal or vertical plane, or both, is drastically affected by the direction of the flare and the manner in which it evolves from the throat, along with the size of the mouth, the size and shape of the throat, and the angles of the straight sides. This is a fairly complicated matter which needs to be taken on a horn-by-horn basis, so the following discussion will assume that the high frequency horn being used is a radial, biradial or "constant directivity" horn.

The horizontal pattern in a well designed radial horn should tend to remain fairly consistent throughout its designated dispersion angle, most often 60° or 90°. (The most common exception to this is the VHF "beaming" in radial horns mentioned earlier in the chapter.) *Here the vertical pattern tends to be the most important remaining consideration. Typically, the vertical pattern in this type of horn tends to be excessively wide when the wavelength is equal to or larger than the height of the mouth* (see Fig. 9.37). With a typical radial or constant-directivity design of 10" height (a common size), excessive vertical spread (in excess of 60°) would begin to occur about 2k and below. With the very compact 1" throat designs commonly marketed, this might be closer to 3k or 4k and below. (Remember that the degree of vertical spread would tend to increase as frequency decreases.) Other horn-mouth heights would begin to lose their ability to control the vertical pattern roughly according to Fig. 9.37.

In a "constant directivity" or "BiRadial" horn with the above-mentioned vertical slot in the throat-design, beaming would begin when the wavelength is equal-to or less-than the width of the slot.

The type of line-array mentioned above is a common configuration designed to allow fairly wide horizontal dispersion and relatively effective vertical pattern control. (A notable concern in this approach is the quality and clarity of their sound in the upper midrange, lack of good transient response, along with the relative inefficiency of using relatively large direct radiators at higher frequencies. A compromise is made here in terms of the accuracy of sound quality in the upper midrange. Well designed horn/driver assemblies tend to be, simply, clearer in this range, and tend to have much better transient response. Nevertheless, a number of multi-way high-level enclosures for high-quality applications make excellent use of this approach.)

Many midrange horns involve a flare which expands only in the horizontal plane. (The straight sides are on top and bottom here). This type of device often tends to exhibit a significant narrowing of the pattern in the horizontal as its frequency increases into the middle of its operating range. Vertical patterns tend to remain less than 60° for wavelengths smaller than the mouth height, gradually narrowing as frequency increases.

"Constant directivity" midrange horns with the previously mentioned "vertical slot" principle tend to avoid the horizontal pattern narrowing up to the approximate range where the wavelength gets smaller than the width of the slot, above which the pattern tends to narrow fairly quickly (again, see Fig. 9.37).

Fig. 9.37. Table of approximate wavelengths throughout the audio spectrum.

Frequency: **Wavelength:**
25-31.5 Hz ___~40'   ~12m
50-63 Hz_____~20'   ~6m
100-125 Hz__~10'   ~3m
200-250 Hz__~ 5'   ~1.5m
400-500 Hz__~30" ~0.75m
500-800 Hz__~24" ~0.6m
800-1k _____~16" ~0.375m
1k-1.6k _____~12" ~0.3m
1.6-2k _____~ 8" ~0.2m
2k-3k_____~ 6" ~0.15m
3-4k _____~ 4" ~0.1m
4k-6k_____~ 3" ~0.075
6-8k_____~ 2" ~0.050m
12-16k_____~ 1" ~0.025m

As a general rule of thumb, wavelengths larger than the height of the horn can be assumed to have a vertical pattern wider than about 60° or-so at the minus 6 dB points. Example: an exponential or radial horn with a mouth 10" high can usually be assumed to have a vertical pattern wider than 60° around 1.6k and below.

With any horn design involving a radial or straight exponential horn, the following general assumptions can be made about its vertical pattern.

If it is less than 4" in height, the vertical pattern will tend to exceed 60° below 4 kHz.
If it is less than 8" in height, the vertical pattern will tend to exceed 60° below 2 kHz.
If it is less than 10" in height, the vertical pattern will tend to exceed 60° below 1.6 k.
If it is less than 14" in height, the vertical pattern will tend to exceed 60° below 1.2 k.
If it is less than 20" in height, the vertical pattern will tend to exceed 60° below 800Hz.
If it is less than 30" in height, the vertical pattern will tend to exceed 60° below 500Hz.

For specific wavelengths, the formula introduced in Chapter 2 is repeated here for convenience.

Wavelength = speed of sound (1130' or 340m) divided by frequency.

Low-frequency and low-mid/mid-bass components figure into the directional characteristics as well—normally above about 200Hz or 300Hz. A low-frequency straight exponential horn of the type in Fig. 9.5 and 9.34 tends to have a pattern which narrows noticeably in the horizontal plane above about 400 Hz. In addition, the flare of the horn itself in the just mentioned design-type will tend to project the horizontal pattern in a way which narrows to below about 60°, typically above 400 Hz—depending somewhat on the horn design. As with other horns, when the wavelength gets shorter than the throat size (commonly in the 10" to 14" range with a horn designed for a 15" driver), the output fails to couple with the horn flare, and behaves more like a direct radiator.

In a low frequency horn, some degree of effective pattern control with, say, a 5' x 5' (1.5m)-square mouth, could begin to be achieved around 125-160 Hz (see again the chart in Fig. 9.37).

How does all this get put together in a practical way? This largely depends on the application. As mentioned earlier, more than about a 40° actual vertical pattern (often *not* quite the same as the "nominal" pattern) at the minus 6dB points can legitemately be considered wide, unless the horns are hung very far overhead and pointed down at the audience (as in many permanent installations). But the real-life behavior of sound generally does not allow this to be consistently achieved (at least not without an relatively tall custom-designed stack of speakers), so as with most engineering pursuits, compromises are made.

Every system, as mentioned, makes some kind of compromise around the crossover points, which is most commonly noticeable in the crossover transition leading up to the HF horn. (Some manufacturers of complete loudspeaker systems, it should be said, have reduced this compromise to the point where it is barely noticeable—though these systems tend to have a relatively wide vertical pattern overall. The narrower the vertical pattern "design goal" is, the wider these variations usually are.) Most often, the compromises become very noticeable in cases where the height of the HF horn has been reduced to cut down on the height of the system. This kind of compromise is generally quite appropriate whenever a system may need to be used in applications where relatively little height is available between the heads of the audience and the ceiling. A compromise of this kind certainly accomodates other practical needs as well, such as conserving space for portable systems within a truck, van or station wagon. (Not too many people want to carry around a horn of the size shown in Fig. 9.16-A, for example).

One approach to vertical pattern control in the midrange and upper midrange, involves vertical stacking of mid and/or high horns, or of direct radiators (line-array). This, again, depends heavily on how much height is available between the heads of the audience and the ceiling. It also depends heavily on practical concerns like the complexity of the speaker-wire feeds, and the time-constraints and expertise of the persons responsible for setup. In a "1-box" type of system designed for relative simplicity and quickness of setup, the pattern variations of the particular equipment often need to be simply accepted. And no portable system accomodates all needs perfectly—no matter what the commercial brochures may say. But the compromises can often be minimized with an understanding of how the equipment tends to behave. (Chapters 12 through 15 include further discussions describing some of the merits and drawbacks of various approaches used in speaker design, and ways in which they can affect the actual process of sound reinforcement "out in the field".

Fig. 9.38. Stacking of horns to achieve narrower vertical dispersion. Shown are typical directional pattern changes when HF horns are stacked directly atop one another. These particular graphs are for JBL model 2370 (which was pictured in Fig. 9.16). Note that the horizontal dispersion remains the same. Also note that in the VHF range, vertical dispersion changes very little—this is because the wavelengths are much too short to achieve any substantial coupling. At relatively lower frequencies, though, the outputs of the horns combine to act as essentially one taller unit. (Important: the components *must* be wired in the same polarity. Stacking units together horizontally tends not to work as well, unless they are splayed into an arc.) (Graphs courtesy JBL)

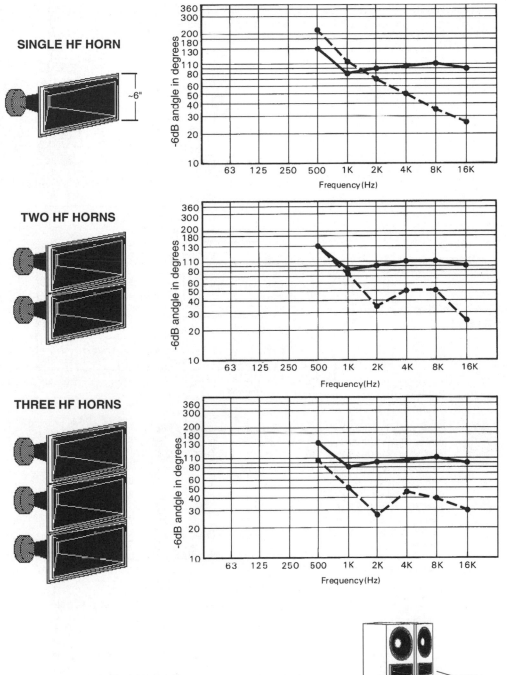

A similar result can be achieved by stacking enclosures as illustrated at right. Units are splayed as depicted in Fig. 9.39C.

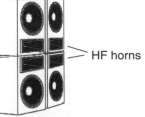

HF horns

Fig. 9.39. Combining multiple speakers and components. Several important factors come into play when combining multiple components. Firstly, in A, note that adding multiple enclosures basically amounts to a 3 dB increase in output capability for each doubling of the number of enclosures.

In B, note that when the wavelength significantly exceeds (2 to 3x or more) the distance between the center axis of two identical components placed adjacent to one another, the response and maximum output capability is increased by upwards of 6 dB per doubling of enclosures. This is particularly applicable to low frequency enclosures set up in an array, but may also come into play in the midrange frequencies when stacking horns as in the previous illustration.

In C, note that on axis, directly along the center axis in front of the array, all frequencies will tend to reinforce. Off to the side, though, some cancellation is likely to occur at different frequencies.

A

Single unit with given output capability

2 units
(+3dB)

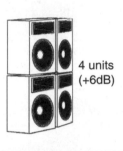

4 units
(+6dB)

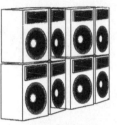

8 units (+9dB), etc.

B

MUTUAL COUPLING OF LF UNITS

```
··············  4 units
wwwwwwww  2 units
————————  1 unit
```

Relative Response 3 dB per division

Frequency

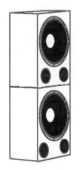

2 LF units:
(up to +6dB in on-axis response compared to single unit, below typically 200 Hz or so, depending on driver size, enclosure design and spacing. Effective low frequency cutoff typically moved downward about 1/3 octave.)

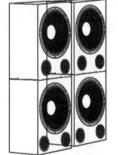

4 LF units:
(up to +12dB in on-axis response compared to single unit, below typically 150 Hz or so. Effective low frequency cutoff moved downward about 1/2 to 2/3 octave, depending on enclosure design.)

C

HORIZONTAL SPLAYING

top view

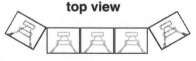

significant lobing error off to sides occurs with a splayed array of this type, resulting in changing frequency response as listener moves off-center.

top view

some lobing error, but more consistent sound quality throughout the listening area—this type of splayed arrangement is generally preferable.

Fig. 9.40. Typical crossover regions. In addition to combining bands according to their frequency response and maximum output capability, the directional pattern of midrange and high frequency components need to be considered, as outlined in the previous several sections of the text. (See the discussion in sections "e" and "f" of this chapter.)

(A)

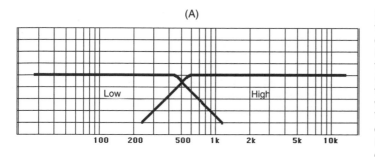

(A) Typical crossover point for traditional two-way theater system with 2"-throat HF horn. With a 500 Hz crossover point, a 15" LF driver tends to maintain at least a 90° pattern up to the frequency range where the high frequency horn is coming into play. Here, (assuming a 90° horn) a full 90° pattern is kept throughout most of the spectrum, with pattern widening beyond 90° toward the lower frequencies. Vertical pattern depends strongly on the height and design of the HF horn as discussed in Figure 9.16. Power handling ability for the high frequency driver is often less than rated wattage here.

(B)

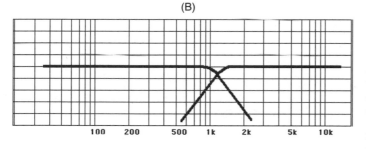

(B) As the crossover frequency is raised, power handling ability for a typical HF driver increases, but a compromise is some pattern narrowing ("beaming") of the cone driver(s) between about 500Hz and the crossover point. For a device such as a stage monitor covering a single mic position, we might accept the "beaming" as OK and use a crossover point as high as 2kHz (or even higher, depending on the HF driver's capability).

(C)

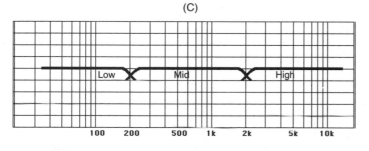

(C) Typical 3-way system crossover points. Here a dedicated midrange unit is used, ordinarily with one or more 10" or 12" cone drivers, or a midrange compression driver on a midrange horn. Moving the mid-to-high crossover point higher than 2k may in some cases allow the HF driver to handle slightly more than its quoted power rating (see again Fig. 9.19), but this depends on the driver design. A midrange compression driver often will have a minimum recommended drossover frequency higher than that shown here. Moving the low-to-mid crossover point upward may allow the mid unit to handle jmore power, but puts extra responsibility on the LF unit. Horizontal pattern ln this type of system often narrows significantly from 700Hz to 2k.

(D)

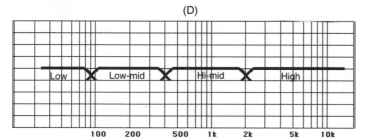

(D) Typical crossover points for a high level 4-way system with 18" subwoofer, 15" low-mid, 10" or 12" hi-mid, and 2"-throat HF driver.

(E)

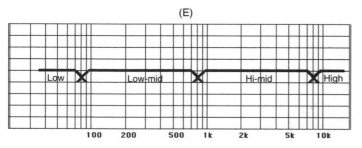

(E) Typical crossover frequencies in a four way system with 18" LF, 15" low-mid, 2" HF compression driver, and VHF unit such as described in Figures 9.23-9.25. (A 1"-throat horn with aluminum or titanium diaphram could also be used for the VHF range.) Though a VHF unit is used, these would of-course still correspond to Low, low-mid, high-mid and high on a 4-way crossover. Moving the low-mid-to-hi-mid crossover point upward would, as is typical, allow the compression driver to handle more power, though a disadvantage would tend to be "beaming" of the low-mid unit below the crossover point.

Fig. 9.41. Commercial example of a four-way crossover. (Courtesy Ashly Audio.)

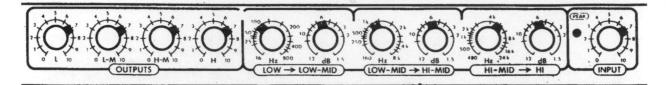

This commercial line of crossovers, commonly encountered "out in the field", is significant in that there is an additional function for tuning the response curve around the crossover point. The reason for this extra control, referred to as the "damping" control (simply labeled dB on the faceplate), is to give the operator an opportunity to adjust the system response exactly around the crossover point. Ordinarily, a 12 dB/octave crossover shows a slight response increase on-axis at the crossover point. This "damping" control was originally developed to deal with the 3dB "hump" in on-axis response characteristic of standard 12 dB/oct. crossovers (which exhibit what is known as a "Butterworth response"). Below, and in the following figure, is shown how this control affects the response.

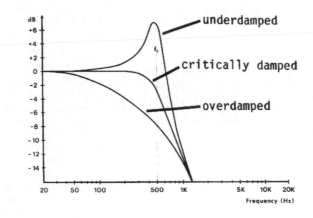

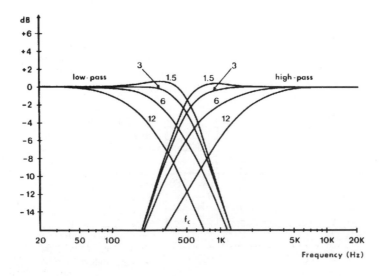

Fig. 9.42. Summed response of the filter characteristics shown in Fig. 9.41.

(A) 12 dB/octave crossoversummed response curves. The 3dB "hump" is the combined on-axis response for a standard 12 dB/oct. "Butterworth response". A setting of 6 dB on the damping control of the 12 dB/octave Ashly crossovers, all else being equal, results in flat on-axis response.

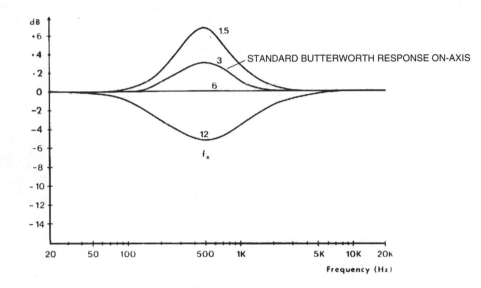

(B) Damping options on the Ashly 18dB/octave crossover. Here the damping function, labeled "dB" on the faceplate, is a carryover from the original Ashly design. Ordinarily, any standard 18dB/octave crossover will provide flat on-axis summation (setting of 3dB on the Ashly design).

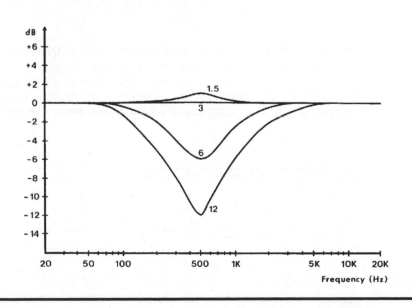

Fig. 9.43. Basic time-alignment of separate components.

In aligning multiple components with a 12 dB/oct. crossover or 18 dB/oct. crossover, a reasonable procedure is to align the "vibrating elements" of the drivers vertically. Assuming the components are properly wired this will usually place adjacent components in the proper phase relationship on-axis at the crossover point.

If the drivers are not aligned vertically, the outputs of adjacent bands in some instances will cause destructive interference in the crossover region. For example, with a 2kHz crossover point and a 12 dB/oct. crossover, a difference of 4" (0.1m) in alignment between the mid and high components would put the two directly out-of-phase on-axis at the crossover point (though a difference of 8" (.2m) would put them back in-phase again). As well, the average ear is most sensitive to differences in time alignment of loudspeakers in the 1.5 to 3 kHz range. Since this is a typical range for a crossover point in many systems, effective time alignment can become additionally important.

Note here that we are talking about the cones or diaphrams of the drivers, *not* the magnets or the voice coils. This would be the average position from which the acoustical energy actually radiates. Obviously it is helpful to know where the diaphram is on a high frequency driver (normally we can assume it is fairly close to the rear cap—see Fig. 9.21.) For a cone driver this position can usually be assumed to be roughly at the top of the dust cap (the center "dome").

Often, we will need to be content with having components out of alignment at the crossover point, as in the low-to-mid transition at right. In the illustrated folded horn, the "acoustic center" is actually significantly behind the physical position of the enclosure, due to the path-length of the folded horn (in this case, the path length to the mouth is roughly 4 & 1/2 ft.(1.5m)—other folded horns obviously may vary).

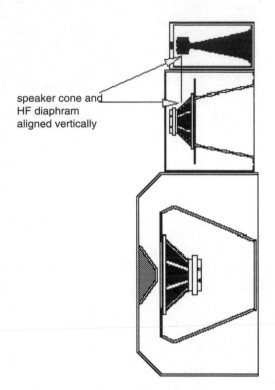

speaker cone and
HF diaphram
aligned vertically

Fig. 9.44. Front panel controls of a 24dB/octave crossover with delay

options. Many 24dB/oct. crossovers have a delay adjustment intended for compensating for differences in the physical alignment of multiple components. The amount of delay available may vary from one manufacturer's design to another. In rough terms, we can figure to use 1.1 millisecond of delay for every foot of difference in alignment, or 1 millisecond for every .34 meter.

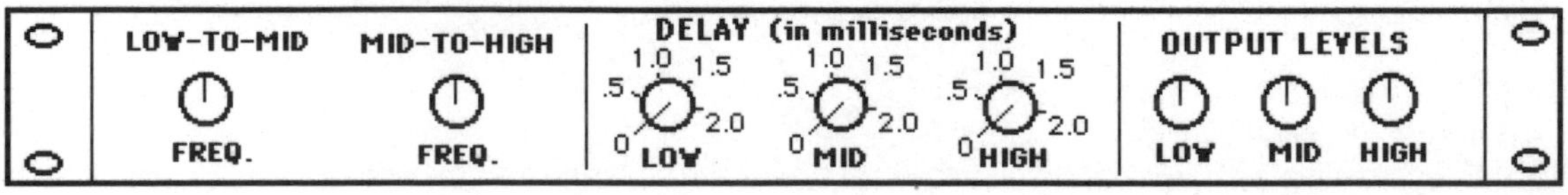

LOW-TO-MID MID-TO-HIGH DELAY (in milliseconds) OUTPUT LEVELS
FREQ. FREQ. LOW MID HIGH LOW MID HIGH

Fig. 9.45. Basic use of delay settings on a 24 dB/oct. crossover. In this example, the cone and diaphram of the mid and high horn are aligned, but there is a path-length difference between the low and mid. When using a crossover with a delay function, as in the previous illustration, we should delay the low frequency output by the amount of time sound takes to travel the distance from the mid and high frequency drivers to the mouth of their respective horns. In this instance no delay would be used on the mid or high crossover outputs.

In any system, the rearmost driver would be used as the reference point and the drivers farther up would be delayed appropriately. In the example at bottom right, the midrange driver is placed farthest back, so a very slight delay would be used on the high output, with a somewhat longer delay on the low frequency output.

The scale below can be used as an approximate guide to how much delay to use in a given situation. We may also wish to make an assessment of what the path length differences are not only on axis, but also at various angles off-axis, then take an average to figure the delay time.

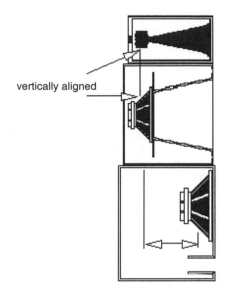

vertically aligned

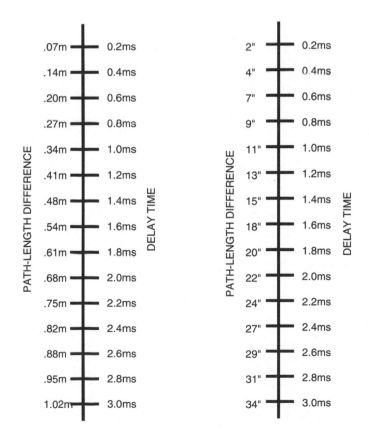

PATH-LENGTH DIFFERENCE	DELAY TIME	PATH-LENGTH DIFFERENCE	DELAY TIME
.07m	0.2ms	2"	0.2ms
.14m	0.4ms	4"	0.4ms
.20m	0.6ms	7"	0.6ms
.27m	0.8ms	9"	0.8ms
.34m	1.0ms	11"	1.0ms
.41m	1.2ms	13"	1.2ms
.48m	1.4ms	15"	1.4ms
.54m	1.6ms	18"	1.6ms
.61m	1.8ms	20"	1.8ms
.68m	2.0ms	22"	2.0ms
.75m	2.2ms	24"	2.2ms
.82m	2.4ms	27"	2.4ms
.88m	2.6ms	29"	2.6ms
.95m	2.8ms	31"	2.8ms
1.02m	3.0ms	34"	3.0ms

Fig. 9.46. Use of crossover output levels. The ouput level controls on an electronic crossover serve as a form of shelving EQ. This allows for adjustment to compensate for different power amplifier gains and speaker component sensitivity, as well as for tuning a system to taste. Generally, one should "rough-tune" a system with the main outboard EQ set "flat"., then use the EQ to "fine-tune" the system. The particular crossover frequencies and curves here are for illustration only.

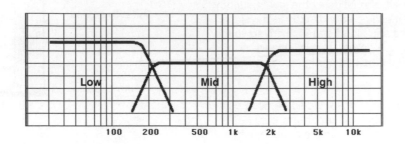

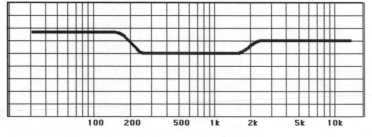

RESULTING OVERALL RESPONSE

Fig. 9.47. Use of a crossover to reduce potentially damaging extreme low frequencies. Using a 4-way electronic crossover on a 3-way system (or a 3-way crossover on a biamplified system) allows the lowest crossover point to be used as a high-pass filter. Here the upper three bands of the crossover itself are used to drive a 3-way system. The "low" output of the crossover is simply not used and the "lowmid" output is used to drive the woofer. (The particular crossover frequencies are again used here for purpose of illustration only. Utilizing a EQ with a variable high-pass filter would eliminate the need for this type of procedure.)

A similar approach would allow a 4-way crossover to be used on a 2-way system, using the highest crossover point to reduce the VHF range above, say, 14kHz or so. (Though music has little energy above this approximate frequency, excess—and perhaps inaudible—energy from synthesizers and other sources can sometimes damage high frequency drivers as well as overdrive power amplifiers.)

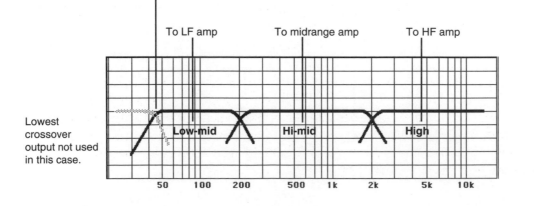

CHAPTER 10

POWER AMPS and IMPEDANCE CONCERNS

The obvious purpose of an amplifier is to produce an output signal closely identical to, but stronger than, the input signal given to it. While amplifiers intended to perform other functions are also used, here we will focus on this basic purpose of supplying an effective output signal from power amplifiers.

The ability of an amplifier to produce output is affected by the circuit's impedance according to Ohm's Law (introduced in Chapter 4). It should be carefully noted that since impedance can change significantly according to frequency (see Fig. 10.4), the output power of an amp can sometimes be significantly affected by this factor.

Each power amplifier, at a given frequency, has a maximum output capability which follows a curve according to the impedance of the circuit. Fig. 10.2 shows two such curves. Note that up to a certain approximate range, as impedance is reduced the curves basically follow Ohm's law. (For a given voltage, half the impedance=twice the current, and thus twice the power as described in Chapter 4.) Beyond a certain point, as impedance continues to be reduced, the maximum power capability first begins to level off, then finally falls off fairly drastically. This is a natural characteristic of amplifier circuits.

Additionally, this curve may vary somewhat at different frequencies (though it is usually published at 1 kHz). Figure 10.2-B shows a typical way in which power capability varies *according to frequency* at different impedances.

Now, having established a couple of the limitations of typical power amplifiers, lets deal with them in a simpler way. Most power amplifiers quote their output specifications into 16Ω, 8Ω and 4Ω according to US Federal Trade Commission guidelines. (As might be expected, some manufacturers are much more conservative in presenting their specs than are others.) While these output specifications do not by any means tell the whole story, they serve as a useful guide in assessing roughly what level of output capability can be expected.

(There are different schools of thought on how to best and most efficiently match power amplifier capabilities to driver capabilities. Generally, most experienced engineers prefer to have power amps which exceed the rating of the drivers, and if necessary use voltage-limiting or power-limiting devices to protect the drivers from being overpowered. Increasingly, loudspeaker manufacturers are designing these features into the equipment. As well, most processor-controlled systems have this type of limiting in one form or another.)

The simplest way of assessing the overall impedance of the circuit is to note the "nominal" impedance rating of the speakers, and how they are wired together. The two basic ways of wiring speakers together are *series circuits* and *parallel circuits*. Fig. 10.3 shows the difference between the two. (In practice, an advantage of parallel circuits is that if one driver fails, the remaining one(s) in the circuit will continue to function. In a series circuit, if one driver fails, the entire circuit is interrupted. In well-designed-and-operated systems, though, total failure of any driver should rarely—if ever—happen. Nevertheless, parallel circuits are normally regarded as the most dependable method, and the majority of modern systems are wired in this way.)

Multiple drivers wired in parallel will present lower impedance to the amplifier output, as follows: For parallel circuits, divide the impedance of each identical driver by the number of drivers. If two identical drivers or speaker enclosures are wired in parallel, the total impedance presented to the amplifier output will be cut in half. Thus, two 8 ohm drivers in parallel will present a total impedance of 4Ω. Two 16Ω drivers in parallel will present a total impedance of 8Ω.

Multiple drivers wired in series will present higher impedance to the amplifier output, as follows: For series circuits, multiply the individual impedance by the number of drivers. If two identical drivers or speaker enclosures are wired in series, the total impedance presented to the amplifier output will be double the individual impedance of each speaker. So two 8Ω loads in series will present a total load of 16Ω to the amp.

Speakers wired in groups of four-or-more can be arranged in a combination of series and parallel (usually called "series/parallel"). Fig. 10.3 shows total nominal impedance calculations for a number of common driver combinations.

Since most manufacturers of power amplifiers quote their maximum output capability into loads of 4Ω and 8Ω, the use of nominal impedance ratings of speakers is convenient. In practice, however, impedance varies greatly according to frequency, so the nominal impedance is often significantly different than the actual impedance in the frequency range being reproduced.

Fig. 10.4 shows a typical impedance curve of a cone driver. Here it can be seen that a typical cone driver will have its lowest impedance in the midrange of the audio spectrum. In rare cases this might allow less maximum power in feeding multiple drivers wired in parallel, especially when a cone driver is used in the midrange. This would generally become a concern only when the midrange needs to be pushed "to the hilt". But this is the exception to the rule. Under most circumstances the published nominal impedance ratings are an adequate guideline in assessing impedance. The impedance rise in the low frequencies, though, is one reason why it is generally preferable for the amplifier rating to somewhat exceed the speaker's rated power when used for low frequency components.

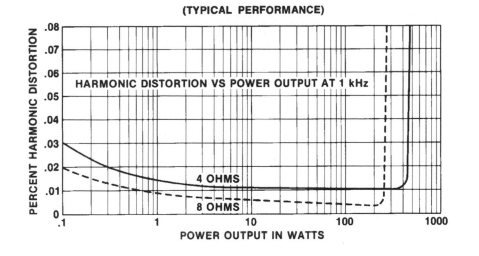

(TYPICAL PERFORMANCE)

Fig. 10.1. Examples of power amplifier output capability.
(Above) Typical curves for a high quality power amplifier at 4 ohm and 8 ohm load, using a 1 kHz signal. Here the curves trace the percentage of harmonic distortion as power output increases. The slight rise at low power levels is typical, and is well below audible levels. The rapid rise at high power output is typical of what happens as a power amp reaches its maximum output capability, beyond which noticeable distortion (clipping) occurs. In this case the amplifier is very conservatively rated at 200 watts RMS per channel into 8 ohms (both channels driven) and at 400 watts RMS per channel into 4 ohms. (Courtesy Altec)

(Below) Example of how maximum power output can vary according to frequency. This set of curves, for the same power amp as above, shows why the ratings from 20Hz-20kHz are normally less than the capability through the midrange frequencies. Note, though, that the rolloff of these curves tends to be outside the range where most of the power is needed, which is normally from about 40Hz and up. The experienced user will recognize that in the VHF range high amounts of power are normally not needed to drive compression drivers and tweeters.(Courtesy Altec)

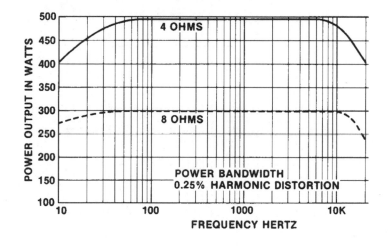

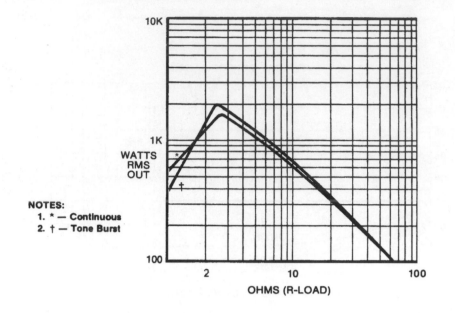

Fig. 10.2. Additional graphs of typical maximum power amp output capability.
Although power capability is most often quoted at 4 ohms, 8ohms and 16ohms, the actual output capability follows a curve, as above. Such curves rise as impedance decreases (roughly according to Ohm's Law) until a certain impedance is reached, below which the output capability *decreases*. The impedance below which power capability begins to fall off varies from one amp to another, and in any given amp may also vary according to frequency. In the above case, note that maximum output at 2 ohms is roughly the same as at 4 ohms. In some cases (where the amp is not designed to be used at 2 ohms) the output ability may actually fall off very significantly below 4 ohms (and overheating of the amp at very low impedances, or in the worst case complete failure may become a problem as well). Below is illustrated a typical set of maximum output curves, according to frequency, of a contemporary high quality amplifier. (Courtesy Crown International).

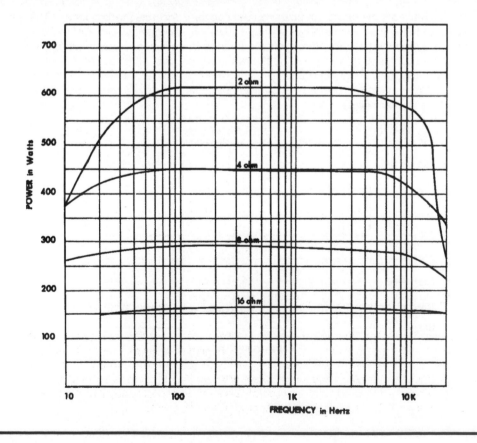

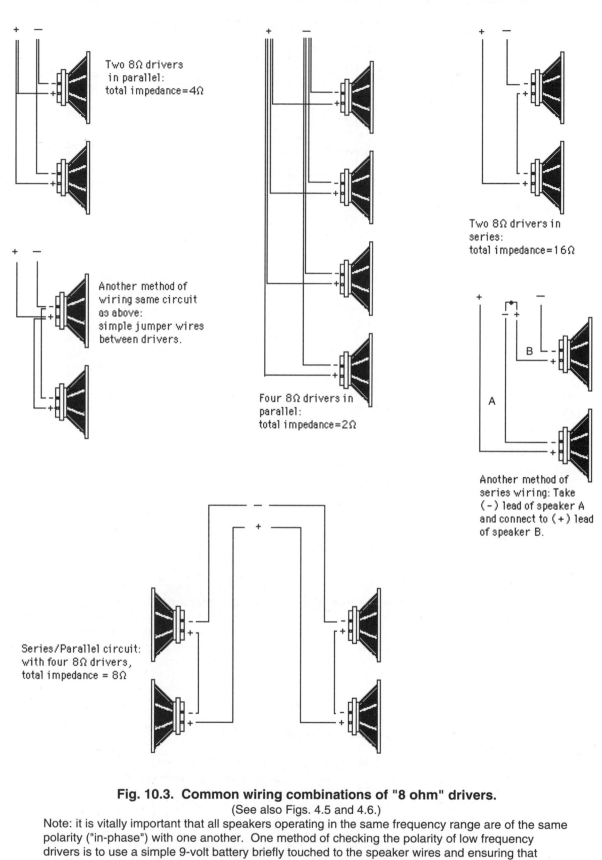

Two 8Ω drivers in parallel: total impedance=4Ω

Another method of wiring same circuit as above: simple jumper wires between drivers.

Four 8Ω drivers in parallel: total impedance=2Ω

Two 8Ω drivers in series: total impedance=16Ω

Another method of series wiring: Take (−) lead of speaker A and connect to (+) lead of speaker B.

Series/Parallel circuit: with four 8Ω drivers, total impedance = 8Ω

Fig. 10.3. Common wiring combinations of "8 ohm" drivers.
(See also Figs. 4.5 and 4.6.)
Note: it is vitally important that all speakers operating in the same frequency range are of the same polarity ("in-phase") with one another. One method of checking the polarity of low frequency drivers is to use a simple 9-volt battery briefly touched to the speaker wires and ensuring that positive voltage to the "+" terminal produces forward motion of all of the speaker cones.
(Additional note: most JBL cone drivers and compression drivers use the black terminal as "+", and the red terminal as"—", the opposite of most other manufacturers.)

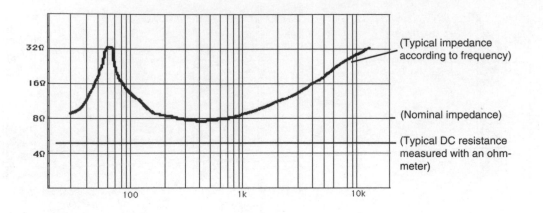

(Typical impedance according to frequency)

(Nominal impedance)

(Typical DC resistance measured with an ohm-meter)

Fig. 10.4. Typical impedance curve of an "8 ohm" low-frequency driver.
The commonly used 4ohm, 8ohm and 16ohm ratings are "nominal" impedance, which essentially means "what we choose to name it". This is for simplicity's sake, and for the vast majority of applications simple arithmetic based on the nominal impedance is adequate to do the job. Most often, the lowest impedance presented to the amplifier will be close to the nominal impedance, as above. In certain cases, though, the impedance in the midrange falls significantly lower than the nominal impedance—this is a judgement made by the particular manufacturer. In several commercial loud-speaker designs this can be as low as 5ohms in the midrange. Ordinarily this would not be a serious issue, unless we are using two such drivers as midrange drivers, in parallel with an amplifier not designed to operate below 4 ohms.

The impedance variations are already taken into account in published frequency response curves, so the only concern here is the impedance relationship with the amplifier. The impedance rise in the lows varies, depending on the enclosure in which it is installed. Several such "humps" might be displayed.

Fig. 10.5. Typical impedance curve of a 16-ohm high frequency driver.
(Courtesy JBL—curve shown for 2445 driver) The peaks and dips shown here, while typical, can vary somewhat in frequency with different drivers, and are also affected to an extent by the horn design. Still, for most applications, simple arithmetic based on the nominal impedance will suffice.

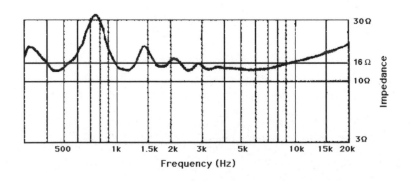

Fig. 10.6. Typical power amp rear panel connections.

(A) Amplifier set in standard two channel mode, sometimes labeled "dual" or "stereo". The illustrated select switch between two channel operation and mono-bridge mode is often located behind a removable panel, to reduce the likelihood of inadvertent switching by a careless hand. (In some cases, a qualified service technician might be required to make the switch.)

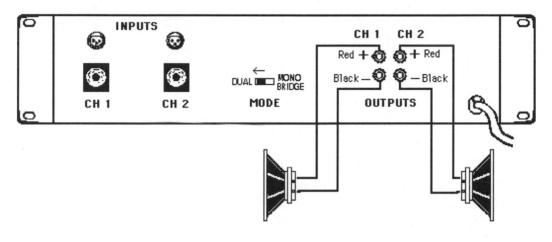

(B) Amplifier wired in bridged mono mode.
When in bridged operation, the optimal impedance of the circuit is double the optimal impedance for standard two channel operation, as shown in Fig. 10.7.

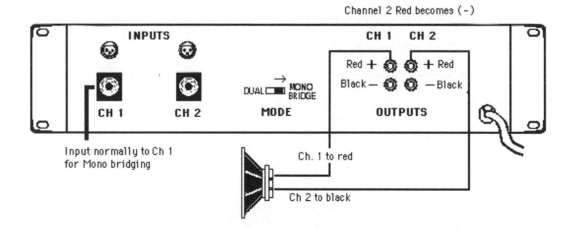

(Note: Some power amplifiers include an additional setting for "Dual mono", which feeds both inputs with the same signal (normally from the "Channel 1" or "Channel A" input jack, but must be wired as in "A" of this figure. A "dual mono" setting, designed to eliminate the need for a "Y" connector, should not be confused with the bridged mode shown in "B".)

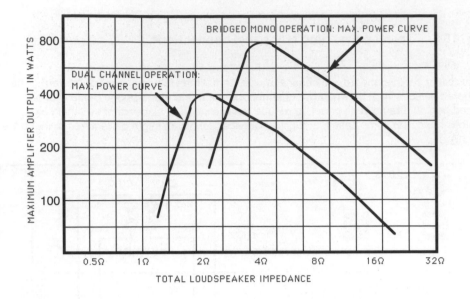

Fig. 10.7. Typical maximum power relationship between standard operation and bridged mono operation. When a power amp is operated in the bridged mode, the red ("hot") output of the 2nd channel operates together with that of Channel 1, but in opposite polarity. This method of operation changes the load impedance requirements. Shown are curves (of a hypothetical power amp) for maximum available output at a given percentage of distortion, say .1%, with both channels operating. As can be seen, twice the maximum power is available in the bridged mode, but the maximum is achieved at double the impedance as compared to standard two channel operation. This is why mono specifications are ordinarily quoted into 16Ω and 8Ω, rather than 8Ω and 4Ω.

The maximum power capablity and its relationship to load impedance will of-course depend on the design of the amp. However, the relationship of these curves to one another is always similar to that shown here. (In other words, if the shape of one curve changes, so will the shape of the other. Likewise, if we move one of these curves with respect to the above graph, the second curve will always move in conjunction with it, and the bridged output capability will always reach its maximum at roughly twice the impedance.)

Fig. 10.8. Typical standard amplifier rack.
A well designed rack of three two-channel amplifiers such as below can typically handle the power-amp requirements for a modest size three-way or four-way high-output mono system along with two channels of stage monitoring. The basic wiring and connector concerns of amplifier racks are further described in Chapter 16.

Fig. 10.9. Commercial examples of power amplifiers. (Top) The Carver PM-1.5, weighing in at a mere 21 pounds yet providing 600W RMS per channel into 4Ω, has found wide use on the "concert tour" as a monitor amp, as well as for midrange and HF amplification. (It's descendant, the PM-2.0T, with similar specs, actually weighs only 12 lbs.) (Above) The Crown Macrotech 2400 is an excellent example of a compact contemporary high output amplifier, delivering over 1000 watts RMS per channel into 2Ω. (Below) The Crown Macrotech 10,000, originally developed for medical magnetic resonance imaging (MRI) technology, is so potent that two of these amps drive the entire sound system at the Indianapolis Speedway (with a third on hand as a spare).

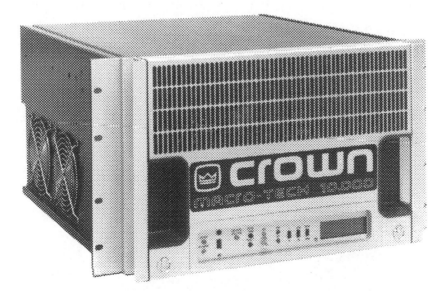

Part Three

SYSTEMS: DESIGN AND USE

CHAPTER 11

GENERAL SYSTEM CONSIDERATIONS

The appropriate design of a system can of course be affected by an extremely wide variety of factors, many of which arc beyond the scope of this book. Certainly, in designing and choosing a system, the overall output level and required frequency range of the system need to be assessed, in order to accomodate the heaviest demands likely to be placed upon the system. Among other things which should normally be considered early in the design stage: the required directional characteristics of the speakers, the number of input channels likely to be needed, what kind of effects, if any, are desireable, and of-course the nature and complexity of the additional tasks it may be required to perform (such as perhaps true stereo output, type of stage monitor system, etc.). As well, concerns relating to system wiring and physical placement of equipment need to be considered.

This chapter briefly overviews some of these basic concerns, and introduces some additional practical matters involved in designing and using systems. While none of the information here (or anywhere in this or any other book) can take the place of experience, good planning ability and common sense, the general descriptions in this chapter and throughout Part III hopefully can serve as a useful guide in the process.

a) General Assessment of System Requirements.

In general, the following things should be assessed before deciding on what equipment to use in a system.

(1) What should be the basic speaker configuration: single or dual clusters, distributed system, etc.?

(2) What are the output requirements: overall output level and the likely distribution of energy through the system's frequency range? (Perhaps emphasis on the low end?, lots of sizzle?, relatively flat response throughout the spectrum?, etc.) Are the output requirements such that the system should be biamplified, triamplified or 4-way amplified?

(3) What kind of basic dispersion pattern is likely to be most useful?

(4) How many input channels will be needed; will submasters be needed, etc?

(5) What type of EQ capability and other signal processing will be useful?

(6) What type of microphones will be most useful within the budget available, and how many?

(7) Is it more important to have versatility, or to have simplicity and ease of operation? (What is the technical and/or artistic skill-level of the likely system operator? Will a compromise need to be made for this reason?)

(8) Aesthetic concerns: what should the system look like? Should it be as inconspicuous as possible or should it stand out? (Some people are impressed by a lot of visible speakers.)

(9) Cost considerations, of course, run across all of these—if budget is limited, where should the money be spent first? Can the system be arranged so improvements can be made as money becomes available?

b) Equipment Selection (General).

To maximize the likelihood of success with a system, thorough consideration should be given to anticipating (as best as possible) the range of situations in which it is likely to be used. With a permanently installed system, while the size of an audience in a given room can change the acoustics significantly, these changes can generally be predicted, or, at the very least, fairly quickly learned once the system is put into action. In many cases, though, the type of audio program the system needs to handle might change radically from one event to another.

With portable systems nearly the opposite can often hold true. The type of environment might change radically from one location to another, while perhaps the type of program might remain similar, if not the same, from one event to another.

The choice of specific equipment of course can vary widely depending on the application. Here is a general overview of the basic concerns about what equipment to use.

Microphones should generally be chosen mainly for:

(1) *The appropriate directional pattern.* With rare exceptions, for sound reinforcement, mics with a unidirectional design are most useful. These include the cardioid, supercardioid and hypercardioid designs discussed in Chapter 5. Usually, cardioid and supercardioid patterns are good all-purpose designs. Hypercardioid mics tend to be additionally helpful when rejection of sound coming from the sides is very important. Rejection of distant sounds in-general (as opposed to sound from the up-close user) is also a relevant concern here. Mics with strong proximity effect (supercardioid, hypercardioid, "Differoid", "Noise-cancelling/differential", etc.) can provide a substantial advantage in high-level applications—but here the mic must be used consistently very close-up or the advantage is lost.

(2) *Their frequency response curves.* Mics ideally should be chosen to reduce equalization needs as much as is reasonably possible. Generally, a matched set of vocal microphones should be used, unless some kind of major overriding concern is involved. EQ needs for various classes of instruments and drums will sometimes tend to lean in certain directions, so it is helpful if these are chosen accordingly. Drums and bass instruments, generally, should have microphones with fairly strong low frequency response. This is particularly true of kick drum and low tom-toms, but also tends to be true of the middle toms. The high-hat mic and drum overheads, if used, should have good very-high-frequency response. Often, the same mics used for vocals can, if necessary, be used for "treble" instruments, baritone instruments and guitar. Beyond these general considerations, such choices are largely a matter of personal taste (though the mics ideally should all be heard together in the same system before making such selections).

Signal processing capability which is needed for a particular application perhaps-obviously involves a number of important judgements at the planning stage.

The *number of input channels* of the mixer should generally include several extra channels beyond the anticipated need, to allow for unexpected guest performers or other additional applications, such as input for tape deck or CD player, etc. Adequate channels should be provided for effects returns as well (usually this means standard input channels, as discussed in Chapters 7 and 13).

The *complexity of the equipment* can be either an advantage or a disadvantage, largely depending on who the system operator(s) will be. If the operator(s) are skilled and technically competent, versatility of EQ controls, aux. send and return options and additional signal processing such as extra compressor/ limiters for submasters and individual channels can be superb and highly effective tools. If the operator lacks reasonable skill and experience, the additional signal processing options can be nightmares.

The *additional signal processing features*, aside from budget-concerns, should depend largely on the skill-level of the operator, as well as on how critical the needs of the application are. A highly critical audience which expects to hear a high-quality musical sound might merit a more intense investment in versatile equipment and hiring of a skilled operator, than might an audience which just needs to hear the very basics. (A serious caution is in order here: Do not underestimate the listening expectations of modern audiences. They may not be able to identify what they hear, but their feelings about the sound might play a strong role in influencing their perception of a given presentation.)

Generally, *all but the most basic systems should have at least one limiter to protect the power amplifiers from being overdriven and the loudspeakers from damage* (ideally, if an active (electronic) crossover is involved, one limiter per crossover output). The limiter(s) should be set up so tampering is not likely, either by placing it in an inaccessible location, or with a security cover preventing access to the controls once the unit is properly set. If the operator is not likely to be relatively skilled, it might be sensible to have the main outboard EQ similarly secured behind a security cover, or otherwise made unavailable to the operator(s). Upon encountering a skilled operator with special requirements, it might occasionally be sensible to make these units accessible for a particular purpose. For special adjustments in system response, it might be much more sensible to make one-or-more additional outboard units available to the operator so the basic system characteristics are not altered for a particular event (which might make harder, or in the most extreme cases disastrous, work for other operators who follow later).

Certainly, *choice of power amplifiers* capable of adequate output is an important concern as well (as discussed in Chapter 10). If amplifiers with ratings well beyond the drivers' capabilities are used, appropriate signal limiting becomes more important, since driver distortion is often less obvious than amplifier distortion, especially to the inexperienced user.

c) Speaker Selection (General).

The choice of dispersion angles of the loudspeakers is a major factor in dealing with the shape of the room and the main audience positions within the room, as well as with the acoustic characteristics of the room. As discussed in Chapter 9, this can be a somewhat complicated situation, since the loudspeaker dispersion patterns commonly vary at different frequencies and since the acoustic characteristics also can vary widely. But here we will reduce it to its very basics.

In most portable systems, it is likely to be difficult to choose the pattern to fit the room, since the room characteristics can change radically from one location to another. Generally, with a portable system involving a single unit on each side of a stage or platform , a 90° horizontal pattern brings reasonably acceptable results on the average. The 90° configuration is largely based on the idea that if the loudspeakers are placed at the corners of a rectangular room, the system can cover essentially the whole room. In practice this approximate degree of dispersion is a reasonable compromise allowing coverage of both wide and narrow rooms. With systems likely to be used in arrays of two or more identical units per cluster, a narrower pattern more on the order of 60° tends to allow more flexibility, allowing the speaker components to be arrayed for either wide and narrow coverage.

For portable systems, it certainly seems sensible to assess in-advance the general types of rooms in which the particular system is likely to be used. If a system is likely to be used in rooms where there there is not much room between the heads of the audience and the ceiling, a system should be chosen so the best possible projection can be achieved within the available height. Generally this would involve a high frequency horn positioned on top. In almost all cases, the HF horn should be placed as far as reasonably possible above the heads of the audience, and, where possible, the midrange component too.

In permanent installations, the placement and directional characteristics of the loudspeakers of-course need to be carefully oriented to the shape and reverberant characteristics of the environment. In a system with critical quality requirements, this may call for the services of a qualified acoustical consultant with appropriate experience and credentials, working in conjunction with a similarly qualified system contractor. Some of the concerns regarding such installations are also offered throughout the following several chapters.

Certainly, a system should be chosen which reasonably well achieves the necessary sound level, as well as the necessary frequency range. Here, as discussed in Chapter 9, there are a couple of additional twists which need to be heeded. One important concern is the difference in tonal quality (i.e., frequency response) between the sound on-axis and at off-axis angles, both horizontal and vertical. Even the best components and system packages have this type of variation to some extent measurable by electronic testing equipment. In some instances the variations are relatively inaudible, but many designs suffer from these variations to a degree which makes them unable to sound similar throughout their stated dispersion angles.

The other concern has to do with maximum output capability at different frequencies. Often the response characteristics of speaker systems changes at high levels due to power compression and other limitations also discussed in Chapter 9. For example, a system with strong response down to, say, 50 Hz commonly will be unable to reproduce 50 Hz at high levels. (Remember the difference between frequency response and maximum output capability.) Care should be taken to ensure that the selected components can reasonably well maintain their "sound" at the levels at which they will be used in the field. If possible, this should involve a listening test of the system in the basic type of environment in which it will be used, prior to a final purchase agreement. At minimum, an "A/B" comparative test of the system should be conducted alongside a system with which one is already familiar.

d) Single Vs. Dual Speaker Systems.

The choice between whether to use a single or dual system revolves around several factors. These factors are the degree of clarity desired, the apparent direction from which we wish the audience to perceive the sound as arriving from, and of-course practical concerns such as the placement options and the difficulty involved in implementing the most desired options. So these concerns need to be balanced in the most effective way possible in any given situation.

With regard to the needed degree of clarity, single clusters tend to be the most desireable option if assessed in terms of articulation alone. They tend to provide the clearest sound for the most audience. This of-course assumes that circumstances allow such an arrangement to be effectively implented. Generally, this amounts to having the opportunity to use a relatively permanent system, or at least the opportunity to erect a scaffold of some kind. As well, the physical structure of the room must allow for an appropriate speaker location; a low ceiling or other physical limitation might immediately rule out such an arrangement.

The apparent direction from which the sound emanates is a subtle, but nevertheless important, consideration. Since effective communication is the main goal in speech reinforcement, a sense of realism that the sound` is coming from the approximate direction of the talker can greatly enhance a person's presentation. Utilizing a single loudspeaker cluster placed approximately above a platfrom, lectern or pulpit can lend strongly to this effect. In permanent installations it is often possible to safely suspend or otherwise mount such a cluster at a significant enough height to minimize potential feedback problems. Since directional hearing is relatively less sensitive in the vertical plane (Chapter 3), the perceived vertical difference is relatively minimal. The result, when combined with the visual image of the person speaking, is the commonly perceived illusion that the sound is emanating from the person speaking, rather than from the actual location of the cluster itself. But, such a cluster must be able to reach the bulk of the audience reasonably effectively, or it becomes self defeating to worry about apparent direction of the sound's origin from the audience's perspective. If budget allows, a delayed distributed system can also be implemented in such a way as to preserve the image that the sound is originating from the talker's position.

Probably the most important argument for using a single cluster has to do with destructive interference (the "comb-filtering" effect mentioned a number of times throughout this book) caused by two or more interacting wave patterns. This tends not to happen to any great extent with a well designed single cluster, and from an acoustical standpoint a single cluster is certainly the preferred option for speech reinforcement. Of course, when a single cluster cannot effectively provide coverage to the bulk of an audience, and a delayed distributed system is beyond the budget limitations, two or more speaker locations must be used, and the comb-filtering simply accepted as an appropriate compromise. In practice, this compromise is not always a drastic one, except in the low frequencies. (In a difficult environment such as a typical medium to large-size house of worship or other large reverberant hall, though, the compromise inherent in using dual speaker locations may be more critical. Given the high cost of such installations, common sense dictates that the decision should be made in conjunction with an experienced sound contractor familiar with modern techniques for assessing acoustic environments and the associated effects on intelligibility of speech.)

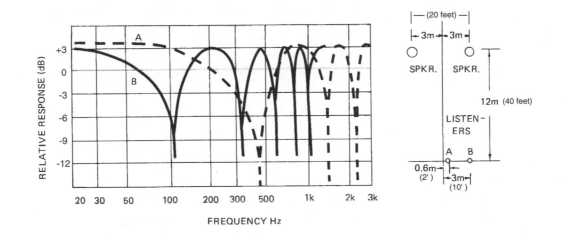

Fig. 11.1. Example of dual-speaker system response in audience. Note how the interference effects of two interacting speaker systems reproducing the same sounds cause frequency response to change from side to side in an audience. In permanent speech reinforcment installations in difficult environments, this points to the advantages of a single cluster mounted overhead. Where two speaker locations are used, whether by choice or necessity, we at least need to be aware that response will change from one location to another. (illustration courtesy JBL Professional) See the following figure also.

With music reinforcement systems (including multipurpose systems handling both speech and music) an additional concern is involved. People often find music more pleasant when it emanates from a relatively broad horizontal area (even if it is reproduced in mono). In a very reverberant environment the room itself causes this, sometimes to excess—here the reflected sound is arriving at the listeners' positions from a variety of directions in a variety of time relationships (kind of a live stereo effect—or more accurately, one of the natural effects which stereo systems mimic).

In music reinforcement, having the sound emanate from a relatively broad area or from two relatively widely spaced sources is consistent with the spread of performers across a typical stage, so the sound image from the split system often coincides well with the visual image from the audience's standpoint. Also, two or more speakers is quite consistent with the normal modern format for listening to music. As well, music reinforcement systems are often run in true stereo, allowing panning of, for example, certain drums or other special effects (though ordinarily a good majority of the audience will miss the "stereo" effects). As mentioned above, there is a substantial comb-filtering here, especially in the lower frequencies. As always, the primary concern is effective coverage. Both single and dual clusters have proven effective in various settings. Oftentimes a center cluster is the best option in providing effective coverage of a semicircular seating arrangement, as in Fig. 14.11. In many cases, though, practical concerns require—like it or not—that we stack or hang a cluster on each side of the stage (this is due in part to the need for stage lighting trusses across the top of the stage, and also due to the difficulty of suspending an adequately large single cluster for most musical applications).

Fig. 11.2. Subjective perception of comb-filtering. (courtesy JBL Professional) Shown is the approximate subjective perception of a listener in Position "B" of the previous illustration. As introduced in Chapter 5, "comb-filtering" also comes into play when sound is reflected off of nearby surfaces and when failing to follow the 3-to-1 rule of microphone use. So while some degree of this type of interference is commonly unavoidable, the combination of interference from multiple speakers, reflections, and poor microphone use, perhaps together with a difficult environment, can sometimes make "mincemeat" out of the resulting sound. Generally we need to get as many of these factors in our favor as possible for a given situation. (As in the previous figure, the frequencies of such interference will naturally change as the position in the audience changes. This of-course also comes into play in the system operator's assessment of the sound from a given position wherever two speaker locations are used (see also Fig. 14.4 and 14.5).)

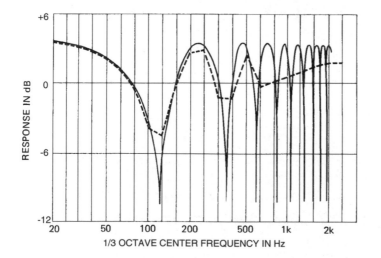

SOLID LINE — MEASURED SINE WAVE FREQUENCY RESPONSE

DOTTED LINE — 1/3 OCTAVE BAND RESPONSE, CLOSELY CORRESPONDING TO SUBJECTIVE TONAL QUALITY WHEN LISTENING TO NORMAL PROGRAM MATERIAL. ABOVE 1 kHz RESPONSE IS ESSENTIALLY FLAT.

Author's note: The use of 1/3 octave bands to represent subjective tonal quality is related to the minimum detectable difference between sine waves introduced in Chapter 3, section"g".

e) Distributed Systems.

Distributed systems are useful in any of a wide variety of situations where the listeners are spread out beyond the effective range of a single or dual speaker setup. In addition to obvious situations such as where the listening area is divided into a number of rooms, distributed systems are useful:

(1) when significant portions of the listening area are obscured by partitions, abutments or overhangs;

(2) when the farther reaches of the audience are at a distance which would required uncomfortable or harmful listening levels in close range of the loudspeaker clusters;

(3) when the environment is highly reverberant.

(4) when the illusion of sound originating from the talker(s)' position needs to be preserved.

Basically, distributed can be described as falling into two categories: *simultaneous distributed systems*, and *delayed distributed systems*. The first approach involves placing a relatively large number of low-level speakers, strategically placed to cover the entire audience. Among the advantages of well-designed simultaneous systems are: relatively even distribution of sound levels throughout the listening area(s), and close time-synchronization of the audio with the visual image of the public speaker or performers. This might be desireable, for example, in a large environment where the talker or performer is also pictured on a video screen for the audience.

A delayed system involves the use of one or more digital-delay units to delay the signal to the loudspeakers farther away from the stage or platform so they are synchronized with the arrival of the sound from the front cluster(s). As well, such a system, as already discussed, allows the image of the sound's origin to be preserved. Some of the factors involving this type of system are briefly outlined in Chapters 12 and 14.

f) Basic Circuit Considerations.

Interfacing the components effectively is important in achieving an acceptable signal-to-noise ratio, and in minimizing distortion through the entire signal chain from microphones to loudspeakers. At its most basic, this means impedances should be reasonably compatible, or be adapted with appropriate transformers, between components.

An effective grounding scheme is an extremely important concern, since major hums and buzzes can be caused by ground loops (discussed in Chapter 16). This type of situation can be a major source of noise in typical sound reinforcement systems, and can by far overshadow noise originating from within the components themselves.

Effective gain structures are also important to the effectiveness of any system from the low-budget to the highest quality systems. This subject was outlined in Chapters 4 and 7.

Check the specs and know what the equipment limits are. Use the specs and live within them unless they are shown to be either under- or overstated, or are otherwise proven irrelevant to the pariticular system. Basic measuring systems used in the field were introduced in Chapters 4 and 10.

g) The Environment.

Beyond the basic concern of system output capability, environments of different sizes tend to present somewhat different challenges in sound reinforcement. In relatively small environments, resonances and feedback-causing reflections from nearby hard surfaces are often the most important obstacles to overcome. In very large environments, resonances tend to be less significant. Here, long reverberation and echoes, and the difficulty of distributing sound over a very large area with reasonable consistency tend to become the most pressing obstacles to effective sound reinforcement.

While the situations in which sound reinforcement is needed often are not hard-and-fast categories, an attempt has been made to present the necessary information in general categories, no-doubt with substatial overlap between them. The following chapter overviews common methods of voice reinforcement in a variety of basic kinds of environments. Chapter 13 overviews music reinforcement in small to modest-size environments, while Chapter 14 deals primarily with reinforcement for audiences of approximately 1,000 and more. Chapter 15 deals with monitor systems. **Because of the obvious overlap of techniques and equipment from one type of application to another, it is recommended that the following four chapters be viewed as an overlapping group.**

CHAPTER 12

SPEECH REINFORCEMENT

General Requirements.

The effective reinforcement of sound—in situations where it is required—obviously plays an integral role in the success of that event. For speech, surely the clarity, understandability and reasonable pleasantness of sound quality in the audience are vital factors. Reasonably effective communication can be achieved with a relatively narrow frequency range of about a decade, or 10-to-1 ratio, of frequencies. A typical telephone, for example, operates within a frequency range from roughly 300Hz to 3.5 kHz. A typical "good-old-fashioned" re-entrant paging horn might operate in a similar range, but with a more substantial emphasis somewhere in the 500-800 Hz range—depending on the design.

While the range required for intelligible speech is relatively narrow, extended lower midrange and high frequency response contributes substantially to pleasant, realistic voice quality (see Fig. 12.1). From a simple design standpoint this extended range is easily achieved. The problems which arise in a basic system most often are related to adequate gain-before-feedback, intelligibility in difficult environments, and effective distribution of the sound to all of the intended audience.

Certainly systems designed for speech reinforcement can be used for music as well, and vice-versa, but generally it can be assumed that the system for music reinforcement will require more signal processing, frequency response extending farther into the low end, and somewhat higher output capability. Many of the costly signal processing and EQ options commonly used for live music reinforcement are simply unneccesary for this type of system, if it is unlikely to be used for any purposes other than speech and perhaps low-level background music.

Fig. 12.1, A and B show typical frequency ranges and very approximate distributions of energy for male and female voices. For the spoken voice, the fundamental usually ranges from about 150-300 Hz for adult males, and about 220-440 Hz for adult females. The harmonics go much higher in frequency, and the sybillant sounds, ("s" and "z"-type sounds), extend upwards from about 3kHz to around 10 or 12 kHz.

What does this mean in terms of the freqency range of loudseakers? Overall, the task can be effectively accomplished with reasonably level response from perhaps 200 Hz through 8 kHz or so. This might be reflected as an overall response spec by the manufacturer of perhaps 80 Hz to 14 kHz or more, depending on the manufacturer. Extended lower frequency response, while not absolutely necessary, serves to enhance "depth" of vocal quality (see Fig. 12.1-C).

Common concerns relating to speech reinforcement are introduced in the illustrations and accompanying captions which follow.

Fig. 12.1

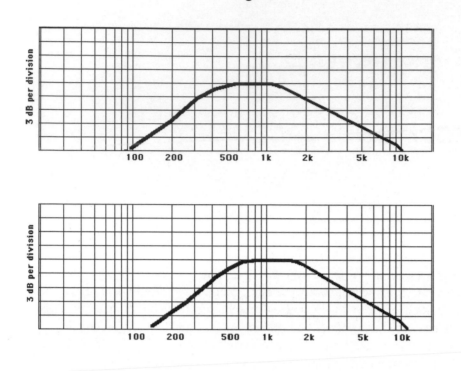

Typical long term average spectrum for male voice. At any given moment in time, the spectrum will vary. This shows only an averaging over time.

Typical long term average spectrum for female voice.

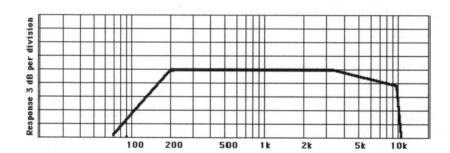

Typical system response required to achieve pleasant, realistic voice reinforcement. The actual system being used may have response farther out toward the extremes of the spectrum, but this is the approximate range actually needed. (Remember that system response incudes loudspeakers *and* micro-phones, as well as any electronic components in the signal chain.)

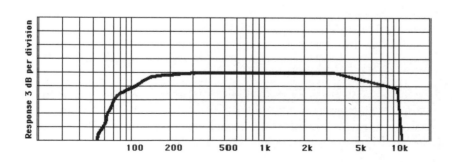

Extended lower frequency response of-course adds "depth" to vocal quality, but can actually be a disadvantage, especially in highly reverberant environments, since the low frequencies normally take the longest to decay in the environment. Minor variations in the response through the midrange generally do not present a problem.

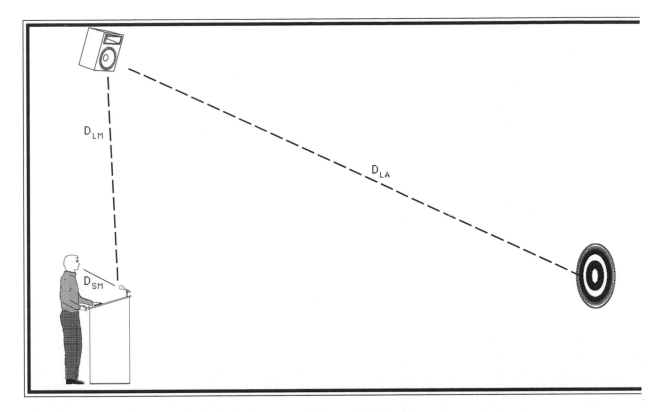

Fig. 12.2. Basic gain relationships in a simple system. The specific mathematics of system gain are somewhat beyond the intended scope of this book. It should be apparent, though, that the smaller the source-to-mic distance (D_{SM}) and the greater the loudpeaker-to-mic distance (D_{LM}), the greater the gain which can be achieved at a given distance to a selected "target" in the audience. In practice the directional patterns of both the mic and the loudspeaker come into play as well, allowing additional gain-before-feedback if they are well aimed and well positioned. However, if more than one mic is open at any given time, the available gain is reduced (two open mics = -3dB, four open mics = - 6dB, eight open mics = -9dB, etc.). (This basic relationship also does not take into account room reflections, which normally add to the "volume" level throughout a room, but detract from sound clarity.)

Fig. 12.3. Effective acoustic distance. The concept of "effective acoustic distance" (also often called "equivalent acoustic distance") is used in the industry to express the perceived distance, based on comparative level, between the person speaking and a given section of the audience. As an example, if we wish the effective acoustic distance (EAD) to be one-half that of the actual distance, a sound level gain of 6 dB must be achieved at the given audience position. If we wish the EAD to be one-fourth the actual distance to a given audience position, a gain of 12 dB at the audience position must be achieved; an EAD of one-eighth the distance from the podium requires a gain of 18 dB, etc. (Remember the inverse square law introduced in Chapter 4.) The required output from the primary loudspeaker (or pair of speakers) can, when necessary, be reduced by using a distributed system.

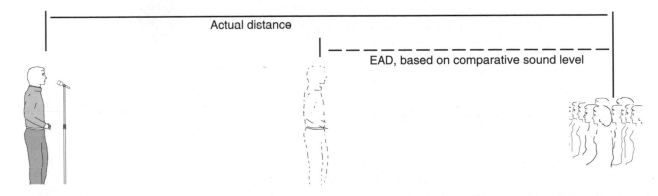

Actual distance

EAD, based on comparative sound level

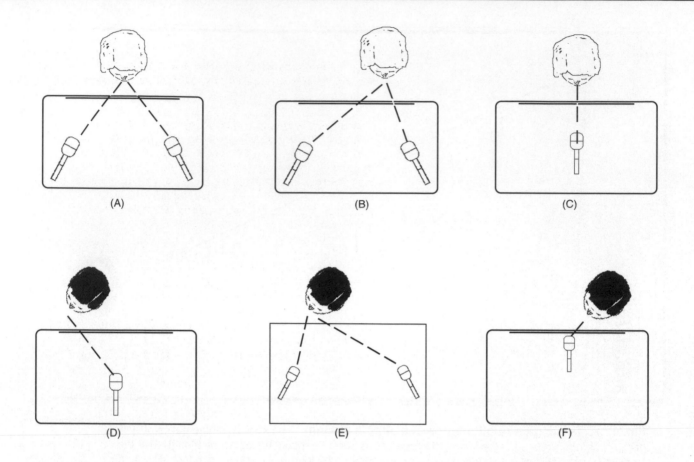

(A)   (B)   (C)

(D)   (E)   (F)

Fig. 12.4. Basic podium miking concerns. As introduced in Chapter 5, when using two mics we need to be concerned about phase cancellation (the "comb-filter" effect). When in position A, all frequencies reinforce, assuming the mics are mixed at the same level and with the same EQ settings. But when the source moves off-center, as in B, some frequencies will cancel, while others will reinforce, thus degrading frequency response. *The farther the two mics are placed from one another, the more severe the comb-filtering will tend to be.* The ideal in terms of frequency response is shown in C, simply one mic.

Of course, the main motivation for using two mics is to effectively pick up the person speaking when he/she shifts position or faces left or right in the process of addressing an audience, as in D and E. (There may also be egotistical reasons for more than one mic.) So in some cases we may need to balance the wish to use two mics against the disadvantage of "comb-filtering", and also against the disadvantage of reduced gain-before feedback (3dB less than one mic). In "E", pickup is more effective but frequency response is compromised.

Ideally, clear instructions to the talker about microphone technique solves this problem, and making adjustments as in F is the ideal. But if two microphones are used for egotistical reasons, they should generally be kept less than about 8" (0.2m) apart to keep the "comb-filtering" to a minimum. At this distance, the positioning may also intuitively assist the talker in staying roughly between the two mics.

If multiple mics need to be spread out farther to deal with talkers who do not have good mic technique, it can actually be an advantage to use three microphones as in G. This arrangement, believe it or not, results in less serious "comb-filtering" than two mics. But it also has the disadvantage of further reducing the available gain before feedback. (At a given source-to-mic distance, the reduction in available gain would normally be 4.8 dB less than a single mic, and 1.8 dB less than two mics.)

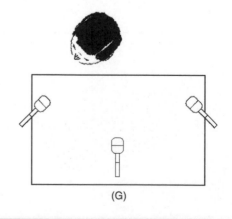

(G)

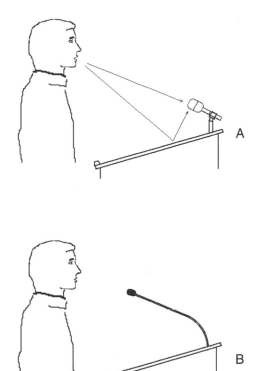

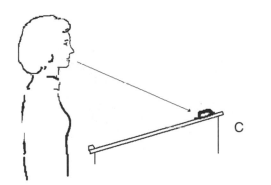

Fig. 12.5. Additional podium mic concerns.

Shown are several side views relating to source-to-mic distance and to mic positioning.

Position A is a reasonable positioning where only a small degree of reinforcement is required. Slight signal degradation occurs because of reflection from the hard surface of a typical podium or pulpit, but fortunately the loss of signal quality tends not to be major. The primary disadvantage here is the relatively small gain which can be achieved before feedback occurs, particularly if a loudspeaker is mounted in the podium itself.

In position B, it should be apparent that much greater gain-before-feedback can be achieved. Here, though, the disadvantage often is varying signal level as talkers shift position and move closer to and farther from the mic. As well, multiple talkers of varying height, many of whom may not have a good idea of how to effectively use a mic, can present further difficulty in terms of signal level. A clear sign placed in a conspicuous spot on top of the podium sometimes helps: for example, "KEEP WITHIN 12" OF MIKE". If an opportunity exists to personally instruct the talkers to move the mic into an appropriate position and attempt to maintain a certain consistent distance (e.g., 6", 12", or whatever is required), the opportunity should certainly be taken.

In C, a "boundary microphone" is shown. Such a mic provides not only a clean sight line, but also virtually eliminates any signal degradation due to reflection from the surface on which it is placed. Where only slight reinforcement is required, this is actually preferable to the arrangement in A. But talkers *must* be instructed not to cover the mic, for example, with their notes.

Below are shown two commercial boundary microphones with unidirectional patterns, Below-left is the Crown PCC-160, which exhibits a supercardioid pattern. The axis is oriented on an angle as shown at bottom center. Below-right is shown the appearance of the Shure SM-91, with a cardioid pattern (actually pictured is the 819, a modest-budget version in the same housing).

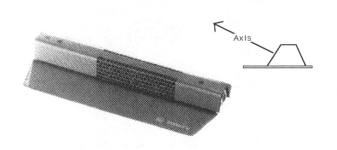

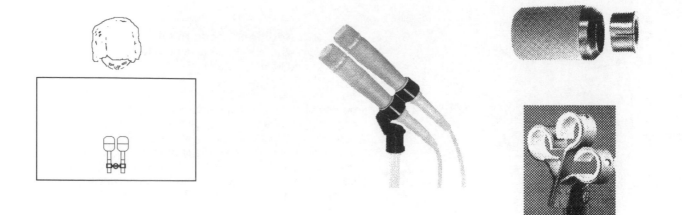

Fig. 12.6. Multiple mic mounts. Multiple microphones mounted in the same position are sometimes used, for several different reasons. A common reason is to provide one "feed" for live reinforcement, and a second for broadcast media. The broadcast feed is then sent to a specially designed distribution amplifier to in-turn separately feed multiple stations covering the same event. Occasionally, a second microphone will be placed both for egotistical reasons, as well as to have a spare feed arriving at the mixer in case, for example, a mic cord fails or is somehow disconnected in the confusion of having many people at an event. When a triple mount is set up, commonly one is used as a live mic, one as a broadcast feed, and the third as an emergency spare to avoid having a technician walk up to the podium itself should there be a failure.

Also shown above are typical accessories, courtesy Shure Bros. Center: A25M double mic mount with two SM-57 mics. At right are the commonly seen A2WS windscreen for the SM-57, and the A27T triple mic mount.

Fig. 12.7. Lavalier / lapel miking. In positioning a lavalier microphone, it is important to know the directional characteristics of the mic. With an omni, as at left, the directional positioning is irrelevant—the only real concern is the distance from the mic to the person's mouth—the mic itself can turn without a problem. With a unidirectional mic, as at right, the most gain-before-feedback is obtained by orienting the axis at the person's mouth, so aiming the mic becomes much more important. (photos courtesy Beyer Dynamic—MCE-5 shown at left; MCE-10 at right)

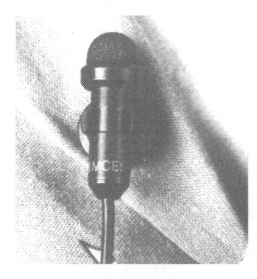

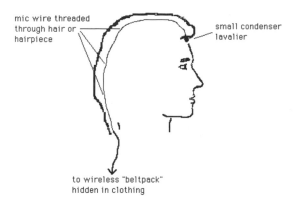

mic wire threaded
through hair or
hairpiece

small condenser
lavalier

to wireless "beltpack"
hidden in clothing

Fig. 12. 8. Theater mic placements. The mic positioning above is generally the preferred option in high quality theater reinforcement whenever a "lapel mic" is inappropriate (for example, whenever the actors need to dance, hug, touch their chest, etc., in the course of a performance). Here the postioning does slightly reduce the pickup of the extreme high frequencies, but provides a very close source-to-mic distance (usually about 6" / 0.15m). A further advantage is that the distance does not vary as the performer turns his/her head. As a result, a consistently high degree of gain can be achieved.

Effective coverage of a stage involves some concerns important to sound quality as perceived by the audience. Probably the most important is that the level and tonal quality of the reinforced sound be kept reasonably consistent from one performer to another. Generally this means that if we put a wireless mic on one person, we need to put one on *all* of the performers with important speaking parts, else a conspicuous difference will be heard once the audience gets accustomed to the sound of the close-up mic(s) placed on the performer(s). If we choose to cover some of the performers with mics placed at a distance, as below, the reinforced sound of any performers with wireless mics needs to be kept to a minimum in order to avoid a radical difference in the quality of their voices.
Normally it is the practice to use supplementary microphones placed downstage just in case a battery runs out on a wireless unit. Boundary mics as shown in Fig. 12.5-C are often used for this purpose. For coverage farther upstage, additional mics can sometimes be hidden behind objects placed in the middle of the set. Another approach, as below, is to use one or more "shotgun mics". (Placements for such mics are further shown in Fig. 12.9.) Supplementary mics such as these most often are kept off unless a wireless unit actually fails.

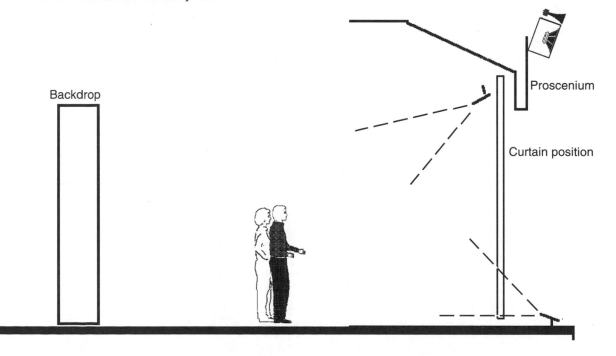

Backdrop

Proscenium

Curtain position

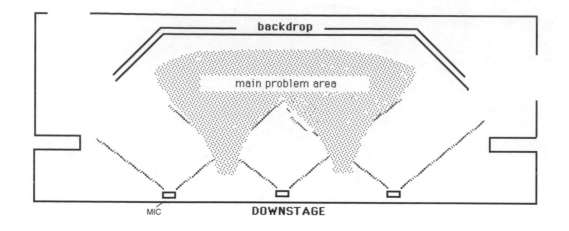

Fig. 12.9. Area Coverage on a theater stage.

Top: When using boundary microphones (as in Fig. 12.5-C) or other cardioid mics for area coverage, there are two main obstacles. Firstly, normally only a very slight degree of gain can be
achieved, due to the large source-to-mic distance. (Actually, some traditionally oriented directors
prefer only slight reinforcement.) As might be expected, several are usually required to cover a
typical stage. But secondly, and much more importantly, very noticeable "comb-filtering" (phase
shifting) often occurs as performers move onstage while speaking or singing, due to the great
distance between the mics. The most conspicuous changes in sound quality tend to occur when the
performer is moving within the shaded area in the illustration, and are most noticeable when the
performer is moving across the stage. (Note that the troublesome areas are where the 3-to-1 rule is
not followed.) In some cases the main problem areas can be covered with additional mics hidden
behind objects on the set. But remember that each time we double the number of open mics, we
sacrifice 3dB of overall gain. With a wireless mic on each performer, the much closer source-to-mic
distance allows many more mics to be used, with greater gain before audible feedback.

Bottom: Several shotgun-type microphones carefully placed in a splayed array can often allow
somewhat greater gain before feedback occurs. Since the mics are placed close together, "comb-
filtering" is minimized. The narrower pattern requires that several be used, and their coverage
angles should overlap somewhat. (It is very important to closely examine the manufacturer's
published polar patterns, since the directional characteristic of this type of mic can vary radically at
different frequencies. Also remember that the more effective "shotgun" mics tend to be fairly long.)
If such an arrangement is placed on the floor, as is most likely, with a bit of extra creativity an
additional object of some kind can often be added to the set to hide the mics from the audience.

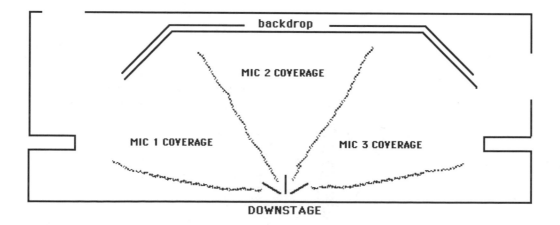

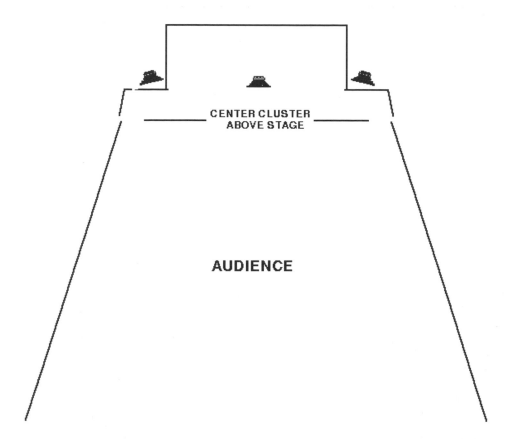

CENTER CLUSTER
ABOVE STAGE

AUDIENCE

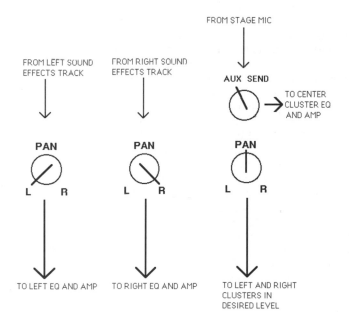

FROM STAGE MIC

FROM LEFT SOUND
EFFECTS TRACK

FROM RIGHT SOUND
EFFECTS TRACK

AUX SEND

TO CENTER
CLUSTER EQ
AND AMP

PAN

PAN

PAN

L   R

L   R

L   R

TO LEFT EQ AND AMP

TO RIGHT EQ AND AMP

TO LEFT AND RIGHT
CLUSTERS IN
DESIRED LEVEL

Fig. 12.10. Primary loudspeaker placements in a theater / auditorium.
The main loudspeakers can be set up either as a single center cluster or dual cluster, or a combination of both. Most systems are designed either one or the other (a center cluster or a dual cluster). If budget allows, though, a combination of both can be utilized. For example, the mixer might be set up to reproduce sound effects or music in stereo, via the dual system. The center cluster could then be used to reinforce voice, either by itself or in combination with the dual system, depending on the directional orientation we wish to achieve. With a standard stereo mixer, a post-EQ aux. send can be used to feed the center cluster.

At left is shown one possible mixer setting for such a combined system.

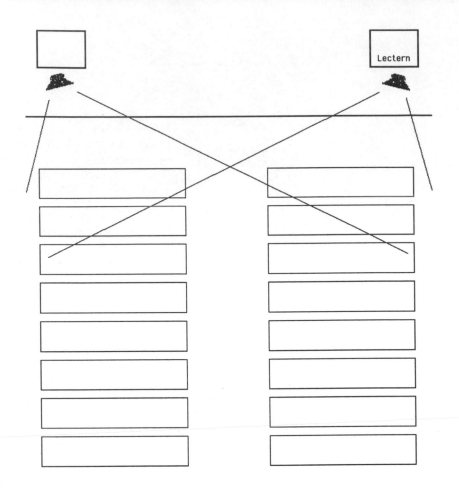

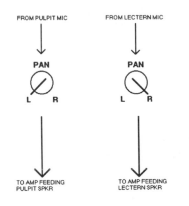

Fig. 12.11. Optional house of worship loudpeaker placements. As always, the primary purpose in speaker placements is to cover the listening area as best as possible. As discussed in the previous chapter, a single cluster suspended overhead is usually the ideal in terms of clarity.

In certain cases, though, we may wish the reinforced sound to be perceived as emanating more-or-less directly from the person speaking. Where there are multiple speaking positions, this can be achieved by locating a primary loudspeaker mounted in or above both the each of the two positions, e.g., pulpit and lectern (or whatever locations and designations are used in the particular house of worship). Where only slight reinforcement is required, a speaker mounted in the podiums themselves can often do the job. Due to the plane of vertical hearing indiscrimination introduced in Chapter 3 (section "f" and Fig. 3.11), the potential also exists to hang the loudpeakers significantly above each speaking position, offering a higher degree of maximum gain before feedback. (The loudspeakers can often be designed to fit into the visual decor by locating them behind a grillcloth in an appropriately decorated structure of nearly any desired shape.) Here the system is set up with a stereo mixer, with the pulpit mic panned to one direction and the lectern mic panned to the other.

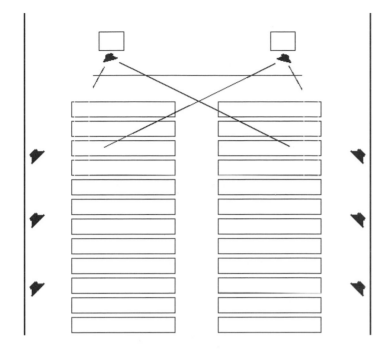

Fig. 12.12. Typical house of worship distributed system placements. At top left, supplementary loudspeakers are placed along the side walls for effective coverage. At bottom, overhead speakers are pointed downward from chandeliers hung from the ceiling.

If we wish to preserve the illusion that the sound is emanating from the front, this can often be done by locating a primary speaker at or above the podium positions as in the previous figure. The supplementary loudspeakers then need to be delayed to synchronize with the arrival of the sound from the primary loudspeakers. As described in Figure 12.13, the delayed signal must arrive at the listeners' position between 5 and 30 milliseconds after the arrival of the sound from the primary speakers, in order to preserve the illusion that the sound is coming from the front of the house of worship.

In Fig. 12.13 is shown the basic signal path for a delayed distributed system. Separate delay channels, equalizers and power amplifiers must be used for each delay "zone" we wish to have. In rough terms, we must have at least one zone for every 20 feet (6m) of distance from the primary loudpeaker.

If we wish to go an extra step, we can actually have the opposite primary loudpeaker on a delay as well, in order to provide more effective coverage of the front pews or seats on the side opposite the person speaking (e.g., in front of the lectern while the pulpit is being used). This would require two extra delay channels, each delayed signal being sent through an additional mixer-channel panned to the opposite side.

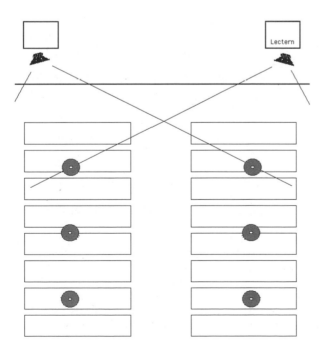

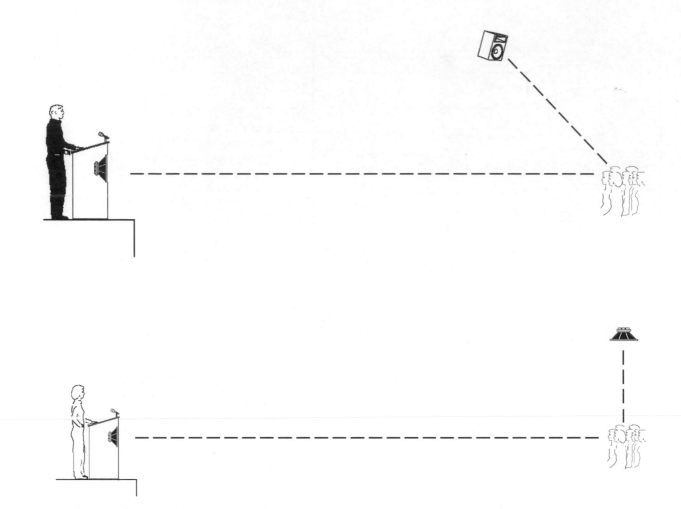

Fig. 12.13. Delayed distributed systems. Due to the "precedence effect", the sound from a delayed supplementary loudspeaker can actually reach the listeners at a louder volume level (upwards to 6 dB louder at the listeners' position) and still be perceived as emanating from the primary loudpeaker. The sound from the delayed must arrive at the listeners' positions between 5 milliseconds and 25 milliseconds *after* the arrival of the sound from the primary loudpeaker, else the effect will not be preserved. (Less than 5 milliseconds and the sound will appear to emanate from the supplementary loudpeaker; more than 25 milliseconds and it begins to sound increasingly like an echo, and sound clarity is drastically reduced.) This can be a somewhat intricate procedure, requiring that sound level meters be used to carefully measure the relative levels of both the main and supplementary loudspeakers in comparison. As well, this system approach requires careful distribution of the listening area into zones which allow these guidelines to be implemented. Below is shown the basic signal flow for such an arrangement.

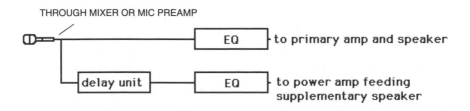

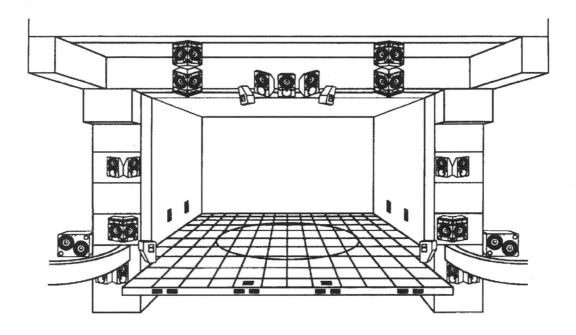

Fig. 12.14. Typical loudspeaker placement options in auditoriums or theaters. (Courtesy Ralph Jones/Meyer Sound Labs) Some of the central concerns involved in the illustrated options were overviewed in the previous chapter.

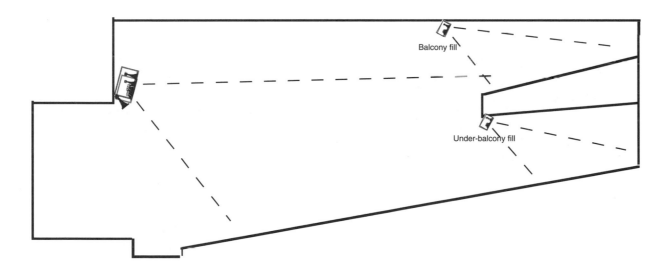

Fig. 12.15. Supplementary loudspeaker placements in a theater or auditorium. Illustrated here is a typical system placement for both a balcony fill and an under-balcony fill. In a high quality installation the supplementary speakers are usually fed with delayed signals. Normally, the distance from the primary cluster to the middle of the balcony is measured, then the distance from the supplementary loudpeaker is subtracted to determine the delay time. (For example, 120 feet to the center rows of the balcony minus 20 feet from the supplementary speaker would be 100 feet, or 113 milliseconds of sound travel time to the average position in the balcony.) Typically 15 milliseconds is added to the calculated time of sound travel to preserve the precedence effect.

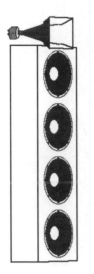

Fig. 12.16. Line array with supplementary HF unit. In many cases a traditional line array can be supplemented with a high frequency horn to assist in providing higher sound quality and more even dispersion high frequencies. Here the line array assists in narrowing the vertical pattern below about 3kHz, thus providing better "projection" without sacrificing horizontal dispersion (recall Fig. 9.10). This type of arrangement is helpful in reducing reverberation off of a reflective ceiling typical of many houses of worship and small auditoriums. Adding the HF horn and crossover to an existing line array can in many instances be a cost effective option allowing an improvement in the sound quality of already existing columns.

Fig. 12.17. Specialized line array. Advanced tapered line arrays are increasingly used to tailor the directional characteristics to the room. Shown is a design for a center cluster installed in a large conference room. Array sections with a 15" LF driver, 2"-throat horns and "slot tweeters" are used here. (Courtesy Ellerby-Beckett, Minneapolis, after Eargle, Handbook of Sound System Design)

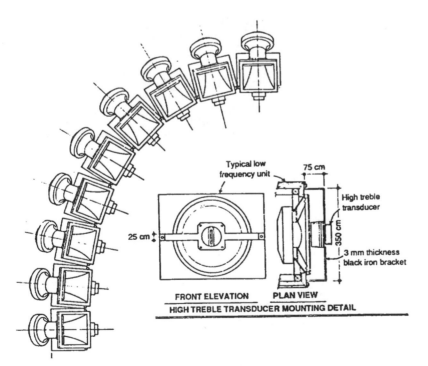

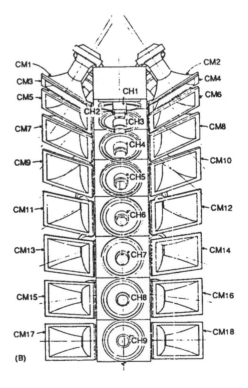

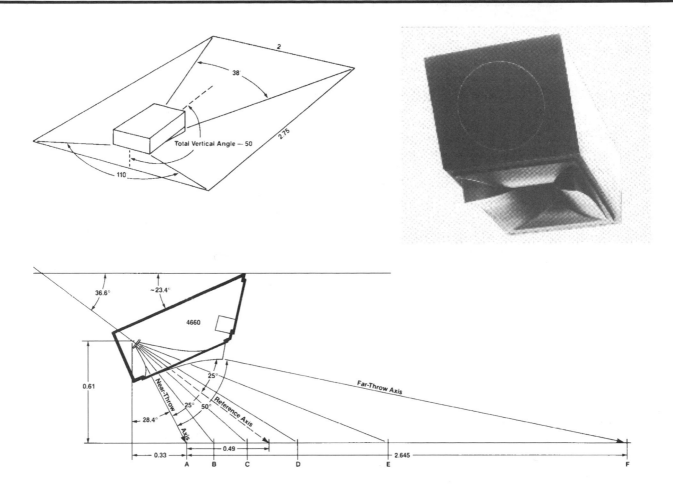

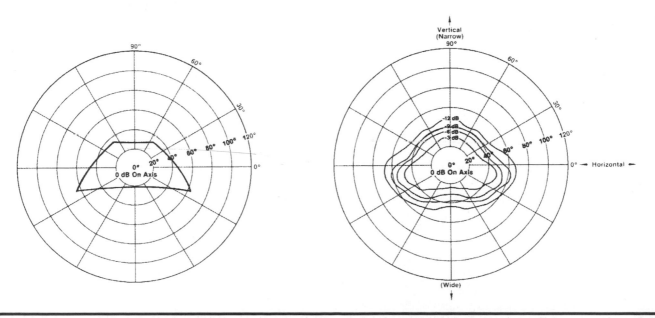

Fig. 12.18. "Defined Coverage" loudsdpeaker. (Courtesy JBL) Here a HF horn with a roughly trapezoidal pattern is used to tailor the directional pattern to the room, with the unit positioned overhead slightly in front of the microphone position. Above right is shown the JBL 4660 as seen from the audience. Below left is shown the target area of the room as "seen" from the unit. Below right is shown the isobar pattern at 8 kHz—this pattern remains remarkably consistent throughout the range of the horn, down to 1kHz.

CHAPTER 13

MUSIC REINFORCEMENT

a) General Requirements.

In sound reinforcement for musical programs, the minimum acceptable standards for system design tend, as might be expected, to expand fairly dramatically from those of a speech reinforcement system.

Firstly, in musical applications the esthetic appeal of the sound tends to be a much higher priority than public address systems—instead of a luxury it is a necessity. Secondly, musical programs are often expected to be substantially louder than speech. Thirdly, when reinforcement of bass instruments is required, at least one to two octaves usually need to be added to the system capability in the low frequency range. (All else being equal, the latter concern alone requires a system of at least two to four times the dimensions of an equivalent system for voice only).

Additionally, versatile mixing equipment with adequate on-board EQ to handle the often highly varying tonal quality of different musical instruments—along with adequate signal processing capability to create audio effects—is likely to be required. Often, additional compressor/limiters, noise gates and/or extra outboard EQs are called for. Also, monitor requirements for musical performers are almost always far more critical than those of a public address monitor.

In a given environment the difference between the sound level for a light musical program and a "heavy" musical program can easily exceed 20 or 30 dB. A moderately light program for casual listening or dance might require an average sound pressure level of around 75 dB to 90 dB SPL in the average audience position, while the demands of a contemporary "high-output" rock act might be 100-115 dB SPL throughout most of the audience. It was explained earlier that, for example, a 20 dB increase in sound power amounts to a hundredfold increase in the demands on a sound system. An additional 10 dB (a total increase of 30 dB) would involve a thousandfold increase in the demands on the amplifiers and speakers. As a result, the effectiveness and efficiency of components for high level systems is of great importance.

The necessary response characteristics for musical voice generally do not require much energy below 160 Hz or above 12 kHz. Systems for reinforcement of a full musical band (including bass drum and bass guitar) typically should have reasonably strong output capability down to perhaps 50Hz or 60Hz. (The difference between frequency response and maximum output capability is extremely important, as discussed in Chapter 9 and in Fig. 13.15.) As always, it should be remembered that the quoted specifications of nearly any system tends to be much wider than the actual needed range.

As well, it needs to be remembered that the actual dispersion angle of loudspeakers may vary substantially at different frequencies (a factor which often is not fully represented in the loudspeaker's quoted specifications). These variations of course have an impact on the consistency of sound quality within the designated angles of the equipment (as discussed in Chapter 9).

b) Vocal Miking.

Selection of mics for a vocals-only system can be a relatively simple matter, often based on personal taste. When choosing such a mic, it should ideally be tested on the system in which the mics will be used, or at least on a system with which one is already familiar, in a familiar environment. As discussed in Chapter 5, the proximity effect of unidirectional mics will tend to boost the lows very substantially when used up-close. Excess low frequencies can if-necessary be easily reduced with a single graphic EQ or with the mixer EQs (this may not be necessary where the speakers do not have strong LF response). In a musical system where the entire band or orchestra is being reinforced, though, expenses can easily escalate if vocal mics are chosen with such strong low frequency response that when used close-up it obscures the necessary low end of kick drum, bass instruments and tom-toms (see also Chapter 17). If on a limited budget, vocal mics should generally be chosen with this in mind. Ordinarily, it is preferable to use a matched set of vocal mics for a given system, using the on-board EQ to adjust for different vocal qualities if necessary. While not a hard-and-fast rule, using matched vocal mics tends to simplify both main system and monitor EQing.

Remember the recommended working angles described in Chapter 5, as well as the general guidelines for microphone use outlined in the same chapter.

Fig. 13.1. Chorus /choir miking. Shown are configurations for miking of a typical chorus. Remember that the 3-to-1 rule (introduced in Chapter 5) is not a hard-and-fast rule. But it should be followed to the best reasonably possible extent, while providing effective pickup of the whole chorus. Fortunately, choral members tend not to shift position much, so whatever comb-filtering does occur tends not to be audible. (Remember from Chapter 3 that the ear tends to be much more sensitive to *changing* phase relationships.)

For situations where hanging a normal-size microphone is inappropriate, most manufacturers of high-quality microphones market small, inconspiuous unidirectional mics specifically designed to be nearly invisible to the audience. A simple length of fishline attached to the back of the microphone is commonly used to assist in keeping hung mics oriented in the proper direction.

Below is an example of the 3-to-1 rule put into practice with a small chorus. (below, courtesy AKG; right and below right, courtesy Shure Bros.)

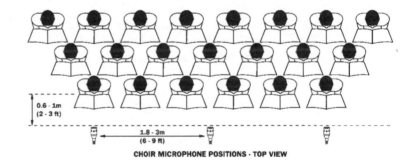

CHOIR MICROPHONE POSITIONS - TOP VIEW

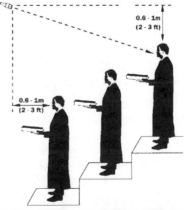

CHOIR MICROPHONE POSITIONS - SIDE VIEW

Fig. 13.2. Commercial examples of vocal mics for hand-held use.
Any of these mics can of course be stand mounted, and each of them also finds use for musical instrument miking as well.

Top left: Sennheiser MD-431, also marketed with an all-black finish as model 531.

Center: Shure Beta 58 and Beta 57. With response characteristics roughly resembling the standard SM-58 and SM-57, but with somewhat stronger VHF response, these mics are part of a newer class of lightweight microphones with lighter-but-stronger magnets. As a result of the stronger magnet, output tends to be stronger, usually requiring the input attenuator to be backed off a bit when used side by side with SM-57's or SM-58's. The Beta 57 also sports a stronger windscreen/head assembly than the SM-57, vastly reducing the potential for accidental damage. (Both the SM-57 and Beta 57 are concert-tour favorites for snare drum and electric guitar as well.)

Bottom: AKG D-330. This mic has found favor among many country artists for hand-held vocal use, though it also finds wide use in other musical styles. (This mic also is a favored podium mic, and is often seen in press conferences worldwide.)

c) Musical Instrument Miking.

Unlike the human voice, which—apart from a certain degree of chest and sinus resonance—is essentially a point source, a musical instrument's sound often emanates from a larger area or from a number of places at once. As a result, microphone positioning is often a key factor in determing the kind of sampling of the instrument's output that will be picked up.

Generally, the closer the microphone needs to be moved to the instrument (to increase signal level and reduce pickup of extraneous sound), the more critical the microphone placement tends to become. As a rule of thumb, the closer the mic is placed to the vibrating element (e.g., a string or reed), the stronger will be the emphasis on the high-frequency energy of the instrument's spectrum (though there are some exceptions to this—perhaps most notably brass instruments.) The closer the mic is to the resonator (e.g., guitar body or horn bell) the stronger will be the emphasis on the fundamentals and lower overtones (lows and low-mids).

For example, placement of a microphone close to the sound-hole of an acoustic guitar produces a high proportion of resonance as well as a reasonably high amount of brightness and string-noise. Moving the mic farther up the length of the neck will further emphasize the string noise, and de-emphasize the body resonance. Moving the mic to the broad end of the guitar resonator may reduce overall intensity, but such a move reduces string noise more than body resonance (and might also interfere with the guitarist's picking arm). Increasing the distance of the mic from the guitar will tend to significantly reduce the lows (part of the reduction in the lows may be due simply to proximity effect), as well as some of the "bite" in the extreme high frequencies, causing the overall sound to be substantially thinner than when miked up-close (if the sound up-close is too "boomy" or "muddy", this might be desireable).

Each instrument of course involves its own set of specifics, which are intertwined with the needs of the performer. (Common sense and a knowledge of the mic characteristics can go a long way here.) When a musician is seated or standing in one location without moving the instrument substantially, the desired sampling and appropriate placement of the mic can often be fairly easily determined by some brief experimenting. When the performer needs to move about to any extent, though, instrument miking can indeed be a challenge. In such cases, obviously one of two approaches can be taken: (1) make the performer come to the mic, or (2) make the microphone follow the performer.

Clip-on microphones and contact transducers can certainly be helpful if the mic needs to follow the performer. This type of approach can easily be used for hollow-bodied stringed instruments and many wind instruments. Figure 13.4 illustrates several approaches involving the fastening of a microphone to an instrument. Wireless mics can further aid this process, though with wireless rigs there

Fig. 13.3. Acoustic guitar. Mic positioning when a guitarist is seated tends to be reasonably simple, since the guitar tends to move very little with respect to the mic. When the guitarist is standing, though, many engineers prefer a mic without proximity effect, to reduce the variations in tonal quality as the guitarist moves. Another common problem with a mic which exhibits the proximity effect happens when the proximity effect combines with the resonance near the sound hole. Low frequency feedback is a common result.

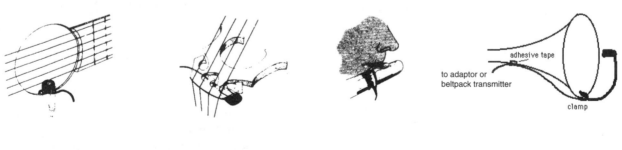

Fig. 13.4. Examples of microphones fastened to instruments. Shown are several common methods of using a clip-on lavalier mic for instrument pickup. The mics illustrated above in A, B and C are the AKG C-567 omnidirectional (a cardioid would generally not be an advantage, as it would be too difficult to effectively aim in this type of use). At right is illustrated the AKG 747, a compact condenser mic with gooseneck and clip, designed for general instrumental miking.

can be a compromise in both financial cost and complexity of setup and operation. Obviously the advantage with a wireless setup is a very high degree of freedom of movement for the performer.

Mics without proximity effect can sometimes be helpful in miking musical instruments, to reduce variations in tonal quality. The tradeoff here would be less rejection of lower frequencies from speakers and/or other instruments (this is likely to be a disadvantage mainly in situations where feedback or ambient sound pickup is a major concern).

Some musical instruments tend to be very directional in their output. Many instruments with a flared bell in their design have a high concentration of high-frequency output on-axis of the direction in which the bell points. This is extremely characteristic of trumpets and trombones. Several approaches can be taken. In high level systems the most common approach approach is to simply point the instrument directly at the mic at very close range, and if necesary rolling off the highs with an EQ (some consider the "brightness" desirable). If the mic has strong proximity effect it may be necessary to roll off the lows as well. Increasing the source-to-mic distance and pointing the instrument slightly away from the mic can in some instances reduce the likelihood of large variations in both sound level and tonal quality when the musician moves the instrument—as well as provide a more representative sampling of the instrument's sound in roughly the way an "average" audience member might hear it acoustically. This of-course depends on the application. Adequate stage monitoring can allow the instrumentalist to tailor the sound by ear—this is one of a number of areas in the actual practice of sound reinforcement where clear communication of objectives between soundperson and musician might be crucial. Another common approach is to mount a small mic in front of the bell as shown in Fig. 13.4. Trumpets and trombones, as well as saxes, can have extremely high output at close range, so the microphone should be able to withstand very high sound pressures without significant distortion (most modern high quality mics have this ability).

When miking musical instrument amplifiers, the directional characteristics of the instrument-speaker need to be considered. Normally, the closer to the center-axis of the instrument-speaker the mic is placed, the brighter the sound will be. When there are multiple speakers included in one cabinet, we of course need to locate an individual speaker behind the grill-cloth and determine where its axis is, in order to make a well considered mic placement.

Fig. 13.5. Flute /sax. The flute mic in a system for a band playing contemporary music is often set very similarly to a vocal mic, in terms of mic stand placement, input attenuator setting, and EQ. So it is often relatively easy to use one mic for both vocals and flute in situations where the sax/flute player is also a vocalist. The sax mic, though, tends to be a different story, since both the mic position and mixer EQ settings are commonly very different than for typical vocal use. Only "in a pinch" should it be used both for vocals and sax. (illustrations courtesy AKG)

Fig. 13.6. Trumpet /trombone. In this illustration (courtesy AKG Acoustics) the recommended position is slightly off-center of the direction in which the bell points and at a slight distance. With a high-level system, many engineers prefer a close-up, on-axis positioning, as in "B" (illustration modified by the author). The disadvantage, though, is sometimes excessively strong proximity effect in the up-close positioning, and sometimes radical variations in tonal quality and volume level as the instrumentalist moves. In small venues, the relatively loud acoustic output of horns may require only slight reinforcement (and perhaps reverb, etc.) through the system itself. In larger venues, though, the variations just mentioned can become much more important. A reasonably well executed monitor system would of-course assist the instrumentalists in a horn section in tailoring their dynamics by ear, for example, to do effective fade-ins and fade-outs.

Fig. 13.7. Acoustic piano. In a pinch, one mic can be used for an acoustic piano, though two mics are the standard for any reasonably high-quality pickup. In the standard two-mic arrangement, one is placed to pick up an averaging of the lower strings, and the other for the high upper strings. This also allows for separate EQing when necessary of the varying character of high and low strings encountered in pianos. Where budget allows, mics with good transient response, such as condenser mics or ribbon mics, can provide an additional advantage, particularly on the higher strings.

In some critical situations, and where time and budget allows, many engineers will use more than two mics. A common grand piano arrangement using a third mic involves two boundary microphones (such as PZM's) placed inside a closed piano top, with a third mic—normally one with strong low frequency pickup—positioned underneath the piano close to the sounding board. With an upright, a similar arrangement can be used with one or more additional mics behind the piano, placed close to the sounding board. (Illustrations courtesy AKG Acoustics)

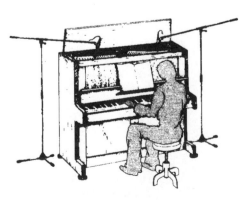

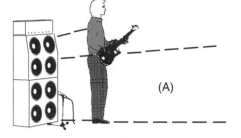

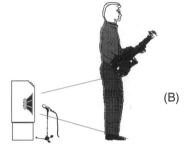

(A)

(B)

(C)

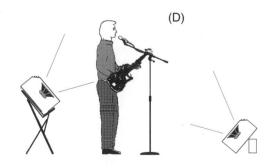

(D)

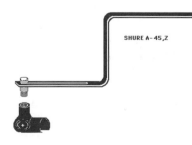

SHURE A-45,Z

Fig. 13.8. Electric guitar.

At top left is shown a traditional guitar "stack", miked for the reinforcement system. While such an arrangement may look impressive, the disadvantage is strong output directly in front of the amp, but little output above about 1k or 2k off to the sides. This presents a serious problem for the person operating the reinforcement system, i.e., loud guitar directly in front of the amp, and very little guitar sound off to the sides. This can make mixing in any but the largest arenas a nightmare.

One approach, when such a stack is necessary for visual reasons, is to modify the cabinets so only the top two speakers operate, and then mike the working speakers.

Ignoring visual concerns, the best overall sound is usually achieved with a compact guitar amp. Modern electronics easily allow the traditional large amp (e.g., Marshall 4x12) sounds to be achieved with a compact stage amplifier. If a "deep" guitar sound is needed, it is easily achieved by using a mike with proximity effect, placed up close to the guitar speaker. (The big cabinets can always be added as "dummies" if desired for visual purposes.)

Still, even a guitar amp with single or double 10" or 12" speakers can easily overwhelm an audience with its upper midrange output, even in, say, an auditorium, when placed as in "B".   Here the high frequencies "miss" the guitarist, who most needs to hear the onstage sound. The vast majority of experienced soundpersons agree that the arrangements in "C" and "D" are preferable when the guitar amp is miked. The guitar amp essentially serves as a stage monitor for the guitar sound, while the reinforcement system distributes it more evenly to the intended audience.

Below is shown the Shure A-45Z, a handy accessory designed to be placed under the top handle or taped to the top of a typical guitar amp. The mike then is easily positioned in front of the musical instrument speaker. Increasingly, direct inputs are used today instead of mics, since the vast majority of guitarists today achieve their "sound" electronically. But this is still a tossup—many good engineers still prefer a mic. (An additional note: hanging a cardioid mic in front of the cabinet puts the speaker at the -6dB angle of the mic. While this can be done in a pinch, best results are achieved by pointing the mic at the speaker.)

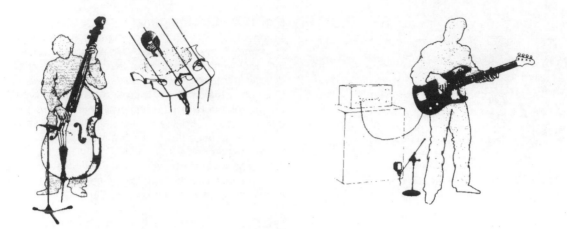

Fig. 13.9. Bass. Increasingly, string bass players are having internal pickups installed in their instruments. When they need to be miked, the two arrangements above left are the most common. Certainly the mic should have strong low frequency pickup, and if possible strong proximity effect as well. The normal method for connecting bass guitar to the reinforcement system is direct input. Occasionally, though, the bass amplifier itself has a certain "sound" considered desirable, in which case a supplementary mic is sometimes used, as shown above right. The direct and miked channels can then be mixed in any desired combination. (Illustrations courtesy AKG)

d) Drum and Percussion Miking.

Miking drum sets is an aspect of sound reinforcement that has traditionally presented something of a challenge to soundpersons, because of the number of sound sources in such a relatively small space. The advent of close-miking and radically altered drum sounds in recording studios created expectations for a similar type of sound in live performance—which can at times be a difficult task. The more recent appearance of synthesized drums and digital samplers has allowed fairly easy replication of studio-type sounds. In some cases this has simplified the task of the soundperson. Acoustic drums, though, are preferred by most drummers and will certainly continue to exist, as will the need to mic them and alter their sound.

The most common alteration of the sound of a conventional drum kit calls for an increased emphasis of both the contact sound (stick meeting drumhead) in the high frequencies, as well as a significant boost of the fundamental frequencies of the drums. Since the fundamentals vary widely from drum to drum, this can often be a complicated task. Effective miking is an important aspect of accomplishing these objectives (along with appropriate muting and tuning of the drums, and appropriate equalizing).

For single headed drums, positioning one mic in each drum as shown in Fig. 13.10 provides both high signal level and excellent separation of the sound from that of other drums. This allows a high degree of flexibility in tailoring the sound of each drum.

Traditional double-headed drums need to be miked from the top in a manner that picks up the sound of the individual drums without interfering with the playing technique of the drummer. Miking as shown in Fig. 13.10 (far right) can in very many instances allow one mic to provide very effective coverage of two adjacent drums of similar character (e.g., two tom-toms).

Snare drums can sometimes be difficult to close-mic, since their sound involves—in addition to the vibrating of drumhead and internal resonance—both the attack sound of the stick on the top head and the broad-band high-frequency sound of the snare underneath. The conventional method of snare miking is to use a mic angled at the top head. To obtain a reasonable proportion of the sound of the snare-spring below (and to add "snap" to the sound of stick meeting drumhead) the upper-mid and high frequencies often need to be boosted at the mixer EQ. This often has the consequence of picking up an excessive amount of the sound the the nearby high-hat—particularly if the drummer's style involves hard strikes on the high-hat in its opened position. An additional mic beneath the snare drum appears at-first to be an easy solution to this obstacle. However, the opposing positions of the mics with respect to the drum causes the fundamental and lower overtones to be picked up in almost exactly opposite phase—potentially causing serious cancellation of the low and low-mid frequencies.

Fig. 13.10. Drums and percussion. (Courtesy AKG) At left is shown a typical complete drum miking arrangement. Note that the snare drum mic, normally a unidirectional mic, is positioned with the axis pointed away from the high-hat. Still, in some cases, pickup of loud high-hat strikes is unavoidable, in which case the snare channel is a good candidate for a noise gate (along with the kick, and any toms with excessive ring).

In a modest-size setup where mics and input channels may be severely limited, it is generally most important to mic the kick and snare (while the snare tends to be acoustically loud, this gives an opportunity to add reverb through the system), and perhaps an overhead mic for overall pickup of the kit.

Below are shown typical mic placements for other drums (illus. partially modified by the author). Remember that proximity effect is strongest on-axis, so we can sometimes change the response by changing the mic's angle. At far right, one mic is used for coverage of two drums of similar character. Here, while the input channel gain may need to be set a bit higher, and the low end boosted a bit more, this is normally offset by the fact that one less open mic is being used. Two adjacent rack-mounted toms or two adjacent floor toms are good candidates for this approach to save on the number of mics and input channels.

Positioning kick-drum mic in front of pedal beater provides stronger pickup of contact sound.

Positioning high-hat mic close to edge tends to emphasise highs of cymbals. For more stick sound, move mic upward.

Two congas can usually be effectively covered with one mic, though in critical situations, if enough input channels and mics are available, one mic per drum allows greater flexibility in tailoring the sound of each drum. Bongos, on the other hand, are so small and close together that one mic is normally preferred. Other percussion should be miked on a case-by-case basis to provide a reasonably effective sampling of their sound.

There are two solutions to this dilemma. One approach is to cut the low and midrange frequencies of the signal from the bottom mic (at the mixer or by an outboard EQ) to reduce the relative effect of the bottom mic on the lower drum-frequencies while still allowing effective reproduction of the snare-spring sound. Another approach is to wire the cable for the bottom mic 180-degrees out-of-phase as shown in Chapter 16, to allow the low frequencies of the drum to be received approximately in-phase by both mics. (Remember to clearly label the cable.) High quality mixers sometimes have a switch on each channel allowing the operator to invert the phase of the input signal. This is one example of a perfect use for such a switch.

The most common method of miking a snare drum is to use a single cardioid or supercardioid simply pointed at the top head as shown in Fig. 13.10. Under ordinary circumstances, this allows for a very respectable snare sound. A noise gate inserted in the snare channel at the mixer would be another way to tame an excessively loud high-hat.

Miking a double headed bass (kick) drum poses an obstacle not entirely unlike that of the snare drum. Kick drums are usually miked from the front, but the attack sound of the pedal beater is, in most contemporary music, a highly emphasized part of their sound. An additional mic can be put behind the drum to access the pedal-beater sound. But this approach has the serious disadvantage of picking up the much louder sound of the snare, drastically reducing the separation of the two sounds at the mixer, and thus the ability to equalize them separately (pedal-beater and snare-spring sounds are usually emphasized in different areas of the audio spectrum). A common solution is to remove the front head to obtain access for a microphone to the inside of the drum. Cutting a hole in the front head is an another approach—this approach is fairly standard today. If it is not possible or appropriate to remove the front head, the pedal-beater sound can be accessed be using a mic mounted on a gooseneck fastened to the rim

Fig. 13.11. Commercial examples of favored kick drum mics. Left to right: Beyer M-88, AKG D-12E, AKG D-112, Electrovoice RE-20/PL-20, Beyer M-380. While these mics are among those widely used for bass drum, it is not necessarily their only use. The M-88, interestingly, is a favored mic on the concert tour for both kick drum and vocals. The D-112 is an updated version of the classic D-12E, with different response in the mid and high frequencies. The RE-20 also finds fairly wide use as a live sax mic, as well as for radio broadcast studios. The M-380, a bidirectional (Figure-8) mic with very strong low frequency proximity effect, is also put to good use on string bass, tuba and other bass instruments. As with any mic, if it works well for a given application, by all means use it—but remember that in the final mix, it is the overall combination of mics onstage which determines how the mix will "fit together".

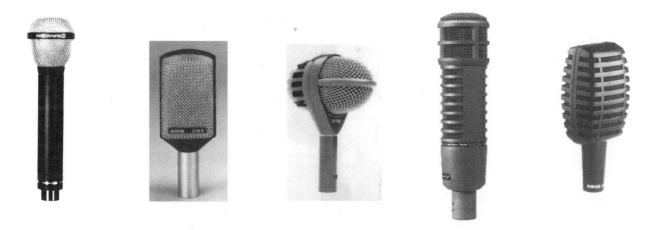

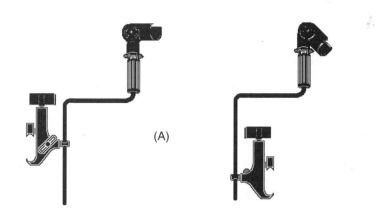
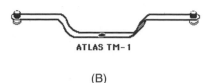

Fig. 13.12. Typical commercial mic-related accessories.
(A) Latin Percussion LP Claw®, widely used for mounting microphones onto the rims of drums and other percussion instruments, shown in two of its many possible orientations.
(B) Dual microphones mounts, Atlas TM-1 and Sennheiser MZS 235 (shown with two MD-421 mics, as might be used for rack-toms). Mounts of this kind are widely used for live stereo recording of performances where the sound of the audience and/or the ambience of the environment are desired on tape.
(C) Atlas LO-2 (black finish version is LO-2B) allows quick disconnect of the mic clip itself.
(D)   Right angle XLR-type plug is a useful accessory for drum vocals and other tight spaces, e.g., tom mics underneath low cymbals, etc. Shown is Switchcraft connector R3F. A few short mic cables with a right angle connector, perhaps just long enough to reach to the bottom of a typical boom stand (say 6' to 9', or 2-3m) allow this configuration to be added wherever needed for a given performance.

of the drum with a clamp of the kind shown in Fig. 13.12.   As indicated, the tradeoff will normally be a substantial amount of snare sound included in the signal from that mic (even with a standard noise gate). The only way around this problem is a noise gate with a carefully tuned control loop as discussed in Chapter 8, and as described in Fig. 13.23.

Overhead microphones as shown in Fig. 13.10 can provide effective pickup of cymbal sounds. Mics with smooth curves in the very-high-frequency range—such as condenser mics—can be helpful here. Overhead mics often are not necessary when tom-toms are miked from the top, as well as when there are a number of vocal mics placed in close range on a tightly spaced stage.

The frequency range and response curves of microphones for drums and percussion, as with other applications, depends on the range of the instrument and the desired shaping of tonal quality. Often, favored microphones for drums are also considered to be desirable for other instruments and vocals, since these are in many cases the highest-quality microphones. Certainly, using microphones with relatively strong low-frequency response for the low-pitched drums (especially kick and low toms) will tend to greatly simplify the equalizing and mixing process.

e) Direct Inputs.

Commonly it is useful to provide direct input (also—and originally—referred to in the industry as "direct injection") to a mixer from instrument amplifiers or electric/electronic instruments such as bass guitar, electric guitar processors, electronic keyboards, synthesized drums and wireless mic receivers.

By using a direct input (**DI**, for short), variations and deficiencies in the sound of a musician's personal amplifier can be eliminated, as can leakage from other on-stage sounds. Since the task of mixing a musical band—particularly in most forms of contemporary music—is greatly complicated by cross-leakage of other on-stage sounds, this approach can be very helpful.

Small units designed to accomplish direct injection (**DI** *boxes*, or ***direct boxes***) can be inserted in the signal path between the instrument output and the instrument-amplifier input, or between the amplifier output and the instrument speaker (with the use of a built-in optionto reduce the signal strength to a level suited to the mixer input—generally this would tke the form of either a switch or a separate input jack). Rack-mountable units with several channels of DI circuitry also are produced by many manufacturers.

This type of circuit should allow the shield ground to be disconnected at the unit, should it be necessary in order to avoid redundant ground paths, known as ***ground loops*** (discussed further in Chapter 16).

A system approach involving direct input allows the instrument amplifier to be completely eliminated, using a stage monitor mix to provide the instrument's sound to the performer. This is shown in Chapter Fifteen.

Additional music reinforcement considerations are introduced in the following diagrams.

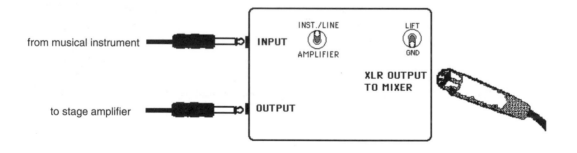

Fig. 13.13. Sample DI-box configuration. Here the signal from an electric musical instrument to a musical-instrument amplifier is sampled, with a copy of the signal sent to the reinforcement system. The switch on many DI-boxes allowing the user to plug in a speaker level output is simply a pad switch to bring a power-amp output level down to an appropriate line level (in this illustration it is labeled as a choice between "inst./line" or "amplifier"). In the line-level position, we could plug in either the direct output of an instrument or a line-level output from a musical instrument amplifier.

The ground-lift switch often needs to be moved to the "lift" or "ground disconnect" position to eliminate a redundant ground path (a "ground loop") to eliminate the audible "hum" or "buzz" which often accompanies this situation. Refer to Chapter 16 for a further discussion of system grounding.

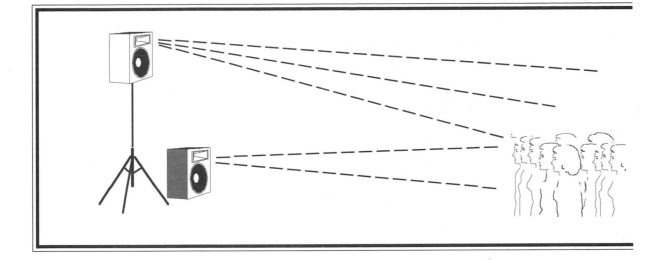

Fig. 13.14. Height orientation. Recall that the higher the frequency is, the less able it is to bend around objects. Generally, the lows and lower mids can easily penetrate audiences, while the higher mids and especially the highs tend to be unable to. Obviously, we need to have the high frequency horn(s), and if possible the mid-frequency unit(s) positioned above the audience's heads to the best extent possible. Wherever possible, it can also be helpful to have a slight downward tilt of the high frequency horn, particularly if it is a radial or straight exponential horn (as opposed to a CD horn).

At right is shown a typical arrangement with a speaker stand inserted into a mount in the accompanying low frequency unit (courtesy Turbosound). The low frequency unit is normally best placed on the floor, not only for weight reasons, but also because up to 3 dB of low frequency capability can be lost when the LF unit is raised off of the floor.

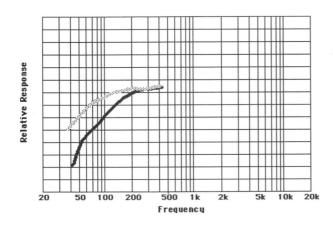

Fig. 13.15. Low frequency output capability. Recall from Chapter 9 that there is an important difference between frequency response and maximum output capability (the latter is usually not published as a curve according to frequency). A typical full range two-way unit may have low frequency response as shown in the dotted line, but its maximum output capability at full power tends to look more like the solid line. Thus the need for a "subwoofer" to effectively reproduce kick drum, bass guitar and low toms.

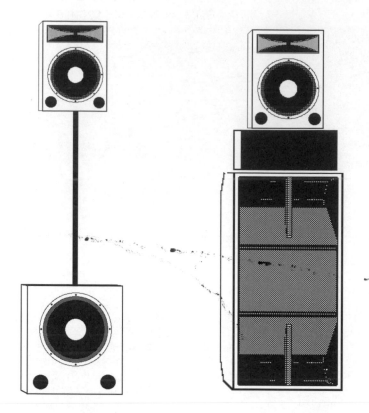

Fig. 13.16. Typical systems with supplementary LF units. Ordinarily, systems of this type are actively crossed over around 125 to 200 Hz, depending on the capabilities of the units involved. At far left is shown a direct radiator "subwoofer". At near left is shown a typical "W-bin" with an 18" driver. A spacer is used to elevate the "full-range" unit to an appropriate height. Below is illustrated the "signal flow" for a basic system of this kind. (See also Fig. 13.19.)

TYPICAL SIGNAL FLOW

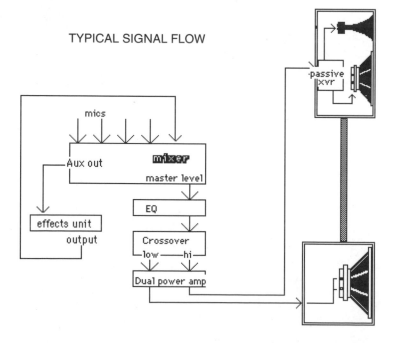

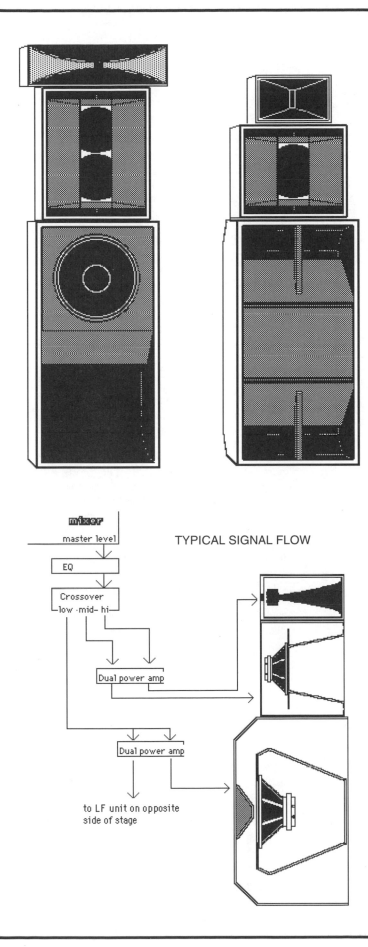

mixer

master level

EQ

Crossover
└low ·mid– hi┘

Dual power amp

Dual power amp

to LF unit on opposite
side of stage

TYPICAL SIGNAL FLOW

Fig. 13.17. Typical traditional 3-way high-level component systems.

Systems such as these are commonly arranged out of separately purchased components widely available out in the field, both new and used. Here a 3-way electronic crossover and two dual power amps are required, in addition to whatever EQ and compression is within budget. The system can also be set up to use one amplifier channel to power both LF units, with the fourth channel designated to monitors.

Typical crossover settings for both these systems would be 200 Hz and 2kHz. The EQ should first be set in the flat position, and the crossover output levels gradually raised until a reasonable tonal quality is achieved. The main outboard EQ can then be fine tuned to the desired frequency response for a given room.

At top-left is illustrated a 2"-throat 90° radial horn, a typical dual 10" or 12" midrange cabinet, and a "scoop", found in both 15"-driver and 18"-driver designs. The normal effective orientation for a dual-driver midrange cabinet of this type is one atop the other, rather than side-by-side, for reasons which were discussed in Chapter 9. Generally only "in a pinch" where low ceiling height is a problem should the cabinet be positioned sideways.

At top-right is illustrated a 2"-throat "constant directivity" horn, a single 12" mid cabinet, and a single 18" folded horn. The CD horn can be a significant advantage, for example, in an auditorium, where the highs usually need to consistently cover a relatively wide vertical angle (say 40°). (Remember that the vertical dispersion with a radial horn tends to narrow significantly as frequency gets higher. This often is fine in a typical room or club where the audience is on the floor, but it can be a problem in covering an audience where the height varies as in the sloped seating arrangement of an auditorium.)

As in many systems, the output capability of the mid and high units in both these sample systems can be increased by moving the crossover points somewhat upward in frequency. But this practice often leaves large gaps in the dispersion capability below the HF crossover point. (Both of these systems, incidentally tend to exhibit some "beaming" in the range from about 800 Hz to 2kHz. The 2"-throat radial horn also tends to "beam" above about 8kHz.)

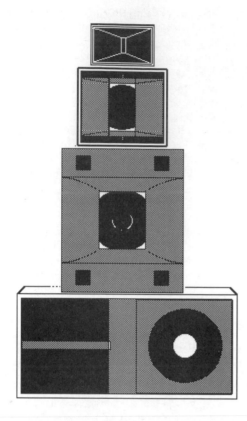

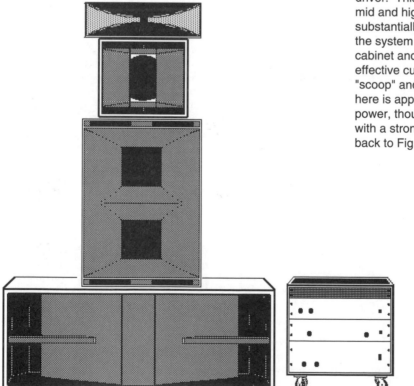

Fig. 13.18. Typical traditional 4-way high-level systems. Here we require a 4-way crossover and at least four power-amplifier channels, plus whatever is required for monitors. Obviously, systems of this type can be put together in a variety of ways, but an attempt should be made to match both the output capabilities and the directional characteristics of the components as best as possible. (The directional characteristics would tend to come into play mainly in the upper mids and highs.)

Typical crossover points for both these systems would be 80-100Hz, 400-500 Hz, and 1.6-2 kHz.

At top left is illustrated a 2"-throat CD horn, single cone driven mid cabinet, single 15" "Perkins bin" for low-mid, and a single 15" or 18" "scoop" for the low end.

At bottom left is illustrated a 2"-throat radial horn, cone driven upper mid, dual 15" LF horn-loaded cabinet for mid-bass (low mid), and a large "W-bin" (6' in width) with an 18" driver. This system has roughly equivalent mid and high frequency capability but has substantially more low end capability than the system above, due to the dual 15" cabinet and the very large "W-bin". The effective cutoff frequency of both the "scoop" and the large "W-bin" illustrated here is approximately 35Hz. At maximum power, though, we may need to be content with a strong 50 or 60 Hz output. (Refer back to Fig. 9.30.)

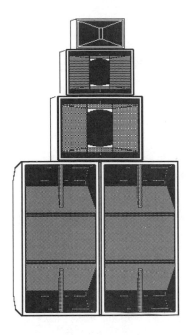

4 units ··········
2 units ～～～～～～
1 unit ━━━━━━

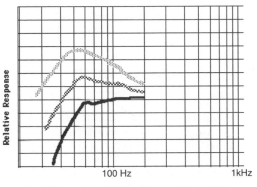

100 Hz   1kHz

Relative Response

TYPICAL LOW FREQUENCY COUPLING
(Note: Response also depends on crossover point)

Fig. 13.19. Supplementing very-low-frequency capability. Left: The use of multiple enclosures in the low end increases the frequency response in the lows, extends the low-frequency "cutoff" to a lower frequency, and of course increases the maximum output capability in the lows.

The actual frequency response and capability will of course vary from one enclosure design to another, but the basic principle of mutual low-frequency coupling normally holds as we add enclosures. Due to the coupling effect, with two units, the on-axis response and output capability is increased up to 6 dB in the lows. The effective low frequency limit is extended almost one-third octave lower. As frequency gets higher, the net increase gradually falls off towards 3 dB.

With four units as opposed to one, the net increase approaches 12 dB in the lows, gradually tapering toward 6 dB as frequency rises. The effective low frequency limit is extended roughly 2/3-octave lower than with one unit.

In order to effectively couple, the units should be placed as close together as possible, in order to act essentially as one larger unit. (They can, if necessary, be splayed into an arc and still achieve coupling in the lows. As a general rule, we can use the figure 6dB per doubling of enclosures whenever the wavelength is at least 2 or 3x the distance between the centers of the enclosures with respect to one another.)

Below: As mentioned earlier, if the units are lifted off the floor (as when they must be hung) we can lose as much as 3dB of the LF capability. We can, though, gain the 3 dB back by placing the enclosure(s) against a solid wall (discounting a bit for the absorption or flexing of the wall). If you guessed that placing LF units against both a floor and wall will result in a 6 dB increase as compared to hanging in free air, you are correct (again discounting a bit for wall absorption). Similarly, placing an enclosure on the floor in a corner will result in a 9 dB increase (assuming, for example, granite walls). This is because the normally omnidirectional lows are forced into a narrower dispersion angle. In most portable applications, though, the advantage gained in seeking such a corner is usually outweighed by other practical concerns, and we may need to be content with somewhere in the middle of the floor.

LOW FREQUENCIES TYPICALLY
3 dB LESS THAN WHEN PLACED
ON FLOOR, PARTICULARLY
WITH AN ABSORBENT CEILING
SUCH AS A 'DROP CEILING'

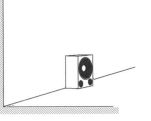

LOW FREQUENCIES UP TO 3 dB
MORE THAN WHEN PLACED IN
MIDDLE OF FLOOR

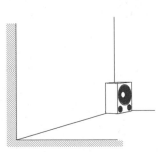

LOW FREQUENCIES UP TO 6 dB
MORE THAN WHEN PLACED IN
MIDDLE OF FLOOR

Fig. 13.20. Sample small system outboard EQ options. Top right: Using a dual 2/3 octave EQ can be a cost effective way of allowing equalization of both main and monotors with a single rack mounted unit. If using a stereo mixer with a sum output, we may wish to also separately equalize voices and instruments by using a patch on each of the stereo submasters, as at right center. Here an additional EQ would be required for monitors.

If using a stereo mixer without patching capability, or without a "sum" or "mono-mix" output as at bottom left, we can use the left output as a vocal sub, take the output through an EQ channel as at bottom right, and return it through an Aux. input. The Aux input *must* be panned the opposite way or a continuous feedback loop will be created. The right output then serves as the "main" and is sent through its own EQ (for the entire mix) and in turn to the crossover and power amplifiers. (If using a "full-range" passively crossed-over system the EQ output will of-course be patched directly to the power amp(s).)

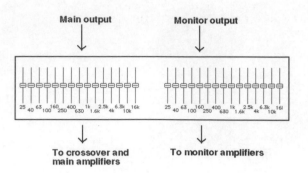

Main output   Monitor output

To crossover and main amplifiers   To monitor amplifiers

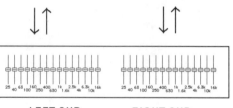

VOICES   INSTRUMENTS

PAN   PAN

To outboard EQ via board's patching jacks

LEFT SUB   RIGHT SUB

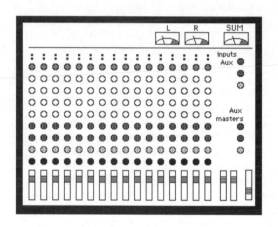

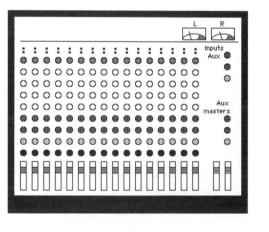

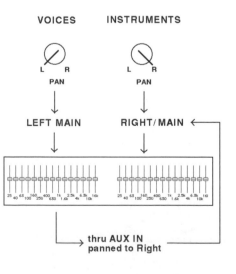

VOICES   INSTRUMENTS

PAN   PAN

LEFT MAIN   RIGHT/MAIN

thru AUX IN panned to Right

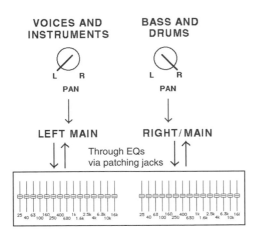

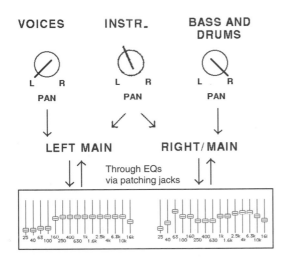

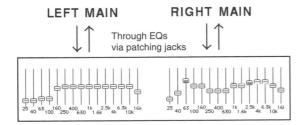

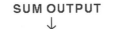

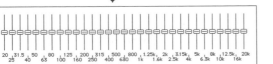

Fig. 13.21. Additional outboard EQ options for mid-sized systems.

When using a typical stereo mixer with a sum output, we may wish to pan voices and instruments to one side and bass and drums to the other. We are still using a mono mix, but using the Left and Right "subs" to allow extra EQ capability and separate control over the level of each category. This is sometimes a desirable option because the low frequencies are often cut when using vocal mics up-close, while the drums commonly require a low frequency boost. Using a graphic EQ to set the basic EQ needs for each category then allows the onboard EQ to be used more flexibly to make individual adjustments.

Another interesting option is shown at center. We can set one EQ curve for voices, and another for drums and bass. Instruments which fall between the two categories in terms of their general EQ needs can be panned somewhere between the two, making use of both EQ curves in combination. This can be useful, for example, when the voice EQ curve has too little bottom end, and the drum EQ curve has two much, say, for a guitar or keyboard.

At bottom is shown what is generally regarded as the ideal with a standard stereo mixer (say 12x2 or 16x2 with "sum" output) when used for live sound. Here the left and right "subs" are separately equalized and used as above, but the main output has a 1/3-octave EQ to tailor the mix to the particular room.

Monitors would of-course require a separate outboard unit. If extra outboard EQs are available, the one instrument which is most often in need of it tends to be the kick drum (though obviously there is no hard-and-fast rule).

Fig. 13.22. Typical patches for submasters.

When using a mixer with submasters for music reinforcement, commonly an outboard EQ is patched into the inserts of each sub, to allow each designated category of instrument or voice to be separately equalized, in addition to the main EQ. (Outboard monitor EQ(s) not illustrated here.)

Shown here is a typical 16x4x2 mixer, and typical submaster groupings. Generally we will use one sub for vocals, one for drums, with the remaining groups designated as desired by the operator for best mixing and EQ convenience. Some operators will actually use one sub in this type of arrangement for the kick drum alone, which tends to have its own EQ needs not shared by any other instrument. The bass guitar is often sent directly to the main mix, not using any sub. If multiple keyboards are being used, we may wish to put all the keys on one sub, and so on. Many soundpersons prefer to designate one of the subs for effects only.

Typically some form of compression is used for dynamic control of the mix, independently of any limiting designed for system protection. At bottom is shown a typical two-channel compressor/limiter, with one channel used for limiting of the overall mix. The second compressor/limiter channel would most often be patched after the outboard EQ for the vocal submaster, since the vocals tend to be most in need of compression for a typical mix. (In fact, when confronted with a system with only one channel of compression, many experienced operators will actually patch it on the vocals and leave the instruments uncompressed, in order to avoid having the vocals "push down" the rest of the mix during loud vocal passages.) Generally the compression should be set to engage only during the loudest passages likely to be encountered, else gain-before-feedback is significantly reduced.

As systems get bigger and as budget allows, additional outboard EQs, additional compressor/limiters (for each submaster and/or for individual instruments or voices which present troublesome dynamics) and noise gates (most often for drums) are commonly added to facilitate the mixing task.

SUB 1 (vocals)   SUB 2 (guit./keyboards)

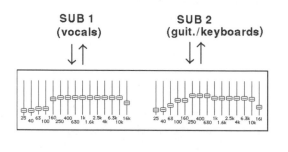

SUB 3 (bass guit.)   SUB 4 (drums)

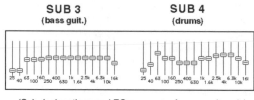

(Sub designations and EQ curves are for example only)

SUM OUTPUT (or choose either Left or Right as Main and pan subs accordingly)

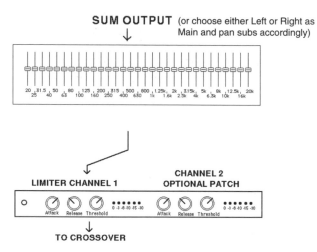

LIMITER CHANNEL 1   CHANNEL 2 OPTIONAL PATCH

TO CROSSOVER

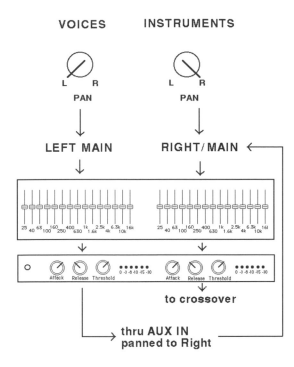

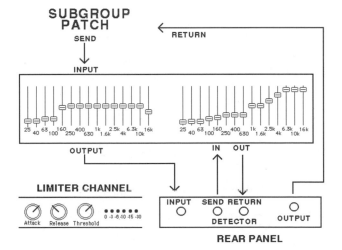

Fig. 13.23. Additional compressor/limiter options. At top-left is shown a patching arrangement similar to that shown in Fig. 13.20, when using a standard stereo mixer without a sum output. Here the vocals are EQ'd and limited separately from the main mix, with the mix also EQ'd and limited to help keep the overall mix under dynamic control. (Remember again that the Aux. input must be panned the opposite way to avoid creating a feedback loop in this type of arrangement.)

When using a stereo mixer with a sum output, we can separately EQ and compress left and right , eliminating the need for compression of the overall mix. As budget allows, compressors are typically added both to the main mix as well as to troublesome instruments and/or voices.

At bottom-left is shown a typical patching arrangement using a detector loop to make the limiting characteristics frequency dependent. Here the output of the left EQ channel is patched in the standard way, i.e., through the compressor and back to the return on the mixer. The detector loop is patched to the right EQ. (Sometimes the detector patch is a TRS format, in which case the appropriate cable needs to be used, and a determination made as to which is the send, the tip or the sleeve.) In this illustration the EQ on the detector loop is set to favor limiting the high frequencies in order to act somewhat like a "de-esser", though any necessary curve can be used. This type of arrangement can often be helpful in keeping the "high end" of the vocals under control, a common problem with vocal compression. But its usefulness is certainly not limited to vocals. Any instrument, or category of instrument on a submaster, where certain frequencies seem to "jump out" in spite of compression, is often a good candidate for a detector patch.

Similarly a detector patch can be used in conjunction with a noise gate to make its triggering action frequency dependent. An example of such a use is on kick drum, to respond only to the pedal-beater sound (1k-4k range).

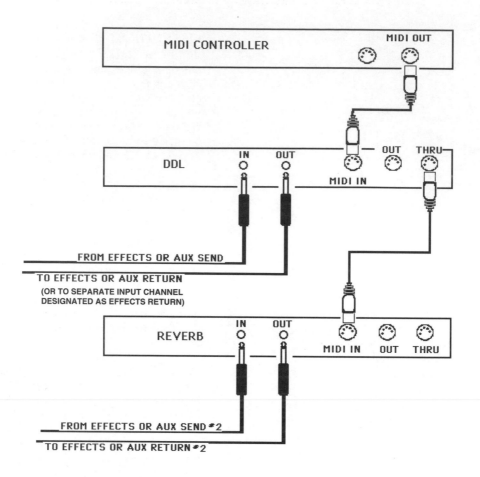

Fig. 13.24. Effects units with MIDI capability. Shown is a patching arrangement for synchronized control of MIDI-capable effects units. We may wish to use such an arrangement to synchronize complicated changes in echo time and reverb for specific musical passages. The units are patched as normal "effects loops", but in this arrangement the MIDI controller allows combined control of the effects settings.

A significant amount of experimentation and advance preparation is usually required here during rehearsal. A series of MIDI programs should be set up in a reasonably logical number progression to accomodate the various needs likely to be encountered in live performance, ranging from short echo and reverb times to long echo and reverb times, and various combinations in between.

The use of this type of setup does not necessarily eliminate the standard manual changes needed to adapt to unexpected song-to-song and passage-to-passage changes in a performance, but it can be extremely helpful for quick changes planned in advance which would involve changing too many settings in a very short time. Properly set up and logged, the special effects are then ready to go at a touch of a button on the MIDI controller. This can be particularly handy when using, for example, multiple reverb units and/or DDLs for different voices and instruments. (The MIDI format allows up to 16 different effects units to be operated under a given program. A specific discussion of MIDI operating techniques would be well beyond the scope of this book, but is normally included in the manufacturer's literature for any MIDI controller. Both rack-mountable and foot-pedal-type units are commercially available.)

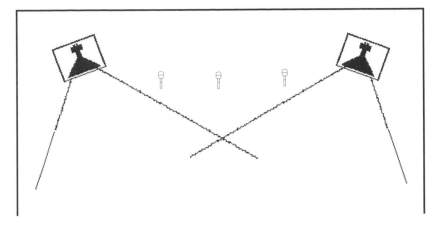

Fig. 13.25. Basic stage setup. Best results in terms of gain-before-feedback are achieved when the "front line" of the stage setup is beyond the outer dispersion angles of the equipment. Stage monitors of-course need to be pointed more-or-less at the mic positions, but they are normally placed at an angle where unidirectional mic response is lower. Not so with the main speakers, which, if placed behind the "front line" of the stage, would be at a much "hotter" angle of mic pickup. Another thing to heed here is the potential for feedback in the lows and lower mids when a mic is situated close to one of the main speakers (no matter how far off-axis it is).

When using a small system without stage monitors, we can allow the "front line" to overlap the outer dispersion angles of the speakers at or just beyond the -6dB points, where the response is much lower than on-axis (recall that most manufacturers average out the -6dB angles in quoting the dispersion) . While reducing maximum gain-before-feedback, this can allow the performers to catch the "edge" of the dispersion pattern without falling into the "hottest" output angles of the loudspeakers. It may be appropriate to set up the stage with the center performer(s) forward just a bit when taking this approach, so they also catch the edge of the pattern.

Below: If a performer is to walk out in front of main speakers it is sensible practice to plan an arc to avoid the area closest to either "stack", in order to reduce the potential for feedback. (Recall the inverse square law from Chapter 4.) To some extent it is also possible for the performer to use the face and/or body to put the mic in a "shadow" when walking directly in front of speakers (mainly the highs are shadowed, but the highs tend to be the frequency range where we are most likely to experience feedback in this situation).

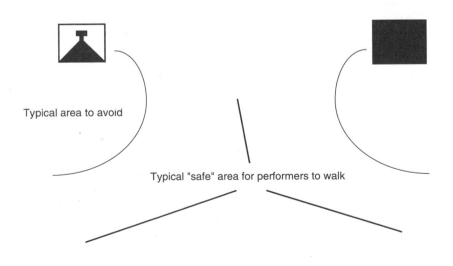

Fig. 13.26. Typical "mid-sized" mixer and house equipment rack setup. Here the house rack equipment is divided into two racks for ease of carrying. The bottom rack contains the crossover, main and monitor EQ's and main limiting, along with an Aphex (one channel on mains, one on monitors). The top rack contains a DDL, reverb unit, four channels of compression (two dual channel units, and a dual 2/3 octave EQ for submaster and/or individual instrument patches. The top rack also contains a patch panel (normally called a "patch bay") on the front of the rack for easy access in patching the equipment when needed. The bottom rack also contains an additional dual-channel 2/3 octave EQ, one channel of which is patched as a control-loop for frequency-dependent limiting, with the second channel available for additional patches when needed. (Not included in this particular system are noise gates for drum channels.)

CHAPTER 14

CONCERT SYSTEMS

General Considerations.

The parameters for system design and use for concerts depend wholly upon the nature of the performance, the size, shape and acoustical characteristics of the performance environment, and of course the required sound level.

Generally speaking, we can regard such systems as similar or expanded versions of systems described in the previous chapter. Systems such as described in the latter portion of Chapter 13 are often quite adequate in providing reinforcement for a typical high school or small college auditorium or gymnasium, as well as for many outdoor affairs. For larger environments or more elaborate stage setups, the system of-course needs to be expanded accordingly.

In a larger arena or large outdoor concert setting, we are more likely to use a modular system involving larger, actively crossed-over "full-range" enclosures with suplementary subwoofers, as well as processor controlled systems as described in this chapter.

Further, in the larger concert environment we are much more likely to encounter long reverberation times, as well as the high frequency attenuation over long distances as described in Chapter 4.

Certainly, safety concerns are more likely to come into play here, due to the heavier electrical requirements and equipment size often needed. Among other things, a separate electrical distribution system independent of the "wall outlets" is standard with any large system. The implementation of any such distribution system should always be supervised by a qualified electrician. Similarly, rigging of enclosure arrays should always be supervised by a competent person familiar with heavy-duty rigging techniques.

Increasingly, for the largest applications, intricate computerized studies of the complex interactions of directional patterns among large numbers of enclosures are being used to tailor the arrays to the environment. There are still some engineers who are adept at arranging portable arrays by eye, but this approach is today being rapidly taken over by the computerized approach. The dimensions, shape, seating arrangement and reverberant characteristics of the arena are plugged into the program and "voila", out comes the shape of the "optimal" array for a given set of equipment. In this chapter, though, we will need to be content with overviewing some of the more basic aspects.

Additional concert sound considerations are introduced in the following diagrams, supplementing material presented in previous chapters. Additional wiring concerns are discussed in Chapter 16.

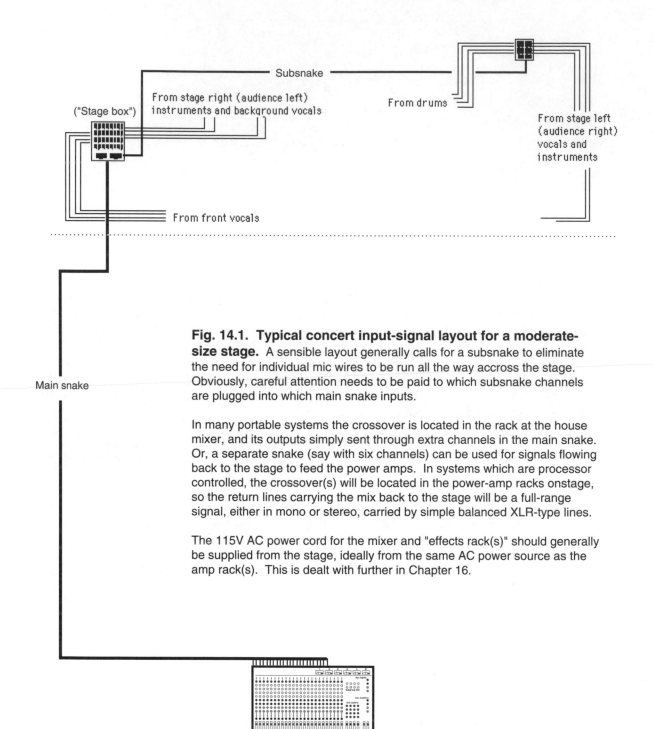

Subsnake

From stage right (audience left)
instruments and background vocals

("Stage box")

From drums

From stage left
(audience right)
vocals and
instruments

From front vocals

Main snake

Fig. 14.1. Typical concert input-signal layout for a moderate-size stage. A sensible layout generally calls for a subsnake to eliminate the need for individual mic wires to be run all the way accross the stage. Obviously, careful attention needs to be paid to which subsnake channels are plugged into which main snake inputs.

In many portable systems the crossover is located in the rack at the house mixer, and its outputs simply sent through extra channels in the main snake. Or, a separate snake (say with six channels) can be used for signals flowing back to the stage to feed the power amps. In systems which are processor controlled, the crossover(s) will be located in the power-amp racks onstage, so the return lines carrying the mix back to the stage will be a full-range signal, either in mono or stereo, carried by simple balanced XLR-type lines.

The 115V AC power cord for the mixer and "effects rack(s)" should generally be supplied from the stage, ideally from the same AC power source as the amp rack(s). This is dealt with further in Chapter 16.

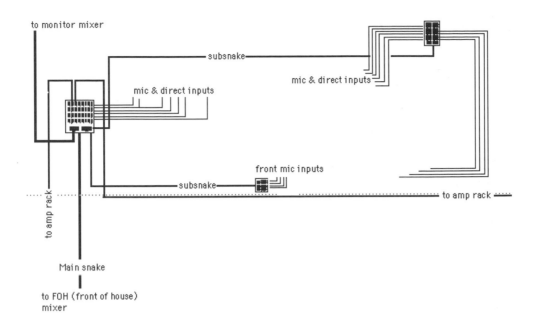

Fig. 14.2. Basic large-stage layout. As stages get larger and more complex, additional subsnakes are generally used. A flow-chart needs to be drawn to match channel numbers on the subsnakes to the appropriate channel numbers on the main snake, and each engineer and/ or stagehand should have access to copies.

Onstage monitor mixers require either a separate snake with "tails" as in the following chapter, or a snake built to match multipin connectors built into the stagebox itself. In larger systems, it is more likely for the crossovers (or processors) to be located in the amp racks themselves, so here we are more likely to be using a simple XLR-type cable for the main signal(s), simply run from the snake to the appropriate input connector on the amp rack(s). The ideal for mixed signals returning to the stage is to use a separate snake (or extra balanced cables taped to the outside of the main snake.

Fig. 14.3. High frequency attenuation due to long cable runs. A 60-meter cable run (approximately 200', typical for a 150' snake plus mic cable and/or subsnake length) will result in some rolloff of high frequencies from a typical low-impedance microphone (with Z usually in the neighborhood of 200Ω). As can be seen, the rolloff is not radical with a 200Ω source (about 0.5 dB at 12 kHz) and in most cases can be ignored. With a microphone or other source having much higher source impedance, the rolloff can become much more significant where extremely long cable runs are involved. In some instances, this may call for slight EQ compensation (or, in certain extreme cases, preamplification of the signal prior to entering the snake). The degree of rolloff, which is due to cable capacitance, is also dependent upon cable thickness and upon the ratio of source impedance to load impedance, as discussed in Chapter 4. (Illustration reprinted from Handbook of Sound System Design, by John Eargle, courtesy Elar Publishing.)

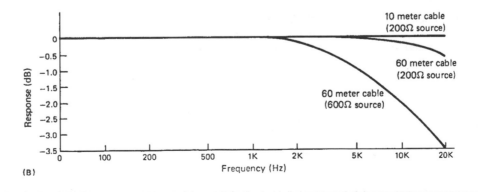

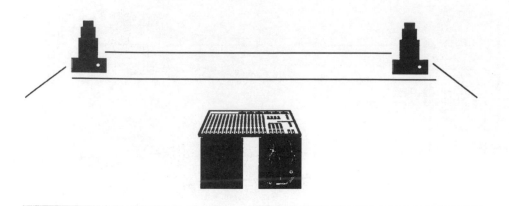

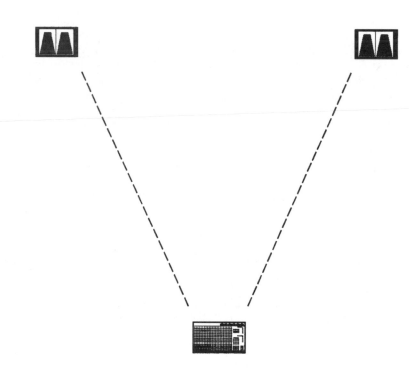

Fig. 14.4. Mixer in center positioning. A mixer placed as illustrated allows the operator to hear the full spectrum in constructive interference as discussed in Chapter 1. Some engineers prefer this positioning. The compromise here is that the engineer is not hearing the most representative sampling of what the audience hears. The operator must take into account, when hearing the mix, that the bulk of the audience off-center is hearing less low frequencies in general. In some cases, the task of mixing actually becomes more difficult here due to the comparatively high degree of low end, which, while perhaps enjoyable, can partially mask some of the subtleties of the mix which the operator needs to hear. (This of-course also depends on how comparatively strong the low frequency output is—but in the studio, for similar reasons, the extreme lows are commonly tapered off while mixing, then boosted again for the final cut.)

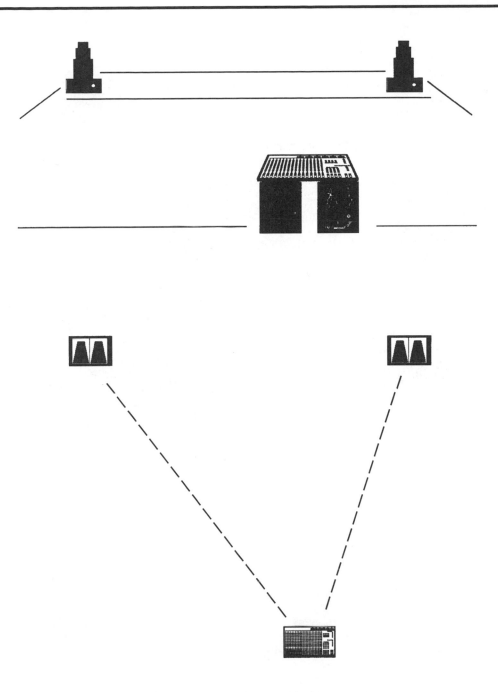

Fig. 14.5. Mixer in off-center positioning. The majority of live engineers prefer a mixing position somewhat off-center. This gives a slightly more representative sampling of what the audience is hearing. One compromise here is that careful attention needs to be paid in certain types of music to avoid boosting the very low end to the point where it is too overwhelming in the center of the audience. It is common practice during sound check to walk over to the center (as well as elsewhere) to determine how much of a difference in sound quality there is as compared to the mixing position. Having made a mental note of this, the more experienced engineer takes it into account during the performance. With practice, a facility is developed for keeping track of the differences in tonal quality commonly encountered in such situations. As well, an ability can be developed to keep the necessary relationship between kick drum and bass guitar, as well as the low end of vocals and other instruments, in their proper proportion to one another despite the usually reduced low end response at the mixing position. Also, in a very large arena, this kind of positioning often tends to put the house system operator(s) more-or-less squarely in the sound-field of one cluster, with the effect of the other cluster comparatively minimized. (This is in part due to the precedence effect briefly described in Chapter 3, which, beyond playing a role in directional hearing, happens to also play an important role in perceived tonal quality.)

Fig. 14.6. Splayed arrays. (Left: courtesy Eastern Acoustic Works; right: courtesy Martin Audio)

These are typical of high quality "flown" arrays for mid-size concert applications. Note that in both these examples the principles of both vertical pattern control (as discussed in Chapter 9) and horizontal dispersion come into play. Stacking the components atop one another tends to narrow the vertical pattern.

It is normal for typical loudspeaker designs for concert applications to be designed for a narrower horizontal dispersion than for typical small systems. With this type of enclosure design it is assumed (at the manufacturer's design stage) that the enclosures will most often be used in arrays of this type, and typical horizontal dispersion averages somewhere in the neighborhood of 50-60 degrees from the midrange through the high end. The combination of such enclosures in arrays then assists in projection in the lower mids (and in the largest arrays, in the low end as well). (Remember that when a long distance "throw" is required, the lower the frequency is, the larger the array which is required to "focus" it in a forward direction towards farther reaches of the audience.)

It is the normal practice to overlap the dispersion patterns in such arrays around the -6dB angles. Since the -6dB angles commonly vary by frequency, we may wish to select a frequency in the upper midrange (or whatever frequency has the narrowest dispersion) as our angular reference. Where the horizontal pattern needs to be narrowed, a flatter, broader arc is used, as at right.

Fig. 14.7. Rigging of a cluster for a circular seating arrangement.
(photos courtesy Turbosound)

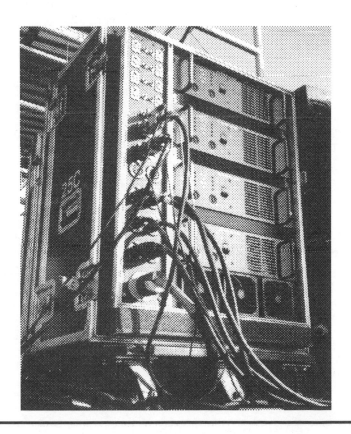

Fig. 14.8. Example of an amplifier rack setup for a large portable system.
(System by Sun Sound, Northhamptom, MA)

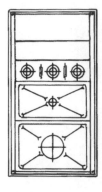

Combination array
(Combi)
1×F2M, 1×F2H,
1×F2T.
Short and medium
throw. Forward gain
reference = 0 dB*.

(A)

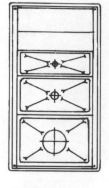

Combination array
using F2V.
Used in systems with
other F2V arrays for
full compatibility.

(B)

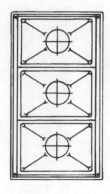

Mid array.
3×F2M.
Medium and long
throw applications.
Forward gain = 9 dB.

(C)

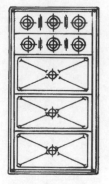

Medium/long throw
extended range array.
3×F2H, 2×F2T.
Mid band forward gain
=9 dB.

(D)

Medium throw
extended range array.
2×F2H, 2×F2V.
Forward gain = 6 dB
for both bands.

(E)

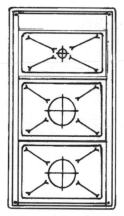

Combination array
2 x F2M, 1 x F2H
Medium throw.
Mid band forward gain
= 6 dB.

(F)

Fig. 14.9. Example of a modular arrangement which can be customized for various pattern-control requirements. (courtesy Martin Audio)
The illustrated commercial system serves as a good "object lesson" on basic techniques of stacking multiple units for vertical pattern control. (These are the enclosures pictured in Fig. 14.6., right-hand photo. This arrangement, incorporating different elements into a single enclosure size, is designed to allow customizing of systems without complicating rigging procedures or visual appearance of arrays. Not shown are compatible midbass and subwoofer.)

Here the concept of "forward gain" is used by the manufacturer to describe the increase in on-axis response at a distance when multiple components in the same frequency range are stacked atop one another. The increase actually involves both better projection in the vertical plane and acoustic "coupling" of the components to increase efficiency and maximum output capability.

The rough specs are as follows:
F2M: midrange horn 13"/335mm high—low crossover point is 220 Hz;
F2H: HF horn 10"/250mm high, with a 2"throat driver—recommended crossover point is 1.5 kHz;
F2T: a splayed VHF array of three "bullet" tweeters where the recommended crossover point is 8 kHz;
F2V: VHF horn, 6.5"/166mm high, with a 1" throat driver, designed for better projection of the VHF range—crossover point is 7kHz.
The enclosures themsleves measure 42"/ ~1m in height.

In "A" and "B", three units are combined to produce "full range" output down to 220 Hz (the 1"-throat VHF horn provides slightly narrower vertical pattern and better wavefront coherence). In "C" is shown stacking of mid-horns to narrow the vertical pattern in the mids. In D is shown stacking of both HF and VHF units. In "E" is shown stacking of HF units and 1"-throat VHF horns. (If we wish to be technical, no acoustic coupling is achieved in the VHF range in "D" and "E" due to the very short wavelengths (8kHz = ~2")—they are stacked for the extra SPL. In "F" is shown stacking of two mid-horns to achieve midrange vertical pattern control (down to about 500Hz) roughly equivalent to the vertical pattern of the 2"-throat horn.

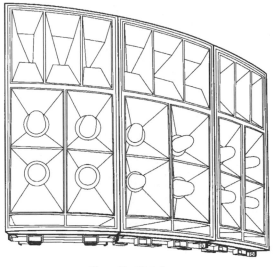

Three-Section Array
40° Vertical Coverage
90° Horizontal Coverage

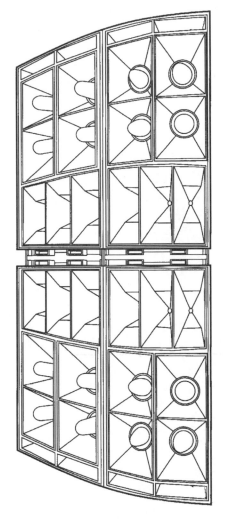

Long-Throw Configuration
20° Vertical Coverage
60° Horizontal Coverage

Fig. 14.10. Large concert "long throw" arrays. (courtesy Meyer Sound Labs) The Meyer MSL-10 represents, at this writing, the consummate "long throw" configuration marketed in a "1-box" configuration, illustrated here without grilles. Even experienced engineers are sometimes amazed at the degree of "throw" achieved by these enclosures. Each measuring 85" high and weighing in at a mere 700 pounds each, fork-lift brackets come as standard equipment. Each consists of 4 horn-loaded 12"/300mm drivers and 3 HF horns with 2"/50mm-throat drivers. The coverage angles here are nominal angles quoted by the manufacturer for simplicity of use (though in measurements the enclosures come remarkably close to the nominal angles).

Note on left that when the enclosures are stacked, the HF horns are placed together, since smaller wavelengths require closer placement to achieve coupling. The low frequency units in the vertical stacking arrangement on left begin to couple vertically with one another below about 200 Hz, further increasing projection in the lows, where the projection also tends to be badly needed in large environments.

(A common problem in very large environments is that the combination of HF attenuation in air, and the lack of adequate pattern control in the lower mids and lows, often results in a "tinny" or "blary" sound (i.e., heavy in the upper mids and mid-treble) at greater distances. Remember from Chapter 9 that in any given frequency range, identical components separated by more than about a wavelength will tend not to couple acoustically, and the patterns will behave more like two separate sound sources. When the wavelength significantly exceeds the distance between the two identical components, they will tend to couple and achieve a narrower pattern along with higher on-axis SPL. Thus the stacking arrangement at left, where the horns are stacked together and where the total height is over 14'*(4m).

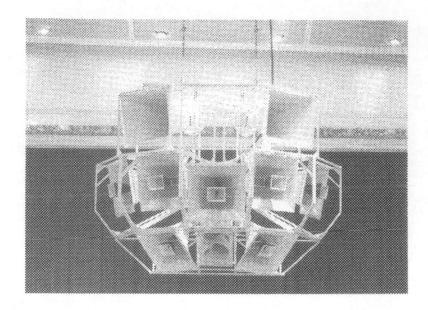

Fig. 14.11. Example of a high quality center-cluster installation. Shown is the installation at the Cincinnatti Music Hall (courtesy Community, Inc./InView Magazine/Installation by Midwest Communications). Utilized are units comprised of Community M-4 4"-throat midrange compression drivers on midrange horns, with a coaxially mounted high frequency horn. The topmost units in the photo are the Community CB-594 bass horn shown in Chapter 9, Fig. 9.34, used here to assist in projection of the midbass. The unit facing downward in the center is a dual 15" midbass unit to cover the floor seating. Subwoofers are located on the floor. An available SPL of over 100 dB from 63Hz to 12kHz, with nearly 20dB headroom, is achieved throughout the entire seating area.

Below: View of the array from the top balcony. This array is designed to be disassembled and removed during symphony orchestra performances where reinforcement is not required.

Fig. 14.12. After the house lights go down. (Photo courtesy Martin Audio)

Fig. 14.13. Commercial high-output systems. (courtesy Turbosound) Left: TMS-3, containing an 18" LF driver, 10" midrange with a patented mid-horn design, and HF horn. Right: TMS-3. This enclosure is, at this writing, the most widely sold high-power enclosure worldwide. Note that the mid horns are arranged in such a way that when enclosures are combined in large arrays, the mid horns couple acoustically, both vertically and horizontally, increasing low-mid projection for larger environments. The HF horn is crossed over at 3.8kHz (wavelength of ~4"), and so does not require stacking to achieve effective pattern control.

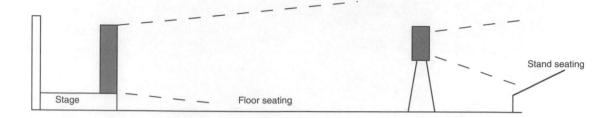

Fig. 14.14. Delayed clusters in large arenas. Due to both the inverse-square law and the attenuation of high frequencies over long distances, delay towers are commonly set up for concerts in large environments such as full-size stadiums. In a typical large arena, the tower is set up so the delayed cluster' height will be between upper and lower "decks" so the sight line to the stage is not obscured.

As with most delayed systems, about 10 to 15 milliseconds is added to the calculated time of sound travel to preserve the precedence effect (described in Chapter 12). Often, such towers will be composed solely of high frequency horns to make up for the high frequency loss in the rear seating, crossed over at perhaps 5kHz or so, and EQ'd to make up for the amount of loss in the particular environment. Amp racks are typically set up at each tower, fed with a line level signal.

A handy way of setting the delay time in a pinch is to have someone hit two drumsticks together through a mic and stand behind the delay tower until the main clusters and delayed clusters are in-sync.

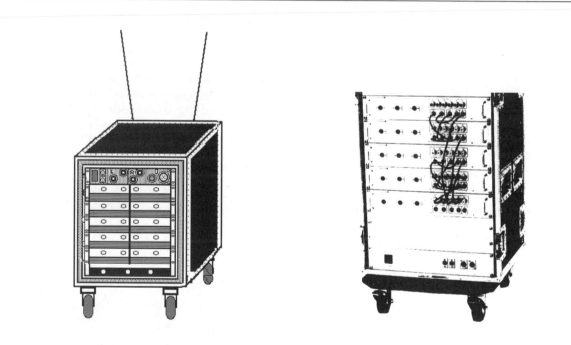

Fig. 14.15. Rack-mounted wireless receivers. The use of rack mountable wireless receivers with a common pair of antennas greatly simplifies situations where many wireless units need to be used. (The antennas do not necessaritly need to be mounted on the rack itself—remote positioning via the appropriate coax cable is often preferable. In some cases a bit of experimentation is required to find optimal positions for the antennas to avoid dropout.) At right is illustrated a back panel of such an arrangement, with jumpers from one unit to another (courtesy Beyerdynamic). This type of arrangement is also highly useful in theater productions involving multiple wireless lavaliers. Ordinarily the units would be situated onstage (out of sight).

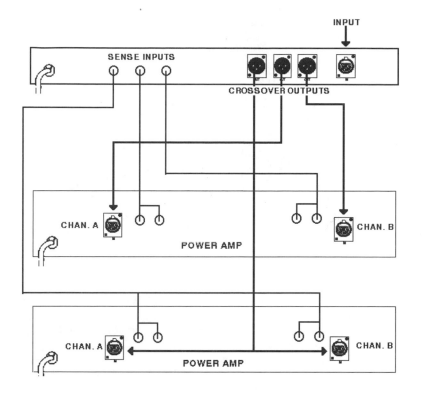

Fig. 14.16. Typical processor-controlled amp/crossover arrangement.
Processor-controlled systems come in a number of forms, one of which is illustrated here. Basically, what is involved is an active crossover, specially designed for a given set of loudspeaker components, as well as (usually) a built-in computerized system for adapting to changing signal levels.

Most often, some form of signal-limiting is designed into this type of unit to reduce the potential for driver failure. As well, many such units include the ability to adapt to high-level signals by changing the crossover points. Such a function, usually referred to as "floating crossover points", moves the crossover points upward when high power levels are sensed. This helps prevent overexcursion of speaker cones and/or HF diaphrams at high power levels.

In the illustration above, the "sense inputs" are designed to monitor the amplifier output levels directly, and the unit is programmed to limit signals according to the power handling capacity and frequency capabilities of each of the units (in this case LF, MF and HF). The sense inputs in this case are wired with standard "dual banana" connectors in parallel with the speaker outputs of the power amps.

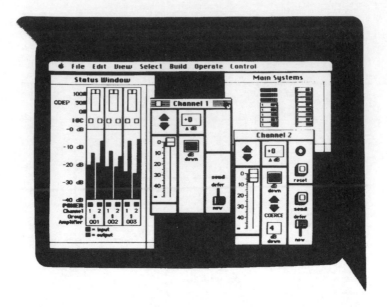

Fig. 14.17. Example of a control/monitoring system for large numbers of power amplifiers. (courtesy Crown International)
Increasingly, in the largest-size systems, monitoring systems are being used to keep track of the signal levels and performance of the power amps. A control system of this type (shown on a Macintosh screen) allows adjustment af amplifier gain as needed, in order to increase or decrease output level of the system to various parts of a large installation (or, if need be, turn various predetermined zones on or off as needed).

CHAPTER 15

MONITOR SYSTEMS

Here the primary concern we generally face is achieving adequate gain-before-feedback. Since the loudspeakers are aimed approximately at the microphone positions, we need to depend upon the directional pattern of the microphone and upon the closeness of the talker or singer to to the microphone if we wish to achieve reasonable gain before continuous feedback occurs.

As introduced in Chapter 7, we can provide stage monitoring controlled by an aux. send from the main mixer. Or we can provide a separate mixer for monitoring purposes, splitting each input signal so they are received by both the main and monitor mixers.

When monitors are controlled from the "house" (main) mixer (a function traditionally referred to as "foldback"), pre-fader aux. sends are used, and generally one or two monitor mixes are provided (occasionally more, depending on the mixer capability). In setting up two mixes we might, for example, provide one mix for the front line performers and another for side fills, tailoring the respective levels to best suit the needs of the particular stage setup. Another common approach is to use one mix for the main vocalist(s), and the second mix for instrumentalists such, for example a horn section.

If the financial budget allows, we might use a house mixer with a matrix (as described in Chapter 7). Here we can use the submixes to provide several additional monitor mixes in addition to those controlled from the monitor sends (i.e., the pre-fader aux.'s). An example of this would be a separate mix for the drummer and perhaps keyboards or brass section. These additional matrix mixes would of-course reflect any changes the operator makes in the house mix which needs to be routed through those subgroups. So if using a matrix, a decision needs to be made as to whether or not the performers wish to hear their instruments change in level when, for example, they play a lead part. (Ordinarily, this is not as attractive as it would at first seem, and such changes can actually be disconcerting to many performers.)

In any relatively large or complex reinforcement system, the optimal approach is generally to use a separate onstage mixer for monitors . Two basic formats are found in monitor mixers. In the first, each of the monitor busses are set up to be post fader on each individual channel. The fader is used to regulate the overall level of each input channel in all of the mixes. A slightly more versatile offshoot of this approach provides a choice between pre and post fader on each of the monitor busses. The other basic mixer design simply provides separate sends for each monitor buss, with no fader on the input channel. Such a mixer serves essentially as a large matrix.

Fig. 15.1. Commercial examples of "wedge" monitors. (Left: courtesy Meyer Sound Labs; right: courtesy Electro-Voice) The Meyer UM-1 is a processor-controlled biamped monitor with horn displaying a 60° conical pattern, thus matching the pattern of the 12" LF cone driver. The EV FM 1202 is a passively crossed-over monitor with a constant directivity horn displaying a 90° horizontal pattern. A 90° pattern would, when necessary, allow two mics to be reasonably well covered by one monitor.

Fig. 15.2. Monitor placements. It should be obvious that the basic positioning of a stage monitor is well off-axis of a unidirectional microphone, in order to make use of the angles of minimum pickup of the mic. In situations where gain-before-feedback is a problem, such as on a loud stage, several things can be done to improve a performer's ability to hear. First off, we can ask that they maintain an extremely up-close positioning to the mic (the proximity effect can if-necessary be compensated with an EQ). We can place the monitor slightly off to the side, pointed towards the ear rather than the underside of the face—gain per-se is not always improved, but the ability to hear the "high end" of the monitor *is*. (Sometimes gain-before-feedback is improved here as well. While the off-to-the-side angle is not at the minimum pickup angle of a cardioid mic, it has the advantage of reducing the amount of sound which reflects off the face and back into the mic when used up close. This can give a slight advantage in the high frequencies.)   Of course if two monitors are available we can place one on each side at an angle. We can also elevate the monitor slightly with some type of spacer, bringing it closer to the performer and achieving a better angle towards the ear.

With any monitor which is very "beamy" (i.e., very hot on-axis), such as a single 12" speaker with tweeter or compact straight exponential horn, the best result is often achieved with the positioning at right. Here the axis of the monitor is pointed at the back of the head, increasing the output towards the ear, and slightly reducing the output towards the mic. (The angle in the illustration, incidentally, is roughly at the -12 dB angle of a cardioid mic, and close to the angle of minimum pickup of a supercardioid or hypercardioid mic.)

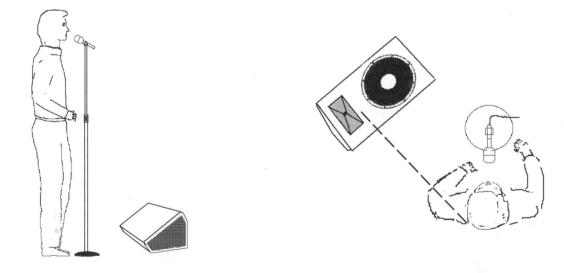

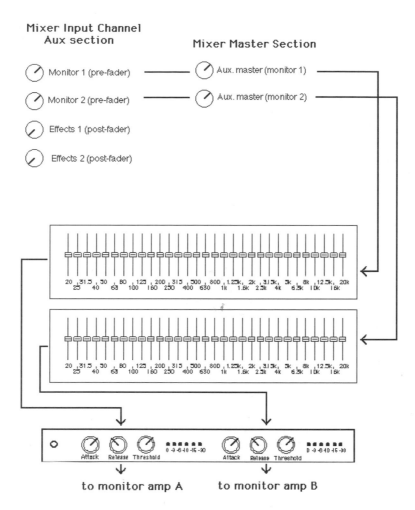

Fig. 15.3. Basic monitor signal flow from house mixer. Generally, a 1/3-octave EQ is the preferred choice for monitor EQ. Basic guidelines for the use of an EQ for feedback control were given in Chapter 6.

The compressor/limiter in this diagram is optional, but can be useful in high level systems—not only in protecting the monitors themselves, but also in keeping stage volume reasonably within bounds. A common problem, particularly where many monitors are used at high levels on a tight stage, is the high degree of monitor sound coming from the stage (usually in the range below about 800 Hz or so). This increases the minimum level at which reasonable control of the house mix can be achieved by the system operator, sometimes to the point where the level of the main mix needs to be overwhelming. A compressor/limiter on the monitors, along with careful attention to the instrument amplifier levels, can often go a long way toward improving the overall sound and simplifying the task of the system operator.

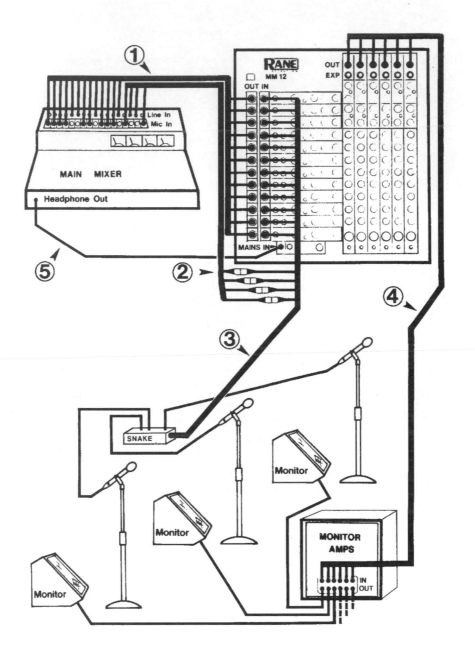

Fig. 15.4. Using a monitor mixer situated at the house mixing position.
(courtesy Rane Corp.) See explanation on opposite page.

Explanation of Fig. 15.4.

The numbers below coincide with the numbers on the accompanying illustration.

(1) A set of jumpers needs to be used to carry input signals from the monitor mixer to the main mixer. Generally this will take the form of a short multicore cable with "tails" and in-line XLR connectors at both ends. (In a pinch, we can also use a set of short mic cables numbered at both ends and tied into a bunch.)

(2) Commonly, not every instrument onstage requires any monitoring, since the stage amplifier essentially serves as the performer's monitor. Whichever channels bypass the monitor mixer are simply jumped across to the main mixer. Occasionally, there may be enough length on the "breakout" of the main snake to avoid the need for such jumpers.

(3) In the Rane MM12 design shown, the "splitter" is built into the mixer itself. In this instance the main snake channels are plugged into the monitor mixer, and the jumpers run across to the main mixer. In some instances where the monitor mixer does not have such XLR outputs on each channel, some type of splitter needs to be used. A set of simple "Y" cords can be constructed in a pinch, but the more effective method is to use splitter boxes as illustrated in Fig. 15.6.

(4) The output mixes (in this case up to six mixes) are patched through outboard EQ's and ultimately back to the monitor amps. This can be accomplished via extra channels on the main snake (if enough are available) or by a separate snake.

(5) This particular monitor mixer allows the headphone output of the main mixer to be patched to a dedicated jack on the monitor mixer with a stereo 1/4" (TRS) patch cord, allowing the operator to listen to the main mix as well. When any of the the "cue" buttons (the equivalent of "PFL") on the monitor mixer are depressed, the main mix is eliminated and the signal from the particular monitor channel is heard. (This does not interrupt the flow of PFL signals from the main mixer, so here the opportunity to sample individual channels on the main mixer is also kept intact.)

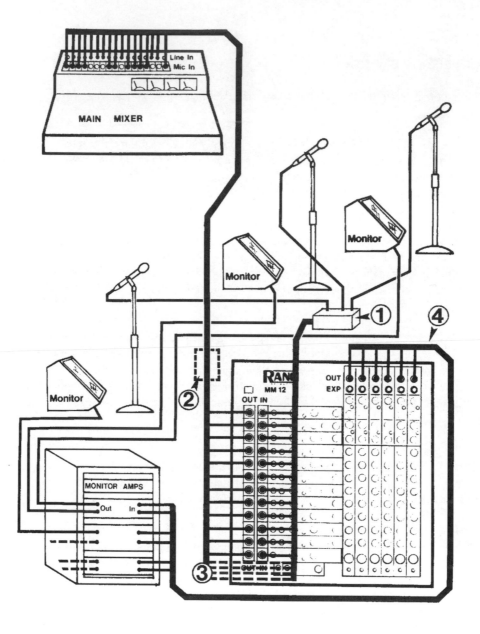

Fig. 15.5. Using a monitor mixer situated onstage. (courtesy Rane Corp.)
See explanation on opposite page.

Explanation of Fig. 15.5.

The numbers below coincide with the numbers on the accompanying illustration.

(1) With a monitor mixer which has outputs for each channel (such as the illustrated Rane MM 12), several appraoaches can be taken.

We can use a subsnake to eliminate the need to run mic lines all the way accross the stage to the monitor mixer, as illustrated. Or, if we are in a low-budget pinch, we can situate the monitor mixer so the mic lines can reach it directly.

(2) Since most snakes of any length involve a stagebox (as opposed to tails at both ends), we are likely to require a jumper snake from the monitor mixer to the stagebox (postion #2 in the illustration, shown in dotted lines). Such a subsnake would need to have tails at both ends. In a pinch, we can use separat mic lines for such a run, but in any high quality system, a multicore cable should be used. (We could also, if budget is a serious issue, modify the main snake so *it* has tails on both ends, thus eliminating the need for an extra subsnake. Obviously, XLR-type connectors would need to be pur-chased and a significant amount of time devoted to this. Chapter 16 presents guidlines for soldering techniques and wiring of XLRs.)

(3) In this illustration, #3 designates channels which do not require stage monitors, which are jumped directly to the main snake.

When a mixer without splitter outputs is used, we need to use a splitter box as in Fig. 15.6, in order to feed both mixers. When such a splitter box is within budget, it is the preferred option no matter what the design of the monitor mixer.

(4) Jumpers from the output of the monitor mixer (in this case up to six) are run from the mixer position to the monitor amps, preferably patched through outboard EQs. The preferred position for the outboard EQs is in a separate rack at the monitor-mix position, as opposed to at the amp rack(s). Basic EQ use for feedback control was described in Chapter 6.

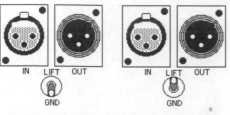

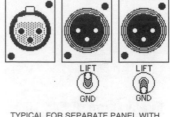

TYPICAL FOR STAGEBOX WITH MULTICORE CABLE
(SNAKE) TO HOUSE MIXER

TYPICAL FOR SEPARATE PANEL WITH
NO MULTICORE CABLE ATTATCHED

Fig. 15.6. Basic splitter configuration for monitor system input signals.

The splitter configuration in this illustration is fairly standard, though occasionally other formats are found. Here, the "ground lift" switch disconnects the shield ground (pin #1) in order to interrupt ground loops and the associated "hum" or "buzz" in system output.

Normally, a high quality splitter box is transformer isolated, as opposed to a simple parallel connection. One reason for this is that in certain mixer designs, changing the setting of the input attenuator can change the level at the other mixer when they are fed with a parallel connection without benefit of an isolating transformer. The other reason is that overall input impedance is reduced, which in critical high quality applications can degrade frequency response, particularly when a long snake is used (e.g. 150' or more).

Below is shown an example of a splitter-box configuration involving multipin connectors in addition to the normal XLR-type connectors. In this instance we would expect to use one multipin connection to feed the main mixer and one to feed the monitor mixer, with the individual XLR-out's to use "just in case". Some splitter boxes are designed with two ground-lift switches on each channel, to allow a choice of whether to lift the shield ground (pin #1) for either the main *or* monitor mixer, or both. System grounding in-general is discussed in the following chapter.

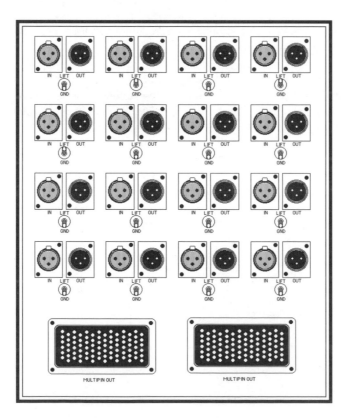

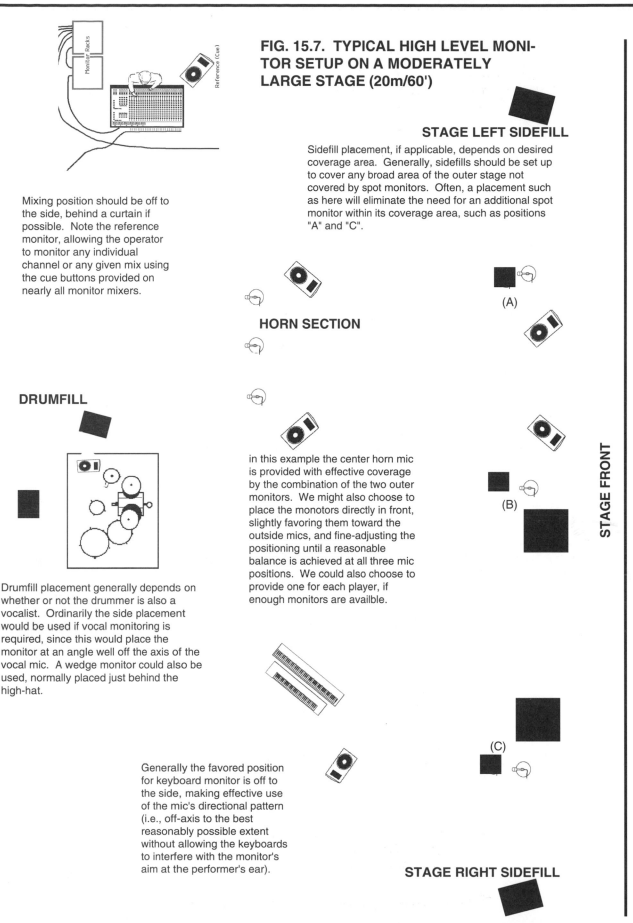

FIG. 15.7. TYPICAL HIGH LEVEL MONITOR SETUP ON A MODERATELY LARGE STAGE (20m/60')

Mixing position should be off to the side, behind a curtain if possible. Note the reference monitor, allowing the operator to monitor any individual channel or any given mix using the cue buttons provided on nearly all monitor mixers.

STAGE LEFT SIDEFILL

Sidefill placement, if applicable, depends on desired coverage area. Generally, sidefills should be set up to cover any broad area of the outer stage not covered by spot monitors. Often, a placement such as here will eliminate the need for an additional spot monitor within its coverage area, such as positions "A" and "C".

HORN SECTION

in this example the center horn mic is provided with effective coverage by the combination of the two outer monitors. We might also choose to place the monotors directly in front, slightly favoring them toward the outside mics, and fine-adjusting the positioning until a reasonable balance is achieved at all three mic positions. We could also choose to provide one for each player, if enough monitors are availble.

DRUMFILL

Drumfill placement generally depends on whether or not the drummer is also a vocalist. Ordinarily the side placement would be used if vocal monitoring is required, since this would place the monitor at an angle well off the axis of the vocal mic. A wedge monitor could also be used, normally placed just behind the high-hat.

Generally the favored position for keyboard monitor is off to the side, making effective use of the mic's directional pattern (i.e., off-axis to the best reasonably possible extent without allowing the keyboards to interfere with the monitor's aim at the performer's ear).

STAGE RIGHT SIDEFILL

CHAPTER 16

SYSTEM WIRING

a) General Considerations.

The very basic concerns in audio wiring involve the following.

Cabling obviously must be adequate to handle the necessary amount of current for a given application. For mic and line level cables, on the order of 26-guage to 22-guage is normally more than adequate (this is typical of most standard mic cables). As discussed in Chapter 5 (section "j"), shielded cable is used in order to minimize electrostatic noise. In high quality applications involving distances of more than a few meters, balanced twisted-pair cables are required for mic level signals. For line level cables, balanced lines often are not absolutely necessary for avoiding noise, since the signal levels tend to be very substantially above the level of electromagnetic fields. But balanced lines *are* needed to achieve maximum flexibility in arranging an effective grounding scheme, discussed in this chapter. For this reason, balanced lines are the industry standard for high quality systems in all but the smallest applications.

For speaker-level wiring, shielding is not necessary or helpful—the normal method is the use of simple two conductor cables. Guages of at least 16 AWG (American Wire Guage) are normally used, and some applications call for the use of upwards of 10-guage or larger. A chart of power losses according to length of the wire, amplifier output power, and speaker impedance is given later in this chapter .

Ineffective system grounding is probably the most commonly encountered stumbling block in elimination of system noise, notably "hum" and "buzz". **Systems must be properly and effectively grounded for very important safety reasons—specifically to reduce or eliminate shock hazards.** Interestingly, though, the very noise we seek to eliminate arises as a result of *too many* paths to ground. This causes "loops" to be created within the grounding paths, which in effect act like antennas. Such loops pick up the surrounding electromagnetic field, and rather than draining it off directly, recirculate it through the system, to be amplified along with everything else we are amplifying. The use of balanced circuitry between components allows these loops to be interrupted in the safest possible way, without interrupting the integrity of the standard electrical ground system via the third pin of the AC electrical plugs.

Finally, the connectors used in any system, as might be expected, are vital links in the signal path of any system. A knowledge of the various connector types commonly used in sound reinforcement systems, and the ability to adapt them to different connector types when necessary, can at times be vital when doing field work. A well-stocked adaptor selection can allow ready adaptation for tape decks, CD players and the like, as well as allow for last minute patches of signal processing equipment and/or power amplifiers when needed.

The locations of other wiring considerations in this book are shown on the last page of this chapter.

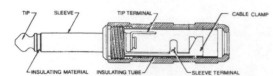

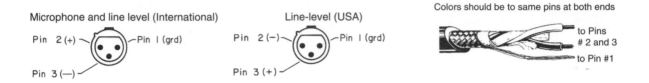

Fig. 16.1. Unbalanced wiring connections. (Left: courtesy ADC; right: courtesy Canare)
When using 1/4" phone plugs, the normal polarity is that a positive voltage applied to the tip should ultimately produce forward motion of a speaker (designated "+"). This polarity is normally maintained throughout any system with unbalanced wiring.

Fig. 16.2. Balanced wiring connections. Balanced mics are normally wired Pin #2 (+) and Pin #3 (-), both in the USA and elsewhere. (On the cable itself, which color is used for which pin is not important so long as it is the same at both ends.) **With line-level cricuits, though, we can occasionally run into a sticky issue.** Contrary to international agreement, because of tradition, **balanced line-level connections in the USA are** (at this writing) **usually wired Pin #3 (+) and Pin #2 (-).** While signal will flow no matter which polarity is used in the components, in high quality applications it can sometimes be important in any system with balanced line-level cricuits to make sure all components are wired for the same polarity. (If they are all made in the US, for example, the same polarity is most likely to prevail throughout.) But the polarity concern can be important, for example, if different power amplifiers are used with an electronic crossover—many power amplifiers have an internal switch which chooses between Pin#2(+) or Pin#3(+). The shield ground should always be wired to Pin #1.

Below: (courtesy Yamaha) Balanced wiring with a 1/4" TRS connector.

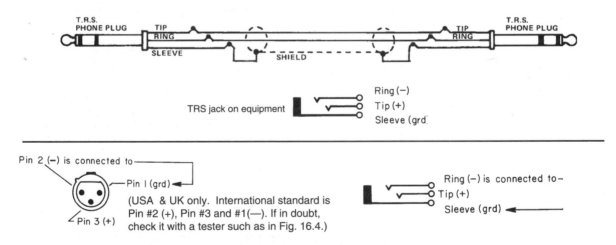

Fig. 16.3. Unbalanced wiring of an XLR-type or TRS connector. (illustration courtesy Carver)
Left: Occasionally an XLR connector will serve carry an unbalanced signal, as with an unbalanced mic. When using an XLR cable to carry an unbalanced mic-level or line-level circuit, an issue similar to that in the previous figure comes into play. **A determination *must* be made as to whether Pin #2 or Pin #3 is "hot" (+).** Internationally, Pin #2 is normally the standard for the "hot", or "high" (+) connection. In the USA and UK, though, the more common configuration, at this writing, is as illustrated here (unfortunately there is no guarantee here either). Note: occasionally we will also find unbalanced XLR outputs on mixers manufactured in the UK (usually Pin#3(+), Pin#1(—)). See also Fig. 16.4 and Fig. 16.13.

Right: Whenever an unbalanced phone plug is inserted into a TRS jack, the ring is shorted to ground and the circuit automatically becomes unbalanced.

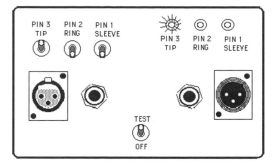

Fig. 16.4. Typical cable tester design. This type of tester is invaluable to anyone doing work in sound reinforcement. Such a unit allows cables to be tested for proper polarity, as well as to detect shorts (two conductors touching each other) or open circuits (broken conductors or connections). As well, we can use such a tester to determine which pins are connected to where on an XLR-type to 1/4" phone cable.

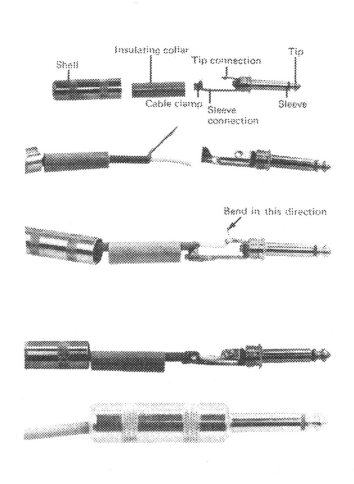

Fig. 16.5. Wiring an unbalanced 1/4" phone plug. (courtesy Yamaha Corp.)

(A) Parts identification.

(B) Slide the shell, then the insulating collar, over the cable end. Strip the outer insulation to a length equal to the length of the sleeve connection. Unwrap the shield, and twist it to for a wire lead.

(C) Postition the outer insulation just ahead of the cable clamp. Strip the center conductor from a point just behind the tip connection. Tin the center conductor and shield (see Fig. 16.6). Bend the shield as illustrated, and solder it to the outer surface of the sleeve connection. (Cool immediately with pliers touched to the back of the sleeve connection.) Insert the center conductor through the hole in the tip connection; solder it and cut the end flush. Bend the end of the tip connector slightly back to help prevent the wire-end from cutting through the insulating collar.

(D) Using pliers, bend the cable clamp around the outer insulation. The clamp should be firm, but not so tight as to cut the insulation.

(E) Slide the insulating collar forward until it is flush with the threads (but not over the threads). Slide the shell forward and screw it tightly to the plug assembly.

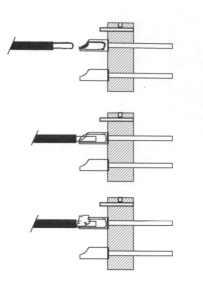

Fig. 16.6. Basic soldering technique. (male XLR-type connector shown) First off, some type of effective clamping method needs to be used to secure the connector itself, since one hand will be holding the soldering tool and the other hand holding the wire. Also, at minimum we should have a small pair of pliers, small diagonal cutters and a solder cleaning tool, as well as some method of checking the cable when finished.

Top: Both connections should be heated with the soldering pencil (or gun) and solder should be melted onto each end of the connection separately (this is known as "tinning"). The surface of the hardened solder should appear fairly shiny. After the solder on both has hardened, the wire should then be touched to the terminal and both heated to the point of melting together.

Center: A correct connection should look roughly like the illustration, and the surface of the solder itself should have a somewhat shiny appearance.

Bottom: If the solder appears "clumpy" or dull (a condition known as a "cold solder joint"), chances are an effective connection has not been made, and the connection generally needs to be redone.

Fig. 16.7. Wiring a TRS phone plug.
(courtesy Yamaha Corp.)

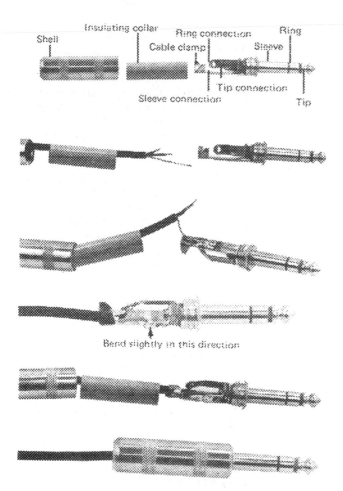

(A) Parts identification.

(B) Slide the shell and insulating collar over the cable end. Strip the outer insulation for a length equal to the length of the sleeve connection. Remove any tracer cords running through the cable. Form a wire lead out of the shield. Hold the cable with the outer insulation just ahead of the cable clamp, and strip the red (or white) conductor just behind the tip connection. Then strip the black conductor just slightly shorter than the tip conection. Tin all leads, and cut the center conductors so approximately 1/8" of bare wire remains.

(C) Solder the shield to the outer surface of the sleeve connection, allowing enough free shield to bend around the other side of the cable clamp. Cool the connection immediately with pliers.

(D) Insert the center conductor leads in their respective connection points, and solder them in place. Trim the leads flush. Bend the end of the tip connection slightly back to help prevent the wire from cutting through the insulating collar.

(E) Using pliers, bend the cable clamp around the outer insulation. The clamp should be firm, but not so tight as to cut the insulation.

(F) Slide the insulating collar forward, until it is flush with the beginning of the threads. Slide the shell forward, and screw it on tightly.

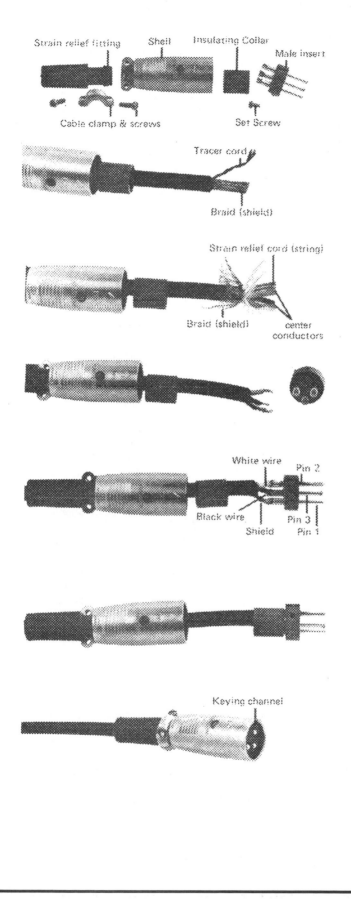

Fig. 16.8. Wiring a male XLR connector.
(courtesy Yamaha Corp.)

(A) Parts identification (ITT/Cannon XLR shown).

(B) Insert the strain relief in the rear of the shell. Then slip the shell onto the cable end, followed by the insulating collar. (This is important—forgetting to slide these parts on in the proper order before soldering is a common error.) Strip the outer insulation about 1/2" back. (Belden #8412 cable illustrated here.)

(C) Cut the tracer cord, unbraid the shield, and cut the excess off the internal strain relief cords.

(D) Strip about 1/4" of the insulation from each of the center conductors. Tin and trim them to about 1/8" of exposed wire. Then twist the shield, positioning it in the correct orientation to mate with the insert. After tinning the shield, cut it to the same length as the center conductors.

(E) Solder the center conductors to their respective pins, using just enough solder to fill the ends of the pins. (The predominant world standards favor mating black to pin #3 and white (or red) to pin #2, though the important concern is that they are the same at both ends of the wire (i.e., that polarity is not reversed). Clean any solder splashes, and inspect for burned insulation or stray strands of wire.

(F) Slide the insulating collar forward, up to the flange of the male insert. The outer cable insulation must be flush with, or covered by, the end of the insert. (If any of the center conductors are visible, the cable clamp may no be able to firmly grip the cable. This is why it is important not to cut the outer sleeve of the cable too far back.)

(G) Slide the shell forward, orienting its internal keying channel with the raised lip on the insert. Secure the insert in the shell with the set screw. Place the cable clamp over the rear of the shell, with careful attention to the clamp's orientation, for thinner cable, the clamp should be turned around so the two lips inside the clamp and shell are aligned in order to effectively clamp the cable. (Different manufacturers have different methods of providing strain relief, but they should always be used in a way which effectively secures the outer jacket of the cable, else the strain of normal use will fall on the solder joints themselves.)

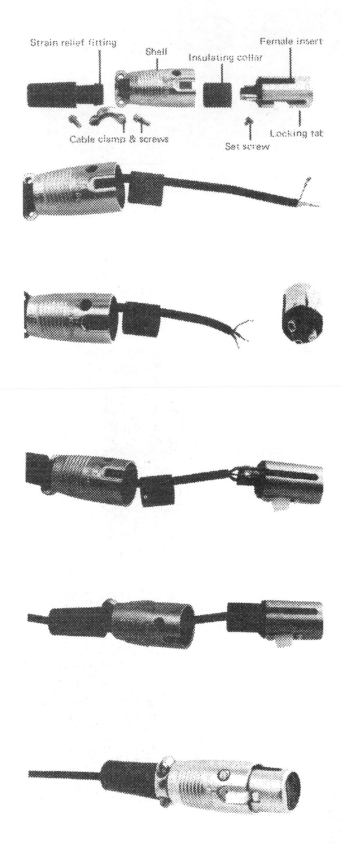

Fig. 16.9. Wiring a female XLR connector.
(courtesy Yamaha Corp.)

(A) Parts identification (ITT/Cannon XLR shown).

(B) Insert the strain relief in the rear of the shell. Then slip the shell onto the cable end, followed by the insulating collar. Strip the outer insulation about 1/2" back. (Belden #8451 cable, a thinner cable with aluminum foil shield, is illustrated here.)

(C) Pull off the foil wrap. Strip about 1/4" of insulation from each center conductor, leaving about 1/4" of insulation between the bare wire and the outer insulation. Tin the bare wire and the outer insulation. Tin the center conductors, and trim them so that about 1/8" of bare wire remains. Then tin the shield conductor, orienting it with the center conductors so they are aligned with the proper pins of the insert. Cut the end of the shield so that is extends 1/16" bayond the center conductors.

(D) Solder the center conductors to their respective pins, using just enough solder to fill the ends of the pins. (The predominant world standards favor mating black to pin #3 and white (or red) to pin #2, though the important concern is that they are the same at both ends of the wire (i.e., that polarity is not reversed). Clean any solder splashes, and inspect for burned insulation or stray strands of wire. Make sure the locking tab is properly inserted into the female insert.

(E) Slide the insulating collar forward, up to the rear edge of the female insert. The outer cable insulation must be flush with, or covered by, the end of the insert. (If any of the center conductors are visible, the cable clamp may no be able to firmly grip the cable. Again, this is why it is important not to cut the outer sleeve of the cable too far back.)

(F) Slide the shell forward, orienting the notch in the shell with the locking tab in the insert. Secure the insert in the shell with the set screw. Place the cable clamp over the rear of the shell, with careful attention to the clamp's orientation. For thinner cable, the clamp should be turned around so the two lips inside the clamp and shell are aligned in order to effectively clamp the cable. (Different manufacturers have different methods of providing strain relief, but they should always be used in a way which effectively secures the outer jacket of the cable, else the strain of normal use will fall on the solder joints themselves.)

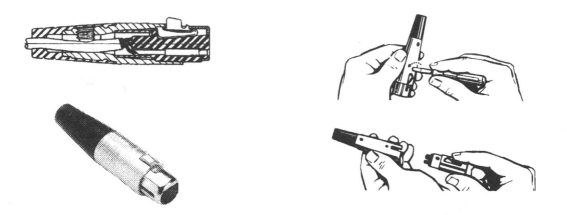

Fig. 16.10. Additional XLR features. As mentioned in the previous two sets of illustrations, it is important that the cable be effectively relieved of any strain on the solder joints themselves. On left is shown another ITT/Cannon design (this company, incidentally, is the inventor of the XLR configuration). In this design the set screw shown in the cross-section clamps the cable in place. The flexible outer jacket then fits over the set screw as pictured. On right is shown the "reverse-thread set scew", to which Switchcraft, Inc. holds the patent. Here the set screw backs into the insert when turned counterclockwise, so it cannot be inadvertently lost.

Fig. 16.11. Several practical methods of dealing with cables. Right (courtesy Canare): A dual cable spool of this type allows convenient division of mic cables into "short" and "long", or however we wish to categorize them. Bottom right (courtesy Canare): a multicore cable ("snake") on a cable spool, with splitter outputs for an onstage monitor mixer. Multipin connector at the end mates to a "breakout" for the house mixer. Below: Incorporating the "stage box" into a road case is another effective method of dealing with snake cable (shown sitting on top of an amp rack).

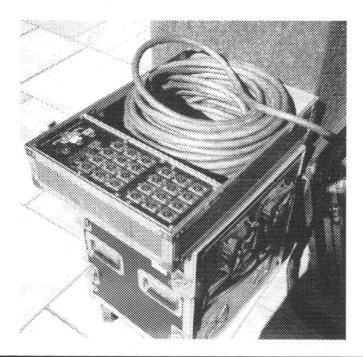

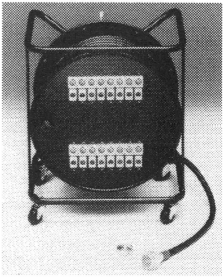

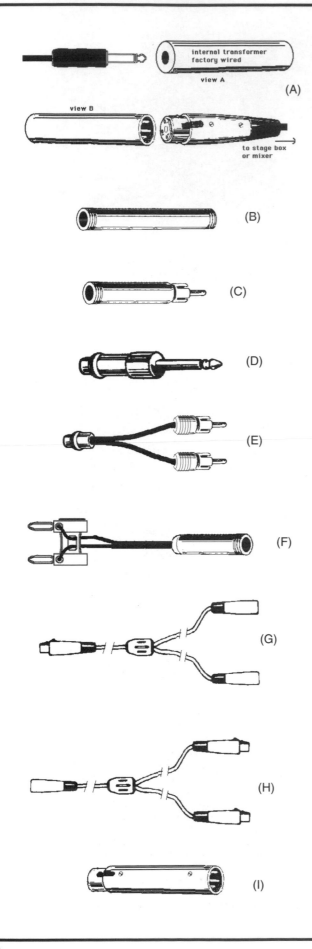

Fig. 16.12. Typical adaptors.

(A) Balanced, low-impedance to unbalanced, high-impedance transformer/ adaptor. These tend to be handy. To name just one common use, an acoustic guitar with internal pickup is easily adapted to a standard mic cable. These are compact and relatively inexpensive (as opposed to a DI box) and are also manufactured with female XLR to male phone plug. Generally, a strong line level will saturate this type of adaptor, though we can usually get away with a low line level. If a strong line level needs to be transformed, use a DI box or other appropriate line-level transformer.

(B) Double female 1/4" phone jack, allows two 1/4" plugs to be joined.

(C) Female phone jack to male "phono" (also known as "RCA") plug for tape deck inputs or outputs, etc.

(D) Female phono to male 1/4" phone plug.

(E) Phono (RCA) "Y" cord, allows tape deck outputs or inputs to be joined with a single mixer input or output. (In this instance we would generally combine this with the adaptor shown in C.

(F) Dual banana (power amp) plug to whatever configuration is being used for speaker wiring (1/4" phone jack shown here for convenience). It is certainly sensible to be prepared to adapt a spare power amp on the spot, if need be.

(G) XLR "Y" cord, female to two males, allows one balanced output to feed two units when necessary.

(H) XLR "Y" cord, male to two females.

Ideally, the adaptors in G and H should be replaced with transformer-isolated splitter or combining boxes, as soon as budget allows. This is particularly true of H, where two mics are combined into one input channel, since the low impedance of the second mic degrades the signal. It can, though, be used with two *matched mics* in a pinch, e.g., for two tom-toms when there are insufficient input channels to handle each individually.

As well, 1/4" phone "Y" cords simply wired in parallel often come in handy.

(I) Mic Pad, for handling very "hot" mic signals on mixers which do not have supplementary "Pad" switches. Typically manufactured with -15dB, -20dB or -30dB attenuation.

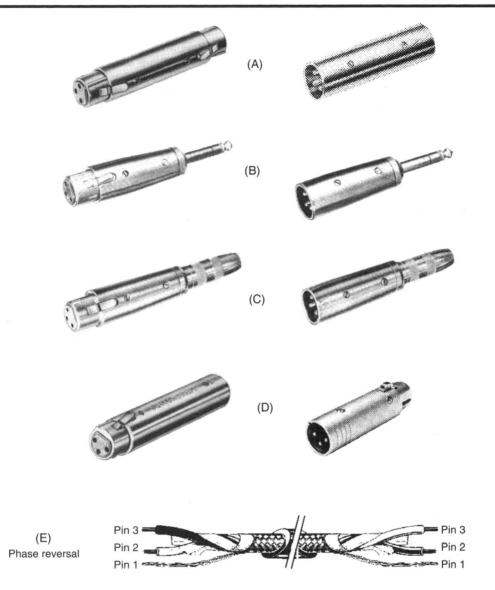

(A)

(B)

(C)

(D)

(E)
Phase reversal

Pin 3 — — Pin 3
Pin 2 — — Pin 2
Pin 1 — — Pin 1

Fig. 16.13. Additional adaptors of importance.

(A) XLR-type "turnarounds" (courtesy Switchcraft) These adaptors are pre-wired to provide a simple turnaround when snake channels are wired in the opposite direction of what we need. This is a common problem, for example, with crossover outputs and other signals headed back to the stage. (Double-female connector is Switchcraft # 389/ or Neutrik #NA3FF; double-male connector is Switchcraft # 390/ Neutrik #NA3MM.)

Note: B, C and D require internal wiring by the purchaser, since the needs vary from one user to another.

(B) XLR to male 1/4" phone plug (courtesy Switchcraft). (Female XLR is Switchcraft #386A/ Neutrik #NA3FP; male XLR is Switchcraft # 387A/ Neutrik #NA3MP.)

(C) XLR to female 1/4" phone jack (courtesy Switchcraft). Both B and C are often necessary adaptors when going from XLR-type cable to TRS phone jacks, or to two-conductor phone jacks. Several such adaptors should be in any audio system operator's tool kit, wherever there is the possibility of encountering, for example, snake cables with phone jacks as return lines to the stage, or wherever else equipment may need to be adapted from one format to another. As mentioned, the international standard is pin #2 (+), though in the US, line-level signals are today usually pin #3 (+), i.e., to tip. A few of these wired pin #2 to tip and a few pin #3 to tip should be carefully labeled and kept around, "just in case". If we need to go from balanced XLR to unbalanced 1/4", the adaptors in C can be preferable to the ones in B. Here we might wire it TRS and, if necessary, unbalance it by inserting a two conductor patch cord. (Female XLR is Switchcraft #383A/ Neutrik #NA3FJ; male XLR is SWitchcraft #384A/ Neutrik #NA3MJ.) After wiring it for your particular needs, it should be carefully labeled (for example: Pin#3-tip, Pin#2-ring, Pin #1-sleeve, or Pin #3 to tip, Pin #2 to ring and sleeve, etc.).

(D) XLR-type "shunt adaptors". (left: courtesy Switchcraft, S3FM shown; right: courtesy Neutrik, NA3MF shown) These are simple XLR extensions, allowing custom wiring for phase reversal, lifting of pin #1, etc.

(E) Phase reversal. As with any custom-wired adaptor, it should be carefully labeled as to its wiring and then covered with clear tape or clear shrink wrap.

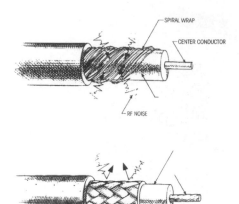

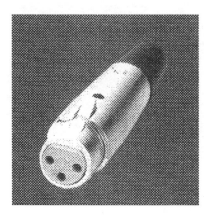

Fig. 16.14. Cable-shield designs. This illustration, courtesy of TEAC Corp., well illustrates the need for effective shielding in any mic or line-level cable, whether balanced or unbalanced. At top left, a traditional spiral wrap is only partially effective in shielding noise out. This is typical of many inexpensive guitar cables and the cheapest mic cables. As well, such a cable may in an extreme case exhibit "microphonics", which is literally noise generated by the cable itself as it is moved or bent. At center is shown a braided shield, generally used for high quality mic cables and patch cords. (In truth, the noise does not entirely "bounce off", but is partially drained off by the shield—the illustration nevertheless makes its point well.) Still, a cheap braided shield may leave small gaps between the braids, so a high quality cable is always in order—it tends not to be a good place to skimp. At bottom is illustrated a metal foil shield. These are very highly effective, but are generally advised only for permanent installations, since the foil may crack with repeated bending. They also tend not to be as flexible as high quality cable with a braided shield, so they seldom sit quite right in actual use. (Snake cables use this type of shield, but due to the large number of conductors involved, the bends they are asked to make are never very sharp.)

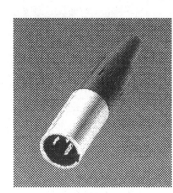

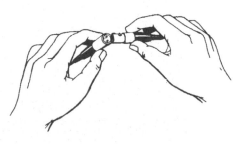

Fig. 16.15. "Tini" QG connectors. (courtesy Switchcraft) This line of connectors (commercially designated Tini QG), shown above in its size relationship to an XLR-type connector, and at right to average-size hands, are increasingly finding favor for connections of lavalier mic cable and other applications where the cable and connectors need to be very lightweight and inconspicuous. Like the XLR-type connector, these also have a locking mechanism designed to make inadvertent disconnection next to impossible.

Fig. 16.16. Typical "multipin" connectors. Top (courtesy ITT/Cannon): "K" series connectors have traditionally found wide use in high level concert reinforcement, particularly for multiple effects patches and amp rack connections.

Center (courtesy Amphenol): Larger multipins such as these are commonly used for snake connections, both at the "stagebox" and for the breakouts (also known as "tails" or "pigtails").

Bottom: A multipin connection at a 40 channel house mixer. Here the road case is sufficiently oversized to allow the breakout to be tucked into the case and the input channel connectors to remain plugged in during transport.

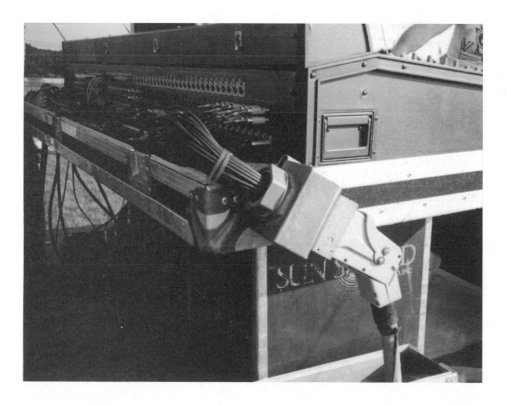

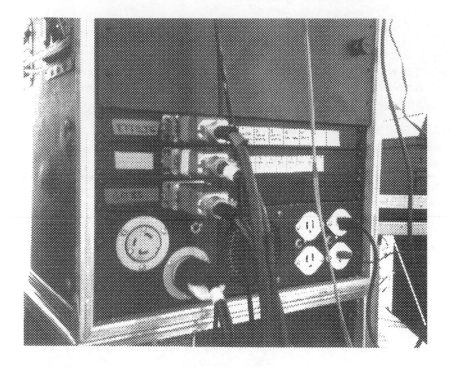

Fig. 16.17. Example of multipin connectors for outboard signal processing and effects patches. This is the rack patching system for the same mixer as in the previous illustration (system by Sun Sound, Northhampton, MA). Separate categories are established for Effects, Compressor/ limiters and Gates. Note that the racks' AC power connection utilizes a twist-lock-type connector to avoid inadvertent disconnection, with provision for jumpers to other racks. Below are the multipin connections at the mixer, with some of the phone plug inserts visible. As they are diligently labeled, repatching them is easily accomplished should it be necessary for a given performance.

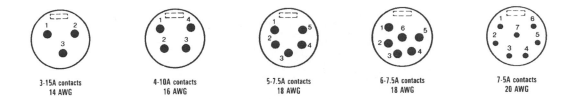

3-15A contacts
14 AWG

4-10A contacts
16 AWG

5-7.5A contacts
18 AWG

6-7.5A contacts
18 AWG

7-5A contacts
20 AWG

Fig. 16.18. XLR pin-configurations. (courtesy ITT/Cannon) XLR-type connectors also find use for speaker lines and other applications other than the standard 3-pin mic/line cable. Shown are the maximum wire guages recommended for each pin configuration (though sometimes we can stretch it a bit in a pinch (e.g., 12 ga. on a 3-pin connector, etc.). We can, for example, use a 4-pin XLR for a biamped monitor system (though soldering and fitting the cable into the connector tend to be extremely tight here). The 3-pin connectors are not uncommonly used for individual speaker lines (here, of course, they should be carefully identified if the cable itself could possibly be mistaken for a shielded cable). When using 3-pin connectors for speaker lines, we can of-course use any two pins we care to, so long as they are appropriately matched and polarized within a given system. The 5-pin through 7-pin connectors normally should be used only for specific low-signal-level applications.

Fig. 16.19. EP connectors. (illustrations courtesy ITT/Cannon) The EP connector is a high level industry standard for multi-way enclosures. Shown at bottom-left in its size-relationship to an XLR, most often used are the 4, 6, and 8-pin configurations, for 2-way, 3-way and 4-way systems, respectively. These are normally wired with the male end at the amp rack and the female end at the enclosure, with male parallel output connectors on the enclosure. This approach also allows for easy extension of speaker lines when necessary. As there is no universal standard, it needs to be established at the system-design stage that a given amp-rack connector's wiring scheme is effectively matched to the wiring at each speaker enclosure.

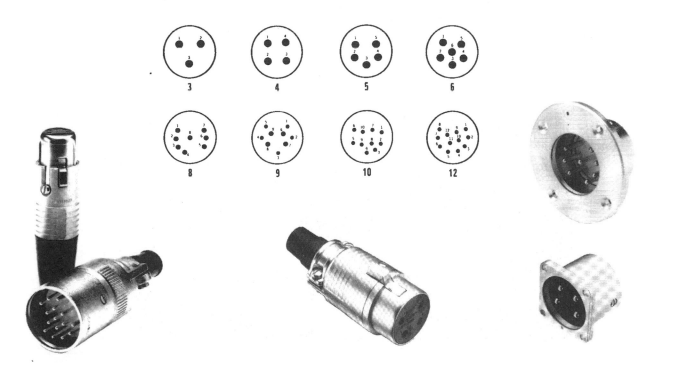

Fig. 16.20. "Speakon" connectors. (courtesy Neutrik) Increasingly finding use today for actively crossed-over systems are connectors of this type, designed by Neutrik, Inc. Marketed in 4-pin and 8-pin configurations, among the advantages are solderless terminals, twist-locking mechanism and cost effectiveness. Other manufacturers have followed with compatible products of the same basic design under different trade names. The 4-pin connector, incidentally, is designed to fit in the same cabinet-cutout as an XLR, and the 8-pin in the same cutout as an EP connector.

Fig. 16.21. Twist-lock-type standard electrical connectors. Many connectors of this type have found their way into existing systems in the field as speaker connectors, due to their durablility, high current-carrying capacity, solderless terminals, and locking mechanism which makes accidental disconnection nearly impossible. If encountering a system using this type of connectors for speaker wiring, keep in mind that the design intent of these plugs is to carry standard AC power suplies. The US National Electrical Code requires that they not be used for speaker wiring in any system, or on any premises, which uses identical connectors wired to carry a standard AC power supply (though some local codes may vary, and the guidelines for temporary installations— i.e. portable systems—are generally more flexible than for permanent installations). These connectors are manufactured in various configurations which are not interchangeable (i.e., it can only be plugged into a mate within its own category). A small sampling is illustrated at right—shown are 125V-15A, 125V-20A, and 125V-30A. (Caution should still be exercised that some idiot does not plug an AC connection—e.g., belonging to a band's stage rack—into your speakers, or say goodbye to the drivers. On the oft-encountered 125V connectors, if we use the silver and green lugs for speaker connections (avoiding the copper lug), this remote possibility is all but eliminated.) Ideally, these should be replaced with connectors designed specifically for speaker wiring.

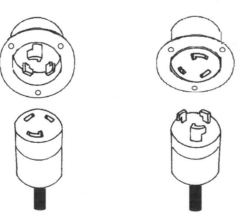

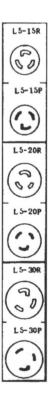

b) System Grounding.

The basic electrical ground for an audio component is depicted in Fig. 16.22. The essential purpose for the standard grounding method is, as should be apparent to most readers, for safety reasons. In an audio system the additional advantage of the AC electrical ground is that electrostatic noise drained off by the shield is ultimately drained off to the earth via the grounding conductors of a properly designed AC electrical system.

Unfortunately, as also mentioned earlier, the main challenge in designing the grounding scheme of all but the smallest sound reinforcement systems is that we need to avoid too many paths to ground. Utilizing too many paths to ground is the most common source of noise in systems that are custom designed by musical bands and soundpersons early in the learning process. System grounding is in itself a fairly complex subject, and ultimately, **any methods used in interrupting a ground path in a system should be double-checked by a qualified electrician**. Here and in the next several illustrations, though, we will take a brief look at system grounding methods in order to get a general idea of what is involved.

In rough terms, the most dependable and safest way to avoid noise associated with grounding is to used only balanced wiring, and interrupt the shield ground at certain points throughout the system. Ideally, all AC power cords involved in a system should go to the same location. In many buildings, the grounding system has slight resistance between widely separated outlets, which can complicate the grounding in the audio system. So outlets should generally be as close to one another as possible (though unfortunately even outlets close to one another can have this problem, which would most often be due to the AC wiring method used in the particular building). Ideally, an independent AC electrical supply source should be used, separate from any other uses in a building (which at the very least means having one or more circuit breakers designated solely for the sound system).

Fig. 16.22. Basic system ground.

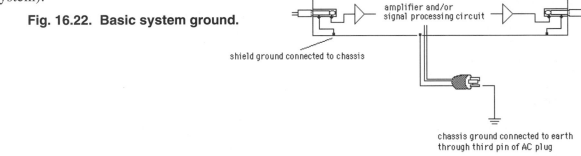

shield ground connected to chassis

chassis ground connected to earth
through third pin of AC plug

Fig. 16.23. Formation of a basic "ground loop". Illustrated is an unbalanced connection between two components, both of which are grounded via the the third prong of a standard three-prong plug. Ground loops of this type are probably the most common source of "buzz" and "hum" in large reinforcement systems. What is required is to interrupt the loops in a safe way without compromising the relative safety afforded by the standard AC electrical ground.

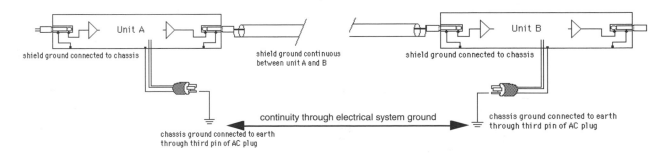

shield ground connected to chassis

shield ground continuous
between unit A and B

shield ground connected to chassis

continuity through electrical system ground

chassis ground connected to earth
through third pin of AC plug

chassis ground connected to earth
through third pin of AC plug

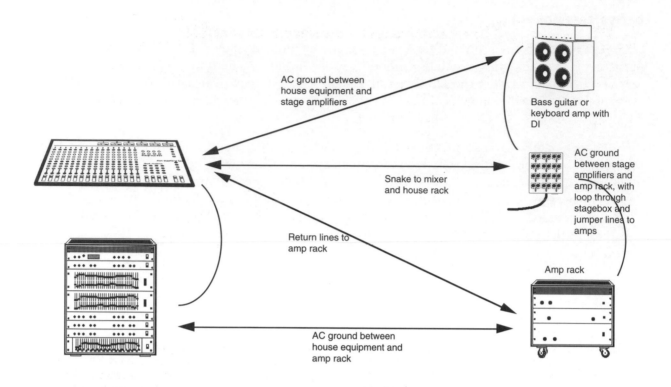

AC ground between
house equipment and
stage amplifiers

Bass guitar or
keyboard amp with
DI

Snake to mixer
and house rack

AC ground
between stage
amplifiers and
amp rack, with
loop through
stagebox and
jumper lines to
amps

Return lines to
amp rack

Amp rack

AC ground between
house equipment and
amp rack

Fig. 16.24. Common ground loops among interconnected components. When using a mixer out in the house position, the most insidious ground loops tend to form between the house mixer/rack and the power amps/stage equipment, due to the length of the snake. This tends to be the most important ground loop to interrupt. Usually we need to interrupt the shield-ground at the direct boxes wherever the musical-instrument amplifier has a 3-prong AC plug. (If it has a 2-prong AC plug, the signal ground should generally be left intact—i.e. the ground should not be "lifted".) As well, we need to interrupt the ground loop along any outputs sent back to the stage, such as crossover outputs and monitor sends.

As well, smaller ground loops form among the interconnected components within a rack, such as an effects rack, as well as between the rack itself and the mixer. Generally these are not as much of a problem, but if budget allows, we should use balanced lines on all of the connections between the board and house (or effects) rack(s). This allows us to interrupt the shield-ground as illustrated in the folowing figures.

Fig. 16.25. Interrupting the shield-ground between components. (Illustration courtesy Yamaha) When the shield-ground is lifted, it should generally be lifted at the beginning of the signal path between components, which would be at the female end of an XLR cable.

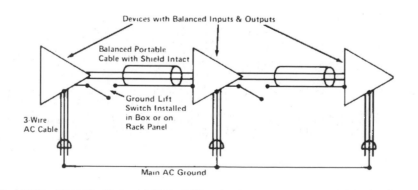

Devices with Balanced Inputs & Outputs

Balanced Portable
Cable with Shield Intact

Ground Lift
Switch Installed
in Box or on
Rack Panel

3-Wire
AC Cable

Main AC Ground

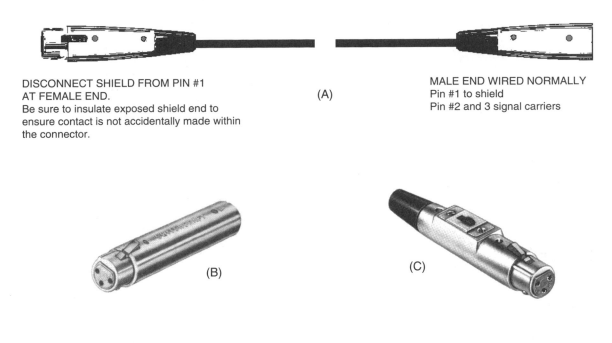

DISCONNECT SHIELD FROM PIN #1
AT FEMALE END.
Be sure to insulate exposed shield end to
ensure contact is not accidentally made within
the connector.

(A)

MALE END WIRED NORMALLY
Pin #1 to shield
Pin #2 and 3 signal carriers

(B)

(C)

Fig. 16.26. Other methods of disconnecting shield ground in line-level cables.
(A) A cable with the shield-ground lifted at the female end should be carefully labeled, and used only for the purpose for which it was designed. This type of cable tends to be most needed on the jumper cables from the crossover outputs or main outputs to the snake (i.e., to the stage from the house mixing position), and also for any monitor sends. With a TRS connector, the same approach can be used, and it should be carefully labeled as to which end is lifted (supplementary color coding never hurts either).

(B) A shunt adaptor (a simple XLR extension) as described earlier, when properly wired, can serve the same purpose as a cable in A.

(C) A short cable wired with a connector of this type at the female end can allow the shield ground to be connected or lifted as needed. Shown is Switchcraft #T3F. Here we would simply wire the end of the shield through the switch. (This can also be handy where we encounter a musical-instrument amplifier with a balanced output, but with no ground-lift switch.)

(D) In systems in which the crossover or monitor EQs have unbalanced outputs a device of the kind shown below can be used to connect the unbalanced and balanced lines. Shown is the ProCo IT-8 (both front and back view), which provides eight channels of isolation transformers, with ground-lift switches. Here we would generally wire an unbalanced cable to an XLR at one end as follows: Center conductor to Pin#3, Shield to Pin #2 (in the US), or center conductor to Pin #2, shield to Pin #3 (in Europe, or wherever DIN/JIS standards prevail). A device of this type would of-course eliminate the need for lifting the shield-ground on the cable itself. (Similar devices, including the ProCo IT-4, have phone-plug inputs as well, eliminating the need for any custom wiring of connectors.)

(D)

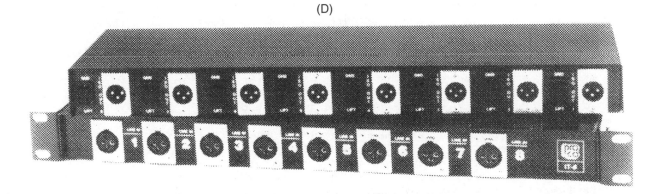

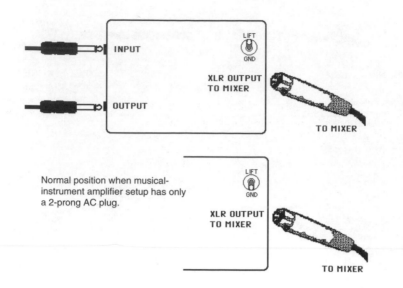

Normal position when musical-instrument amplifier setup has only a 2-prong AC plug.

Fig. 16.27. D.I. (direct injection, a.k.a., direct input) box. Generally, when a DI box is used to connect a grounded musical-instrument amplifier to a snake via a balanced XLR-type mic cable, the ground-lift switch needs to be in the "lift" or "off" position. Such a switch is designed to disconnect Pin #1 of the XLR connector on the unit. When the stage amplifier setup uses only a 2-prong AC plug, though, we generally should leave the switch in the "ground" or "on" position.

Fig. 16.28. AC ground lifts. In the past, 3-prong-to-2-prong adaptors of this type have been used to disconnect a 115V AC ground in order to interrupt ground loops, particularly when the system involves a crossover and/or EQs with unbalanced phone-plug outputs. This today is a questionable practice, since most crossovers and EQs today are manufactured with the opportunity to use a balanced output.

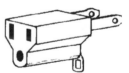

This type of adaptor should be used only with the utmost caution. Firstly, **the AC power ground should *never* be disconnected on an entire system.** Secondly, even if we lift the AC ground, for example, on the effects rack, but leave the power amp rack grounded, the shields of the microphone cables and return lines to the amp rack must then handle part of the system AC grounding. While this is often enough, suppose there are just one or two line level returns to the stage. Are we willing to depend on the shield ground of the mic cables and snake to handle the necessary current if something shorts out onstage? This type of interruption of a ground loop, while sometimes appropriate in a temporary arrangement, should be replaced as soon as feasible with balanced circuitry and 3-prong AC plugs (without adaptors) on all equipment so designed, and instead interrupt any ground loops at the line-level shield-grounds. (A unit such as in Fig. 16.26-D can adapt unbalanced crossover or EQ outputs to balanced circuits with "shield-ground lifts".)

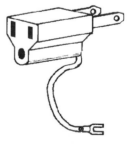

Note: Use of the illustrated adaptor is not permitted in Canada.

Note: Even if implemented in a temporary installation where there is no time to rewire the system with balanced circuits and shield-ground lifts, the use of any of these adaptors should be checked by a qualified electrician to ensure safe system grounding via the mic and line-level cables to the AC ground. (The US National Electrical Code defines a qualified person as one "familiar with the operation and construction of the equipment and the hazards involved". With any audio system, this would mean *both* the audio equipment and the AC power concerns.)

Fig. 16.29. AC circuit tester. A circuit tester of this type, available at most hardware stores and electrical supply houses, can be useful in checking standard outlets to assist in determining they are properly wired. If any type of fault is detected by a tester of this kind, the outlet should not be used.

Fig. 16.30. Interconnecting balanced and unbalanced circuits. Arrows indicate optional connections, e.g., for "ground lift".

UNBALANCED TO BALANCED, SINGLE CONDUCTOR WITH SHIELD

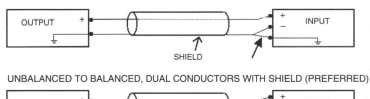

SHIELD

UNBALANCED TO BALANCED, DUAL CONDUCTORS WITH SHIELD (PREFERRED)

BALANCED TO UNBALANCED, DUAL CONDUCTORS WITH SHIELD (PREFERRED)

Power Loss in 25' and 100' Cables at Various Load Impedances

Wire Gauge A.W.G.	Power Lost in Dual Conductor Cable (in Watts)					
	25' 4Ω RE: 175W	25' 8Ω RE: 100W	25' 16Ω RE: 200W	100' 4Ω RE: 175W	100' 8Ω RE: 100W	100' 16Ω RE: 200W
6	0.875	0.251	0.252	3.39	0.988	0.997
8	1.31	0.376	0.377	4.99	1.47	1.49
10	2.18	0.629	0.634	8.08	2.42	2.49
12	3.40	0.992	1.00	12.1	3.74	3.89
14	5.30	1.56	1.59	17.7	5.69	6.05
16	8.12	2.44	2.50	24.7	8.42	9.25
18	12.2	3.76	3.91	32.4	12.0	13.9
20	17.8	5.73	6.10	39.4	16.4	20.4
22	24.8	8.47	9.33	43.3	20.7	28.3
24	32.5	12.1	14.0	43.0	23.9	37.2

Wire guage AWG	Loss in Watts			
	25' 4Ω RE: 350W	25' 8Ω RE: 200W	100' 4Ω RE: 350W	100' 8Ω RE: 200W
6	1.8	0.50	6.9	2.0
8	2.6	0.75	10.4	3.0
10	4.4	1.3	17.2	5.0
12	7.0	2.0	26.7	7.9
14	11.0	3.2	41.1	12.3
16	17.2	5.0	61.9	19.0
18	26.8	7.9	91.1	29.0
20	41.4	12.4	129.5	43.4
22	62.3	19.1	174.6	62.5
24	91.6	29.1	222.2	86.5

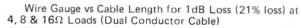

Wire Gauge vs Cable Length for 1dB Loss (21% loss) at 4, 8 & 16Ω Loads (Dual Conductor Cable)

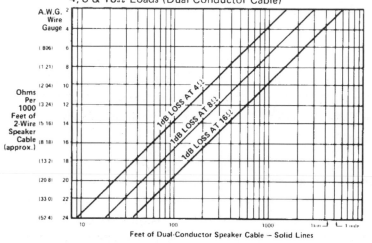

Feet of Dual-Conductor Speaker Cable — Solid Lines

Fig. 16.31. Power losses in various guage cables according to length.
(courtesy Yamaha Corp.) These calculations take into account both wires of a speaker cable.

Other wiring considerations were introduced in the following locations:

Fig. 1.2.   Basic system signal flow.
Fig. 1.7.   Typical crossover applications.
Chapter 4(f).   Output to input impedance relationship.
Chapter 5(j).   Balanced and unbalanced mic circuits.
Fig. 5.16.   Balanced and unbalanced mic wiring.
Chapter 5(k).   Microphone impedance.
Chapter 5(l).   Phantom powering of condenser mics.
Fig. 7.6.   Mixer input channel connections.
Fig. 7.7.   Mixer output section connections.
Fig. 7.8.   "TRS" insert configuration.
Fig. 10.6.   Power amplifier connections.
Fig. 13.17.   Typical 3-way (triamplified) system signal flow.
Fig. 13.20.
through
Fig. 13.24.   Sample patching arrangements for outboard equipment.

CHAPTER 17

THE ENGINEER AS ARTIST

Now that all the miscellaneous setup procedures and other aspects of sound system work are taken care of for the moment, it finally comes down to a person (or persons) behind the mixer to assist in making it all sound good. While the process is inherently a subjective one, there are nevertheless general guidelines which many experienced engineers tend to follow, and which can serve as a useful starting point.

a) General guidelines.

Perhaps most importantly of all, balance is the key to a good mix, no matter what type of event is being handled. If you refer back to the chart of frequency-related subjective qualities in Chapter 6, you may notice that the one word used most often is "fullness". When any one area of the spectrum, from roughly 40 or 50 Hz on through to 12 kHz or so, is missing to any great degree, it is possible to describe the result as lacking fullness. The implication here is that what most people regard as a pleasant "mix" contains a broad range of energy throughout the musical spectrum, in some reasonable degree of balance.

Beyond this, of course each sound within a mix will tend to contribute its own aspect of that balance, each within its own frequency range. So first, it may be helpful to overview some frequency-related qualities as they often relate to the basic equalization task. It seems appropriate to reassert some basic guidelines for equalization, which also were introduced in Chapter 6:

• The overall frequency response is caused by the combination of the frequency response curves throughout the system, from the sound source to the microphones right through the system to the loudspeakers, and beyond into the acoustical realm of the audience.

• An adjustment of an EQ control will have effects well beyond the center frequencies or shelving frequencies (how far depends on the "Q", or bandwidth, of the filter).

• Since the response curves of different mic designs vary widely, the EQ needs can change widely from one mic to another. Oftentimes better results are obtained substituting a microphone with a more suitable response curve. Sometimes a similar objective can be achieved simply by altering the microphone positioning to obtain a more suitable sampling of the sound source.

• All equalization changes in individual voices or instruments will be heard in comparison to the tonal qualities of the other sounds included in the mix. For. example, if we boost all of the HF controls on the mixer input channels by a certain amount, or reduce the mids in a certain range by the same amount on all the channels, we more-or-less end up back where we started—such across-the-board adjustments are often better accomplished with the house outboard EQ and/or crossover output controls.

• Since EQ changes are always relative, as opposed to absolute, the folowing general guidelines are phrased in terms of which ranges of EQ adjustment tend to "add" or "reduce" certain subjective characteristics of the sound, rather than in terms of specific recommendations for EQ settings. And of course, since these are subjective qualities, they are readily subject to debate—the following are intended only as a starting point.

First and most basically, let's break the spectrum roughly in half: too little energy below about 600 Hz will result in a generally "thin" sound, while too much energy below 600 Hz or so will generally result in an overly "thick" sound. Now let's break the spectrum roughly into thirds: too much energy below about 200 Hz will result in a generally "muddy" or "boomy" sound, while too little energy in this range will tend to sound "thin"; too much energy in the 200-2k range will generally cause the mix to sound to sound too "middy" (should this be a surprise?), or to lack "drive", while too little energy in this range will usually cause the mix to lack "fullness" and deprive it of much of its musical character; too much energy above 2kHz or so will tend to cause the sound to be overly "bright", while too little energy above about 2k will usually result in a generally "dull" sound.

b) Speech and Musical Voice.

A large amount of energy between 100 and 160 Hz can cause a voice to sound "boomy", which may or may not be desireable, but which can definitely be a hindrance when present in excess.

A modest boost in the 160 Hz to 250 Hz range can add depth, fullness, thickness, or warmth (warmth usually at around 200-250 Hz) to a voice, but in excess can make it sound muddy, or muffled.

The 250-600Hz range also plays a role in fullness and warmth but in a slightly different way. An excess of this range can cause a voice to sound "clouded". The lower-mid of a 4-band EQ usually falls in this range—a modest cut here often clears up a "cloudy" vocal sound.

If a voice needs to be harder sounding, "punchier", or clearer, boosts over part-or-all of the 800 Hz-2 kHz range often solve this. If, on the other hand, the voice(s) have too much of this characteristic (blary or excessively hard-sounding), all or parts of this range may need to be cut somewhat. (The mid of a 3-band EQ or upper-mid of a 4-band EQ often covers this range.)

The range from about 2kHz through 6kHz is a range critical to vocal clarity and to the effective articulation of consonants. If a system is deficient in this range, a modest boost of all-or-part of the range can sometimes increase clarity and intelligibility. It can, though, easily be overdone to the point of annoyance, a *reduction* in clarity and ultimately listening fatigue. A boost in the 4k to 6k region adds bite to the sound, also tending to cause it to appear to be closer and more intense (within limits). Ordinarily, a boost in this region is not needed, since this is the most sensitive range of the ear for the vast majority of people. In musical mixes, where clarity and articulation are not the main objectives, part or all of this range is sometimes cut somewhat, with the intent of taking some of the edge off of the vocal sound—and also allowing the snap of drums and/or the "bite" of other instruments to "cut through" more readily. (In some cases, a cut in all or part of the region from 2k to 6k may simply represent compensation for an unneeded "presence-peak" in a mic's response.)

A boost in response at about 6-12kHz generally adds an additional breathiness or sibilance to vocal quality. (A compressor circuit known as a "de-esser" can be used to retain breathiness without the excessive sibilance sometimes heard with the sounds "s", "c", "z" and "t".)

c) Bass Instruments.

For bass instruments, EQ adjustments in the following ranges tend to induce the following subjective characteristics.

Boost in the 50-200 Hz range,	adds depth
Boost in the 80-160 Hz range,	adds"boom",low overtones & 2nd octave fundamentals
Boost in the 160-500 Hz range,	adds higher overtones and 3rd & 4th octave notes
Boost in the 400-1k range,	adds "solidness"
Boost in the 800 Hz-3k range,	adds clarity
Boost in the 1.6-4k range,	adds "snap"
Boost in the 3k-and-up range,	adds "edge", "bite", string noise buzz"(~5k-and up)
Boost in the 8k-and-up range	adds "zip" (to, say, a synthesized bass sound)
Cuts in any of the above ranges,	reduce any of the above characteristics.
Cut in the 40-80 Hz range,	reduces "murkiness"

The lowest fundamental of a bass guitar or string bass in the standard tuning is "E"-41Hz. The fundamental of thc "E" two octaves up (highest string, 7th fret) falls at about 160 Hz. Harmonics go upwards to at least 2k, with string noise and buzz above 4k or so.

Piano fundamentals go as low as 30 Hz. But in the actual acoustic sound of the piano, very little energy (essentially none that is audible) is present at this pitch, so what is heard at the very lowest notes is the "missing fundamental" (Chapter 3). Organ-pedal bass (and sometimes synthesizer) fundamentals are able to go as low as 16 Hz, but significant energy seldom goes below around 32 Hz (the first overtone—second harmonic—of the lowest notes). Significant energy down to about 32 Hz can, when necessary, provide an "earthquake-like" sound fairly convincingly. (The need for a sound reinforcement system to be able to reproduce substantial amounts of energy at frequencies below this is fairly unusual and relatively very difficult, and even when the system is capable of it, generally it should be used only as a special effect. In fact, it is increasingly becoming common practice in high level concert reinforcement systems to use an auxiliary send to feed the "subwoofers", since strong energy below 80Hz or so tends only to be necessary for bass guitar, kick drum and certain special effects.)

d) "Treble" Instruments.

The term "treble" is used loosely here. Instruments which play primarily in the treble clef are, of course, a very broad category of sound sources, but the following guidelines often tend to hold true in equalizing them. For full-range instruments, such as piano, organ, synthesizer, harp, etc., and for baritone instruments, use this section along with the previous one as an initial guide.

Boost in the 100-200 range,	adds depth (or, to the extreme) "boomy" or "muddy"
Boost in the 200-300 range,	adds "warmth" or "body"
Boost in the 400-1k range,	adds "opaqueness" or (to the extreme in a relatively narrow band)"hollow" or "hornlike"
Boost in the 800-3k range,	adds clarity, or (to the extreme) "blary"
Boost in the 4k-6k range,	adds"edge",sharpness,"presence","bite" (clarity here too)(also adds "brightness")
Boost in the 6k-and-up range,	adds buzz, sizzle, zip or sparkle
Cuts in the above ranges,	reduce the above characteristics
Cut in the 200-500 range,	reduces "darkness"or "muffled sound"
Cut in the 800-2k range,	reduces "hardness"
Cut in the 2k-5k range,	reduces "brashness" or "tinny-ness"
Cut in the 8k-and-up range,	reduces excessive "zip", "buzz" or "sizzle"

e) Drums.

The following adjustments involve, as always, a combination of microphone selection, microphone placement, and equalization.

Kick/Bass Drum:

Boost in the 40 Hz to 100 Hz range,	adds depth or "thump"
Boost in the 80-160 Hz range,	adds depth or"boom"
Boost in the 800-1.6k range,	adds "solidness", or "thock"
Boost in the 1k- 5k range,	adds "klock", "crack", "click" ("click" towards 4-5k)
Boost in the 4 k-and-up range,	adds "tick" or "slap"
Cut in the 250 to 630 Hz range,	reduces "cardboardlike", "boxy" or hollow sound also tends to bring out both depth and beater contact sound.

Snare Drum:

Boost in the 125- 250 Hz range,	adds depth
Boost in the 250-400 Hz range,	adds "pop" (if the drum is very well muted)
Boost in the 500 Hz-1k range,	adds solidness (if the drum is very well muted)
Boost in the 300-800 Hz range,	adds "ring" (if the drum is left unmuted)
Boost in the 800 Hz-3k range,	adds "bang"
Boost in the 3 k -6 k range,	adds "snap" or "bite"
Boost in the 4 k -10 k range,	adds snare-spring sound ("CH", or "TSCH")
Cuts in any of the above ranges,	reduces the above characteristics
Cut in the 125 Hz-and-below range,	reduces excessive "thump"
Cut in the 400 Hz-1k range,	reduces ringing overtones, "boing", or "boxy-ness", depending on drum muting; helps to bring out depth and "snap"

Cymbals:

Boost in the 3 k-8k range,	adds "sh" and/or "ch" sound, or "crash" sound
Boost in the 6 k-and-up range,	adds "s" "sizzle" or "splashy" sound
Cut in the 800 Hz-3k range,	reduces "blary" sound
Cut in the 2.5 k-5k range,	reduces "brash" sound
Boost in the 300-600 Hz range,	brings out a "gonglike" sound, especially hi-hat

Tom-toms:

Boost in the 100-300 Hz range,	adds depth (depending on the tom's size and tuning)
Boost in the 300-800 Hz range,	adds ring (if the drums are left open)
Boost in the 600 Hz-1.6k range,	adds solidness (if the drums are well muted)
Boost in the 1.6k-5k range,	adds "crack"
Boost in the 4k-and-up range,	adds "tick" or "slap"
Cuts in any of the above ranges,	reduce any of the above characteristics
Cut in the 400-800 Hz range,	reduces ringing overtones, brings out both depth and bite

Recall from Chapter 2 that the overtones of drums are more closely spaced than harmonics. This gives substantial flexibility to the operator, with the help of a patched outboard EQ, to tailor the sound of drums, especially the kick drum, to the mix. Say the kick drum fundamental in a particular tuning is about 30Hz. This would place the lower overtones at roughly 48 Hz, 63 Hz, 70 Hz, 80 Hz, 88 Hz, 105 Hz, and 108 Hz, with other overtones extending on upwards in frequency. (See again Fig. 2.8. This figure described the frequency relationship of overtones of a symetrically stretched circular membrane. In practice there may be even more frequencies than this, depending on how the drum is tuned and muted. With a musical instrument tuned to 30 Hz, the next frequencies would only be 60 Hz, 90 Hz and so on upwards.) Similarly, the sound of pedal-beater or stick meeting drumhead involves many frequencies as well, offering a flexible opportunity to tailor this aspect of the sound as well.

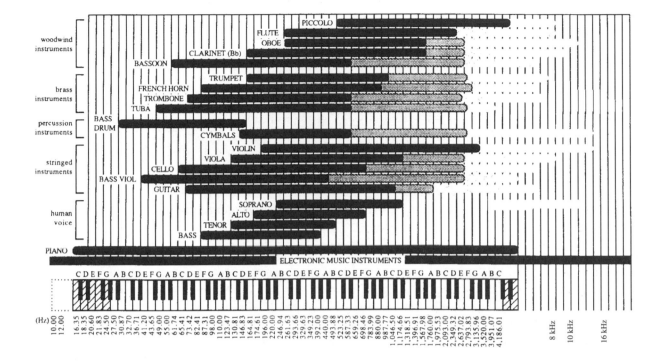

Fig. 17.1. Frequency ranges of instruments and musical voice. These ranges are included here for general reference only. The black bands show the fundamental frequencies of musical notes within the particular instrument's range—these will of course change as different notes are played. The grey bands loosely describe the higher harmonic ranges (with the exception of drums and cymbals, whose overtones are not harmonics). The white bands approximately show the upper frequencies that are typically involved (again, not necessarily harmonics). The white bands typically involve more continuous spectra of closely packed frequencies, such as sybilances and other frequencies which provide "edge" to the sound, such as the "bite" of string windings and so forth. In practice, the black, grey and white bands tend to overlap each other somewhat.

While it is helpful to know them in general, the ranges themselves often have relatively little to do with the task of the engineer. Note, for example, that the fundamental frequencies of cymbals can be as low as 150Hz or so, yet the vast majority of the cymbals' contribution to a typical mix tends to be well above 1kHz. Similarly, while piano and synthesizer fundamentals can go very far down in frequency, the actual frequencies we are reproducing with a rein-forcement system tend to be much higher (though the notes are still heard as such because of the "missing fundamental" characteristic of hearing explained in Chapter 3).

Also note that the very highest energy involved in acoustic instruments and voices does not go substantially beyond 12kHz or 14kHz at the high frequency extreme. The white bands tend to involve what are known as "continuous spectra" of closely packed frequencies. There may be more emphasis in certain approximate frequencies than others, but the comparatively tight-knit nature of these bands tends to allow us to shape their character fairly readily. This is, for example, one way in which mics impart their own character to sounds, but we can also do this with a reasonably flexible outboard EQ.

So overall, what tends to be important, is how the energy of the voices and instruments is distributed within the audio spectrum, thus the general characteristics described in the previous several sections.

f) Other EQ basics.

A few additional notes on EQing here. Most or all of the possible set of harmonic components are present with different instruments and voices, even if they seem at first to be lacking. For example, a breathy voice usually has some clarity in the upper mids (say from about 1k to 3k or so), though obviously not as much as would be present in a voice which we would characterize as "clear". Often this can be resolved by a simple boost in the appropriate range (easily accomplished with a sweepable midrange control in this case). But one of the problems we often encounter is that in adjusting for radical deficiencies, feedback can be created. If we need to boost the upper mids in the example of the "breathy" voice given above, we create a broad peak in that frequency range, which can limit the amount of gain before feedback. As well, we may find in this kind of situation that since the "ch" and "s" sounds overlap somewhat with the range where we can normally increase "clarity" or "hardness", the result may in some cases be an overly harsh sibilance. So we need to find a balance between the two concerns in this particular situation. Similarly, at the other extreme, an excessively "hard" sounding voice can usually be softened somewhat in the upper mids, though if done to excess, we may end up overly lacking in the "ch" sounds. Again, a reasonable balance of concerns needs to be found.

Another common situation, as mentioned in Chapter 6, occurs where the voice (or instrument) resonance changes radically from one note to another. It may, for example, be fairly easy to deal with an overly hard-sounding or a thin voice by cutting the upper mids and/or boosting the lower mids. But what happens when the voice then becomes overly soft, for example, in falsetto parts? Here we would need to either find an averaging which works reasonably well from one extreme of vocal quality to the other, or be prepared to adjust the EQ every time different vocal parts come up (a difficult task at best).

Typically, if a low-cut (high pass) switch is available, it will be used on everything except low-pitched drums (kick and large toms) and bass guitar. Further, we may find that a low frequency cut on the onboard EQ is appropriate for vocals and other instruments miked up-close due to proximity effect of the mics. When using a mixer with submasters, a patched outboard EQ on the appropriate subs can accomplish this purpose when necessary. Another thing to keep a sharp ear for is the overwhelming lows and very high frequencies often present in electronic keyboard sounds—if an extra outboard EQ is available we may wish to severely cut everything above about 12k-or-so and below about 80 Hz on such instruments.

g) Organizing a mix.

First off, we need to organize a reasonably sensible arrangement of input channels on the mixer, as well as a reasonably well labeled and sensible designation of any aux. or effects loops.

Musical mixes vary, as would be expected, according to the type of music and according to the particular artistic expression we wish to impart to it. But overall, we can look at a typical musical mix from a few different vantage points. Firstly, the overall tonal quality of the music—this will tend to be a function not only of the mics and onboard EQ settings that are used, but also of how the main outboard EQ and crossover outputs (if applicable) are adjusted, as well as of what proportion of the sound originates onstage. As the output level of the system is increased to the point where it begins to mask the onstage sounds, an increasing degree of control of the overall sound is possible, up to the limit of becoming excessively loud. Typical obstacles here are excessive stage monitor volume, musical-instrument-amplifier levels, and sometimes very loud acoustic instruments (brass, heavy crash cymbals, loud snare drum hits, etc.).

Secondly, we can view the mix in terms of how it fits together, and also in terms of what needs to stand out, in what way and at what time. A number of ways have evolved out of the contemporary studio for allowing a number of different components of the mix to stand out *together* without obscuring one another. At its simplest, this can be done by putting the emphasis of individual components of the mix in somewhat different frequency ranges. For example we might put a bit of extra emphasis on the drum "contact" sounds (stick meeting head) in the 3k to 6k range, and put a bit of extra emphasis on the vocals in the 8k to 10k range. (If we were to put extra emphasis, or de-emphasis, on everything in the same EQ range, this would preferably be done with the main outboard EQ, and would affect the overall tonal quality, but usually not significantly affect the relationship of the components of the mix to one another.)

Thirdly, we need to view the mix from a dynamic perspective. When budget allows for adequate outboard signal processing, this task can be greatly improved. Typical methods of keeping a mix under dynamic control are separate compressors on vocals, kick drum, keyboards and/or anything else which presents overly wide dynamic shifts. As well, noise gates tend to be most useful on kick drum, and are a highly useful luxury for the other drum channels, particularly on rack toms mounted on the kick drum itself (which tend to ring every time the kick drum is struck) and also on other drums which are left relatively unmuted. Where budget does not allow for noise gates (and sometimes even when it does allow for them) appropriate muting of drumheads can be helpful to the task of maintaining a "tight" drum sound. Generally, most contemporary mixes require a very tight sound on the kick drum, usually a tight sound on the snare (here the reverb unit usually adds any additional duration), and a moderate degree of decay time on tom-toms. Different musical styles may of-course vary from this basic guideline.

Fourthly, and very importantly, we need to view the mix on a timeline. We can conveniently break this up into two basic aspects, short term and long term.

In the short term (i.e., from note to note), a typical mix needs to be "filled out" with delay and reverb. In a medium-to-large-size hall, the acoustic environment usually adds the reverberation, oftentimes far more than desired. (Still, the engineer often will add some reverb for the benefit of audience in close range of the speakers, checking the amount through headphones if need be.) In a smaller, "dry" room the reverb unit plays a vital role in filling in the gaps between notes and in generally "thickening" the mix. And the use of delay (echo) units has of course become fairly standard in many musical styles as an effect, which also helps to "thicken" the mix, giving the music an additional "spaciousness".

Generally, echo is added only to vocals, and to instruments which are not part of the "rhythm section" (i.e., excluding drums and bass). The normal practice is to keep the delay time roughly in sync with the timing of the music, i.e., ordinarily to an eighth, quarter note, or half note. This tends to be the most satisfying to the vast majority of people, as it complements the natural rhythmic flow of the music. (The main exception to this tends to be music involving triplets within a quarter note, such as a "shuffle" or a "boogie". Here we would most often set the delay to roughly two-thirds of a quarter note, thus synchronizing the delay time with the rhythmic emphasis.)

Reverb, as mentioned, is commonly added to snare drum, vocals and to other instruments according to taste and musical style. Usually a relatively short reverb time is used on songs with a quick pace, with the longer reverb times being reserved for ballads and special effects.

EQing the reverb itself often poses an interesting dilemma. Ideally in a contemporary mix, at least two reverb units should be used (assuming there are enough aux busses on the mixer), one for drums and one for vocals and instruments. Commonly, though, we need to get by with just one, since all but the largest mixers tend to have just two post-fader auxes (and like it or not, the vast majority of modest budget performances are put within this limitation). Since a typical reverb program will cause the low frequencies to take longer to decay than the highs, we are faced with a bit of problem on the snare reverb as it is usually implemented. If we do not roll off the lows of the snare reverb, we are left with a very long "booom" long after the shimmery highs on the reverb have decayed. This in itself is simple to deal with. Simply roll off the lows and low-mids on the reverb so they dont stand out, thereby tightening up the bottom end of the snare sound. Many digital reverb units have a high-pass filter which allows the same thing. Of course a compromise is made when we wish to add a full-spectrum reverb sound to other instruments and/or vocals. One way to minimize the compromise here is to add a bit of reverb to the echo (at the echo return channel), thereby filling out the echo and extending it a bit outward in time. This procedure also takes the edge off the delay when staccato notes or inadvertent "bleed" of drum beats through vocal mics are involved, softening the echo. Carefully done, the effect can be an excellent enhancement, and it is possible with practice to learn to fill out the mix with tasteful combinations of reverb and appropriately timed echoes. (Be careful, though, of inadvertently sending the echo or reverb back into itself by using the wrong aux send, or a feedback loop will be created.)

In the long term (i.e., over the course of a performance or set of songs), a few additional factors come into play. To begin with, anything done the same way at the same sound level and with the same EQ settings will ultimately be boring, almost regardless of how interesting the actual musical changes are. While this should be obvious, it is a common obstacle to effective performances. Musical groups, having worked out their particular dynamics in a rehearsal setting, are oftentimes not in the best position to judge how this works in a live setting, particularly when the sound requirements and/or audience expectations are critical. This normally puts some responsibility on the soundperson to assist in the process. (Some bands do seem to master this aspect, but in practice even many of the highest quality musical groups run into this problem—their dynamics are either too severe or too monotonous, or simply inconsistent. Given a choice between the two extremes, most soundpersons would prefer a band which keeps its dynamics fairly steady, so the input attenuators can be left more or less the same over the course of a performance. Nevertheless, it is sensible practice to leave some additional "headroom" to accomodate the increase of vocal levels and instument levels as the excitement of a performance builds.) Another common issue for soundpersons occurs when, for example, a guitarist or keyboard player chooses to intentionally alter their stage level with a knob or foot pedal when playing lead parts. While at first this seems to make sense, the problem occurs when these adjustments are not done exactly right—so we run into situations where the soundperson may actually be *reducing* the fader on lead parts, or "riding the fader" to attempt to keep up with inconsistent changes. A compressor can help here, but seldom completely solves the problem.

For most musical performances, what is required over the longer term is certain periods of excitement and other periods of comparative relaxation, then perhaps a rebuilding of intensity, and so on. While the musical band does its own part toward this end through their song selection and their own dynamic influence, the soundperson can also assist in this process. Commonly we will find that bands will adjust inconsistently when these changes are implemented. For example, the bass guitar may reduce by a certain amount on a ballad, and suddenly the kick drum will be way out in front of the rest of the mix. This and other similar changes in the mix of course require constant attention from song to song on the part of the house system operator. Overall, we may find that reducing the master fader a bit on ballads and bringing it back upwards a bit on stronger songs can be helpful. These changes should, though, generally be made in moderation. It can be helpful to make such changes in the signal path *after* the compressor(s) for the musical program, so we do not end up pushing the mix too far into compression on the "strong" songs. (Where we can do this will often vary from one system to another, depending on how the main compression is patched.) As well, we can increase the overall system level in very subtle increments at key points in a musical program—again the key here is *subtle*. (Do not, though, attempt to make level changes in the signal path after any limiters meant for loudspeaker protection.)

Finally, doing a mix for a live show, like it or not, often comes down to doing what many engineers jokingly refer to as "damage control". Unexpected dynamic changes, missed cues or missed communication (by both band and soundperson) and numerous other unpredictables can and often do come into play. And the task then becomes to make something of it all which can be reasonably well appreciated by the audience, and minimizing the errors which are common to live performance. One of the things we can do, for example, is when an unexpected part comes up or when a part is missed, *make the adjustment gradually, or wait till the next measure of the music to bring the fader up*. When starting off a show without an effective sound check, first make sure the important vocals are audible and reasonably presentable as quickly as possible, then work on cleaning up the mix and bring up instruments and drums gradually, so the changes do not overly stand out to the audience.

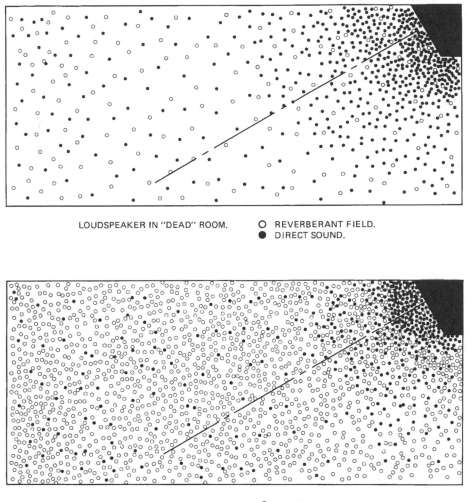

LOUDSPEAKER IN "DEAD" ROOM. ○ REVERBERANT FIELD.
● DIRECT SOUND.

LOUDSPEAKER IN "LIVE" ROOM. ○ REVERBERANT FIELD.
● DIRECT SOUND.

Fig. 17.2. Illustration of reverberant fields in "dry" and "live" rooms. (Courtesy JBL Professional) The task of the soundperson is obviously affected by this factor. When in an overly dry room, we can of-course add reverb electronically. Dealing with excessive reflections or reverberation, when confronted with such situations (gymnasiums, certain auditoriums, large houses of worship, etc.), can sometimes be nightmarish. This may be particularly true when using a modest-size portable system in such environments, where there may not be a significant opportunity to alter a system specifically to deal with the environment.

Since a high degree of reverberation also increases overall level, stage amplifier volume, generally speaking, should be kept comparatively low, along with overall system output (this would generally hold true for any "loud" environment). Simply increasing volume levels almost never helps, though moving stage amplifiers and monitors closer to performers' ears usually does help. An increase in clarity throughout the audience can often be achieved by increasing the very high end output somewhat (usually from 4kHz and up). This is because the high frequencies tend to decay more quickly in such situations. As well, if we have a system with fairly strong low frequency capability we may wish to try reducing the lower midrange and midbass, and emphasize kick drum and bass guitar in a comparatively low frequency range (say 40Hz to 80Hz).

An audience tends to be a very good absorber of sound, reducing or eliminating reflections from the floor, and thus tending to change the reverberant characteristics. Often, an increase in midrange output is needed as an audience becomes denser.

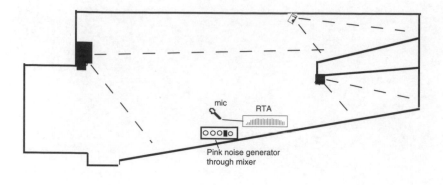

Fig. 17.3. Use of random noise for system equalization. Many engineers use a combination of a vocal microphone with which they are familiar (i.e., "Check 1-2-3-4") and recorded music with which they are familiar, noting the sound in various points throughout the room, and EQing the system accordingly. Beyond EQing a system by ear, system response in a given environment can be adjusted using "pink noise" in conjunction with a "real-time analyzer" (RTA), or "spectrum analyzer" and a mic with reasonably flat response. Pink noise produced by a generator consists of equal long-term-average energy throughout the audio spectrum, according to a logarithmic scale ("white noise" follows a linear scale and is not ordinarily used in audio work).

This is not as simple a procedure as it might at-first seem (except perhaps outdoors). To begin with, readings may need to be taken in a number of places. Though a certain approximate curve is usually sought for speech reinforcement and perhaps other curves for music reinforcement, these are largely dependent on taste and are thus very debatable ("flat" is not always preferred). In addition, there is no absolute standard due to the nature of reverberation indoors (the highs decay more quickly), the varying directivity of different component designs, and the normally varying ratio of direct-to-reverberant sound throughout a room. With a large portable system, a common practice is to determine a certain approximate curve to set onsite, EQ the system until the desired RTA curve is roughly achieved, then make adjustments according to taste if necessary.

Index

Learning Resources
Centre